THE ZINOVIEV LETTER

THE ZINOVIEV LETTER

THE CONSPIRACY THAT NEVER DIES

GILL BENNETT

OXFORD
UNIVERSITY PRESS

OXFORD
UNIVERSITY PRESS

Great Clarendon Street, Oxford, OX2 6DP,
United Kingdom

Oxford University Press is a department of the University of Oxford.
It furthers the University's objective of excellence in research, scholarship,
and education by publishing worldwide. Oxford is a registered trade mark of
Oxford University Press in the UK and in certain other countries

© Gill Bennett 2018

The moral rights of the author have been asserted

First Edition published in 2018

Impression: 1

Published in the United States of America by Oxford University Press
198 Madison Avenue, New York, NY 10016, United States of America

British Library Cataloguing in Publication Data
Data available

Library of Congress Control Number: 2018938180

ISBN 978-0-19-876730-5

Printed in Great Britain by
Clays Ltd, Elcograf S.p.A.

Dedicated to the memory of three distinguished scholars and good friends,
who all played a part in this book and are sadly missed

Peter Freeman (1937–2006)
Tony Bishop (1938–2012)
Keith Jeffery (1952–2016)

Acknowledgements

Many people have helped me with this book. In particular, I should like to thank those supportive friends and colleagues who have read it in draft and offered constructive comment: Jim Daly, Professor George Peden, Professor Patrick Salmon, and Professor David Stafford. I have enjoyed, as always, the encouragement and friendship of Professor Christopher Andrew and Lord Hennessy of Nympsfield. I am grateful to the Foreign and Commonwealth Office Historians, and to the FCO generally, for facilities and help; to the Cabinet Office Knowledge and Information Management Unit; to the staff of The National Archives; and to colleagues across Whitehall who have ensured the book's smooth progress. I owe the biggest debt to Bill Hamilton of A.M. Heath, whose idea it was and who has encouraged me at every turn. Many thanks also to Matthew Cotton at Oxford University Press, and to all his team.

Contents

List of Illustrations

List of Abbreviations

@	Alias/also known as, in intelligence context
ARCOS	All-Russian Cooperative Society Ltd
BBC	British Broadcasting Corporation
C/CSS	Chief of the Secret Intelligence Service
Cheka	Soviet security and intelligence service, 1917–23
CIA	Central Intelligence Agency, US foreign intelligence service
Cmd/Cmnd	Command Paper
Comintern	Communist International
CPGB	Communist Party of Great Britain
CPSU	Communist Party of the Soviet Union
DBFP	*Documents on British Foreign Policy 1919–1939*
DBPO	*Documents on British Policy Overseas*
DG	Director General of the Security Service
DNI	Director of Naval Intelligence
DVPS	*Dokumenty vneshney politiki SSSR* (Foreign Policy Documents of the USSR)
ECCI	Executive Committee of the Comintern
EU	European Union
FAPSI	Federal' naya Agenstvo Pravitel'stvennoy Svayazi i Informatsii, Russian Federal Agency for Government Communications and Information
FBI	Federal Bureau of Investigation, US domestic intelligence organization
FO/FCO	Foreign Office/Foreign and Commonwealth Office (from 1968)

FSB	Federal'naya Sluzhba Bezopasnosti, Russian domestic intelligence service
GC&CS	Government Code and Cypher School
GCHQ	Government Communications Headquarters (from 1946)
GOCs	General Officers Commanding, i.e. commanding officers in the British armed services
GPU	Godudarstvennoye Politicheskoye Upravleniye, Soviet security and intelligence service within Internal Affairs Commissariat, 1922–3
GRU	Glavnoye Razvedyvatel'noye Upravleniye, Russian military intelligence organization
HN	History Note, i.e. 1999 report on Zinoviev Letter published by the FCO
HQ	Headquarters
IIB	Industrial Intelligence Bureau
IKKI	Ispolnitel'niy Komitet Kommunistischeskogo Internatsionala (Executive Committee of the Comintern)
ILP	Independent Labour Party
INO	Inostrannyi Otdel, foreign department of Cheka
IPI	Indian Political Intelligence
ISA	Intelligence Services Act, 1994
ISC	Intelligence and Security Committee
KGB	Komitet Gosudarstvennoi Bezopasnosti (Soviet security and intelligence service, 1954–91)
MI1(c)	Early name for Secret Intelligence Service
MI5	Security Service, UK domestic intelligence agency
NARA	US National Archives and Records Administration
NATO	North Atlantic Treaty Organization
NKID (Narkomindel)	Narodnyi Kommissariat Inostrannykh, People's Commissariat of Foreign Affairs
NKVD	Narodnyi Kommissariat Vnutrennikh Del, People's Commissariat for International Affairs, incorporating state security 1922–3 and 1934–43
NSY	New Scotland Yard

OGPU	Obyedinennoye Gosudarstvennoye Politicheskoye Upravleniye, Soviet security and intelligence service, 1923–34
Politburo	Political bureau of the Central Committee of the CPSU
PQ	Parliamentary Question
PRO	Public Record Office
PS	Private Secretary
PUS	Permanent Under-Secretary
PUSD	Permanent Under-Secretary's Department, FO, responsible for liaison with the secret intelligence agencies
RVF	Russian Volunteer Fleet
SIGINT	Signals Intelligence (interception and codebreaking)
SIS	Secret Intelligence Service (also known as MI6)
Sovnarkom	Sovet narodnykh kommissarov, Soviet Council of People's Commissars
STD	Soviet Trade Delegation in London
SVR	Sluzhba Vneshnei Razvedki, Russian foreign intelligence agency
TNA	The National Archives (UK)
USSR/SSSR	Union of Soviet Socialist Republics

Introduction

The Impact of the Zinoviev Letter
on British Politics

No one knows for certain who wrote the letter supposedly addressed to the central committee of the Communist Party of Great Britain (CPGB) on 15 September 1924 by Grigori Zinoviev,[1] head of the Comintern or Communist International, the propaganda arm of the Bolshevik Russian regime. The text of the Zinoviev Letter—in English—was transmitted to London in a telegram from the Riga station of the Secret Intelligence Service (SIS),[2] arriving at SIS head office on 9 October. No original of the letter was ever found: the CPGB denied receiving it, in the post or by any other means, and there is no evidence that they did. Zinoviev denied writing it, and there are good reasons to believe him. Alternative copies that have turned up in various countries appear to be retranslations of the version received by SIS. Yet this document—which may never have existed in the form of an original letter and was almost certainly not written by Zinoviev—has haunted politics, especially Labour politics, in the United Kingdom ever since.

Since the 1920s, scarcely a decade has passed without a mention of the Letter in print. There have been several cross-Whitehall investigations into its provenance and exploitation. More than ninety years later, political commentators still tend to refer to it as if everyone

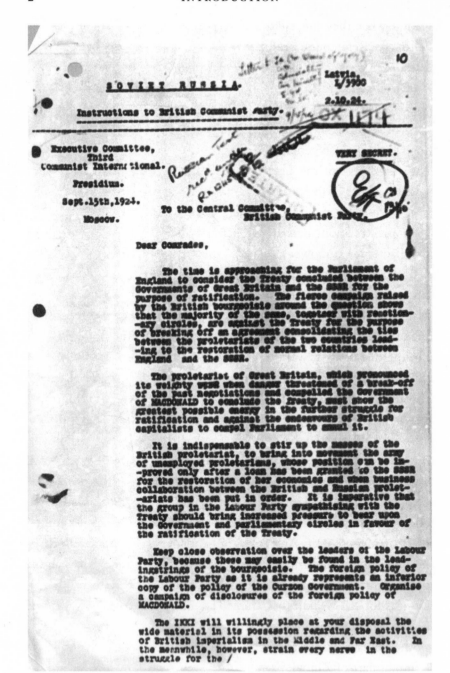

Figure 1. First page of Zinoviev Letter as received in SIS

knows what they are talking about. An article written during the European Referendum campaign in 2016 referred to the Zinoviev Letter, comparing the *Daily Mail*'s treatment of Prime Minister David Cameron to its treatment of the first Labour Prime Minister Ramsay MacDonald during the 1924 election campaign.[3] In the spring of 2017, accusations by Prime Minister Theresa May of foreign interference in the British general election campaign prompted comparisons with the effect of the Letter in the 1924 campaign.[4] The Zinoviev Letter, which David Aaronovitch has called 'the great British conspiracy',[5] refuses to go away. This book seeks to explain why.

In 1924 relations between Britain and the Bolshevik government that had come to power after the October 1917 Revolution in Russia were strained. Western powers, particularly those like Britain with empires targeted by Bolshevik propaganda, had struggled in the aftermath of the First World War and the Russian Civil War[6] to find a way of interacting with a regime dedicated to the overthrow of capitalism. On the one hand, it was the avowed policy of the Communist Party of the Soviet Union (CPSU) to encourage the spread of communism to other countries, inciting proletarian revolution through propaganda, subversion, and espionage. At the same time, for economic reasons Russia wanted to normalize relations and be treated as a regular trading partner. The Zinoviev Letter received in October 1924 seemed a typical example of the tactics employed by the Soviet regime in pursuit of these twin policies. It exhorted the CPGB to greater effort in stirring up the British proletariat, in order to bring pressure on Parliament to ratify Anglo-Soviet treaties that would grant a much-needed loan to Russia and restore 'business collaboration' between the two countries' proletariats. It went on to admonish the British communists for the weakness of their 'agitation-propaganda' work in the British armed forces, who in the event of war must be ready to 'paralyse all the military preparations of the bourgeoisie'.[7]

It was part of Zinoviev's job to stir up revolution overseas, and he had signed many similar letters to communist parties in Europe, Asia, and even in the United States. Western governments had copies of these, obtained by their intelligence services and shared with each other. Other documents on these lines, received earlier in 1924, testified to the Comintern's view that the CPGB was underperforming. What was surprising about the 15 September letter was its timing: for it arrived just when the first ever Labour government in Britain, in power since January 1924, had run into serious trouble. Indeed, on 8 October, the day before SIS received the letter, the government was defeated on a Liberal amendment to a Conservative motion of censure in the House of Commons, and the Prime Minister, J. Ramsay MacDonald, had asked HM King George V to dissolve Parliament so that a general election could be called.

Within a fortnight of its arrival in London, copies of the Zinoviev Letter had reached Conservative Central Office and the Tory-controlled press. It was published in the *Daily Mail* on 25 October—four days before the general election—together with a note of protest drafted in the Foreign Office and issued, according to MacDonald (who served as Foreign Secretary as well as Prime Minister), without his authorization. This was a gift to Labour's political opponents, who in the last stages of the election campaign could portray MacDonald's government as both incompetent and in thrall to the 'Reds' in Moscow. Despite this, on 29 October 1924 Labour polled over a million more votes than they had in the election of December 1923 that had put them in office. But the Conservatives, who had healed damaging internal divisions and reformed their party machinery, gained 48.3 per cent of the total vote to Labour's 33 per cent, while the Liberals, the traditional party of opposition, slumped to 17.6 per cent.

The Zinoviev Letter may, as all parties claimed, have damaged the Labour vote; it did not lose them the election. But that view was not shared by many of MacDonald's ministerial colleagues, the trade unions, or the wider Labour Party. They felt cheated and humiliated by what had happened, sentiments that were exacerbated by the mystery surrounding the whole affair. In the febrile atmosphere following electoral defeat, it was only too easy for Labour supporters to blame dirty tricks by a reactionary Establishment, in which they included the intelligence services, the civil service, and the press as well as Conservative Central Office. Early enquiries were contradictory and inconclusive, and a steady stream of scandals kept the story alive. The fact that successive investigations made it more likely that the Zinoviev Letter was a forgery did not diminish its political potency. Each decade seemed to bring a new 'revelation' that reignited suspicions about what happened in 1924. The Letter was to rear its head again in successive general elections, in the context of atomic espionage, the treachery of the Cambridge Spies, internal divisions within the Labour Party, and even the Falklands War. There were a number of official enquiries, including a major investigation in the late 1960s in the aftermath of Kim Philby's defection[8] and the publication of a book on the Letter by the *Sunday Times* 'Insight' team that claimed to have solved the mystery.[9]

The Zinoviev Letter has not only haunted British politics, it has haunted my career as well. As an official historian working for the Foreign and Commonwealth Office (FCO) for more than forty years, my job involved, among other things, investigating and explaining historical conspiracies, and debunking them where possible, though the most persistent ones never go away. When I joined the FCO in 1972, new questions had been raised recently about the authorship of the Letter, based on material found at Harvard, and this was followed by a rash of articles speculating on the authenticity of the Letter and deploring the archival obstacles to discovering the 'truth'. Later, when a new set of documents was released by the Treasury in 1992, it added further fuel to the fire.[10] Nothing that was published had laid the matter to rest satisfactorily.

Why has this curious document had such a lasting impact? One reason lies in the history of the Labour Party itself. Established in 1900, by 1924 it had replaced the Liberal Party as the principal opposition to the Tories: a remarkable achievement. Nevertheless, during the first 100 years of its existence Labour was in power for only twenty-three. When Labour governments took office, they struggled against the assumption that the Conservatives were the natural party of government. Powerful media, financial, and business interests tended to support the Conservatives. Some right-wing individuals and organizations were less than scrupulous in the methods they used to try and prevent Labour coming to power, and to attack them when they did. At the same time, Labour governments faced damaging splits in the ranks of their own party, with strong criticism from left as well as right. During the two world wars, party politics and party divisions were suppressed to an extent by the need for national unity, but peace-time saw the resurgence of old habits at all points on the political spectrum.

Long intervals between periods in office cause problems for any political party. Incoming ministers usually lack experience of govern-ment, of working with the civil service, the military, and the intelligence agencies. In Labour's case, these elements of the British Establishment were suspected by many party members of being not just innately conservative, but actively hostile. In particular, some Labour ministers suspected the intelligence agencies—which had been in existence roughly as long as the Labour Party—of undermining them behind the scenes. This did not stop ministers from working professionally and harmoniously with those agencies during all Labour administra-tions (nor from trying to use them for the detection of industrial sub-version from the Left). But 1924 was never forgotten, and the Zinoviev Letter returned to haunt both government and officials at times of trouble and vulnerability.

Another key element was the ambivalent relationship between the Labour Party and the Soviet Union. From Ramsay MacDonald's first administration in 1924, Labour governments rejected the totalitarian nature of the Bolshevik regime that had come to power so violently in 1917. They were committed to changing society through reform rather than revolution; and after the Second World War, the threat posed to British and Western interests by the Soviet bloc meant that Cold War considerations predominated in Anglo-Soviet relations. Yet there remained within the wider Labour movement a certain residual fellow feeling for the Soviet regime, an admiration for the first real government 'by the people for the people', that ministers could not ignore altogether. In practice, successive Labour governments were often actively hostile to the Soviet Union: but there was always an element in the party who felt they *ought* to get on well together.

This ambivalence went both ways: Soviet leaders tended to prefer Conservative administrations in Britain, and to be suspicious of, if not openly hostile to, their Labour counterparts. As Conservative Foreign Secretary Sir Austen Chamberlain remarked in 1927, the Soviet government was more ready to shake hands with him than they were with Labour ministers: 'They regarded Conservatives as their natural enemies, but the more moderate among the Labour leaders they looked upon as traitors.'[11] This remained true when Labour came to power in 1945: Stalin would far rather have dealt with Winston Churchill than with Clement Attlee. The tension between the advantages of 'normalized' political and economic relations, and the clash between Soviet communism and Western capitalism, were felt in Moscow as well as in London. Set against this context, the ghost of Zinoviev was never quite exorcized.

Of course, the relationship changed over time and according to the international context. The first two Labour governments, in 1924 and 1929–31, held office at a period of global economic dislocation and growing resentment on the part of those on the losing side in the First World War. The Soviet Union combined an active programme of hostile propaganda, espionage, and subversion, aimed both at Britain and its Empire, with the pursuit of normalized relations at intergovernmental level. After a major political and economic crisis in 1931 that led to the formation of a National Government under Ramsay MacDonald, there was no further Labour government until 1945. In the meantime, many on the left were alienated by the Stalinist purges of the 1930s; others, like the 'Magnificent Five' Cambridge spies,[12] committed themselves secretly to communism; still others maintained stubbornly that the Stalinist regime was not as black as it had been painted.

During the Second World War, the Soviet Union was the staunch ally of the Western powers from 1941 to 1945 and made an enormous contribution to Allied victory. It was, however, no surprise to those Labour ministers like Clement Attlee and Ernest Bevin, who had served in Churchill's War Cabinet, that the Russian wartime ally turned into a Soviet enemy as the Cold War unfolded during the early post-war years. Attlee, and his colleagues in the government formed following Labour's resounding victory in the 1945 general election, found that they had to spend a great deal of time combating communist threats both overt and covert, within Britain and overseas, at the same time as carrying out their ambitious domestic reform agenda.

Labour's defeat in 1951 was followed by another long period out of office, and the government formed by Harold Wilson in 1964 had to start from scratch in building good working relationships with Whitehall, and indeed with the Soviet Union. They succeeded in both, but not without considerable turbulence and distrust under the surface. A sharp increase in hostile Soviet espionage activities within the United Kingdom during the 1960s contributed to the atmosphere of suspicion. At the same time, Wilson made great efforts, with American encouragement, to foster good relations with Soviet leaders to secure their good offices with Hanoi in trying to bring an end to the long-running conflict in Vietnam. Despite the Soviet invasion of Czechoslovakia in 1968, the political advantages of engaging with the Soviet Union made Wilson unwilling to adopt too antagonistic a stance—a major reason why tackling Soviet espionage in the UK was left to his Conservative successor, Edward Heath.

But it was on the domestic front that the legacy of the Zinoviev Letter caused the most disturbance during the Wilson government of 1964–70. Ministers, and Wilson in particular, were on high alert for attempts to undermine the government, whether from right or left. Very sensitive to press criticism, they accused each other and officials of leaks (though most leaks came from No. 10). This affected their relations both with the civil service and with the intelligence establishment, though Wilson had a high regard for both. But insecurity and paranoia, in a rather febrile political and economic atmosphere, created the perfect climate for the ghost of Zinoviev to reappear.

A number of articles and books were published on the Letter during this period, and in 1967 a major official investigation into the authenticity and handling of the Zinoviev Letter was launched, carried out by a retired member of MI5. In fact, this investigation was prompted more by the spy scandals of the 1950s and 1960s than by accusations of political conspiracy. But it is directly relevant to the central question of the impact of the Zinoviev Letter on successive Labour governments.

The atmosphere of suspicion continued during the second Labour government of 1974–9, after the Conservative administration of Edward Heath had taken decisive action against the Soviet Union by expelling 105 of their intelligence officers in 1971.[13] Though there was little mention of the Zinoviev Letter in this period, the increasing paranoia of Harold Wilson, until his resignation in 1976, was a source of tension within the government and Whitehall. His replacement as Prime Minister, James Callaghan, did not share Wilson's suspicions of plots against him by domestic or foreign agencies, but rumours spread by conspiracy theorists that the security services were involved in a disinformation and destabilization campaign to discredit both Labour and Liberals were unsettling to the party.[14]

By the time Labour came to office again in 1997, after another long period of opposition, the Cold War had ended and the Soviet Union was no more. The Red Menace had dissipated with the crumbling of the communist underpinning of the Eastern bloc, and the early years of the Blair government saw the beginning of a new, promising period of Anglo-Russian relations. And yet the shadows of the past had not been dispelled entirely. The revelations of a former KGB archivist, Vasili Mitrokhin, provided new evidence of the extent of Soviet espionage during the Cold War.[15] Meanwhile, the intelligence landscape in Britain had been transformed by legislation between 1989 and 1994, putting the security and intelligence services onto a new statutory basis under parliamentary oversight, their heads named openly for the first time. Though secrecy remained an imperative, there was a greater willingness to discuss intelligence matters with the aim of increasing public understanding of the importance to national security of the work done by the agencies. The government's increased emphasis on open government, given concrete form in the Data Protection and Freedom of Information Acts,[16] created a climate in which intelligence matters could be discussed rather more openly than in previous years.

It was this new climate of openness, together with the end of the Cold War and the dissolution of the Soviet Union, that enabled the search for the Zinoviev Letter to make significant progress. One of the first acts of the MacDonald government in January 1924 had been to recognize *de jure* the Soviet Union, a move that had outraged many on the right. The traditional British ruling parties—Conservative and Liberal—thought the Labour government would be a brief aberration after which normal service would resume. Similarly, traditional ruling interests—political, financial, and military—throughout Europe and the wider world thought the communist regime in Russia could not endure. In both cases, they were wrong. The British political landscape had changed definitively, with Labour replacing the Liberals as the opposition to the Conservatives; the Soviet Union lasted until 1991.

And the ghost of Zinoviev continued to walk. In 1998 Nigel West, intelligence historian (and as Rupert Allason, a Conservative MP 1987–97), published with retired KGB Colonel Oleg Tsarev *The Crown Jewels: The British Secrets at the Heart of the KGB Archives*, purportedly based on material passed to Moscow by Philby and others.[17] The publication of *Crown Jewels*, which includes a chapter on the Zinoviev Letter, provoked much press speculation and a number of Parliamentary Questions. The late Robin Cook, then Foreign Secretary, was surprised at first at the way in which, seventy-five years later, the episode clearly retained such political resonance, particularly in his own party. However, he soon accepted not just the need for an investigation, but for greater openness about the sources of the evidence.

Some questioned the need for the continued closure of SIS records, presumed to hold the keys to the mystery.[18] On 12 February 1998, in a written parliamentary answer to Liberal Democrat MP Norman

Baker, who had asked if the Foreign Secretary would 'release for public scrutiny the files held by MI6 relating to the Zinoviev Letter', Robin Cook stated that having reviewed the arguments, he recognized that there was an 'overwhelmingly strong reason' for the continued permanent retention of SIS records under Section 3(4) of the Public Records Act 1958,[19] based on the 'unshakeable commitment' not to reveal the identities of those who cooperated with the Service. 'This essential trust would be undermined by a perception that undertakings of confidentiality were honoured for only a limited duration. In many cases, the risk of retribution against individuals can extend beyond a single generation.'[20]

The Foreign Secretary added, however, that he wished to be as open as possible, and so had commissioned the FCO Historians to write an account of the Zinoviev affair based on full access to SIS as well as FCO records. As Chief Historian of the FCO, it was my task to undertake this investigation, which extended to the records of all the UK's intelligence agencies, as well as to those of a number of Whitehall departments. The search led me to Washington and Moscow as well as Whitehall. At that time, the UK had close relations with the government of the Russian Federation, signing a memorandum of understanding on archival cooperation with them in 1998. Evidence from the Russian archives and cooperation from the Russian foreign intelligence service (SVR) provided important pieces of the Zinoviev jigsaw.

The key questions about the Letter's origins, handling, and immediate impact were covered in some detail in the FCO's 1999 report, *The Zinoviev Letter of 1924: 'A most extraordinary and mysterious business'*.[21] Yet although I was able to bring a lot of previously unseen material out into the open in this publication, I was unable to dispel completely the clouds of mystery surrounding the Letter. I was forced to conclude, like the redoubtable former MI5 officer, Miss Milicent Bagot, who had carried out the investigation in the 1960s, that there were too many gaps in the evidence, and variant interpretations, for the truth about the Zinoviev Letter to be established beyond doubt.[22] Like Miss Bagot, I concluded the Letter was almost certainly a forgery, but was unable to say with certainty who forged it. Equally, there were many possible candidates who might have leaked the Letter, though the idea of a coordinated conspiracy among civil servants or intelligence officers seemed to me, both then and now, very unlikely. If there is one thing long experience of government has taught me as a historian, it is that misfilings and mistakes are far more common than conspiracies, and that interdepartmental coordination is more aspirational than real. To quote Cass Sunstein, conspiracy theorists 'typically overestimate the competence and discretion of officials and bureaucracies, which are assumed to be capable of devising and carrying out sophisticated secret plans—despite abundant evidence that in open societies government action does not usually remain secret for very long'.[23] Even in closed societies, it can be hard to keep secrets for ever.

Twenty years later, it is time to revisit this extraordinary story, and to examine the reasons why it continues to have such strong political resonance in Britain. The 1999 report, based on privileged access to closed as well as open archives, remains authoritative in its detail, and it makes sense to draw on it closely in order to make best use of the intelligence material consulted in its preparation. But the report was necessarily specific in scope and limited in circulation, and since then more evidence has become available. In order to understand the Zinoviev Letter mystery in its broader political context, and explain its enduring fascination, we need to revisit the key questions—what was it? why was it controversial? and was it a forgery?—in the light of subsequent scholarship. I have moderated, rather than changed, my views since 1999, and while it remains impossible to establish the facts conclusively, there are some new and interesting things to say about this extraordinary document.

The longevity of the Zinoviev Letter controversy is indeed remarkable, considering that today the global, political, and intelligence context, in both Britain and Russia, is very different from what it was in 1999; just as in 1999 it was quite different from 1924. In the 1920s, fear of the spread of what was perceived as an alien and savage doctrine, Bolshevism, provided the focus not just for the politics of Left or Right, and so for the civil servants and intelligence agencies who served the government, but for the ordinary concerns of many in the aftermath of the First World War. Though the 'Red Peril' was over-taken from the late 1920s by the threat from Nazi Germany, against which the Soviet Union was to be a key ally in the Second World War, Britain and other Western powers continued to see communism as alien and threatening, a perception that underlay forty years of Cold War between East and West after 1945.

In the 1990s, the collapse of the Soviet Union and reunification of Germany created hopes of a more peaceful and less polarized world in which Russia and the former Warsaw Pact countries would coexist in a normalized, mutually beneficial relationship with Britain and her Western allies. Those hopes have, indeed, been largely realized; but they have been accompanied by new tensions, economic, social, and political, that have made the twenty-first-century world appear increasingly dangerous and uncertain. In this context, the investiga-tion of a political controversy nearly 100 years ago may seem arcane; but its continuing relevance, at a time when the distinctly ahistorical terms 'post-truth' and 'fake news' have become common parlance, will soon become clear. The Letter retains its power to intrigue and perplex, nearly a century after it was (never) written.

I

One Version of the Truth

Wednesday, 8 July 1998: Moscow

A visit to the Public Affairs Centre of the Russian foreign intelligence agency, the Sluzhba Vneshnei Razvedki (SVR). Greeted by someone whose business card describes him merely as an 'expert', I and my own personal expert, the principal Russian interpreter of the Foreign and Commonwealth Office (FCO), wait politely in a small room in an attractive eighteenth-century villa in central Moscow. A door opens, and admits Oleg Tsarev, former KGB colonel and co-author with Nigel West of a book called *The Crown Jewels: The British Secrets at the Heart of the KGB Archives.* The 'Crown Jewels' was the KGB's unofficial term for material handed to the Russians by British pro-Soviet spies, including the 'Cambridge Five', Kim Philby, Guy Burgess, Donald Maclean, Anthony Blunt, and John Cairncross. Published earlier in 1998, *Crown Jewels* had caused some disquiet in Britain. Even though, as the former KGB double agent Oleg Gordievsky pointed out, the book contained little that was new, a 'mere peep through the curtain', it showed, as historian Alistair Horne wrote in *The Times*, 'the other side of the hill of the most damaging traitors in British history'.[1]

A particular focus of parliamentary and media attention was chapter II of *Crown Jewels*, on the Zinoviev Letter. This document, purportedly sent by Bolshevik propaganda chief Grigori Zinoviev to the British Communist Party, exhorting it to greater revolutionary effort, had been used to smear the reputation of the first Labour government in 1924, and had been controversial ever since. The chapter in *Crown Jewels* set out in some detail the activities of an extraordinary character called Vladimir Orlov, former intelligence chief under tsarist, Bolshevik, and White Russian authorities, who supplied information simultaneously to a number of governments (including the British) and ran a forgery bureau in Berlin. According to one of Orlov's colleagues, the Zinoviev Letter had in fact been written by a former tsarist officer, Ivan Dmitrievich Pokrovsky, at the suggestion of a British intelligence officer called 'Captain Black'. On the basis of the evidence in its files, *Crown Jewels* stated, the KGB's predecessor, the OGPU or Unified State Political Directorate, had concluded that 'everything pointed to Ivan Pokrovsky as the author of the Zinoviev Letter' and that he had 'played a key role, together with British Intelligence, in the fabrication and despatch of the Zinoviev Letter'.[2]

The Crown Jewels was the latest in a long series of books and reports asserting the 'truth' about the Zinoviev Letter. The episode remained a sore spot for the British Labour Party even in 1998. But Labour MPs were not the only ones to ask questions in response to the new publication. Why should the British public have to learn about its history from traitors? All this had happened in 1924: surely it was time for the facts to be set out from official British sources. When, as Chief Historian of the FCO, I was commissioned to produce a report for the Foreign Secretary, Robin Cook, I realized that my researches would not be complete without a visit to Russia. His Excellency Yuri Fokine, then Russian Ambassador in London, proved very supportive and smoothed my approach to the relevant authorities. Since I neither spoke nor read Russian, my friend Tony Bishop, senior analyst of Soviet and Russian affairs in the FCO, who had interpreted for every British Prime Minister since Harold Macmillan, travelled with me.[3] Now, somewhat to our astonishment, we were talking to Oleg Tsarev, who greeted me with a sweeping, and perhaps ironic, bow. Our discussion was brief: he signed my copy of *Crown Jewels*, mischievously, with the words 'from a comrade in arms'. I asked him, as he departed, whether the account of the Zinoviev Letter given in the book was accurate. 'It is', said Colonel Tsarev magisterially, 'one version of the truth.'

The meeting with Tsarev was staged and dramatic, intentionally no doubt, yet nonetheless impressive. I now realize that his final comment, together with the fact that I already knew from British sources that a number of the details about the Zinoviev Letter given in *Crown Jewels* were wrong, led me to discount rather too readily other aspects of the OGPU account. At the time, however, I merely felt privileged to have had the chance to discuss the Russian version of the Zinoviev Letter story with an inside source. It was clear from the meeting that the SVR regarded *Crown Jewels* as 'their' book: they preferred, they said rather engagingly, to brief journalists or authors since no one believed them if they published the information themselves. In the detailed diary I kept of my visit to Moscow, I noted that the encounter had been 'a stunning success within the parameters I'd envisaged'.

During our week's stay in Moscow, Tony and I also had meetings with other senior figures, such as the head of the Federation Archives and Academician Yakovlev of the International Democracy Foundation. As many former ministers would agree, Tony's post-meeting analyses of what was said, of body language, and the general mood music were as enlightening and valuable as his interpreting. For most of our stay, however, Tony and I worked hard in the archives, principally at the Russian Foreign Ministry and in the Russian Centre for the Preservation and Study of Documents of Contemporary History (formerly the Institute for Marxism–Leninism; once, taking the lift by mistake to the basement, we found disembodied heads of Lenin and Marx rolling in the dust). We examined the records of the Politburo and the Comintern,[4] of the Commissariat of Foreign Affairs, and even of the Communist Party of Great Britain (CPGB), of which the Russian Centre held a full set. I was not so much of a spare part as I had feared, since apart from the CPGB archives, which were of course in English, many of the records were in German, not Russian—a reminder of the fact that the Bolshevik leaders who had seized power in the revolution of October 1917 had spent years in exile, many of them in Germany.

Everywhere we went, the collections were guarded by enormously knowledgeable lady archivists, who despite their deliberately formidable manner were proud to show us extra nuggets that they thought we 'might like to see'. Some of these made the hairs rise on the back of our necks, such as notes—cocooned in many layers of tissue paper—bearing Stalin's original signature, and a small collection of papers seized from Zinoviev's home and office when he was arrested in 1936. Tony's hand was shaking as he explained the significance of a rough note in Zinoviev's papers in which he awarded himself '2½' for effort out of the 5 that represented top marks in the Russian educational system. Despite his undoubted brutality, it was hard not to feel sorry for Zinoviev, who had been one of the original supporters of Lenin in exile but whose star was already beginning to wane in the Bolshevik firmament in 1924; he was to be disciplined and rehabilitated more than once before being executed in July 1936 for allegedly plotting the assassination of Stalin.

When the archives were closed, Tony showed me round Moscow and its environs. He was an unparalleled guide: he not only knew what everything was and its history, but usually a good story about it based on his long years of travelling with ministers and senior officials. (On the plane to Moscow, he had presented me with a list of useful phrases, complete with phonetic guide to pronunciation, that he had prepared previously for Michael Portillo.) Under his tutelage I drank shots of vodka at good 'people-watching' vantage points, ate traditional Russian food (including in one restaurant that, according to Tony, had been a favourite of Stalin's), and marvelled at the architectural wonders of Red Square. We went to the opera at the Stanislawski Theatre, drinking Russian champagne and eating smoked roe and 'pike-perch' on black bread in the interval. Tony explained that the mirrored area between the auditorium and the foyer is so large because for more than six months of the year the audience would need space to divest themselves of heavy outer clothing and boots before entering. In the interval couples strolled up and down in this area, arm in arm, reflected multiple times in the huge mirrors. We also visited the amazing shopping centre built in layers underneath Manezh Square by Mayor Yuri Luzhkov, where the window displays of a 'hunting shop' depicted dramatic scenes from Russian history, such as driving back the Mongolian hordes, with papier mâché figures set against the painted backdrop. A beautifully painted blue and white porcelain chess set had pieces that were called 'Muscovite mafiosi', complete with mobile phones and bodyguards!

Venturing out of the city, we visited the Novodevichy ('New Maidens') monastery, founded in 1524 to celebrate the taking of Smolensk from Lithuania by Basil III. And of course a visit to Moscow would not be complete without a trip on its palatial and spotless Metro, with marble ticket halls, chandeliers, and uplit pillars. This spirited us up to the top of the Lenin Hills (now called Sparrow Hills), where couples in wedding outfits came for a blessing and photographs. I gazed over Moscow, visited the small green church where Pushkin was married, and bought a wonderful set of interlocking Russian dolls that I still display at home. The outer is a caricature of Boris Yeltsin, complete with both hammer and sickle, and Russian star and flag; within are Gorbachev, Brezhnev, Khrushchev, Stalin, Lenin, and a tiny Tsar.

I have not been back to Moscow since 1998, so I know that a lot of things will have changed since that visit. But this account of my trip is not intended merely as a description of tourist attractions. Apart from the copious notes Tony and I had taken that were to prove invaluable in piecing together the Zinoviev Letter mystery, the visit, even if brief, had given me some valuable insights. After many conversations with British Embassy staff, I wrote in my diary that it was 'easy to see how people get the bug serving here, and spend their careers trying to get back to Moscow'. As the Ambassador said, behind the politics and economics Russia is endlessly fascinating because it is so *human.* I also felt that, less than ten years after the collapse of the Soviet Union, many contradictions lay underneath the surface:

> Moscow has a buzz, amid its stunning architecture, amazingly swift restoration programmes and increasingly lively social life; but it's also got an undercurrent of savagery, a dangerous excitement and brutality hovering under the veneer of progress and freedom visible outside. The view of the Kremlin as you walk from the hotel to the Embassy[5] along the river, sun on the golden domes, is uplifting and inspiring— but you feel that it would not take much to tip you, it and most of Moscow through the oubliette into chaos, violence and dog-eat-dog society in every sense…I'm bowled over by Moscow and the Muscovites.

These judgements were certainly not profound: I am not a Russian specialist. But the thoughts that prompted them were important in helping me to understand the environment in which the events of 1924 had taken place. The documentation I had seen, and the ever-present sense of dramatic history with which Russia was imbued, impressed upon me the importance of looking at the context in which the Zinoviev Letter was written, and the use that was made of it, from the Russian as well as the British side. In 1924 the Bolshevik revolution, Russia's withdrawal from the First World War, and the ensuing brutal civil war were very recent memories, as were the mass starvation and deprivation that created the conditions for the fall of the Romanov dynasty. Bolshevik rule, and the newly created Soviet Union,[6] were in their infancy, fragile and facing internal and external opposition. The need for constant vigilance against threats both real and perceived, together with the exertion of the iron control over civilian life necessary to the success of the Bolshevik regime, meant that aggressive intelligence methods were part of the fabric of the Soviet state.

As both Lenin and Stalin[7] recognized, it was helpful to encourage within the Communist Party of the Soviet Union (CPSU) and the wider populace the idea that there was a consistent campaign by Western governments to undermine the Soviet Union. This was not

a difficult concept to sell when the activities of 'Western spies' during
and after the revolution, including the so-called 'Lockhart Plot' in the
summer of 1918,[8] remained very fresh in Russian minds, and when the
civil war, in which Western governments had supported White Russian
forces against the Bolsheviks, had ended only three years earlier. The
threat of Western subversion was a useful tool in maintaining order
and authority in diverse and unwieldy Soviet territories, as well as
enabling Stalin to dispose of political opponents who could be shown
to have 'factional tendencies' that threatened party unity; it also
reflected genuine apprehension on the part of the Bolsheviks.

As the material brought out of Russia by the former KGB archivist
Vasili Mitrokhin has shown, in order to understand the working of
Soviet intelligence 'it is frequently necessary to enter a world of smoke
and mirrors where the target is as much the product of Bolshevik
delusions as of real counter-revolutionary conspiracy'.[9] But that does
not mean that all anti-Bolshevik conspiracies were a delusion. The
regime faced a constant stream of attacks both overt and covert from
anti-Bolshevik elements throughout Europe, including Russian monarchists who wanted to place a new tsar on the throne, former tsarist
military officers, discontented émigrés and nationals of countries
with a grudge against the Soviets (like Poland), not to mention well-
financed agents and agencies sponsored by governments—including
that of Britain—who resented Russian subversive influence in their
territories. The Bolshevik regime felt impelled to spend enormous
amounts of money on espionage and counter-espionage, as well as
on 'agitation' and propaganda. The results of that global effort of
intelligence collection may have been valuable, but they were also
destabilizing, in more ways than one: they encouraged the idea that
the Soviet Union was under constant threat, but they also numbed the
impact of intelligence that could have been genuinely useful.

This was already true in the 1920s, although even more so in the
1930s and 1940s, as officials remained unwilling to bring unwelcome
news to Stalin, and the increasingly autocratic leader refused to believe
intelligence that did not accord with his own preconceptions. When

disaster did strike, as it did when Hitler invaded Russia in June 1941, it compounded the idea of Russia as victim. After Allied victory in 1945, the terrible price that the Soviet Union had paid for its decisive contribution to that victory made Stalin and later Soviet leaders both determined to secure Russia's status as a major power, and sensitive to the idea that Western capitalism would continue to seek to undermine the USSR and profit from post-war recovery at its expense.

I thought of all these things when, in July 1998, I visited the Alexandrov Gardens under the Kremlin wall, where wedding couples queued up to lay flowers at the flame of the Unknown Soldier. There were the impressive monuments to the 'heroic cities' of the Second World War: Leningrad, Murmansk, Sebastopol, Kiev...places where millions of Russians had lost their lives. In 1924, the 'Great Patriotic War' lay in the future, but pride in the achievements of Soviet communism, suspicions of Western capitalism, and a belief in the importance of espionage, subversion, and propaganda were very much in the present.

On my return to London, I used what I had found in the Russian archives to complement material from British sources, both from the publicly available Cabinet Office, Foreign Office, and Treasury files, and also from the archives of the UK's principal intelligence agencies, to which I had privileged access. Not only was it valuable to be able to cross-check different accounts of the same events, but it was also important to identify what the gaps were, both in British and Russian records. The deeper I probed, the more inconsistencies were revealed, and the more intractable were the problems: was the Zinoviev Letter really written by Zinoviev? If so, did the British Communist Party ever receive it? If it was a forgery, who was responsible? Was it, as Tsarev and West said, Pokrovsky? Or was it part of a Moscow plot to discredit Zinoviev? Was it Vladimir Orlov or, as the 1967 book by the *Sunday Times* 'Insight' team alleged, one Alexis Bellegarde? Were the British intelligence agencies involved in its fabrication, or in giving it to the press, or in using it against the Labour Party, or all of these at once? What part did Foreign Office officials play, or Conservative Central Office?

It was clear that despite the valuable extra material from Moscow, and indeed from Washington, I would not be able to answer all these questions conclusively. The report published by the FCO in 1999 made a lot of evidence publicly available for the first time, but it could only represent my best judgement based on what I had found—my version of the truth. The report was generally well received, although inevitably some commentators were not satisfied. There were some differences of interpretation: on 4 February 1999 *The Guardian* head-line read 'Zinoviev letter was dirty trick by MI6', while *The Times* affirmed that 'MI6 did not write the Zinoviev Letter'. Overall, how-ever, the report's verdict that the Letter was almost certainly a forgery was accepted, as well as the conclusion that some members of the British intelligence establishment probably played some part in its manipulation for political purposes, although there was no evidence of an institutional conspiracy. *The Independent* quoted my comment on why the Letter still had so much resonance in 1999: 'It's not quite sex, lies and videotape but it's certainly sex and spies. It's a fairly potent combination.'[10]

I knew in 1999 that the report must begin by setting the Zinoviev Letter in its contemporary context. Twenty years later, that is even more important. In order to bring this complex story up to date, it is necessary first to set the scene in 1924: in Britain, where a Labour government was in power for the first time; in the Soviet Union, where the Bolshevik regime sought to establish itself more firmly both at home and internationally; and in the conspiratorial world of espionage and political trickery that is the essential backdrop to the whole episode.

1924: the first British Labour government

The Labour Party had formed a government in January 1924 (much to their own surprise),[11] when both the Conservatives and Liberals were split and saw a (short-lived) Labour administration as a chance for them to regroup and to prove that inexperienced socialists were incapable of running the country. The Conservatives were in disarray over the issue of free trade, which had provoked Prime Minister Stanley Baldwin to call what turned out to be a disastrous election in 1923. The Liberals were split into rival factions led by two former Prime Ministers, Herbert Asquith and David Lloyd George, both of whom thought Labour's inevitable failure would show the Liberals to be the real party of radical reform. In the event, both sets of Liberals had miscalculated badly, and it was to be the Conservatives who profited from their period out of office in 1924.

The dominant figure in the Labour Party was J. Ramsay MacDonald, in whose back room the Labour Representation Committee had been formed in 1900.[12] The illegitimate son of a Highland ploughman and a dressmaker, MacDonald had cut his political teeth in the Fabian Society and Independent Labour Party. Elected leader of the Parliamentary Labour Party in 1911, he had resigned and been vilified for his opposition to the First World War, yet returned as leader in 1922: handsome, eloquent, a man who, according to his biographer, 'combined respectability with panache'.[13] MacDonald took up the challenge of forming the first Labour government with both trepidation and determination. Cabinet making was not easy: it was difficult to find enough men with ministerial potential. He took on himself the twin roles of Prime Minister and Foreign Secretary, and enlisted some senior Liberals to contribute wisdom and experience to his untried team (a change of allegiance that, according to Attorney General Sir Patrick Hastings, 'resulted in the practical severance of all social acquaintanceship', even if the language and values of the two parties differed little).[14]

MacDonald had no intention of satisfying his political opponents' hopes that Labour would soon show itself unequal to government. Conscious of the need to hold in check the more radical wing of the Labour Party, and to stay in power long enough to demonstrate competence, he and his colleagues were for the most part unexceptionably moderate in their policies. In practice, the government enjoyed frequent

Figure 2. J. Ramsay MacDonald, first Labour Prime Minister

support from the Liberals,[15] and occasional help from the Conservatives, with whose leader, Stanley Baldwin, MacDonald was on good terms. The Chancellor of the Exchequer, Philip Snowden, differed little in his approach from his Conservative and Liberal predecessors since the end of the First World War, and was approved of by the Treasury for his belief in sound finance.[16] On a number of domestic issues, like housing and the creation of the National Grid for the distribution of electricity, Labour's record was impressive.[17]

But the most noteworthy achievements were in the realm of foreign policy, where MacDonald knew his administration had the opportunity to make its mark. As his biographer noted, 'The sight of a Labour foreign secretary grappling successfully with problems which had baffled a Curzon or a Balfour would do more to disprove the charge that a working-class party was unfit to govern than would any conceivable action which minority Government could take at home.'[18] Indeed, of the two major offices he held, it is generally agreed that MacDonald paid closer attention to the Foreign Office at the expense of the premiership. Lord Haldane, who served as Lord Chancellor in the Labour government, wrote that while MacDonald 'understood the Continent as none of his predecessors had done', he 'did not care about other matters. He left them to us, with the result that they seemed not to have the attention of the Prime Minister.'[19]

Two of the most pressing international issues that were destabilizing economic recovery in Britain and Europe, as well as threatening the post-war peace, were Germany's inability to meet debt repayments exacted by the victorious powers after the First World War, and the linked issue of French fears of a resurgent Germany, which had led them to send occupation forces into the Ruhr region in 1923.[20] MacDonald, with long experience in the contentious world of international socialism, proved a far-sighted and skilful statesman, successfully carrying through the negotiations already in train for an international agreement on German reparations, and beginning to lay the foundations for a European security protocol under the banner of the League of Nations.[21]

It was the Labour government's Russian policy that was to prove its downfall. Western powers, particularly those like Britain with empires targeted by Bolshevik propaganda, had struggled in the aftermath of the First World War and Russian Civil War to find a way of interacting with a country whose government was based on an alien ideology but which nevertheless sought international legitimacy. Although MacDonald held no brief for communism, he felt that the way to moderate the excesses of the Bolshevik regime, and to create a mutually beneficial relationship, lay through rehabilitation: to treat Russia as a regular trading partner, encourage the Soviets to pay their debts and fulfil their obligations, and include them in the international community. In a sense this was only continuing the policy of previous governments: Lloyd George's Liberal coalition had signed a trade agreement with Russia in 1921, despite vociferous opposition, including from Winston Churchill (who referred to the Soviet delegation as a 'nest of vipers').[22] But relations had quickly soured as the Bolsheviks maintained a campaign of subversive propaganda throughout the Empire. A formal protest by Foreign Secretary Lord Curzon in May

1923 against Comintern tactics and the behaviour of the Soviet Trade Delegation in London (STD) achieved little save to compromise British cryptographic operations by alerting the Russians to the interception of their diplomatic traffic.[23]

During the 1923 election campaign both Labour and Liberals had pledged to restore relations with the Soviet Union if they won, and MacDonald referred in public to the 'pompous folly of standing aloof from the Russians'.[24] One of his Cabinet's first decisions was to recognize the Soviet Union *de jure* on 2 February 1924.[25] This was designed to please the Labour left as well as to normalize Anglo-Soviet relations, and Moscow was invited to send representatives to Britain to 'draw up the preliminary basis of a complete treaty to settle all questions between the two countries'. Negotiations began in April 1924, and by early August, after a brief breakdown in the talks, agreement had been reached on two draft treaties, a general Anglo-Soviet treaty and a commercial treaty, with provision for a third whereby the British government would guarantee a loan to the Soviet Union if the latter had accepted provisions for compensation to British prerevolutionary bondholders and property owners. The Cabinet agreed on 30 July 1924 that the draft treaties should be put to the Soviet government, together with an offer to recommend to Parliament the guarantee of a loan if the Russians agreed to the property claims terms and fulfilled their treaty obligations.[26] The drafts were signed at the tenth plenary meeting of the delegations on 10 August 1924, and tabled in Parliament for ratification to be voted on after the summer recess.[27]

The negotiations had been difficult from the start, and dogged by hostile press comment. MacDonald expressed growing dissatisfaction with the proceedings and the criticism of his government that accompanied them.[28] Preoccupied with European issues, he had opened the London Anglo-Russian Conference on 14 April, then largely delegated the conduct of the talks to his Parliamentary Under-Secretary, the radical Liberal Arthur Ponsonby. He also excused Sir Eyre Crowe, Permanent Under-Secretary (PUS) in the Foreign Office, from any involvement in the negotiations, since Crowe had 'put it formally and repeatedly on record that he entirely disapproved of and protested against the whole proceeding'.[29] Although the exemption did not apply to other officials—members of the FO's Northern Department were prominent in the British delegation[30]—none of this indicated that the Prime Minister had much confidence in a successful outcome.

MacDonald knew that his government would encounter significant political difficulties in securing parliamentary approval for any agreement that involved a loan to the Soviet Union, which was opposed by both Conservatives and Liberals; but as Ponsonby told MacDonald and Snowden on 18 July, 'without a loan there would be no treaty and without a government guarantee the City would not issue a loan'.[31] If the government wanted a positive outcome to the Anglo-Russian negotiations, it had no choice but to push ahead on the understanding that if the treaties were approved, a loan would be guaranteed. And MacDonald, even if distracted and doubtful of success, did want a positive outcome: for the sake of Party unity, for the economic benefits of normalizing trading relations with the Soviet Union, and for the kudos attached to one of the first policies his government had announced, an answer to Asquith's criticism that the treaties were 'crude experiments in nursery diplomacy'.[32]

Labour's recognition of the Bolshevik regime and attempt to negotiate treaties that included a loan for the 'Reds' gave their political opponents a powerful weapon to use against the government during the parliamentary recess in the summer of 1924. By that time both Conservative and Liberal Party organizers had begun to feel, after six months of a Labour government, that it was about time the political landscape was reset to its 'normal' configuration. In particular, Baldwin, his fellow ex-ministers, and Conservative Central Office had made good use of their time out of office by reforming the party organization and working hard on their legislative programme for when they regained power.[33]

During the summer of 1924, the Conservatives orchestrated a virulent press campaign against the draft Anglo-Russian treaties, while many Liberals could not stomach the idea of extending a loan to the Bolsheviks. The idea that the government was in thrall to its extreme left wing began to take hold among the wider public, while continuing high unemployment further damaged Labour's reputation. Things were already bad when the Campbell Case made them worse. John Ross Campbell, a leading Scottish communist, was the assistant editor of the *Workers' Weekly*, in which an article was published on 25 July 1924 calling on the armed forces to join together and form 'the nucleus of an organization that will prepare the whole of the soldiers, sailors and airmen, not merely to refuse to go to war, or to refuse to shoot strikers during industrial conflicts', but to 'go forward in a common attack upon the capitalists and smash capitalism for ever'. This article, and a similar one of 1 August, was sent to the Director of Public Prosecutions after indignant representations from the armed services; Campbell was arrested on 5 August and charged under the 1797 Incitement to Mutiny Act with 'seducing members of HM forces from their allegiance'. The decision to prosecute caused an immediate uproar in left-wing circles: at its Executive Committee meeting on 7 August, the CPGB denounced this 'iniquitous action on the part of the Labour Government against a working class organization at the behest of the Naval and Military authorities'. Indignation also spread throughout the wider Labour movement, with many pointing out that most Labour MPs had at some point made statements on the same lines as those printed in the *Workers' Weekly*.

MacDonald realized quickly—but too late—the political implications of their decision to prosecute Campbell. The Cabinet decided on 6 August to withdraw the prosecution,[34] but the damage had been done. MacDonald's handling of the affair, including making a parliamentary statement that appeared to contradict directly the Cabinet minutes, discredited him with colleagues and created an impression of government weakness and incompetence, as well as inflaming CPGB and Labour opinion.[35] The government's opponents were quick to exploit its confusion, which came at the ideal moment in the campaign against the draft Russian treaties. When Parliament was recalled on 30 September 1924 in connection with the Irish boundary dispute,[36] the Conservatives mounted an attack. They moved a vote of censure, and the Liberals tabled an amendment calling for an enquiry into the Campbell affair. On 8 October, after a long and bad-tempered debate in which both MacDonald and the Attorney General, Sir Patrick Hastings, struggled to mount a coherent defence of their actions in the Campbell Case,[37] the government was defeated.

MacDonald had warned the House that if defeated he would resign: 'It will', he said, 'be the end of what Hon. Members on all sides of the House will agree has been a high adventure—the end of a Government which, I think, has contributed much to the honour of the country, to our social stability, and which, when the country has an opportunity of passing a verdict upon it, will come again.'[38] He gave the impression that he was almost relieved at what had happened, telling HM King George V that the motion of censure was 'one of the moves in a game which made our position for further fighting intolerable'.[39] Yet MacDonald immediately threw himself vigorously into campaigning for the general election. Always sensitive to criticism, he was stung by the attacks on his probity (though he had brought much of them on himself), and was ready to defend his government's record.[40] MacDonald had every intention of fighting to win, basing his campaign on Labour's achievements since January 1924.

1924: a significant year in Soviet politics

From the perspective of the Soviet government, the timing of the Zinoviev Letter seemed inauspicious, though opportune for opponents of the regime. Lenin, the determined and charismatic figurehead of the Bolshevik movement, died on 21 January 1924, the day before MacDonald took office as Prime Minister. This confluence of events nearly overwhelmed the only pro-Labour (and partly Soviet-funded) British newspaper, the *Daily Herald*, which had to cover both at a time when a rail strike meant it was short of paper.[41] Lenin was succeeded by the *troika* of Zinoviev, Lev Kamenev,[42] and Josef Stalin, which had assumed increasing authority since Lenin suffered strokes in 1922 and 1923. All three were members of the Central Committee of the Communist Party and its Politburo, the body that exercised ultimate authority in the Soviet Union.[43] According to Boris Bazhanov, Stalin's assistant and secretary to the Politburo, Kamenev, Zinoviev, and Stalin met the night before each Politburo meeting, ostensibly to approve the agenda but in practice operating as 'a secret government which decided—in advance—all important matters... In fact the *troika* decided how each question should be resolved at tomorrow's session, agreeing even on what roles each would play in the discussion... everything the Politburo was to decide was predetermined.'[44]

Stalin himself had served as the Party's General Secretary since 1922, recognizing that the road to absolute power lay through control of the machinery of government. By 1924, he was already emerging

Figure 3. Bolshevik leaders: l–r, Stalin, Rykov, Kamenev, and Zinoviev

as the dominant figure in the *troika*, working ruthlessly behind the scenes to gather power into his own hands and eliminate opponents. For the present, however, he still needed the support of Zinoviev and Kamenev to sideline Trotsky, whom he saw as his most dangerous rival.[45] And despite the fact that Lenin's so-called 'testament', written at the end of 1922 with a postscript calling for Stalin's removal from the post of General Secretary, was made known to the party leaders in May 1924, Zinoviev and Kamenev supported him, urging the committee to retain Stalin in his post:

> Thinking, with amazing naivete, that Stalin was no longer a threat because Lenin's testament would considerably diminish his weight in the Party, they agreed to save him.[46]

By the early 1920s, the Bolsheviks' belief that the proletarian revolution would soon spread across the globe had been tempered by experience. After the heady success of the October Revolution, the collapse of European empires during the First World War, and the establishment of the Comintern in 1919, efforts to inspire and support successful uprisings in other countries had proved disappointingly ineffective. The Politburo had been forced to accept that capitalism was not in danger of imminent collapse. Pressing ahead with an undiluted policy of promoting global revolution could only isolate Russia at a time when it badly needed help from and trade with other countries to restore its own shattered economy. At least temporarily, it was necessary to take a more long-term view. Stalin was prepared to accept the idea of 'socialism in one country', the USSR, and to concentrate on establishing and enforcing absolute party control of the state, while others, including leading figures in the Comintern, insisted that the overseas struggle must continue.

Although Soviet government representatives maintained consistently when challenged that the Comintern was a party organ over which they had no control, it is clear that the Politburo determined its political strategy, just as it determined that of the government itself.[47] The Comintern may have been an embarrassment at times; it was, as one account of Bolshevik diplomacy put it, difficult for the Narkomindel to 'maintain friendly relations with a government which Comintern was working simultaneously to overthrow'.[48] But as Robert Hodgson, the British Chargé d'Affaires in Moscow,[49] observed to the Foreign Office on 3 October 1924:

> The 'Comintern' is the instrument which the party has fashioned for the purpose of bringing about, through world revolution, the universal dictatorship of the proletariat: the Union of Soviet Republics is the image in whose likeness the world—when the efforts of 'Comintern' have been successful—is to be recreated.[50]

Since his appointment as head of the Comintern's Executive Committee in 1920, Zinoviev had maintained a flow of international correspondence to keep other communist parties up to the mark. He had played a key part in encouraging the abortive revolution in Germany in October 1923,[51] and the records of the Executive Committee contain many examples of draft instructions to communist parties in countries where the prospects for revolution seemed promising.[52] Although Zinoviev's influence was already declining (he was to be removed from his Comintern post for 'factional activity' in 1926), he remained in 1924 an important figure in the Soviet hierarchy. An inexhaustible plotter, his devotion to the party, eloquence, and zeal seemed undiminished, although his schemes to promote revolution globally through the Comintern were subject to scrutiny by the Politburo and not always approved.[53]

It seems unlikely that Zinoviev and his comrades would have regarded Britain as ripe for revolution in 1924. The formation of a Labour government in January 1924 had posed something of a dilemma for the Bolsheviks. The Comintern had allocated only £2,500 to the CPGB for the election campaign in 1923,[54] with £10,000 allotted to Labour, a modest sum (although Deputy Commissar for Foreign Affairs Maxim Litvinov warned this would damage the Labour Party if discovered).[55] While it was encouraging that a left- rather than right-wing administration should be in power, the Comintern view was that the 'pseudo-socialist' leaders of the Labour Party were likely to 'endeavour to arrest the historic process of the advent to power of the British proletariat'. Zinoviev and the Executive Committee were not sure whether they wanted to bring the Labour government down, or make use of it.[56]

Nevertheless, Labour's early formal recognition of the Soviet government, offering the prospects of international legitimacy and a hopeful precedent for other countries to follow, was clearly welcomed in Moscow, and even the Comintern accepted that an attack on the new British government would be counterproductive. A letter of 18 March 1924 from the Executive Committee to the CPGB instructed that open anti-government action was 'only permissible should the Government commit some grave infringement of the rights of the working classes'.[57] A further memorandum by Zinoviev dated 26 March 1924 spelled out the twin strands that underlay Soviet policy in the early months of the Labour government: British communists should use the government to achieve their own ends where possible, while organizing a 'real united front' with 'advanced sections of the workers' to 'politically take the imperialist Labour Party by the throat' when the time was right.[58]

The arrival of the Russian delegation in London in April 1924, to begin negotiations on Anglo-Soviet treaties and a possible loan, seems to have produced a moratorium on inflammatory instructions from the Comintern. Nobody expected Zinoviev to stop making fiery speeches about the inevitability of the proletarian revolution: but the evidence suggests he refrained, or was prevented, from sending instructions to the CPGB once the Anglo-Soviet negotiations began. Apart from a letter of 7 April exhorting the CPGB to organize mass demonstrations for May Day, no further missives from Zinoviev appear to have been sent until the Letter of 15 September.[59] According to a report received by the Secret Intelligence Service (SIS) from Berlin on 11 June 1924, once the Soviet delegation arrived in London no propaganda literature was sent to England: 'The Bolsheviks appear to be paying more attention to Central and South Eastern Europe and to the North.'[60] It seems the Soviet government, like the British Foreign Office, wanted to avoid 'unnecessary incidents' during the negotiations.[61] Just as the attempt to negotiate a set of Anglo-Russian treaties was controversial within MacDonald's own administration and the wider British political landscape, it also caused friction within the Bolshevik regime. Before the Anglo-Soviet negotiations opened, there had been disputes in Moscow over the composition of the Soviet delegation, while the Chargé d'Affaires in London, Christian Rakovsky,[62] who was to lead the talks from the Russian side, feared that inflammatory statements by Zinoviev ruined any chance of success from the start.[63]

Yet the Russians badly needed the negotiations to succeed: however defiant the statements by Zinoviev and other party firebrands, the Soviet economy was precarious, agricultural prospects poor, and a settlement with the West was needed to restore international confidence and enable recovery. Although the Labour government in Britain might be incurably bourgeois, it offered something the Bolsheviks wanted: normalization of Anglo-Soviet relations, trade opportunities, and above all a loan. Only in England, wrote Rakovsky, 'will we be able to combine the solution of our debts with getting credits and loans'.[64] A treaty would demonstrate publicly that the Soviet Union was a power with influence and stature, a member of the concert of nations—even if its *raison d'être* was the spreading of a political ideology that undermined those nations. At the same time, they hoped that trade and better political relations would prevent the formation of any new Western anti-communist grouping.[65]

MacDonald's resignation on 8 October came as a surprise in Moscow. Addressing the Comintern Executive Committee two days later, Zinoviev commented that it was 'indeed a remarkable thing that the British Parliament is being dissolved because of a communist, Campbell, and because of a treaty with Russia'. He was disposed to take a positive view of events, expressing the opinion that during its short period in power, the government had not compromised itself 'in the eyes of the working masses of Britain'. Not only had the Labour Party gained in authority, there were signs of an encouraging radicalization in the trade unions and the left wing of the party:

> It is often said that we are marching very slowly, but it certainly cannot be called slow when within nine months an attempt of such world historical importance is made and the immediate result is already so clear to the working class...I think that the British worker will now have a great appetite for power...Even if MacDonald wins—I do not believe he will, but it is possible—the appetites of the workers will also grow. They will demand that the Labour Government should be a real workers' government.

Zinoviev went on to discuss what the CPGB tactics should be in the forthcoming election, and on the same day, 10 October, instructions were dispatched to the Central Committee of the CPGB urging support for Labour candidates in general, together with 'sharp criticism of the conduct of the MacDonald Government'.[66] While Zinoviev and his colleagues continued to inveigh against the 'adoption of *bourgeois* politicians as Labour candidates', however, the Politburo clearly would have preferred MacDonald to stay in office and push the Anglo-Soviet treaties through Parliament. When the Central Executive Committee of the Soviet Union met on 18 and 19 October to debate foreign policy, party discipline ensured that a resolution approving the treaties passed unanimously, even though some delegates were unhappy about the level of concessions required from the USSR. Georgi Chicherin gave every impression of confidence in the future.[67] If the Anglo-Soviet treaties were ratified by Parliament, efforts to destabilize Labour and promote revolution could be renewed—but not yet.

The conspiratorial context

The political context in both Britain and the Soviet Union is the essential backdrop to the Zinoviev Letter. It also demonstrates some interesting parallels between the Labour government and the Bolshevik regime. Yet another common factor was that in 1924 both faced an array of forces, both domestically and internationally, who opposed not just Labour or Bolshevik policies, but their ideology and the fact that they were in government at all. Such opponents might act openly, through political speeches or the press. While in the Soviet Union the press was fairly tightly controlled by the Bolshevik regime, in Britain rival press barons with strong political connections, such as Lords Rothermere (*Daily Mail, Daily Mirror, Evening News*) and Beaverbrook (*Daily Express*), were generally right-of-centre in approach and prided themselves on their ability to influence public opinion. Only the *Daily Herald* (partly Soviet-funded, and distrusted by MacDonald) and *The Manchester Guardian* were sympathetic to, though not uncritical of, Labour.

Other opponents of the Bolshevik and Labour governments had access to and were willing to use more clandestine tools. In Britain, the MacDonald administration and the wider Labour Party suspected this deeper layer of treachery and conspiracy, but had little practical experience of dealing with it. The Bolsheviks, with longer experience of power (and opposition) were well aware of it, since they made use of its tools themselves. In both cases, these suspicions—even if not all were well founded—were to affect profoundly the way in which both Labour and the Bolsheviks reacted to the Zinoviev Letter affair. Clearly a parliamentary democracy and a regime that had seized power by revolution had different tools at their command to deal with internal and external threats against their authority. Yet Labour and the Bolsheviks had more in common than might at first appear. Both faced opposition from the forces of global capitalism (what the spy Sidney Reilly called the 'Occult Octopus'[68]), a range of vested interests, political, financial, and administrative, able to operate internationally, through like-minded organizations in Britain, Europe, and the United States, gathering information to further their cause and using their commercial muscle to influence policy. They were well resourced and could employ organizations and individuals who had their own agenda, but whose services were available at a price, to collect information or indeed to spread disinformation.

Alarmed by the threat to profitability posed by what they saw as communist-inspired industrial unrest, capitalist interests did not hesitate to tap into the world of espionage, both state-sponsored and mercenary: the interlocking and international networks of information and disinformation that flourished in the particular conditions of early post-war Europe and post-Revolution Russia; and the cast of players on the espionage stage, of passionate but rarely undivided allegiance. This book is not the place for a detailed description of secret intelligence in Britain and the Soviet Union. But it is impossible to understand the Zinoviev Letter and its impact without exploring this world, and the way it overlapped with the realm of politics.

The first Soviet post-Revolution security and intelligence agency formed in December 1917 was the Cheka, whose methods and organization owed much to the legacy of its tsarist predecessor, the Okhrana, as well as to the Bolshevik leaders' own experiences of underground activities.[69] In 1920 a foreign department of the Cheka was formed, the INO (Inostrannyi Otdel), responsible for identifying, infiltrating, and destabilizing counter-revolutionary groups in other countries working against the Soviet regime, for monitoring the espionage activities of other states, and for collecting intelligence overseas, including penetrating foreign agencies. On the formation of the Soviet Union in 1923, the Cheka evolved into the OGPU or Unified State Political Directorate, integrating the counter-intelligence services of the constituent republics of the USSR; still later it was to become the KGB. In parallel, focusing on both internal subversion and overseas counter-revolutionary activities, was military intelligence conducted by the Fourth Department of the Red Army staff, later to be called the GRU (Glavnoye Razvedyvatel'noye Upravleniye); though distrusted by Stalin and his security chief, Dzerzhinsky, the Fourth was a powerful arm of Soviet intelligence.[70]

The OGPU's top priority was to penetrate White Russian émigré organizations, and to conduct operations against those Western governments that supported counter-revolutionary activities. This was a broad target, since White Russians who had fled after the Bolshevik revolution had settled in communities across Europe, particularly in Berlin, Paris, and Warsaw, as well as the Baltic States, forming 'inter-communicating centres of counter-revolutionary plotting, propaganda and intelligence'.[71] According to a history of Soviet intelligence published by the SVR, OGPU's Berlin station was, for example, conducting operations against Germany, Austria, Britain, Bulgaria, Czechoslovakia, France, and Romania, and had 'managed to penetrate directing bodies of counter-revolutionary organizations of White emigration, as well as government organs and special services of Germany'. OGPU agents were in every Soviet diplomatic and trade mission: their objective,

> to obtain secret information of interest for the Centre. At that time there was not a clear-cut distinction between 'legal' and 'illegal' intelligence: the same intelligence officer could work first under a cover of an official Soviet representative and operate as well under a foreigner's name on his next service mission.[72]

OGPU agents were also stationed at every port and border crossing to watch Russians travelling abroad and foreigners arriving. But there were disadvantages to such a far-reaching and pervasive system: it was open to penetration from other countries' intelligence organizations, and to the activities of what were sometimes called double agents, but which were in fact intelligence mercenaries, offering their services—including forgery—not just to the highest bidder, but to anyone who would pay.

The case of Vladimir Gregorievitch Orlov @[73] K. W. Orbanski, master of duplicity and forger par excellence, who plays a central but mysterious role in the Zinoviev Letter affair, is a good illustration of the interconnected complexities of the Bolshevik and anti-Bolshevik intelligence world. Orlov had been at one time a Greek Orthodox missionary, a General Criminal Investigator for the tsarist regime (in which capacity, according to an SIS note, he may have played a part in forging the notorious anti-Semitic 'Protocols of the Elders of Zion') and then head of the Bolshevik Criminal Investigation Department. Escaping from Russia in 1918, he worked as an intelligence adviser to White Russian Generals Wrangel and Denikin. When their cause proved hopeless, and realizing the potential for cashing in on all his connections, Orlov set up an office in Berlin in late 1920 (housed and financed by the German authorities), supplying reports on Bolshevik activity in and outside Russia, as well as on Russian monarchist activities, to anyone who would pay. In 1921 he reached an agreement with the monarchist Russian HQ in Paris, and was connected with tsarist ex-officers throughout Europe (although since the OGPU had penetrated the monarchist network, it seems likely he retained contacts with Moscow as well). Indeed, Orlov boasted that his customers included 'Red, White and Blue' Russians,[74] various German government, military, and industrial organizations,[75] and British, French, and Polish intelligence agencies. Orlov provided documents—genuine and forged—for anyone who would pay for them. No one trusted him, but many found him useful.

One of Orlov's customers was the British Secret Intelligence Service; indeed, after being introduced to Sir Mansfield Cumming by Sidney Reilly in 1920, he was employed by SIS in the early 1920s, with the designation Z/51, and went on a mission to collect evidence on Soviet activities together with fellow spies Sidney Reilly, Paul Dukes, and Malcolm Maclaren.[76] At first, his intelligence was rated highly by SIS, who apparently subsidized his bureau. But although SIS found some of Orlov's information useful, they did not approve of his working methods. As SIS complained, Orlov would never divulge his sources of information, so that it was very difficult to tell whether reports provided by him were genuine or not. SIS knew the identities of some of Orlov's contacts throughout Europe, and considered them to be 'persons of most doubtful reliability'. Some of those who worked with him in Berlin, such as Harald Sievert, Alexander Gumansky, and Sergiy Druzhelovsky—all of whose names recur in the Zinoviev Letter story—certainly fell into that category. Although SIS ceased to employ Orlov as a paid agent from 1923, however, they did not lose contact with him.

If they had known about them, these were precisely the sort of operations of which the British Labour Party would have been deeply suspicious. To the Labour movement, British intelligence was part of a hostile 'Establishment' that encompassed the monarchy, armed forces, traditional ruling parties, big business, and the civil service. For their part, members of the intelligence community, like officials responsible for defence and foreign policy, were unsure in January 1924 of what to expect from an incoming Labour government. Even those with no firm allegiance to the Conservative or Liberal parties were nervous of what a wholly untried Labour administration might bring, and any connection with what was generally regarded as a murderous Bolshevik regime in Russia enhanced these apprehensions.

On both sides, it was soon clear there was little to fear. MacDonald's socialism was essentially moderate, although there remained many implacably opposed to it, whether in Conservative Central Office, the editorial offices of the *Daily Mail*, or business organizations like the Federation of British Industries and the right-wing Industrial Intelligence Bureau.[77] As for the Labour government, MacDonald appeared amused when Sir Wyndham Childs, the Assistant Commissioner of Police responsible for Special Branch, asked him shortly after taking office whether the Prime Minister wished to receive regular reports on revolutionary movements in Britain, like his predecessor. MacDonald replied that little of this material was likely to be unfamiliar to members of the government, or to anyone who read the *Workers' Weekly*:

> He thought, however, that it might be made at once attractive and indeed entertaining if its survey were extended to cover not only communistic activities but also other political activities of an extreme tendency. For instance a little knowledge in regard to the Fascist movement in this country... or possibly some information as to the source of the *Morning Post* funds might give an exhilarating flavour to the document.[78]

Childs was not amused; but he did include in future reports details of extreme right-wing activities to counter the charge of political bias, and he continued to forward the reports of revolutionary activity. MacDonald did not circulate them routinely to the Cabinet, although Home Secretary Arthur Henderson found them useful and was appreciative of the intelligence supplied by Childs on trade union and communist activities during a period of industrial unrest in the spring of 1924.[79] However, MacDonald was not allowed to see his own Special Branch file, nor, apparently, was he given full information on the activities of the Government Code and Cypher School (GC&CS), while his colleagues received none.[80]

The British intelligence establishment so much distrusted by the Labour Party was in reality a group of agencies: MI5, responsible for domestic security and counter-espionage, and MI1(c) or the Secret Intelligence Service (SIS), the overseas intelligence agency, both formed from the Secret Service Bureau set up in 1909; the GC&CS (precursor of GCHQ), formed in 1919 from the Naval and War Office codebreaking branches that had enjoyed outstanding success during the war and were responsible for signals intelligence (SIGINT); Indian Political Intelligence (IPI), formed in 1909 and run jointly by the Indian government and the India Office in London, set up initially to monitor Indian seditionaries worldwide but much expanded during the war; and finally, Special Branch of Scotland Yard, which had three divisions dealing with secret service matters, under the overall control of Assistant Commissioner Sir Wyndham Childs—SS1 (liaison with SIS), SS2 (liaison with Chief Constables and dealing with revolutionary organizations in the UK other than those of alien or Irish origin), and a branch under a Deputy Assistant Police Commissioner used for acting on information received through the police force.[81] All the agencies were funded from the Secret Vote administered through the Foreign Office, and the FO had direct ministerial responsibility for SIS and GC&CS. For Labour critics, therefore, the Foreign Office was synonymous with British intelligence.

There was particular suspicion in Labour circles of the Foreign Office and its mandarins, and a sizeable faction in the party had lobbied for parliamentary control of foreign policy. MacDonald himself had declared in the *New Leader* in August 1923, 'We intend to end the bureaucracy at Foreign Office.'[82] In office, however, he showed no signs of doing this. Indeed, he worked closely and harmoniously with his officials, who welcomed him warmly in contrast to his predecessor, the capricious and demanding Lord Curzon. Alexander Cadogan, at that time a First Secretary, remarked that it was 'odd that we should have had to wait for the Labour Party to give us a gentleman'.[83]

MacDonald was well aware that some officials held strong views of their own that might conflict with his. In particular, there were a number—in addition to Sir Eyre Crowe—who were strongly opposed to Bolshevism, including those working in the very department that dealt with Russia. The head of Northern Department, J. D. (Don) Gregory, belonged to a luncheon club whose chief toast was to the liquidation of the 'Bolos', and wrote in his memoirs that Bolshevism was a disease that 'must be treated either pathologically, or violently'.[84] He also agreed, after the Labour government's recognition of the Soviet Union, to a request from fourteen White Russian organizations in Britain that he should receive E. V. Sabline, the tsarist representative in London, as their spokesman, and discuss with him unofficially any matters affecting their interests. Yet despite his anti-Bolshevik sympathies, much of the official documentation in Gregory's hand is balanced, cautious, and by no means prejudiced against the Russians, and indeed the FO's views on Anglo-Russian relations were generally more moderate than those of the politicians they served. MacDonald clearly felt sufficiently secure in his own authority to accept, or at any rate ignore, his officials' views, as long as their briefing and reporting displayed no sign of partiality. It was also unavoidable: serving as both Prime Minister and Foreign Secretary and under severe pressure, MacDonald had to rely heavily on his officials, and in particular on Crowe. In the aftermath of the Zinoviev Letter affair, his loyalty to officials, and to the intelligence agencies, was to be severely tested.

Though all the elements of the British intelligence establishment had a discrete function, they tended to overlap and even duplicate their activities, as the Secret Service Committee complained when it met between 1919 and 1922.[85] To some extent this was inevitable. The three principal agencies—SIS, MI5, and GC&CS—had been forced to downsize after the end of the First World War as staff were demobilized and budgets were cut. They were just beginning to expand again in the early 1920s, principally to counter the Bolshevik threat of subversion and propaganda in Britain and throughout the Empire. Although MI5's responsibility was the safety of Britain and SIS's the gathering of overseas intelligence, the line between the two was ill-defined when it came to Bolshevik subversion and espionage.

> So, for example, SIS might receive valuable information from overseas sources about plans by an international organisation to foster industrial unrest in a British industry; while information from British businessmen might cast valuable light upon foreign espionage activities overseas. Cross-fertilisation between the agencies enabled a large body of useful evidence against Bolshevik and other targets to be compiled, and facilitated a number of successful operations.[86]

Both agencies used sources of information that tended to overlap: SIS had agents within Britain, while MI5 (and Scotland Yard) sent agents overseas in pursuit of their own objectives.

All had contacts within the extensive émigré community, both in Britain and in continental Europe, an invaluable connection when White Russians were involved at some stage in most channels of communication concerning the Soviet Union and anti-Bolshevik activities. The idea of Bolshevism as an 'infection' that must be prevented from spreading was common in the 1920s, particularly among those who had served in the First World War and had been horrified by the October Revolution and the massacre of the Romanovs, as well as by Russia's withdrawal from the war and armistice with Germany. White Russians sat together with British subjects on the committee of various welfare organizations in London. There were a number of prominent anti-Bolsheviks with links to Russian monarchist organizations, married to Britons, such as Ariadne Vladimirovna Tyrkova-Williams, wife of Harold Williams, foreign editor of The Times (and formerly its correspondent in Petrograd); she was in direct contact with the monarchist General Kutepov, living near Paris, while her husband was a close friend of Sir Samuel Hoare, future Cabinet Minister and British Ambassador in Madrid, who had worked for SIS in Russia during the First World War. At the same time, there were close contacts between White Russians. Inevitably, there were many points of contact between Russian émigrés and British officials and members of the armed forces who had served in Russia before, during, and after the Bolshevik revolution, when the Western allies refused to release the Bolshevik government from the obligation undertaken by the tsarist regime to continue fighting until the end of the war.

The closeness and complexity of these interconnections are less surprising than they look. In the early 1920s, the social circle in which all these people moved was a restricted one. Many who had served in the armed forces during the First World War and had returned to civilian life retained close contacts with former comrades who now worked in the secret intelligence agencies. Former soldiers who had now gone into political life retained their military contacts. Senior officials in government departments, City financiers, captains of industry, newspaper proprietors, political activists—all tended to belong to the same social network. Many of these men (the community was exclusively male) had been to the same schools and universities, and belonged to the same gentlemen's clubs. While political views varied, these men tended to be of a conservative persuasion, with a small and often a capital 'C'. The environment was one that promoted trust and confidence, but with the potential for connivance, as well.[87]

A useful illustration here is another key figure symbolic of the Zinoviev mystery, British businessman Donald im Thurn (the German-sounding surname is deceptive), who was to make strenuous efforts to ensure that the Letter was made public and used to the advantage of the Conservative Party—and his own.[88] Im Thurn had served in Military Intelligence during the First World War, and in MI5 from 1917 until 1919. He then moved into the City, but continued to lunch regularly with Major William Alexander of MI5 at the Hyde Park Grill.[89] He had good contacts with both current and former members of SIS, including Lt Col. F. H. 'Freddie' Browning, a director of the Savoy who had left the Service in 1919 but retained close links. Both Im Thurn and Browning were on good terms with the former Director of Naval Intelligence, Admiral Reginald 'Blinker' Hall, and his successors. Im Thurn also had close contacts with Conservative Central Office, a number of Tory MPs, and leading newspaper editors, and was the director of the London Steamship and Trading Corporation, run by White Russian émigrés; he was a friend of Ariadne Tyrkova-Williams, and in contact with the London agents of the Anglo-Russian Volunteer Fleet, which was controlled by ARCOS, the body that handled all Soviet trade and financial matters in Britain.[90]

There are many more components to the conspiratorial context than can be described here. Some will emerge as the story of the Letter unfolds. But even this brief survey shows how complex, confusing, and often impenetrable were the networks of political, financial, commercial, and clandestine interests in Britain, in Europe, and in the Soviet Union in the early 1920s. These relationships, whether personal, political, or ideological, were not necessarily sinister, but they make an already complicated picture even more so. It was into this situation that the Zinoviev Letter was let loose in October 1924 'like a flash of lightning in a dark night', as one account put it.[91]

2

In Search of the Red Letter

Dispatch, arrival, and distribution

On Thursday, 9 October 1924, a decoded telegram containing Report L/3900 from the Secret Intelligence Service's station in the Latvian capital of Riga arrived at SIS headquarters, at that time based in a modest villa in West London. The report, dated 2 October, contained the English text of a letter of 15 September 1924,[1] addressed to the Central Committee of the Communist Party of Great Britain (CPGB) by Grigori Zinoviev, President of the Executive Committee of the Comintern, propaganda arm of the Soviet government. Stamped with file number CX 1174[2] and headed 'Very Secret', the report was headed 'Soviet Russia: Instructions to British Communist Party'. The letter within was signed by Zinoviev as 'President of the Praesidium of the IKKI' (Ispolnitel'niy Komitet Kommunistischeskogo Internatsionala, the Executive Committee of the Comintern), with further signatures by Clydeside docker Arthur MacManus and the Finnish communist Otto Kuusinen.[3]

The report transmitting the Zinoviev Letter was one of a series. Conditions in the Soviet Union, and the regime's combination of internal repression and international paranoia, meant that it was difficult for Western intelligence agencies to operate inside Russia (although a good deal of information was received from diplomatic and commercial representatives).[4] British secret intelligence operations targeting the Soviet Union were coordinated from surrounding states like Latvia; Riga was a key centre for agent-running into Moscow.[5] The source cited in report L/3900 was 'FR3/K', the designation for an agent who was part of a network that had been producing reports from Moscow for several years, including copies of other letters written by Zinoviev to communist parties in other countries as well as to the CPGB.[6] The SIS Head of Station in Riga, Rafael Farina, obviously thought the report important, since he sent a follow-up telegram on 8 October asking for confirmation it had been received.[7] But in London, no one seemed to think it particularly urgent or significant. It took a week for the telegram to be deciphered and sent over to SIS from the Government Code and Cypher School, then housed in Queen's Gate, Kensington.

The letter in Riga's report began by referring to the impending consideration by Parliament of the draft Anglo-Russian treaty that had been negotiated with so much difficulty in London between April and August 1924.[8] The British proletariat, it said, had 'compelled' the Labour government to conclude the treaty, and now must 'show the greatest possible energy in the further struggle for ratification and against the endeavours of British capitalists to compel Parliament to annul it'. The letter was critical of the MacDonald government for being 'in the leading strings of the bourgeoisie', its imperialist foreign policy 'an inferior copy' of that pursued by the preceding Conservative government in which Lord Curzon had been Foreign Secretary. Nevertheless, the immediate priority for the British Communist Party was to 'strain every nerve in the struggle for the ratification of the treaty'. Ratification was essential, since the normalization of relations with the Soviet Union would be even more effective in 'revolutionising' the British proletariat than a general uprising; that might happen in the future, but first there had to be a 'struggle against the inclinations to compromise which are embedded among the majority of British workmen'. The latter, the writer observed, were too apt to believe in evolutionary change and the peaceful extermination of capitalism.

The detailed wording of the Zinoviev Letter is important. For one thing, it showed that the author had a good grasp of the political situation in Britain (and of the mood of the British working classes) at that particular time. Once the letter became public, Labour's opponents would portray it as a general incitement to mass revolt against capitalist oppression and mutiny in the armed forces—the kind of inflammatory provocation that had been seen in previous Comintern missives, and very much in Zinoviev's line. But the letter of 15 September 1924, though scolding the CPGB for its weak performance, particularly in agitation-propaganda work among the military, was not a general exhortation to revolution. It was a very time-specific set of instructions.

In SIS headquarters on 9 October 1924, the Zinoviev Letter landed on the desk of Major Desmond Morton, a much-decorated First World War artillery officer who had served as an ADC to Field Marshal Haig, and had become an intelligence officer in 1919 when the presence of a bullet lodged permanently near his aorta cut short his regular army career.[9] Morton, an enigmatic bachelor of military bearing and friend of Winston Churchill, was SIS's Head of Production ('Prod'), responsible for coordinating the collection of overseas intelligence and collating the product. He was one of a small group of officers working at SIS headquarters in the house at No. 1 Melbury Road, Holland Park, that had also been the home of the first Chief or 'C', Admiral Sir Mansfield Cumming, who died there on the sofa in June 1923. A new Chief, the flamboyant former Director of Naval Intelligence Admiral Sir Hugh 'Quex' Sinclair, was now in charge.[10]

By October 1924 Desmond Morton had more than five years' experience in handling material relating to Bolshevik activities, working with colleagues in MI5, like the head of counter-espionage, Major Joseph Ball,[11] and with Special Branch at Scotland Yard. Morton considered himself wise in the ways of Soviet espionage and propaganda, and had a file full of inflammatory instructions from Moscow. He claimed, at the time and later, that he saw nothing special about the report containing the Zinoviev Letter, and marked it on to Nevile Bland[12] and J. D. Gregory at the Foreign Office, as well

Figure 4. Desmond Morton of SIS

as to the Admiralty, War Office, Air Ministry, Scotland Yard, and MI5. (This was a normal distribution list for SIS material on Bolshevik subversion.) Major Malcolm 'Woolly' Woollcombe, another former soldier, head of SIS's Political Section, and the FO's liaison officer in SIS, circulated the copies on 9 October, edited to remove details of origin; at this stage the FO did not know the Letter had come from Riga. The document, Woollcombe said in his covering note, contained 'strong incitement to armed revolution and clear evidence of intention to contaminate the Armed Forces' and constituted a 'flagrant violation' of Soviet treaty obligations. 'The authenticity of the document', he wrote, was 'undoubted'.[13]

When the Foreign Office received the Letter from SIS on Friday, 10 October, everyone on the distribution list had seen similar examples before. That day William Strang, a Second Secretary in Northern Department, discussed the copy intended for his head of department with Captain Hugh Miller of Scotland Yard, who agreed it looked very similar to other Bolshevik documents seen by his section. Sir Wyndham Childs also believed the Letter was nothing out of the ordinary, and did not feel the need to draw it to the attention of the Home Secretary.[14] When Strang marked the document on to Gregory on Monday, 14 October, however, he confessed that although the Letter was typical of Comintern aims and methods, it was 'difficult for the department to advise' on what should be done with it when 'Anglo-Soviet relations are unfortunately an issue in domestic politics in this country'. Publication, or protests in Moscow, might be embarrassing to the British government and even to some sections of the Soviet government, but would make little difference to the Comintern or stop them from sending secret instructions to the CPGB. Gregory agreed: 'I very much doubt the wisdom of publication. The authenticity of the document would at once be denied, and it would probably be the last of its kind which we should receive.'[15]

When Nevile Bland showed his copy of the Letter to the Permanent Under-Secretary on 10 October, Crowe recognized immediately the sensitivity of its timing and content. MacDonald had already left London on a campaign tour leading up to the general election: he travelled alone, with a typist but no assistant or adviser, incredible though that may seem today. Crowe was left in charge of FO business, responsible for keeping the Foreign Secretary (who in this case also happened to be the Prime Minister) informed. He decided to seek further confirmation from SIS of the authenticity of the Letter before forwarding it to MacDonald. On Monday, 13 October, Crowe received a letter from SIS containing assurances that the Letter was indeed genuine. These assurances were based on a report by Desmond Morton of a meeting on 10 October with one of his informants, W. B. Findlay @ Jim Finney @ 'Furniture Dealer', who had infiltrated the CPGB. Findlay, who had served for sixteen years with the 6th Dragoon Guards, had joined MI5 briefly before joining the industrial intelligence network run by the right-wing magnate Sir George Makgill, who then shared his services with Desmond Morton of SIS during the early 1920s.[16]

According to Morton, Finney indicated that the CPGB had indeed received a letter from Zinoviev in the same terms as that dated 15 September, and had held a meeting of the Central Committee in the last week of September to discuss it. In the light of this apparently independent confirmation of the authenticity of the Letter, Crowe recommended to MacDonald on 15 October that a formal protest should be made to the Soviet government and the press given full details:

> It is quite true—and we have always felt—that we get nothing out of the Soviet Government by any remonstrances simply because these quite shameless liars merely deny everything however clearly established. On the other hand, there is much force in the view that our best and only defence against these treacherous proceedings is publicity. It does not seem fair to our own people that our knowledge of these Russian machinations should remain for ever concealed.[17]

The Prime Minister agreed, stressing, 'We must be sure that the document is authentic.' Any protest must be 'so well-founded & important that it carries conviction & guilt'. If not, he added prophetically, 'it will do harm'. MacDonald sent the papers back to the FO on Friday, 17 October, where Northern Department began to prepare a draft letter of protest to the Soviet government.

Crowe, reasonably enough, interpreted the letter from SIS as constituting 'absolutely reliable authority' that the Zinoviev Letter had been received and discussed by the CPGB. But when, in 1998, I examined the SIS archives, I discovered, as the MI5 Sovietologist Milicent Bagot had discovered thirty years earlier, that those assurances were built on shaky ground. Morton claimed that when he met his informant on 10 October, Finney had elaborated on an earlier report, indicating that the Central Committee of the CPGB had met during the week of 29 September–4 October to discuss instructions from Moscow. In fact, the original report from Finney made no mention of a letter from Moscow or of a committee meeting, but stated merely that the CPGB had decided to 'do all in their power to make whatever government was in power to be the promoters of the Revolution'. Yet Morton's minute of 11 October, on which the SIS assurances to

Crowe were based, specified that the Central Committee had met to consider a letter of instruction from Moscow concerning 'action which the CPGB was to take with regard to making the proletariat force Parliament to ratify the Anglo-Soviet Treaty'; instructions that also 'insisted on distrust of the Labour Party and MacDonald, with whom the International was disgusted in that they had shown that their policy was little different from that of a bourgeois government'.[18]

Morton's version of Finney's information fits the 'real' Zinoviev Letter very neatly—far too neatly. In her report on the Letter, Bagot tried to put a charitable construction on it:

> It is...difficult to imagine how an experienced agent could have omitted from his original report such an important matter as the receipt of a directive from Moscow, if he had known of it. The most likely explanation seems to be that he was asked 'loaded' questions by Morton, who is known to have been working on the Riga report and had no doubt put the two together in his mind.[19]

Bagot's explanation for Morton's conduct is not implausible: he *had* just been dealing with the Letter, marking it on to the FO the day before he met Finney. And it would have been entirely in character for Morton to embellish his account of Finney's report to strengthen his own, and SIS's, judgement in authenticating the Letter, the content of which was undeniably consistent with similar messages.[20] It was Morton's job to coordinate intelligence on Bolshevik subversion and espionage, and SIS's responsibility to pass relevant information on to the FO and other departments. All the intelligence agencies operated on the principle that when they passed information on it should be taken as authoritative. As Sir Wyndham Childs explained to the Labour committee of enquiry into the Letter, 'that is the method under which Secret Service is conducted, and any other method would end in disaster, because if one earned the reputation of breaking one's word the sources of information would absolutely dry up'.[21]

Morton and Woollcombe, circulating the Riga report containing the Zinoviev Letter, would not have expected it to be challenged. But Morton's conduct does raise questions. Writing to Joseph Ball in MI5 in July 1924, enclosing copies of reports containing the text of Comintern letters to CPGB dating from December 1923 and March 1924,[22] Morton had stated:

> I have a whole file full of similar ones... There is no doubt that the actual copies of these letters destined for the Central Committee of the Communist Party go from Moscow to Berlin, and from Berlin to London in the ARCOS bag; that they are then sent round by hand to their destination. Presumably they are not delivered openly at King Street [CPGB HQ], but of that side of the business we know nothing. I will not capitulate what it is we are out to do, as I think my description on the telephone must have made it quite clear to you.[23]

There is no record of the telephone conversation between Morton and Ball, so the last sentence of the letter remains ambiguous. It could mean simply that what Morton, and SIS, were 'out to do', with MI5's help, was to keep a close watch on communications between the Comintern and the CPGB, and on ARCOS, in order to monitor subversive activities and identify those involved with it. That was, after all, their job, and when Milicent Bagot interviewed Desmond Morton in 1969 it was what he claimed. Yet if Labour's suspicions about the loyalties of the intelligence community were justified, Morton's remark to Ball could also mean that both men were using, or planning to use communications between the Comintern and CPGB to discredit the government. It is also possible that they already suspected, or knew, that the Letter was in fact a forgery.[24]

Nor was Morton being entirely frank with Ball: it was not true that SIS knew nothing about the way in which Comintern letters arrived at CPGB headquarters. They had at least one informant with access to that information, but did not share with MI5, or Scotland Yard, knowledge of the existence or identity of such informants. What is more, MI5 and Scotland Yard had their own informants in the CPGB. Childs, writing to Nevile Bland a few months later, claimed that 'if it was a question of backing agents against agents', and one agent stated that a special meeting had been held to consider the Zinoviev Letter, he could 'produce from equally reliable sources evidence to the exact

Figure 5. *Punch* cartoon by David Low, 1924

opposite'.[25] In this context, any discussion of the actions or motivation of Morton and other members of the intelligence community must, in the absence of hard evidence, remain speculative.

Leaks, rumours, and dirty tricks

At the same time as the report from Riga arrived in SIS headquarters, rumours about the existence of a 'Red Letter' had begun to spread in London. According to the diary of Donald im Thurn, on 8 October he met a contact called 'X' who told him that 'his old enemy Apfelbaum' (Zinoviev) had boasted in Moscow 'a few days ago' that he was 'entering on a great propaganda war in England and Germany' and had sent instructions to Britain for use when the Anglo-Soviet treaty was signed.[26] Although im Thurn was later to claim that he had been given the text of the Zinoviev Letter on 9 October and passed it on to a 'trusted City friend' who gave it to the *Daily Mail*, it is clear both from his own diary entries and other evidence that this was not true. Im Thurn never managed to get hold of a copy of the Letter himself, even if he succeeded in convincing some of his contacts that he had, and attempted to secure some financial reward for his information.[27] He told a member of SIS on 18 October that 'if there were sufficient time he could probably get a copy from Moscow by sending a man there but that to get the original in London would cost perhaps £10,000'.[28] But he never secured one, as his contacts in MI5 and SIS realized, though they seem to have fed him titbits of information for their own purposes.

As the *Sunday Times* 'Insight' team put it, 'im Thurn's main difficulty was that he had to keep on bluffing the authorities into believing he did possess the letter when in fact he did not'.[29] It seems likely, however, that his 'trusted City friend' was former senior SIS officer Freddie Browning, who was in a much better position to get hold of the Letter than im Thurn was. Browning told im Thurn on 27 October that he had on 23 October given a copy to Thomas Marlowe, editor of the *Daily Mail*.[30] Marlowe, according to an article he published in *The Observer* on 4 March 1928, had also received a copy of the Letter from 'another friend', and sent a circular letter to other editors, telling them that they could satisfy themselves about the authenticity of the Letter by asking the FO, Home Office, Admiralty, or War Office.[31] Scotland Yard was later informed that the *Daily Mail* passed a copy on to the *Morning Post*, whose Foreign Editor sent it to the FO, where a comparison of texts revealed 'several slight differences in the wording', giving the impression 'that the D[aily] M[ail] version was merely a slightly altered version of the FO copy made evidently with the sole object of making it appear to be an independent translation'.[32]

Im Thurn was only one of many claiming to have seen the Letter, and trying to use of it for political ends. Once copies began to circulate in Whitehall, leaks were inevitable, and the circle of knowledge widened greatly when on 22 October a copy was circulated by MI5 to all General Officers Commanding (GOCs) of military commands. Sir Warren Fisher, Permanent Secretary to the Treasury and Head of the Civil Service, later made a statement recording his impression that 'a number of Generals and Admirals had been talking of [the Zinoviev

Letter] in Service clubs and that is how it got round to the *Daily Mail*'.[33]
In parliamentary corridors, in the City, in the gentlemen's clubs, in
military messes, and in newsrooms there was talk of a document that
could discredit the government and undermine the Labour vote in
the forthcoming election. In this largely conservative environment—
with a large and a small 'c'—there were many who welcomed such an
opportunity, and word spread of the Letter's supposed contents,
encouraged by the well-connected White Russian émigré community.

   There were also rumours in the press of a forthcoming 'revelation':
on 22 October the *Manchester Evening Chronicle* reported that sensational developments in connection with the name of Zinoviev might
be expected at the end of the week, while both the *Morning Post* and
the *Daily Mail* reported that a man who had been sentenced to death
by Zinoviev had called at Conservative Central Office the previous day.
The latter story was supported by a White Russian journal published
in Paris, which stated that the allegedly escaping Russian, 'M', had
eluded Soviet Chargé d'Affaires Rakovsky's attempts to detain him,
and that his extradition had been demanded by the Russian authorities.
The story proved impossible to corroborate.[34] Yet concrete sightings
of the supposedly incriminating document were rare. Im Thurn, who
was apparently informed personally on 21 October by both Alexander
of MI5 and Sinclair, the SIS Chief, that the Letter was about to be sent
to military commands, noted in his diary: 'Cannot rely on getting
copy. What the hell! Must play all I can on FO fear of publication.'[35]

   Meanwhile, in the Foreign Office, the departmental draft of a note
to the Soviet Chargé, protesting at the Zinoviev Letter, was amended
extensively by Crowe and sent off to MacDonald in his Aberavon
constituency on Tuesday, 21 October, with a covering minute saying
that the draft 'puts the case squarely' and that the note could be published 'as soon as it has reached M. Rakovsky's hands'.[36] But MacDonald
had gone to Bassetlaw in Nottinghamshire to campaign on behalf
of his son, Malcolm, and did not return to Aberavon until Thursday,
23 October. According to his own account, he looked at the draft
early the next morning and sent it back to the FO.

What happened on 'Zinoviev Friday'?

MacDonald's amended version of the draft note of protest to the Soviet government reached the Foreign Office just before 11 a.m. on 24 October 1924.[37] Earlier that morning, Crowe had received information from SIS that reporters had visited the Admiralty to enquire about a letter from Zinoviev that, they understood, was about to be published.[38] This was clearly preying on his mind when Crowe received the draft returned by MacDonald, which the Prime Minister had 'entirely revised and largely rewritten in his own hand'. Crucially, MacDonald had not initialled it at the bottom. According to his diary, this was deliberate, as he intended to review the draft when it had been copied and sent back to him.[39] Crowe, however, insisted, when discussing MacDonald's revisions with Bland and Gregory, that once amended the note should be put into final form and dispatched to Rakovsky and the press without further reference to the Prime Minister. It would appear that some officials felt uneasy about this. In 1928, when the Treasury investigated the scandal caused by foreign currency dealings on the part of Gregory and other FO officials at the time of the Zinoviev Letter episode,[40] Strang told the Board of Enquiry:

> I said I thought the Prime Minister himself ought to sign it and if he did not do so the purpose of the note would be frustrated. I thought the public, which was not instructed in office ways, would misunderstand and would not realise that the Prime Minister's responsibility was engaged. Gregory said that could not be helped; that Crowe had been perfectly explicit on the subject and one of his reasons for haste was that the *Daily Mail* had got this letter and was going to publish next morning whatever happened. I then took the note up to the Registry and said: this is to be copied at once, do so and let me have it. The clerk said it was not initialled. I said I know that and explained it had to go off nevertheless. He brought it down to me I think somewhere about one o'clock. I took it in to Gregory, he signed it. As he signed it he said: this is an important signature: I agreed.[41]

Although Strang's evidence was given more than three years later, it is perhaps not surprising if he remembered vividly the events of that fateful afternoon, Friday, 24 October 1924. After giving his instructions, Crowe had left the FO to have lunch with MacDonald's Private Secretary, Walford Selby. As for Gregory, if he did consider his an 'important signature', he did not hang around to see the note safely dispatched, disappearing immediately for a long weekend once he had signed it off ('in the absence of the Secretary of State'). Strang, a relatively junior officer, and FO Librarian Stephen Gaselee were left to deal with the matter—most officials having left for the weekend. Although unhappy at what they considered irregular procedure, they sent the final version of the note, together with the text of the Zinoviev Letter, round to the Soviet Embassy at 4 p.m. and gave a copy of both to the press at 6.[42]

As soon as he received the British note and the copy of the Zinoviev Letter, Russian Chargé Christian Rakovsky swung into action, sending urgent telegrams to Moscow that evening asking for instructions. Georgi Chicherin, Soviet Commissar for Foreign Affairs, immediately arranged for copies of the British note to be circulated within the Commissariat and to the Politburo, commenting to the latter that it was 'strange that MacDonald is dealing a blow to his own party by emphasising the role of the Comintern and of Moscow in general in Britain's internal affairs'. He also told Zinoviev that 'the whole of Britain is awaiting a telegram from you', and that he must issue a denial.[43]

In London, Rakovsky did not wait for instructions but drafted a reply to the British note on the evening of 24 October and sent it to the FO the following morning; it was published in the press on 26 October. It stated 'in most categorical terms' that the Letter was 'a gross forgery... Not only the contents but the heading and signature of the document definitely prove that it is the work of malicious individuals who are inadequately familiar with the constitution of the Communist International.'[44] Writing again to Litvinov on the morning of 25 October, Rakovsky said that during the 'extremely tense election campaign and with political feelings running high, this document has

ANNEX C

/106/38.

IN No.
ANSWER
DATE
OUT NO.
FOREIGN OFFICE, S.W.1.,
October 24th, 1924.

Sir,

I have the honour to invite your attention to the
enclosed copy of a letter which has been received by the
Central Committee of the British Communist Party from the
Presidium of the Executive Committee of the Communist
International, over the signature of Monsieur Zinoviev,
its President, dated September 15th. The letter contains
instructions to British subjects to work for the violent
overthrow of existing institutions in this country, and
for the subversion of His Majesty's armed forces as a means
to that end.

2. It is my duty to inform you that His Majesty's
Government cannot allow this propaganda and must regard
it as a direct interference from outside in British
domestic affairs.

3. No one who understands the constitution and the
relationships of the Communist International will doubt
its intimate connection and contact with the Soviet Government. No Government will ever tolerate an arrangement with
a foreign government by which the latter is in formal
diplomatic relations of a correct kind with it, whilst at
the same time a propagandist body organically connected
with that foreign government encourages and even orders
subjects of the former to plot and plan revolutions for its
overthrow. Such conduct is not only a grave departure from
the rules of international comity, but a violation of

specific/

Monsieur C. Rakovski,
    etc., etc., etc.

Figure 6. Foreign Office note

specific and solemn undertakings repeatedly given to His
Majesty's Government.

4. So recently as June 4th of last year the Soviet
Government made the following solemn agreement with His Majesty's Government.

" The Soviet Government undertakes not to support with
"funds or in any other form persons or bodies or agencies or
"institutions whose aim is to spread discontent or to foment
"rebellion in any part of the British Empire........ and to
"impress upon its officers and officials the full and con-
"tinuous observance of these conditions".

5. Moreover in the Treaty which His Majesty's Government recently concluded with your Government, still further
provision was made for the faithful execution of an analogous
undertaking which is essential to the existence of good and
friendly relations between the two countries. His Majesty's
Government mean that these undertakings shall be carried both
in the letter and in the spirit, and it cannot accept the
contention that whilst the Soviet Government undertakes obligations, a political body, as powerful as itself, is to be
allowed to conduct a propaganda and support it with money,
which is in direct violation of the official agreement. The
Soviet Government either has or has not the power to make
such agreements. If it has the power it is its duty to carry
them out and see that the other parties are not deceived.
If it has not this power and if responsibilities which belong
to the State in other countries are in Russia in the keeping
of private and irresponsible bodies the Soviet Government
ought not to make agreements which it knows it cannot carry
out.

                                                        6./

Figure 6. *cont.*

6. I should be obliged if you would be good enough to let me have the observations of your Government on this subject without delay.

I have the honour to be,

with high consideration,

Sir,

Your obedient Servant,

(*in the absence of the Secretary of State*)

J. D. Gregory

Figure 6. *cont.*

gone off like a bomb'. He suspected Gregory of involvement in 'intrigue against us' and even in drafting the 'apocryphal document', though he doubted that Gregory would have dared to send the note of protest without MacDonald's consent. 'We are', he said, 'doing everything possible to assume the offensive and compromise our enemies. However, it is difficult so far to say whether we shall succeed in changing public opinion during the three days between now and the elections.'[45]

It is clear from the Russian documentation that the Zinoviev Letter, as well as the British note, came as a complete surprise to Rakovsky. On 26 October, he asked the Commissariat of Foreign Affairs for 'fresh data confirming the falsity of such an (?alleged) statement by Zinoviev'; he was realistic enough to understand that the Comintern might have acted without his knowledge. The Bolshevik leadership were inclined to sideline the Commissariat of Foreign Affairs and to disdain conventional diplomatic channels, using the Comintern as an instrument of foreign policy when they wished.[46] There was certainly considerable confusion in Moscow. As Litvinov later explained to Rakovsky, the Foreign Ministry received the British note before they received the text of the Zinoviev Letter, and were confused, suspecting 'an electioneering stunt on the part of MacDonald'. Initially, they were inclined not to reply until after the elections, 'in order not to upset his electoral applecart', but then 'news of the forged document of course obliged us to alter our decision and give an immediate reply'. The Zinoviev Letter itself, said Litvinov, was 'a shameless forgery'.[47]

Meanwhile, MacDonald was still in Aberavon, unaware of the storm that was about to break over his head. On the afternoon of Friday, 24 October 1924, neither Crowe nor Gregory seems to have considered asking him whether they should, in fact, send off the note to Rakovsky, or tell him that they were going to do so. When Selby mentioned it to Crowe over lunch at the Travellers Club, he was given the firm impression that 'Sir Eyre Crowe had definitely made up his mind on the subject, and that the less Mr Selby or anyone else said on the subject from that moment onwards the better'.[48] In fact, no one in the Foreign Office seems to have thought it necessary to forewarn the Foreign Secretary (and Prime Minister), away from London campaigning and unaccompanied by advisers, of the impending publication of the Zinoviev Letter and of the note of protest addressed to the Soviet government in his name. Whatever the misunderstanding about the status of the draft, MacDonald was surely justified in his anger at this lack of consultation.

Although there were no computers or mobile phones in 1924, telegrams were both common and swift; and even the postal service, with several deliveries a day, was remarkably fast. What is more, MacDonald was, as he said later, at the end of a telephone all afternoon. Even if Crowe assumed his minister's authority to dispatch the note, it seems extraordinary that he did not inform MacDonald it would appear in the press the following morning, at a time when the Prime Minister was addressing a succession of political meetings at which he was likely to face questions about it. In fact, a reporter from the *Daily News* asked him that very evening, 24 October, 'if he authorised the issue of the Despatch issued today', and was told by a bemused MacDonald that 'the Foreign Office never issues despatches unauthorised'.[49]

Publication and protest: London and Moscow

The Zinoviev Letter and the British government's note to the Soviet government in response were published in the *Daily Mail* on the morning of Saturday, 25 October 1924, under the heading 'Civil War Plot by Socialists' Masters: Moscow orders to our Reds'.[50] The accompanying report stated that a 'secret letter of instruction from Moscow to the British Communist Party', signed by Zinoviev, had been delivered to MacDonald 'some weeks ago', thereby creating the impression in the minds of the public that the government had only protested at the letter when forced to do so by the threat of publication. It was a story guaranteed to play on widespread fears about Bolshevism, and to exploit a good deal of confusion in the mind of the general public about the difference between the Labour Party and the communists. Marlowe had tipped off his fellow editors in advance to ensure maximum coverage, and a media storm ensued. A statement to the press by Arthur MacManus, insisting that he had never put his name to any such letter, was ignored.[51] MacDonald, still in Wales, sent a telegram to Crowe, demanding to know what had happened and insisting that he had not intended the note to the Russians to be dispatched before he had seen it again. In his anguished reply, Crowe insisted that he had had no doubt that the Prime Minister approved it for dispatch:

> No doubt as to your having approved it had crossed my mind. I remembered that you had wished us to make quite sure of the authenticity of Zinovieff's letter. I had gone into this with care and was entirely satisfied on the point. We had evidence not only of the letter being sent from Moscow, but of its having been received here. This is, as a matter of fact, now further confirmed by the *Daily Mail* having succeeded in obtaining the document, presumably from some venal informer in the

Communist camp here. When you returned the draft with your very important—and to my mind excellent—amendments, there was no indication that you did not regard these as final ... If anyone is to blame for your intentions having been misunderstood, it must fall on myself. But in the circumstances as I have explained them, there appeared to me no question of interpreting your intentions otherwise than I did.[52]

Crowe added that he remained convinced that it would not have been right to delay publication:

What then would have been the impression if—as would inevitably happen—it was discovered that the Foreign Office had been in possession of the incriminating document for some time but had concealed this fact and refrained from all action? Would it not have been said that information vitally concerning the security of the Empire had been deliberately suppressed during the elections which were meanwhile to be affected by Bolshevik propaganda?

'In all sincerity', Crowe concluded, he remained of the view that 'however inconvenient the incident may have proved', the consequences of not acting would have been 'infinitely more serious'.

Crowe's letter did not reach MacDonald until the evening of Saturday, 25 October. Meanwhile, as MacDonald later told the Treasury enquiry in 1928, 'I did not know whether there had been a revolution in Moscow or what on earth had happened and I could not find out.'[53] In fact, what was going on in Moscow was a meeting of the Council of People's Commissars (Sovnarkom), held at 6.20 p.m. on 25 October. The record of its proceedings, which reached SIS in translation from Riga in report L/3981 of 6 November, was cited as proof of the authenticity of the Zinoviev Letter, so it deserves a little attention. Kamenev was in the chair: Chicherin read out the texts of the Letter and of the British note in reply, and reported that he had asked Zinoviev for an explanation. Zinoviev had 'categorically declared' that the Letter was a 'deliberately distorted' version of a letter drawn up by MacManus and sent to the CPGB, which 'owing to the criminal negligence of certain of the workers of the IKKI, or the treachery of some one of the British Communists, became known to the British political police'. Zinoviev pointed out certain key differences in wording, including passages that had presumably been 'inserted by officials of the British Foreign Office or persons concerned in the affair'.

'Undoubtedly,' declared Chicherin, 'we have to deal here with an instance of carefully planned provocation, directed simultaneously against the Labour Party and the SSSR.'

> The Conservatives, who are the chief enemies of the Labour Party, owing to their contact with the Foreign Office have strained every effort to have a note presented to us on the matter of this unfortunate letter. MacDonald and the Labour Party have suffered a severe blow. Considerable damage has been done to us also...The first step of the NKID is of course absolutely to deny the accusations levelled against us, especially as the British Government is hardly likely to possess any direct proof that the letter was actually signed by Zinoviev, sent from Moscow, and actually received by the British Communist Party...we cannot accuse the British officials of distorting the text, as this would hardly exonerate the IKKI, or the Soviet Government from the accusation of interference in the internal affairs of the British state; the whole question must be kept on the plane of the authenticity of the whole letter.[54]

It was, Chicherin told Sovnarkom, 'essential to rout the enemy completely, destroy the accusation, and once and for all make an end of all attempts to hold the Soviet responsible for the activity of the IKKI'. It would appear that Chicherin, like Rakovsky, knew nothing about the Letter, but could not discount the possibility that it might actually have come from the Comintern. In a telegram of 29 October to the FO, British Chargé d'Affaires in Moscow Robert Hodgson observed that in the Russian press there was an 'uncertain tone in attacks on authenticity of letter possibly due to knowledge that it is impossible in view of published views of leading figures in Communist International to assert that no such letter could have been despatched. At best, this particular one may not have been sent.'[55] Litvinov, who assumed from the outset that the Zinoviev Letter was a forgery, wrote to Rakovsky on 27 October that it had all been done 'very cleverly, from the drafting of the forged document itself, the phraseology of which really does remind one of the Comintern's, to the choice of timing which left very little time for denial and spelling out to the electors the purpose of the forgery'.[56] For the Soviet Foreign Ministry at least, the Letter itself was seen as an obvious piece of political trickery designed to damage Labour's fortunes in the general election; they assumed that Foreign Office officials were implicated, if not responsible.

What is clear from both Russian and British documentation is that what the Bolsheviks were worried about was the possible effect of the Letter and the British protest on their future relations with the UK and other Western governments. At the Sovnarkom meeting Sokolnikov, Commissar for Finance, spelled out the situation:

> The whole question lies in the result of the elections. If the Labour Party wins, then it is clear that the incident will be settled to our mutual interests, and may even serve our cause, as undoubtedly the Labour Party will carry out an effective comb-out of the diplomatic tricksters in the British Foreign Office. It will be quite another matter if the Conservatives win. Then not only is the collapse threatened of the Anglo-Soviet treaty, but also an improvement in our relations with England is open to doubt... If England turns her back on us, we must reply by the conclusion of a series of agreements, consolidating our position, even making concessions to Japan, who might become our serious ally against England and America.[57]

Both the SIS station in Riga and SIS headquarters, meanwhile, interpreted the record of the Sovnarkom meeting as further proof of the authenticity of the Zinoviev Letter.[58] Zinoviev's claims that it was a mutilated version of a letter from MacManus were brushed aside, although discrepancies of translation could not account for the differences pointed out by Zinoviev, still less the fact that according to him it was MacManus, not Zinoviev, who had sent a letter to the CPGB. But Sinclair wrote to Crowe on 6 November that 'the reference to mutilation evidently refers to the discrepancy between our translation of the Russian original and that received by the British Communists'.[59] Two days later, Crowe passed the information about the Sovnarkom meeting on to MacDonald, and later told Lord Haldane he believed 'that in his heart of hearts' the Prime Minister was convinced, 'although he—perhaps naturally—did not say so'.[60] This was wishful thinking on Crowe's part.

Meanwhile, on the weekend of 25/26 October MacDonald remained in Wales. Struggling to restore the credibility of his government and defend its record, he found it a desperate experience. Worst of all, he felt humiliated. Nevertheless, MacDonald accepted Crowe's assurances that he had acted in good faith:

> He had no intention of being disloyal, indeed quite the opposite, but his own mind destroyed his discretion and blinded him to the obvious care he should have exercised...Still, nothing untoward would have happened had not the *Daily Mail* and other agencies including Conservative leaders had the letter and were preparing a political bomb from it.[61]

Some commentators have been less convinced of Crowe's loyalty. Michael Jabara Carley, calling him 'mendacious and presumptuous', considers Crowe a primary suspect in a 'cover-up and collusion to oust Labour', in terms of means, motive, opportunity, and circumstantial evidence.[62] Yet Crowe's views on the Bolsheviks were well known to MacDonald (and indeed shared by other FO officials); the two men worked closely and, apparently, harmoniously together. Brought up in Germany, and as anti-Bolshevik as the next FO man, Crowe was nevertheless an old-school official scrupulous in his loyalty to his Minister. It is hard to detect from the day-to-day performance and correspondence of a man who was, after all, the most senior FO official any desire to undermine MacDonald or the government.

Crowe's handling of the draft protest note seems odd, high-handed even. But to me, the documentation suggests a man who was overwrought, overworked, and unwell, rather than someone politically motivated. He was already in ill health, and had only six months left to live. Although the idea that the Zinoviev episode 'killed' Crowe has been refuted by his biographers, he was clearly deeply upset by the implication that he had failed in his duty and let MacDonald down, even if he 'neither believed nor acknowledged that he had made a mistake'.[63] Since January 1924 he had been carrying an even greater burden of responsibility than usual, as not only was MacDonald Prime Minister as well as Foreign Secretary, but he left a good deal of the policy formulation to his officials.[64]

While MacDonald may have been reluctant to believe that FO officials had acted improperly, he was becoming increasingly suspicious about the Zinoviev Letter itself. In a campaign speech in Cardiff on Monday, 27 October, he revealed something of his unease:

> All I say is this: so far as I know, the letter might have originated anywhere. The staff of the Foreign Office up to the end of the week thought it was authentic, honestly believed it was authentic. I have not seen the evidence yet. All I say is this, that it is a most suspicious circumstance that a certain newspaper and the headquarters of the Conservative Association seem to have had copies of it at the same time as the Foreign Office, and if that is true how can I, a simple-minded, honest person who puts two and two together, avoid the suspicion—I will not say the conclusion—that the whole thing is a political plot?[65]

MacDonald's dawning suspicions gave him no peace and elicited no sympathy. As *The Manchester Guardian* put it, if the Letter were a hoax, the FO had made an 'egregious blunder'; if it were genuine, he could not accuse his enemies of a plot. The US Ambassador in London, having previously praised the 'firm tone' of the British note of protest to Moscow, now condemned MacDonald:

> There is nothing meaner than a mean man. The first impression of satisfaction at the Premier's courage in issuing a note of censure to the Bolshevist government is abated by his endeavour again to ride two horses at once, and in order to do that, to throw implied blame upon those who have faithfully served him.[66]

If MacDonald was increasingly suspicious about the provenance of the Letter and the way in which it had been handled, Crowe was also anxious. A series of communications from SIS between 25 and 27 October, intended to convince the FO that previous assurances could be trusted, failed in their purpose. Statements that the Soviet government was bound to deny that such documents were genuine, or that the Letter could have been signed in MacManus's name even if he were not present, were hardly conclusive; nor was the response to Rakovsky's terminological objections to the Letter, since it was clear Comintern documentation was inconsistent.

On 27 October *The Manchester Guardian* published a report that the Executive Committee of the CPGB, after a special meeting at King St., had issued a statement that they had never received the Zinoviev Letter, which they were satisfied was a clumsy fabrication. On the same day, Major Woollcombe went to the FO for a long talk with Crowe, who put a series of questions to him—questions that might more usefully have been posed when the Letter first arrived. Had the Letter been received in Russian or English? (Crowe was told SIS had a copy of the Russian text, although in fact they did not receive it from Riga until 12 December.) Could SIS's CPGB source give more information about the supposed discussion of the Letter by the Central Committee? (No, as the members of the Committee were scattered round the country on election work.) Did Sir Wyndham Childs know about the informant? (No, and he must not be told.) Could the informant's material be made public? (No, 'the risk would be too great'.) How did the *Daily Mail* get hold of the Letter? (Probably through one of the military or naval commands.) And finally, would Woollcombe explain things personally to the Prime Minister? The answer to the final question was yes, if the Chief of SIS agreed, but in fact it was decided that Gregory, with Strang, should travel down to Aberavon later that day. The decision no doubt reflected MacDonald's unwillingness to have direct contact with members of SIS.[67]

'Come into the plot'

If Crowe's part in the Zinoviev Letter affair may conceivably be attributed to ill health and excessive zeal, the part played by the head

J.D. GREGORY

Figure 7. J. D. Gregory

of the FO's Northern Department, 'Don' Gregory, is much harder to explain. The Labour MP E. D. Morel, a vocal critic of MacDonald's foreign policy and of the Foreign Office in general, named Gregory in a series of articles and speeches in November 1924 as responsible for an unparalleled act of treachery in his handling of the Letter. Although Morel died shortly afterwards, his accusations helped to sustain Labour suspicion of the FO about the affair.[68] In 1928, a Treasury Board of Enquiry was to look closely into Gregory's activities in 1924,[69] but he was so closely involved in events at the end of the Labour government that a part of the story must belong here.

Gregory was involved with a woman called Aminta Bradley Dyne—born Maggie Bradley in Liverpool in 1887—whose husband Musgrave, had been at school with Gregory; she claimed to know

Lady Gregory, 'Don' Gregory's mother.[70] Gregory's FO colleagues, some of whom knew her from a brief spell working at the FO during the First World War, regarded her as his mistress, and in the 1930s they were to live as man and wife, but it was not a straightforward liaison. Gregory was on good terms with the whole family and went on holiday with the Dynes and their son.

Whatever their relationship, Gregory and Aminta spent a great deal of time together in the early 1920s. They arranged to buy large amounts of foreign currency, which they then sold before having to pay for it—a not uncommon form of speculation, but hardly proper for a Foreign Office employee. In late 1923 or early 1924 Gregory had introduced Aminta to a stockbroker named Alfred de Waal, formerly of military intelligence; Gregory had been recommended to de Waal by Owen O'Malley of Northern Department, and by Charles Blennerhassett, a former intelligence officer who was now a stockbroker. Musgrave Bradley Dyne, Blennerhassett, Gregory, and probably de Waal as well had all travelled on Russia's borders in the early post-war period. They all had intelligence connections and links with the Baltic States, and in 1924 were all based in London: not surprising, perhaps, but certainly intriguing in the context of the Zinoviev Letter mystery. Gregory's and Aminta's financial dealings were spectacularly unsuccessful. By 1927, Aminta owed nearly £40,000—over £2 m today—to de Waal's company, Ironmongers, who eventually sued her. Since she and Gregory seemed to have entangled their finances inextricably, the proceedings thereby set in train the public shaming of Gregory and other FO officials. It was to cost him his career.

In 1924, however, he was still a senior FO official involved centrally in the conduct of British policy towards the Soviet Union. In December, six weeks after the fall of the Labour government, a former servant of Aminta's, Violet Digby, swore a deposition stating that 'about the 21st October' Mrs Dyne and Gregory had 'lost a lot of money through speculating in francs and that Mr Gregory would have to leave the Foreign Office and get a job elsewhere'. Violet went on to describe what had happened during the few days from 25 October—the day that the Zinoviev Letter and the British note signed by Gregory were published in the press:

> Mr Gregory pretty well lived there...they went out to lunch together and he generally came to tea and left about 7. On Saturday, October 25th, Mrs Dyne called attention to Mr Gregory's photo in the paper. She went out to lunch. On the same day Mrs Dyne spoke to the Bank Manager and asked him if he would wait. She mentioned a sum of 60,000 francs and said it would be all right. About this time Mrs Dyne said 'Mr Gregory did it when the Prime Minister's back was turned'. On Monday 27th October Mrs Dyne said that Mr MacDonald had got thrown out and that Mr Gregory had made his name. Mr Gregory should have come to lunch but Mrs Dyne said he had phoned up to say he had to go to Cardiff to see Mr MacDonald. On Tuesday night the 28th October, Mr Gregory came and a man aged about 40 came in who Mrs Dyne said was a Russian. His name began with V and ended with 'ski'. Gregory said, laughing, 'Come into the plot'. They then went into a room together. They stayed until about 8 when Gregory and the Russian left. They appeared to be very pleased and Mrs Dyne said 'Come on, 50-50, halves'. This was on the Wednesday night, October 29th...Mrs Dyne after the election said that she was glad the Labour people were out of it. Gregory said they were 'no darn good'.[71]

At the time, all this seemed rather far-fetched. MacDonald, when told of the deposition, thought it a 'silly document', containing incredible allegations. He consulted Crowe, who 'dismissed it as a mere *canard*'. As MacDonald told the Treasury Board of Enquiry in 1928,

> I do not know what Crowe's frame of mind was, but I should imagine it was rather the frame of mind that I had too. That was that the Zinovieff letter was the absorbing thing...I did not regard the specu-lation story as being of very much value, and I could not quite make it out, because I started with the prejudice in favour of the Civil Servant. That a man who came through stage by stage until he became the head of this Northern Department—I did not believe that man could have done that.[72]

MacDonald did challenge Gregory, who denied the story, stating that Mrs Dyne was 'an old friend' and the so-called 'Russian' a 'very great friend', M. Ciechanowski, the Polish Chargé d'Affaires in London. He repeated his denials to J. H. Thomas, who had served as Colonial Secretary in the MacDonald government, and who was leading the Labour Party's own investigation into the affair. Thomas told Gregory that a number of wild allegations were circulating, including that 'the hand of Rome can be traced in this' (Gregory was a Roman Catholic). But Thomas, too, found it incredible that a man like Gregory could be involved in currency speculation, and was happy to accept Gregory's word that it was a case of a servant who was 'not suited' and acting out of spite. Thomas told the Board of Enquiry in 1928 that he had assured a Labour Party meeting he was 'satisfied there was no vestige of truth in it to connect Gregory with the Roman Catholic side or that there was any dealings in francs or roubles or anything else. It was simply the imagination of a girl who had a grievance and thought she could take advantage of it by the publication of this Zinoviev document.'[73]

No further action was taken in 1924–5: Crowe died in April 1925, and Gregory, who had lied to MacDonald, Crowe, and Thomas, was promoted to the rank of Assistant Under-Secretary. The story disappeared down a rabbit hole until 1928, when Gregory's evidence remained contradictory and mendacious. But even with the further details that emerged from the Board of Enquiry, it remains difficult to see where the truth of all this might lie. If they were trying to make a killing in some way from the Zinoviev Letter, not only were Gregory and Aminta hopelessly inept, but it is hard to say how they could have benefited from its publication financially. Gregory was certainly in a position to have sold a copy of the Letter, if he wished; but there were already a number of copies circulating, and Thomas Marlowe, editor of the *Daily Mail*, denied firmly that he had paid Gregory any money for anything.

The Russians certainly suspected Gregory. In *Pravda*, Karl Radek drew attention to Gregory's role under the previous government in connection with Curzon's protests about Bolshevik propaganda: 'Mr Gregory has had some experience in presenting the Soviet Government with forged documents with a very serious air.'[74]

Rakovsky wrote to Litvinov on 13 November that he had 'received some very serious information concerning Gregory's part in this whole story'. He conceded Gregory was unlikely to have been involved in any forgery, but 'there are indications that he earned capital—and not only political capital—from sending the note and from its publication in the press (or from passing the document to *The Daily Mail*)'. Two weeks later, Rakovsky wrote that although MacDonald seemed unwilling to blame Gregory for sending out the British response to the Zinoviev Letter on 24 October, 'Gregory's role is clear; he was in a position to fool ten MacDonalds and make it look as he was against going into print but that this was recommended by Sir Eyre Crowe.'[75] But these letters, and other reports, deal in supposition and rumour, not facts, and add little to the information that was to emerge in 1928. Gregory was a known anti-Bolshevik, and so an obvious suspect.

No official record has been found of Gregory's visit to MacDonald in Wales on 27 October 1924, except in respect of a response to a second note from Rakovsky received in the FO that morning and published in the press at the same time. This note, which Gregory took with him to Aberavon, repeated that the Zinoviev Letter was an 'impudent forgery', and demanded an 'adequate apology' and the 'punishment of both the private and official persons involved in the forgery'. Whatever MacDonald's suspicions regarding the Letter, he resented and rejected any implication that Foreign Office officials had been involved. Gregory was told to return the note to Rakovsky as unacceptable. He did so the following day, 28 October, explaining that the Prime Minister considered it 'inadmissible interference in our domestic affairs' and must be withdrawn.[76]

This was the beginning of a somewhat farcical series of exchanges over the next few days between Gregory and Rakovsky, described by the latter as a 'tragi-comedy', in which the Russian note was re-presented several times and returned by Gregory. In the official file, Gregory's account of these proceedings is entirely professional, claiming that relations with Rakovsky were 'of the friendliest nature without any personal animus on either side'. However, in a letter to

Translation:
GREGORY: "IT'S THE THIRD TIME I AM TAKING THIS TRIP TO RETURN RAKOWSKY HIS DAMNED NOTE. I AM ALL IN A SWEAT OVER IT."
CHAMBERLAIN: "WHAT, SENT IT BACK AGAIN? WELL THEN, WE'LL JUST HAVE TO MISLAY IT SOMEWHERE AMONG OUR PAPERS"

Figure 8. Gregory tries to return Rakovsky's note

Litvinov on 29 October, Rakovsky described Gregory as seeming 'very perplexed', insisting that 'he was not in any way involved in this matter, that he was required to answer for his superiors, that he was tired of his work, that he wanted to go off to somewhere in America, that we had been wasting our time over the past four months in seeking to conclude a treaty, etc.'[77]

Whatever Gregory's state of mind, events were now moving fast. Tuesday, 28 October 1924, the day before the general election, saw a rash of statements and counter-statements, both public and private. In Berlin, *Die Rote Fahne* (*The Red Flag*) published a report stating that a letter of guidance had been sent from Zinoviev to the German Communist Party concerning the forthcoming German general election, without any denial of its authenticity; while in *Pravda* Karl Radek insisted that MacDonald could 'not have believed the authenticity of this worthless paper'.[78] An intercepted telegram from the French Ambassador in London to his foreign ministry reported that the letter had been obtained in Riga by *un agent du Foreign Office* who had sent it to the FO and Scotland Yard; a member of the Conservative Party had got hold of it and passed it to the *Daily Mail*. The Ambassador did not, however, consider that the results of the election would be affected: '*les paris sont nettement en faveur des conservateurs*' ('the opinion polls favour the Conservatives').[79] On the same day, the French government granted *de jure* recognition to the Soviet government, a move welcomed by the Bolsheviks as an 'offset against the Zinoviev letter episode and against the results of the elections in Britain', although, as William Peters reported from Moscow, the communist leaders attached little importance to the French, who were unlikely to offer much financial assistance nor increased trade.[80]

In Moscow, according to a report received by SIS from Riga on 19 November, a meeting of the Collegium of the Soviet Foreign Office was held on 28 October, at which Zinoviev was present, and in defiant mood:

> Speaking plainly, an apology from the British Government in the affair of my letter, even if one is forthcoming, is really of no importance to us at all. Everyone knows that we are conducting propaganda, and will continue to do so in the future, until either we win or ourselves are crushed. This is a matter of fighting for our existence. The only question is whether British bankers wish to risk this, in the hopes of securing huge profits through entering into trade relations with us.[81]

Zinoviev repeated this point in an interview with a foreign journalist printed in *Pravda* on 28 October, arguing that while there was nothing in the Letter that the Comintern had not said at some point to foreign communist parties, 'the instructions regarding military preparations in England were scarcely timely'.[82]

Meanwhile, in London, Rakovsky received a mysterious letter from someone who claimed to be 'in a position to put before you thirty documents which will be used to discredit Russia', and asking for an interview to offer his services, inspired by a desire to 'expose the persons occupied in the manufacture of forged documents'.[83] Albert Inkpin, General Secretary of the CPGB, wrote to Gregory asking for a copy of the Zinoviev Letter, 'inasmuch as no such letter as that referred to by you has ever been received by the Central Committee of the

Communist Party of Great Britain, and that the alleged signatories to the communication have repudiated all knowledge of it'. A similar letter was sent to Gregory on behalf of MacManus; Inkpin sent copies of both letters to MacDonald, asking him to ensure that copies of the alleged communication were forwarded immediately, and sent all the correspondence to the press.[84] *The Times* published a report on MacDonald's handling of the Letter, under the heading 'Prime Minister's Defence', together with a message from MacDonald himself, stating optimistically that 'At the end of the hardest fight I have ever known, the signs of Labour victories are unmistakeable'. MacDonald himself made a final speech in Aberavon on the morning of Tuesday, 28 October, declaring:

> The Red plot, whether it is authentic or it is not, is safely in the hands of the Government. Tomorrow we can make a red letter day. The red plot may be dead, but the red letter day is in front of us.[85]

For MacDonald and his colleagues, 29 October 1924 was to be Red Letter Day in the worst sense. When the votes were counted the Conservatives had gained 161 seats, while Labour lost 40; the Liberals, in third place, lost 119. The fact that nearly a million more people had voted for Labour than in December 1923 made the result even harder to bear. Britain's first Labour government had ended in confusion, suspicion, and humiliation.

3

Enquiries and Investigations, 1924–1925

'The story of the Zinoviev letter should be indelibly written on the minds of us all.'[1]

The outcome of the general election on 29 October 1924 left both the British and Soviet governments in a state of confusion and uncertainty. This was caused not so much by the result, which was disappointing if not entirely unexpected, but by their perception of the part that the Zinoviev Letter might have played in it. The few days between its publication in the *Daily Mail* on 25 October and polling day on the 29th had left no time for either the Labour government or the Russians to work out exactly what was going on. Both were convinced the Letter had been a significant factor in the election. Rakovsky reported to the Russian Foreign Ministry on 30 October that nearly all the British press had treated the Letter as authentic: 'we were not able to dispel this and it influenced the result of the elections'.[2] Lord Rothermere, proprietor of the *Daily Mail*, told his rival Lord Beaverbrook on 1 November that the Letter had cost Labour something like 100 seats.[3] The truth was immaterial: it was the perception that mattered. The first Labour government was defeated, the Liberals decimated, and the Conservatives triumphant; the prospect of Anglo-Soviet treaties being ratified by Parliament was remote.

There were many in Moscow as well as London looking for someone to blame.

For Ramsay MacDonald, and the rest of his Cabinet colleagues, it was a question of reputational damage as well as loss of office, and a feeling that the ground had been cut from under their feet. Not only had the Zinoviev Letter been used against them ruthlessly by their political opponents, the confusion about the publication of the note of protest, which MacDonald claimed he had not authorized, added to the humiliation. For many ministers, for the wider Labour Party, the trade union movement, and even for the CPGB, the bitter experience of electoral defeat fuelled suspicion of an Establishment conspiracy. It was a breeding ground for dissension and recrimination.

For the Russians, reputational issues were also involved: though they insisted the Letter was a forgery, its very existence was an affront to the Politburo and the Comintern, as well as the Foreign Ministry and security and intelligence apparatus. The Letter, and the British response to it, had caught them on the hop, suggesting worrying security failures in a supposedly tightly controlled system. At a time when the CPSU was engaged in a power struggle that Stalin was determined to win, government ministers, party officials, and Comintern Executive Committee members alike wanted to know how the whole debacle had happened. For a regime built upon revolutionary foundations, the affair also served to confirm the existence of an international anti-Soviet conspiracy, and factional disputes within Bolshevik ranks intensified the depth of feeling. On top of this, with Labour out of office the Bolsheviks had to work out how best to deal with their Conservative successors. 'We must', Litvinov wrote defiantly to Rakovsky on 31 October, 'right from the start show that we are not intimidated by the Conservatives coming to power.' It is clear, however, that the Soviet government was worried about the course the new British government might follow.[4]

In the aftermath of the British general election, therefore, a lot of people wanted to know more about the Zinoviev Letter. During the next twelve months, a series of enquiries was carried out both in

Russia and Britain by those seeking to get to the bottom of the episode. Some were commissioned or carried out by government ministers and civil servants; some by intelligence organizations; and some by non-governmental bodies, such as the CPGB and TUC in Britain. All had a vested interest in deflecting blame for the Zinoviev incident from themselves onto others. All wanted to make sure it could not happen again.

Cabinets, communists, and trade unions

Two days after the election, on 31 October, the Cabinet met to discuss the results and decide when MacDonald should offer the government's resignation to the King.[5] The mood in the Cabinet room in 10 Downing Street was at once sombre and resentful. MacDonald seemed disposed to sorrow rather than anger, looking 'pale and serious', as if 'uncertain what his reception was going to be'. His fellow ministers, however, wanted someone or something to blame for what they regarded as a humiliating defeat. Discussion soon focused on the Zinoviev Letter: according to the Deputy Cabinet Secretary, Tom Jones, 'all agreed that up to Friday night [24 October] all was going well with the Party prospects', but that when the Letter was published in the *Daily Mail* on 25 October, 'the people lost confidence in us; the women were frightened; speakers felt paralysed'.[6] Some considered the episode a mean political trick, perpetrated by the right-wing press, Conservative Central Office, Foreign Office mandarins, or the Secret Service—or all of these at once. Others were more sympathetic to MacDonald's reluctance to condemn the behaviour of officials. All demanded a full explanation from the Prime Minister: was the Letter genuine, or a forgery? Had civil servants conspired to unseat the Labour government? What part had the Secret Service played?

Tempers rose: according to Tom Jones there was an 'interminable delay' in obtaining an FO dossier on the Zinoviev Letter, during which MacDonald tried but failed to give a convincing account of what had happened in respect of the note of protest that had been published with the Letter on 25 October. He appealed for calm, insisting there had been 'no bad faith' on the part of the civil service. But many remained unconvinced, and the bitterness and frustration provoked by nine months of what they saw as constant right-wing undermining of Labour's achievements, combined with the strains of office, now came to the boil.

After a heated discussion—according to Jones, MacDonald had more than once to appeal to his colleagues to keep their tempers— the Cabinet agreed that a committee formed of the Lord Chancellor (Viscount Haldane), the Lord President of the Council (Lord Parmoor), Home Secretary Arthur Henderson, and the Prime Minister himself should 'examine at once the question of the authenticity of the Zinovieff letter, with a view to reporting to the Cabinet at its next meeting'. Parmoor and Charles Trevelyan, President of the Board of Education, wanted the enquiry to examine the conduct of civil servants as well, announcing that they were 'quite prepared to blow up the FO if they could get rid of the spy system'. But Colonial Secretary J. H. Thomas warned that 'they were sitting on a volcano', and it was agreed that the Cabinet minutes should not record anything about investigating the conduct of civil servants. Nor was there to be any mention of the government's resigning until the committee had reported.[7]

Although at the meeting MacDonald remained non-committal about the provenance of the Letter, it is clear he felt there were many questions that needed an answer. While the Committee of Enquiry conducted its investigations, he made some enquiries of his own. Late on the evening of Sunday, 2 November, MacDonald went to see the Soviet Chargé, Rakovsky, who had tried yet again to persuade the FO to accept his note of 27 October stating that the Zinoviev Letter was an 'impudent forgery' and demanding an 'adequate apology'.[8] MacDonald insisted that he was still not prepared to accept the Russian note: it not only said the Letter was a forgery, but implied that it may have been forged by an FO official, something he rejected entirely; 'there was no analogy between his accusation by implication and our definite complaint against the Russian officials with proofs'.[9]

MacDonald recorded this meeting in a brief minute.[10] The Russian account is both more expansive and more intriguing. According to Jan Antonovich Berzin of the Soviet Trade Delegation, who was present, MacDonald and Rakovsky spoke at some length about the Letter itself, a discussion not reflected in MacDonald's record. MacDonald asked if it were really true that Rakovsky had not known anything about the Letter before a copy was sent to him on the evening of 24 October together with the British response. The Soviet Chargé answered 'with a categorical statement that we knew absolutely nothing about it'. MacDonald also asked yet again why the Russians considered the Letter to be a forgery, dismissing arguments about textual inaccuracies as 'inadequate'. Rakovsky and Berzin pointed out that 'it was not a question of us having to prove that the document is false, quite the contrary'; rather, it was for the British government to prove it was genuine.

The Russians then asked MacDonald if he could show them the Zinoviev Letter, which they said they had never seen:

> At that moment MacDonald seemed to want to show us the document. He picked up some sort of brief-case but then hesitated and did not open it. The likelihood is that he decided not to reveal his secrets to us mainly because they do not actually have an original of the letter concerned but only a copy of it.[11]

Berzin and Rakovsky concluded from this that MacDonald was sure the Letter was a forgery, but did not want to investigate further. Neither conclusion was quite correct, but if Berzin's account is accurate (and there seems little reason to doubt it), the meeting was revealing about the way MacDonald's mind was running.

There was another element to the discussion that Sunday evening. Rakovsky told MacDonald he had been approached by a 'Mr Singleton', who claimed to have 'whole files of different forged documents, drawn up with the purpose of compromising various left-wing groups in the

Labour movement in Britain and the Continent'.[12] According to Berzin, Rakovsky subsequently sent MacDonald copies of some of these documents, but if he did they did not find their way into the official archive. When Captain Hugh Miller of Scotland Yard wrote to Nevile Bland at the FO asking if he might see the documents he understood had been sent to MacDonald, Bland replied that the FO had received none.[13]

The day after his meeting with Rakovsky, MacDonald made a final attempt to elicit the truth about the Letter while he still had access to confidential sources. He submitted a list of questions to SIS through Crowe, focusing particularly on the textual objections raised by the Russians, as well as the 'Mr Singleton' story. The replies to most of his questions were not available until after the government had left office. It was made clear, however, that the issue of textual inaccuracies was a red herring. Inconsistencies were not unusual in Comintern documents, even before translation, and Riga had already told SIS head office that according to one of their agents Zinoviev's secretaries had no clear instructions.[14] As for Singleton (who under the name of Henry Lawrence had been employed by Sir George Makgill to investigate communist subversion),[15] MacDonald was informed that the organization through which 'Singleton' claimed his forgeries were processed, the 'Imperial Union', was 'part and parcel of the White Russian organisation' and was one of the names used by the intelligence and forgery bureau based in Berlin and run by Vladimir Orlov. SIS assured MacDonald they had taken 'special steps to be fully informed regarding the organisation and its agents, with the object of protecting itself against the possibility of being taken in by such agents and methods', though in the light of Orlov's wide and varied connections, this seems rather overconfident.[16]

None of this took MacDonald, or his Committee of Enquiry, much further. Nor did they get any help from Assistant Commissioner Sir Wyndham Childs of Scotland Yard, whom they interviewed as part of their investigation. Asked about the Letter, and whether he knew whether it had been received by the CPGB, Childs insisted—with the disdain reserved by some policemen for 'secret service'—that he was not qualified to express an opinion:

> I made it abundantly clear that under no circumstances could I question its authenticity as I had no means whatever to go upon as I knew nothing about the sources from which it was obtained and cared less. The document was secured by the Foreign Office organization and their opinion must overweigh that of any other living person, otherwise the Secret Service would be an impossibility.

Childs said he had no idea whether the Letter had been received by the CPGB, as the Home Secretary had refused him a warrant to intercept MacManus's correspondence, and if the Letter had been locked in the CPGB safe, 'neither I nor any other organization connected with the Secret Service would have been aware of the fact'. Pressed by the Prime Minister, he did offer the opinion that it was odd that the Comintern should 'select that particular psychological moment' to send such a letter:

> I should much more have expected a letter from the Third International to the Communist Party of Great Britain, admonishing them to damp down all propaganda in this country until after the election, pointing out that the fate of the Treaty and the loan hung in the balance.

However, Childs observed, 'one could not budget for the mentality of the Bolshie as he was quite as capable of doing stupid things as well as anybody else'.[17]

In the absence of any new or conclusive evidence about the authenticity or otherwise of the Letter, the Committee of Enquiry—which declined to take statements from Inkpin and MacManus of the CPGB—could only inform the Cabinet when it met again at 3 p.m. on Tuesday, 4 November 1924, that it had found it impossible on the evidence before it to reach a conclusion.

> We have had enough evidence to show us the existence of habitual attempts in Russian matters to pass off forgeries as authentic documents and to use such for political purposes. The copy of this particular document, the original of which has not been seen by or produced to

us or any Departmental official, did not reach the Foreign Office till the 10th October, and was immediately dealt with, in spite of the fact that the General Election was on from the time of its receipt. Whilst it was going through the usual Departmental processes, and diplomatic action upon it was being considered and prepared, the Foreign Office was informed on the 24th ultimo that a copy of the letter had been for some time in the hands of a section of the Press and that on the following morning it was to be published. No enquiries had been made by those in possession of this copy to find out what view the Departments took of the letter or what action had followed upon its receipt. We do not hesitate to say that the evidence submitted to us gives no support to the allegation that leakage of information took place through some Department. By the nature of the case, some time must elapse before important pieces of evidence bearing upon the existence and the history of the document can be thoroughly examined and tested.[18]

It did not take long to decide that the Prime Minister should submit the government's resignation to the King 'forthwith', and issue that evening a statement to the press. Interestingly, there was a subtle change between the wording agreed at the Cabinet meeting and that issued, reflecting the uncertainty felt about the evidence. The text agreed at the meeting read that the committee had examined the authenticity of the Letter 'so far as material was available in the Departments concerned'. A note on the Cabinet minutes, however, stated that after MacDonald had considered the wording 'very carefully', the statement was changed to read: 'The Committee...after hearing the Departments concerned' found it impossible to reach a conclusion.[19] MacDonald wrote a final minute, giving instructions that the FO note of 24 October to the Russian government should be withdrawn formally, since it was prepared on the assumption of the authenticity of the Zinoviev Letter, 'and the Cabinet did not accept that view'. However, he left office before any action could be taken: and a further communication from Rakovsky of 8 November, saying that MacDonald had 'drawn incorrect conclusions' from their meeting on 2 November, fell to the incoming Conservative government for reply.[20]

Stanley Baldwin, leader of the Conservative Party, was asked to form a government on 4 November when MacDonald resigned. Baldwin was, Tom Jones noted in his diary, 'obviously excited': he had felt for some time that 'things were shaping themselves towards the disappearance of the Liberal Party, but I did not think it would come so quickly. The next step must be the elimination of the Communists by Labour.'[21] (Baldwin had for some time favoured a two-party system with Labour as the Conservatives' principal opposition.) The new government, with Austen Chamberlain as Foreign Secretary, took shape over the next two days. Baldwin and Chamberlain were not unsympathetic to MacDonald's plight. They understood the power of rumour and suspicion to destabilize politics in a way that impacted on all parties. The Red Letter affair, however much it may have furthered Conservative interests during the campaign, was both unsavoury and troubling. The new Prime Minister and Foreign Secretary wanted to shut the matter down.

This was a view that found favour in the Foreign Office, particularly in the Northern Department, where recent events had clearly

THE NORTHERN DEPARTMENT OF THE FOREIGN OFFICE, 1924

Figure 9. FO Northern Department, 1924 (Gregory in middle of front row)

been bruising. First Secretary Owen O'Malley, in a memorandum of 7 November, advised that the best course would be 'to allow the recent controversy to end if this can be done without loss of dignity', rather than pursuing tit-for-tat correspondence with Rakovsky. The new Foreign Secretary could, O'Malley thought, 'excuse himself on grounds of good taste from all detailed comments on the action of his predecessors not strictly relevant to the foreign policy of the new government'; and on the question of hostile Soviet propaganda, that policy could be 'at once and easily defined as one of absolute continuity with the policy of the late Prime Minister'. 'It seems to me', O'Malley concluded rather disdainfully,

> that this kind of line would be not undignified, would quite sufficiently whitewash the Foreign Office and leave it open to the new government to adopt a line recommended on previous occasions by this department, namely, to ignore everything connected with Russia as completely and as long as the Russians will allow us to do so...Russia has been much in the public eye lately, and the probability is that public opinion is ready for some other form of entertainment.[22]

On taking office Chamberlain immediately asked the FO to prepare a history of the Zinoviev affair, as well as a memorandum suggesting lines of future policy towards Russia. The first was essentially a compilation of FO minutes and notes since the receipt of the Letter on 10 October; the second an amended version of O'Malley's memorandum of 7 November. (There was no mention in the latter of 'whitewashing' the FO, a phrase that looks suspicious, though it may merely have reflected distaste for the whole controversy.) Attached to the memorandum were the drafts of two further notes to Rakovsky, stating that the information in the government's possession 'leaves no doubt whatsoever in their mind of the authenticity of M. Zinoviev's letter and His Majesty's Government are therefore not prepared to discuss the matter'.[23]

When the new Cabinet met formally for the first time on Wednesday, 12 November 1924, Chamberlain used the documents provided by his officials to give his colleagues 'a full narrative of events in connection with the Zinovieff letter, as well as the grounds on which the Foreign Office felt convinced of its authenticity'. The Cabinet agreed to set up a new committee of enquiry, chaired by Chamberlain and comprising ministers experienced both in foreign affairs and the law: former Foreign Secretary Lord Curzon, now Lord President of the Council; former Lord Chancellor Lord Birkenhead, now Secretary of State for India; the new Lord Chancellor, Viscount Cave, who had fulfilled the same role in 1922–4; and Viscount Cecil, formerly a junior FO minister and now Chancellor of the Duchy of Lancaster. They also decided to refuse an application by Vickers to supply £7,500,000 of arms and ammunition to the Soviet government.[24]

Meanwhile, a good deal of activity had been taking place in Moscow. As Robert Hodgson reported to the FO, the receipt of the British note of protest at the Zinoviev Letter had been a 'positive bombshell and was followed by feverish activity in high Soviet circles'.[25] There was a certain amount of indignant public posturing for the benefit of an internal Russian audience. Trotsky published an article in *Pravda* on 30 October, expressing surprise at what he called 'the idiocy which pervades the whole story from beginning to end':

> How a document so nonsensical, so politically meaningless, a document which cries aloud that it is a forgery could become the focus of the attention of the leading political parties of the oldest civilized country in the world, a country of centuries of world supremacy and of parliamentary regime—that is what is verily incomprehensible...These people are, according to their own standard, educated: they have gigantic political experience, both their own and their ancestors. Whence, therefore, this gross, this politically illiterate credulity?...their conduct in this whole unpleasant business is not due only to hate, intrigue and venality but also to idiocy and blindness...The whole essence is that *they do not understand us*...At the same time, *we understand them*.

Trotsky's eloquence provoked a curious and rather revealing response from Henry Maxse of the FO's Northern Department, who thought

Trotsky had a point about the differences in mutual understanding between British and Russians:

> The Soviet leaders—both Jews and Russians—seldom react in the same way as leaders of Western peoples. If I might venture on a speculation, this difference arises primarily from a complete abnormality (the Western outlook being normal) which however is common to all Russians and nearly all Slavs. In so far as the abnormality is specifically Bolshevik, it is perhaps more in the inherited instinctive disposition of the Jew that 'every man's hand is against him', than in the Russian disposition (less instinctive than acquired) of hatred of the oppressed for the oppressor...it is, generally speaking, among the Jews that the extremists are found, whereas the evolutionaries are more often Russians—witness Zinoviev and Lenin.[26]

These two documents show clearly the mixture of incomprehension and apprehension with which the Foreign Office and the Bolsheviks viewed each other. But the differentiation between Jews and Russians, linking Jews to revolution and conspiracy, was not merely a prejudice of FO officials (although it did reflect the idea promoted by the British press of Bolshevism as an 'infection'). In Bolshevik circles, too, the Jewish identity of both Trotsky and Zinoviev had long been held against them in factional infighting.[27] Patrick Ramsay, Counsellor in the British Embassy in Stockholm, forwarded to the FO on 1 November information from a Swedish press correspondent in Moscow reporting rumours that the Zinoviev Letter had been 'possibly concocted in Moscow' by a group, headed by Trotsky, that was 'systematically endeavouring to compromise the British Labour Government'. The correspondent added that there were sharp divisions on foreign policy in the CPSU, where Chicherin was 'accused of being too much of an evolutionist'.[28]

Whatever the differences between 'revolutionaries' and 'evolutionaries', all the Soviet authorities were clearly keen—like the British Conservative government—to try and close down the Zinoviev Letter incident, while at the same time establishing better control over the activities of the Comintern. As a report sent to Scotland Yard by

SIS noted, in the aftermath of the Zinoviev Letter incident 'every responsible worker is now regarded as a possible traitor'.[29] Felix Dzerzhinsky, the notoriously fearsome OGPU chief, had been worried for some time about foreign penetration of Soviet missions abroad and the organs of state in Russia itself, as well as about the leakage of important documents. According to a report from agent FR3/K (source of the Zinoviev Letter) sent on to SIS from Riga, on 29 October Dzerzhinsky had interrogated the chiefs of Comintern departments about their internal organization and arrangements for handling documents, apparently leading to a decision that in future the more secret papers would not be given to typists for transcription but to more senior officials. Though Zinoviev continued to swear he had not written the Letter that had caused all the trouble, the episode suggested a certain laxness in security. Whoever wrote the Letter knew far too much about the internal workings of the Comintern for comfort.

The report added that two Executive Committee workers had been arrested on suspicion of mishandling documents, although they were freed for lack of evidence. Kuusinen, one of the alleged signatories of the Zinoviev Letter, had also been cross-examined twice by Dzerzhinsky, but was adamant that a document could not have been copied within the Comintern; it must have happened after it had been handed over to MacManus. Further reports indicated that some senior figures in the party were taking the opportunity to attack Zinoviev on the grounds of Comintern inefficiency. Karl Radek, in particular, had launched a campaign against Zinoviev, 'reproaching him for the disorganisations' in the Comintern.[30] Meanwhile, Chicherin was busy making his own enquiries about the Letter, instructing Litvinov to check whether the forger might have been Ignacz Trebitsch Lincoln, a Hungarian Jewish adventurer and con man whose extraordinary career included serving as an Anglican curate in Kent and, briefly, as a liberal MP in 1910. Lincoln was, said Chicherin, a 'specialist in the forgery of diplomatic documents, was once deported from Vienna and now lives in Riga…Radek could work this up most impressively.'[31]

Everyone, in short, blamed each other. Yet in none of these reports was it stated or admitted that Zinoviev *did* write the Letter dated 15 September 1924, although it was generally accepted that its tone and content were consistent with Comintern style. For the Bolshevik authorities, it was the repercussions of the Letter that mattered, not its authenticity. They clearly suspected that the whole affair had been devised by the leaders of the extensive network of White Russians who still hoped to overthrow the Bolshevik regime—and since Soviet intelligence had penetrated many White Russian organizations, they knew what they were talking about.

One issue on which Politburo, Comintern, and government ministers were agreed was the importance of making use of a planned visit to the Soviet Union by a British Trades Union delegation. A 'fraternal' invitation had already been extended at a meeting of British and Russian trade unionists in September, but on 26 October Zinoviev sent a telegram to the TUC on behalf of the Comintern Executive Committee, describing the Letter as a 'gross falsification' and asking the TUC's General Council either to send a special commission, or to use the visit already planned to 'investigate the question regarding the authenticity of the alleged document'. 'The decision of this commission', Zinoviev promised, 'will be accepted by us as final.'[32]

The TUC delegation spent much of November and December in Russia (an oblique reference to it is made in the first 'Tintin' book, published in 1929 by the Belgian cartoonist Georges Rémi ('Hergé'), *Tintin in the Land of the Soviets*).[33] Headed by former TUC Chairman Arthur Purcell and Fred Bramley, secretary to the General Council, its members included an interpreter in both Russian and German and two others who knew one or both languages. Stung by the impact of the Zinoviev Letter controversy in Britain, the TUC was as keen as the Bolsheviks to get to the bottom of the 'Red Letter'. In Moscow, the delegation was greeted warmly and offered every facility, including, apparently, a demonstration of how forged documents could be produced. On 7 December, some members of the delegation had an interview with Chicherin, whose remarks in recounting the conversation to Litvinov give a good indication of the confusion prevailing in the Russian Foreign Ministry:

> From the letter itself I consider that it was not brought from Moscow. I also said that there are certain trails. One trail leads to Gregory, his actress, White Guards linked with them, and Scotland Yard... Another trail leads to Trebitsch Lincoln, and a third leads to Berlin. They told me that there were rumours in London that the Letter was received officially from another government and they thought it likely that this referred to the German government... It is highly important, in order to discredit the Conservative cabinet, to establish accurately the origin of the forgery.[34]

In their search for the Letter, the TUC delegation wanted access to Comintern archives, and after a meeting with Zinoviev in the Kremlin on 19 November, three members of the delegation had made an apparently unannounced visit to the Secretariat.[35] In its report the TUC delegation stated that it had examined Comintern Executive Committee minutes between June and October 1924, and had found no letter from Zinoviev in the terms published in the British press on 25 October. They also examined outgoing correspondence, daily registers, and other documentation, concluding that 'no document of such importance or confidential content as the "Zinoviev" letter would have been sent out without the matter being first submitted to the Executive Committee, and from the minutes seen of these meetings there is not the least reason to suppose that—had the "Zinoviev" letter been a genuine production of the Comintern—its subject and composition would have been kept from the Executive Committee's knowledge'.[36] The Report did draw attention to two other documents: a letter to the CPGB of 12 September from MacManus, enclosing a copy of a speech by Zinoviev, and a 'letter of an extremely secret character' that was 'neither seditious nor inflammatory' but contained 'some pungent criticisms of certain prominent figures in the British Labour and Trade union movements'. But neither, the report stated, could have formed the basis for the Letter that Zinoviev was supposed to have signed on 15 September.

Although the report was not published until 1925, its conclusions had been trailed from November 1924 onwards. In general, the British press were dismissive of the delegation's findings and discounted the assurance by its members that they were 'absolutely satisfied' the Letter was a forgery. The Russians, critics said, would have found it easy to pull the wool over the delegates' eyes, showing them only what they wanted them to see.[37] It is impossible to refute this: it is undoubtedly true that the Soviet authorities controlled the delegation's access, and according to one account, Comintern files had been 'hastily cleansed' before the TUC delegation inspected them.[38] In addition, evidence that the delegation submitted a draft of its Report to the Soviet Legation in London before publication cast doubts on its impartiality.

On our visit to Moscow in 1998, Tony Bishop and I bore all this in mind when we examined the substantial and well-maintained Comintern Executive Committee archive. But like the TUC delegation, we found no draft or final letter of instruction to the CPGB during the summer or autumn of 1924 (though we did see a number of similar drafts to other communist parties). We also examined the records of Politburo meetings, and found no reference to any instructions to the CPGB, or any document resembling the Letter from September until the middle of November. In addition, the list of attendees at the Politburo meetings confirmed Zinoviev's story that he had not been in Moscow at the time when the Letter was supposedly signed and sent (although this would not necessarily mean the Letter was not genuine). All these records are kept meticulously, numbered and including printed agenda as well as minutes. Though it is impossible to be certain that nothing was omitted or concealed, our overwhelming impression was that the lack of discussion of the Letter in both Politburo and Comintern reflected the bemusement felt by the Bolshevik authorities at the crisis caused by a document that they did not recognize as having been sent.

Back in London, the new Conservative government paid no attention to the views of the TUC delegation. The Committee of Enquiry into the authenticity of the Zinoviev Letter set up by the Cabinet on

12 November took only a week, like its Labour predecessor, to reach its conclusions. (This was slightly longer than Sir Wyndham Childs had predicted, when in giving evidence to the MacDonald committee he had concluded: 'Prime Minister, it is quite clear to me that if a new Government sets up a committee of enquiry into authenticity, the committee will last precisely two minutes. It will send for the officer who presented the document to you, the officer will say "I have not a shadow of doubt that the document is authentic" and there that committee of enquiry will begin and end.'[39])

At the next Cabinet meeting on 19 November Chamberlain stated that 'after hearing all the necessary witnesses' the committee were 'unanimously of opinion that there was no doubt as to the authenticity of the letter', and indicated 'in broad terms' the proofs that had convinced them of this. The Cabinet adopted the committee's conclusions, and approved the dispatch of two notes to Rakovsky, one declining to discuss further the authenticity of the Letter, and one informing him that 'after due deliberation' HM government found themselves unable to recommend the draft Anglo-Soviet treaties to Parliament.[40] On receipt of the notes on 21 November, Chicherin told the Politburo that the Cabinet's decision was as if a 'British bomb has just been thrown at us', and that Chamberlain's note marked 'the start of attacks against us by Britain's combative Tory regime'.[41]

Despite Chicherin's fears, Baldwin and Chamberlain clearly hoped that the adoption of the Committee of Enquiry's findings would put an end to controversy over the Zinoviev Letter and Anglo-Soviet relations in general. For like any incoming administration, the Conservatives now had to tackle a number of pressing issues. They faced a range of economic problems, including rising food prices, a housing shortage, and preparations for a return to the gold standard.[42] Most immediately, however, came a crisis in Egypt: on the day of the Cabinet meeting on 19 November, General Sir Lee Stack, Governor General of the Sudan and Sirdar of the Egyptian Army, was shot and killed while being driven through Cairo. Stack's death inflamed an already tense situation in Egypt, where there was growing nationalist agitation, against British rule in

Egypt itself as well as against the Anglo-Egyptian condominium in the Sudan.[43]

In this context relations with the Soviet Union were not a priority, and the Zinoviev Letter was an unwelcome distraction as the government drafted the King's Speech for the opening of the new Parliament. When the Debate on the Address opened on 9 December 1924, however, government ministers discovered that whether they liked it or not, Russia and the Zinoviev Letter would occupy as much parliamentary time as the Egyptian crisis. Labour MPs, licking their wounds after their electoral defeat, had no intention of letting the new government off the hook about the role played by the Letter in the campaign. Chamberlain and his colleagues were forced to discuss their policy towards the Soviet Union, and to give out far more details than they at first intended about the Committee of Enquiry, when pressed to explain what were the 'proofs'—indicated to the Cabinet only in broad terms—that had led its members, after 'hearing all the necessary witnesses', to reach the unanimous opinion that there was no doubt as to the authenticity of the Letter. No trace has been found of the identity of the witnesses, though presumably they were similar to those examined by MacDonald's committee, including FO officials and Scotland Yard. But between the Cabinet meetings that marked the appointment and conclusion of Chamberlain's Committee of Enquiry, he and his colleagues had received evidence that convinced them conclusively that the Zinoviev Letter was genuine.

Soviets and spooks

On 17 November 1924 Sinclair had sent to Crowe a document giving 'five very good reasons' why SIS considered the Letter genuine, and which evidently helped to convince the committee. This rather curious document, which the FO handed over to the Committee of Enquiry, was essentially an elaborate restatement of the argument in the SIS letter to the FO of 9 October: in effect, the FO and Cabinet ministers should accept SIS's assurances 'because we say so'. But a close look at the 'five very good reasons', apparently drawn up with the assistance of SIS's Riga station, shows that, like the corroborative assurances given by Desmond Morton in October, they were based on rather shaky foundations.[44]

The first reason given for the authenticity of the Letter was 'Because of its source':

> It came direct from an agent *in Moscow* for a long time in our service, and of proved reliability. He is an official in the Secretariat of the 3rd International, who works directly under Zinoviev and has access to his secret files. He made a copy straight from Zinoviev's Russian original, and passed this copy direct to us.

This was a combination of wishful thinking and information from Riga. The Letter came from a sub-agent, FR3/K, who allegedly worked in the Comintern Secretariat: SIS did not know his identity, then or later, and were already doubtful enough to have commissioned an analysis of his reports, comparing them with information from other sources; another source in the Baltic States had also become suspicious about Riga's output, and tested the system by feeding in a story that later appeared as a report from Riga.[45] FR3/K was one of a group of eleven sub-agents run by FR3/Riga, many of whose names were not known, raising the question, as the official historian of MI6 observes, 'whether they ever existed at all'.[46] Miss Bagot, in her 1970 report, admitted that no satisfactory answer had been found to the crucial questions of the identity of FR3/K, whether he was driven by 'mercenary or political motives', and if the latter, on whose instructions.[47]

The second reason was 'Because of direct independent confirmation', citing the 'independent and spontaneous' confirmation received in London from informants connected with the CPGB and with ARCOS, together with the record of the Sovnarkom meeting on 25 October. As we have seen, the information from Morton's contact in the CPGB was suspect, as was that from ARCOS apparently communicated through im Thurn.[48] The Sovnarkom meeting, although illuminating, contains no admission that the Letter was genuine. The same objection applies to the third reason, 'Because of subsidiary confirmation', a reference to the evidence of 'frantic activity on the part of leaders in Moscow' and the arrest of two Comintern employees.

The fourth reason, 'Because the possibility of being taken in by "White Russians" was entirely excluded', was particularly confident in its formulation:

> Not only have we made it our special business to be acquainted with the methods and personnel of the various White Russian and other forging organisations, especially the main one in Berlin, with the object of preventing ourselves from having forgeries planted on us; but *in this particular case we are aware of* the identity of every person who handled the document on its journey from Zinoviev's files to our hands. A forger would probably have produced an alleged original—as the known forging agencies have every facility for reproducing documents, on official paper and complete with signature and every detail.

In view of the complexities and divided loyalties of the 'forging organisations', the first part of this seems overconfident; the second downright false, since SIS did not know the identity of everyone who had handled the Letter. And an 'original' would surely have aroused more suspicion than the form in which the Letter was received by SIS: if the intention were to plant a forgery on British intelligence and make sure that it was accepted as authentic and disseminated widely, the surest method would be to make sure that it was received from a source that was tried and tested.

The fifth reason was 'Because of the subject matter':

> It was entirely consistent with all that the Communists have been enunciating and putting into effect. Instructions similar in substance have recently been sent by them to the German, Danish and Norwegian Communist Parties. It was merely application in detail of their general policy.

This was unarguable and far more convincing. But it did not take into account evidence that the Comintern had refrained deliberately from sending inflammatory instructions to the CPGB during the negotiation of the Anglo-Soviet treaties and their forthcoming consideration by Parliament. It is true that SIS and the FO had evidence of similar letters sent to other countries' communist parties; but that does not prove the authenticity of this particular Letter, and their availability would also have made it easy for any potential forger to acquire a model for use in Britain.

Sinclair's letter to Crowe finished with a statement designed to reassure both the FO and the Committee of Enquiry: 'If it was a forgery', 'C' wrote, 'by this time we should have proof of it.' As Childs had told MacDonald's committee, secret service is an impossibility if its assurances are not accepted by government departments. But in the light of all the evidence, it is hard to take Sinclair's confident assertion at face value. SIS received a lot of intelligence about anti-Bolshevik activities, including from forgery bureaux run by people like Vladimir Orlov, but it was often ambiguous and of doubtful provenance. Conflicting reports were received from different sources, and the forgers themselves served more than one master. It would have been extremely difficult for SIS to be absolutely certain the Letter was genuine; nor to be certain it was a forgery—unless, of course, they already knew it to be one. It is certainly conceivable that one or more SIS officers—someone like Desmond Morton, for example— could have known, or suspected, the Letter to be a forgery, but vouched for it nonetheless.

There is no solid proof of this, and if there were official involvement in the dissemination and political manipulation of the Letter it would not necessarily mean those officials knew the Letter to be forged. In my investigations in 1998 I found no evidence of institutional con-spiracy in the handling of the Zinoviev Letter affair, and I have found none since on re-examining the evidence and looking for more. There are plenty of unanswered questions: but intelligence agencies are organizations that depend upon the proper maintenance of secrecy. One cannot expect to find everything explained, written down, and tabulated. As Milicent Bagot conceded, it is only too easy in hindsight to attribute shortcomings, such as failure to investigate what now appear to be obvious leads, to evil intentions when they may have been due merely to lack of expertise.

Nevertheless, while the activity going on in SIS headquarters during November and December 1924 does not support the idea of any general conspiracy to mislead the FO or ministers, it does suggest that Sinclair and his senior officers were far less confident in their judgements about the Letter than they told the FO. At the same time that the note giving 'five good reasons' for the Letter's authenticity was being prepared, SIS were making their own further enquiries about the provenance of the Zinoviev Letter. Despite their confident assertions to the FO, they were increasingly uneasy about the role that Orlov and his connections might have played, and about the reliability of the intelligence they had been receiving from Riga. By the beginning of November 1924 SIS had begun to receive reports from overseas stations that the Letter was a fake, probably originating in the Baltic States. By the end of the month Morton was writing to MI5 that 'we are firmly convinced this actual thing is a forgery'. A source connected with Orlov's forgery ring in Berlin told Frank Foley, head of SIS's Berlin station,[49] that the Letter had been written by a non-communist in one of the Baltic States, who had passed it to a British communist while informing Scotland Yard. The source declined to name the author of the letter, though claiming to be convinced it was not Zinoviev.[50]

Disturbing information had also been received from a former tsarist naval officer and representative of the Russian Central Monarchist Council in England, who had been introduced to Desmond Morton in late October 1924 through a War Office contact. This officer, who claimed to control a large secret service organization 'with representatives in every government office in Moscow', produced samples of the kind of documents he could obtain. Some of these were identical to reports received from the SIS station in Riga, suggesting that the naval officer's network shared the same sources of information, and perhaps the same agents. He also claimed to have had an agent who was Zinoviev's principal adviser on British affairs in the Comintern

Executive Committee, and said that at the time of the Campbell case back in August[51] he had instructed the agent to provoke a serious mistake on the part of Zinoviev. Morton's contact expressed the view that this agent had fled with a copy of the Letter to Britain, where he contacted the *Daily Mail* and Conservative Central Office. Similar rumours were rife in Moscow, where press reports suggested that the head of a 'highly secret department' of the Comintern had flown to London with a collection of documents and 'put himself under the protection of the Conservatives'.[52] All this was uncomfortably close to the press reports during the last week of October.[53]

Although SIS's Riga station had helped willingly in drafting assurances of the Letter's authenticity for the FO, it had not been particularly helpful in its responses to requests from headquarters for extra information. Asked to produce a blank sheet of Comintern notepaper, Riga replied that it was too difficult; supplies were carefully checked. Nor, despite the fact that Woollcombe had assured Crowe on 27 October that SIS already possessed the Russian text of the Letter, did Riga produce until 12 December the Cyrillic text from which it claimed to have translated the version sent to London on 8 October. By the time this arrived, SIS had already received a different Russian version through a circuitous route (involving the Yugoslav police, US intelligence in Paris, and Colonel Stewart Menzies, head of the military section of SIS). Morton sent copies of this text to MI5, and it was also sent to Riga: the view in London, Morton wrote, was that it was a retranslation back into Russian of the English version of the Letter that had been published in the press.

If it had not caused a political crisis, the Letter and its source would not have received this kind of scrutiny: but now, everything that SIS learned seemed to cast further doubts. Naturally, SIS did not reveal to the FO that they had any suspicions about the Letter or were conducting further investigations. For the Committee of Enquiry, the 'five good reasons' in the document that Sinclair sent to Crowe on 17 November provided the certainty they sought. For the Baldwin government, it provided a *vade mecum* for statements during the Debate on the King's Speech that opened in the House of Commons on 9 December 1924.

The King's Speech had contained only a brief reference to Russian matters, expressing the hope for future good relations and trade between Britain and the Soviet Union. In his response as Leader of the Opposition, MacDonald, although admitting in his diary that he felt 'nervously worn out and stupid',[54] was in ironic form, expressing surprise at the 'mild and friendly paragraph about Russia': after the violent language used against him and his party during the election campaign, he had, he told the House, expected something more 'spirited'. (In response, Baldwin said that in the matter of angling for votes he always 'tried to fish with clean bait'.) MacDonald then moved on to the Zinoviev Letter, suggesting that 'a newspaper' (the *Daily Mail*) might have had a copy even before the FO received theirs, and used it purely as an electioneering stunt, to 'create a certain panic in the minds of old ladies'. (At this, Nancy Astor, the first woman MP, protested 'Oh!', but MacDonald said he was 'not using that expression in reference to sex'.[55]) The most suspicious thing, he said, was that a newspaper should have precisely the same copy of the Letter as the FO, and hang on to it until the psychological moment in order to induce panic and produce a large majority for the Conservatives.[56]

MacDonald's demands for a further enquiry were brushed aside by Conservative ministers, but other Labour MPs asked more pointed questions. On 10 December both the Deputy Leader of the Party, J. R. Clynes, and the Scottish MP Neil Maclean pressed the government to produce the evidence that had convinced its Committee of Enquiry that the Letter was genuine. Chamberlain missed the first two days of the debate,[57] and in his absence it fell to the Home Secretary, Sir William Joynson-Hicks ('Jix'), to respond. Joynson-Hicks, a former solicitor described by the cartoonist David Low as 'the most intolerant, narrow-minded and dictatorial of anti-democrats',[58] was known for the strength of his anti-Bolshevik sentiments. On this occasion, however, he made a moderate, and rather telling, speech about the Letter, which, he said, had only become significant because MacDonald thought it important enough to address a protest to 'the representative of a friendly nation' (laughter in the House).

Joynson-Hicks then named the members of the Committee of Enquiry (the Cabinet having decided on 3 December that 'in view of the peculiar circumstances attaching to the matter of the Zinovieff Letter' this could be done, though it must not create a precedent),[59] but insisted that it would be impossible to make public either the evidence or the identities of those who had provided it, 'for reasons of safety to individual life'. (Rakovsky rather mischievously sent a note to Chamberlain after reading this, offering to guarantee, 'in the interests of truth', the 'unhindered departure' from the Soviet Union of the person who supplied the Letter to the British government, but Chamberlain declined to rise to the bait.[60]) In regard to relations with Russia, Joynson-Hicks continued:

> If Russia wants to be friends with this country, let her begin by stop-
> ping her propaganda all over the world. We are told that she is a friendly
> nation. We are told that she desires friendship with this country... What
> right has she, if she is a friendly Power, to propagand against us, and to
> try to make our rule futile in every country in the world where we
> rule? Before she wants a treaty with us, let her stop that.

MacDonald, as the Home Secretary pointed out, had made almost identical statements about Russia when he was Prime Minister.[61]

When the debate resumed on 15 December, Austen Chamberlain had returned, and knew he was going to have to respond to Labour members who continued to demand answers about the Zinoviev Letter. He seemed tired and a little rattled: he spoke of European issues and Egypt before turning to Russia, and did his best to shut down the issue of the Letter. MacDonald had not, Chamberlain conceded, delayed unduly in dealing with it, as some newspapers had alleged; both he and MacDonald were agreed on the loyalty and devotion of Foreign Office officials; Chamberlain accepted that MacDonald had not authorized the note sent to Rakovsky on 24 October. He wished, he said, to avoid controversy. MacDonald thanked him, though observing that it was 'a little bit late'; J. H. Thomas added that

Chamberlain may have vindicated MacDonald, 'the most maligned of statesmen', but was in effect saying 'We have got our reward, and we are content to sit here and enjoy it.'[62]

Chamberlain then addressed the issue of the Committee of Enquiry, prefacing his remarks with a statement about the importance of secrecy (Sinclair had written to Crowe on 12 December, asking him to ensure that when the Letter was discussed in the House of Commons special care should be taken to safeguard SIS sources):

> Obviously there are, and there always will be, strict limits imposed on any minister who is speaking of information that comes under the head of Secret Service. It is of the essence of a Secret Service that it must be secret, and if you once begin disclosure it is perfectly obvious to me, as to Hon Gentlemen opposite, that there is no longer any Secret Service and that you must do without it. I must, therefore, be careful as to what I say.

He then went on to paraphrase fairly closely for the House of Commons the letter SIS had sent to Crowe on 17 November, stressing the independence of the corroborative evidence: 'the sources from which we obtained this information were not casual visitors to the Foreign Office who arrived with a document to sell'. Echoing Sinclair's confident assertion, Chamberlain insisted that it was impossible that the FO had been 'hoaxed' by a 'vulgar imposture':

> The Foreign Office and our Secret Service have probably a closer knowledge of these manufactories and manufacturers of forgeries than even hon Members opposite. We know them, and the fact that we know them is a guarantee that we are not taken in ... I am not going to argue this matter.[63]

1925: 'The Bolshevik Plotters in our Midst'

Neither the parliamentary debate nor the turn of the year put an end to the controversy over the Zinoviev Letter.[64] In Britain, internal investigations continued within the Labour Party, where J. H. Thomas conducted an enquiry between January and March 1925 that did not reach any firm conclusions. Further enquiries also continued in the trade union movement and the Communist Party. September 1925 saw the publication both of a Labour Party report on the Zinoviev Letter, declaring that MacDonald had been entirely justified in his handling of it, and of the CPGB's *History of the Zinoviev Letter: Facts about the Infamous Letter*, with a commentary by MacManus. Yet neither of these moved the debate on, or produced new evidence sufficient to prompt renewed official consideration of the issue. Meanwhile, the government continued to receive regular reports from the intelligence agencies about Bolshevik activities. The British Communist Party remained under scrutiny, and a raid by Special Branch on the CPGB's King St. headquarters in October 1925 led to the arrest of a number of communist officials and the seizure of large numbers of documents.[65]

Rumours and allegations about the Letter continued to appear in the press. On 23 April 1925, the *Daily Herald* published an article entitled 'From the Workers' Point of View—on the Track of the Zinoviev Letter', telling its readers that those seeking the truth about the Letter should be looking to Berlin. It mentioned the involvement of 'Gutschinski' or 'Druscheviski', apparently alternative names for Sergiy Druzhelovsky, a forger who was to provide new information about the Zinoviev Letter during his trial in Moscow two years later. For the moment, such press 'revelations' were at once ephemeral and tantalizing, keeping the subject of the Letter in the public eye while not providing any conclusive evidence.

Within the British intelligence establishment, too, the Zinoviev Letter clearly still rankled: SIS, investigating 'forgery factories', noticed that the Soviet authorities now seemed to be encouraging forgers to concoct documents on genuine notepaper, so that they might be 'planted' and subsequently denied with proof that they were not genuine. In January 1925, Captain Miller of Scotland Yard passed on to SIS an unnamed informant's report that there were representatives of foreign news agencies in the Soviet Union, paid by the Bolsheviks and organized by Zinoviev, to fabricate 'news' for English, French, and German newspapers, as a counter-move to the publication of anti-Russian reports.[66] In May the SIS Chief sent out a circular instructing all stations to

> use every precaution in accepting as genuine any alleged Communist document that may be offered to you...The only facts which can be considered in future as in any way proof of authenticity is [sic] the complete story of the manner in which the alleged document has been obtained, and the hands through which it has passed between those of the alleged writer and the SIS representative.[67]

Meanwhile, both MI5 and SIS continued to investigate the possible penetration of Special Branch by a network working for Soviet intelligence, run by Daily Herald journalist W. N. Ewer and including a former Scotland Yard officer, Arthur Lakey @ Allen. The full extent of this penetration, extending to SIS and other agencies, did not become apparent until 1929, but it was already clear that there were active Soviet-funded networks in Britain with connections to ARCOS and in Europe.[68]

Throughout this period the Soviet civilian and military intelligence organizations, the OGPU and the Fourth Department, were also involved actively in international operations against 'White Guards', or any groups opposed to the Bolshevik regime. Not only did they keep a close eye on anti-Bolshevik elements throughout Europe, often by establishing a presence in Soviet diplomatic missions, but they also mounted elaborate deception operations using agents provocateurs. The most significant of these were the OGPU's 'Syndicate' and 'Trust' operations: the former targeted Boris Savinkov, who was running from Warsaw and Czechoslovakia an organization dedicated to the overthrow of the Bolshevik regime,[69] while 'The Trust' was the name of a fictitious organization based largely in Paris, the 'Monarchist Association of Central Russia', which had fooled a number of leading anti-Bolshevik figures. Savinkov was lured over the Russian border in 1924 to his death, as was Sidney Reilly in 1925.[70]

Reilly's brutal execution by the OGPU on 5 November 1925[71] presents the opportunity to deal with the many rumours and theories that it was he who commissioned, forged, posted, or guaranteed the authenticity of the Zinoviev Letter. A number of accounts express confidence in his involvement in the episode: Michael Kettle called the forging of the Letter 'the high water mark in Reilly's whole career'; Gordon Brook-Shepherd concluded that he was 'one of a chain of half a dozen persons, official and unofficial', who ensured the Letter's publication in the Daily Mail; Richard Spence suggested that Reilly might be the same person as 'Singleton', and also 'Captain Black' operating in Riga.[72]

Sidney Reilly, the so-called 'Ace of Spies', was a 'complex, unpredictable and undoubtedly self-serving individual mired in deception and conspiracy', who had worked for SIS for a few years from 1918 and was in contact with Desmond Morton until at least 1922. He certainly moved in the circles where such forgeries were common currency. He knew Vladimir Orlov well, and had good connections in anti-Bolshevik circles.[73] But despite all the allegations, Reilly's most authoritative biographer, Andrew Cook, is doubtful of his involvement with the Letter (not least because he was in New York for most of 1924),[74] and Milicent Bagot, in her 1970 report on the Zinoviev Letter, examined all the evidence and discounted it. With a man like Reilly, it seems unwise to be categoric: my own view is that he may well have known something—perhaps quite a lot—of what went on, but played no significant part in it.

During 1925 the Bolshevik regime, once the prospect of Anglo-Russian treaties had been rejected by the Conservative government, increased its efforts to secure trade deals with other European partners, while stepping up its subversion, espionage, and propaganda activities in Britain and the Empire. The year 1925 was critical in the power struggle within the Bolshevik leadership, as Stalin sought to extend his own authority and diminish that of potential rivals, especially 'old' Bolsheviks like Zinoviev. The Comintern's powers were reduced, and with it Zinoviev's influence, though the scale of subversive activities overseas belied the idea that this indicated a more moderate approach by the Soviet regime.

In this context the Baldwin government continued to find that while relations with Russia were not a priority, they were unable either to ignore them or to deal with them satisfactorily. This was largely due to a section of right-wing Tory backbenchers who conducted a sustained anti-Bolshevik campaign backed up by sometimes hysterical press coverage that whipped up public opinion. Yet while some called for the severance of relations with the Soviet Union, and the press demanded the restriction of Soviet visitors to Britain, neither policy seemed practical or attractive to Chamberlain and the Foreign Office. As Gregory noted in a minute of 2 May 1925,

> We all have, I think, a feeling that we *ought* to do something about this question of Bolshevik agents, and yet, though I have discussed it up and down with the Department, we can none of us think of anything that we can do! The real difficulty, it seems to me, is that we shouldn't necessarily exclude the danger of propaganda or outrage, even if we were to tighten up still further our regulations in regard to the admission of *Russian* Bolsheviks. A real terrorist would clearly have taken great pains to conceal his identity and nationality, and therefore, in this respect, we are entirely dependent on Scotland Yard for protection...It is certainly very annoying, even disquieting, to feel that we are constantly letting in Russian Communists, but, so long as we maintain official relations with the Soviet Govt., it is unhappily inevitable.[75]

Although Chamberlain and his colleagues were aware of the threat posed by Bolshevik espionage and propaganda, they also understood the need, in an international context focused on disarmament and the peaceful settlement of disputes, to encourage trade and not be outflanked by their European partners in negotiating contracts; 1925 was, after all, dominated by international discussions on mutual security and the peaceful settlement of conflict, leading to the Locarno conference in October and the signature of the Locarno Treaties in London on 1 December.[76] The Locarno Pact—which secured for Chamberlain the Nobel Peace Prize and a knighthood—was regarded as a significant achievement by the British government, but was bound to be seen from Moscow as yet another example of the Western powers ganging up against Russia.

Some British businessmen called for an increase in trade with Russia. Chamberlain, in a note to the Home Secretary of 5 May 1925, complained that his life was 'made a burden by commercial interests': but despite outrageous Bolshevik propaganda, he did not think much would be achieved by restricting Soviet visitors to Britain, or accusing the Soviet Embassy openly. 'We may', the Foreign Secretary wrote, 'easily make fools of ourselves in this matter, and apparently some people would wish us to do so.' The best policy was 'no breach unless we are forced to it, and no pinpricks on our part. But if there is real cause and a first-class case, strike and strike hard.'[77]

What would constitute 'real cause', however, was difficult to determine. As Chamberlain observed in July 1925, when the FO was considering how to reply to a Parliamentary Question, the agreement reached with the Soviets in 1923 on restricting propaganda had contemplated occasional breaches, 'whereas we are confronted with a continuous infringement'. Maxse, in a minute of 21 July, pointed out that 'if we are to call Mr Rakovsky's attention to breaches of the propaganda agreement as they arise and with any show of plausibility at all, we shall have to some extent to disclose our secret sources of information'. Chamberlain agreed, and proposed to reply that no useful purpose would be served, or friendly relations promoted, by 'a constant stream of detailed complaints'.[78]

Nevertheless, both official and public anxiety at the scale of Bolshevik subversion in Britain grew, creating an environment in which the Zinoviev Letter was never forgotten. In July 1925, MacDonald asked the FO if he might see the original draft of the note to Rakovsky of 24 October 1924, 'as there was a small committee of the Labour Party...who desired to be satisfied on one or two points'. The FO Librarian, Gaselee, thought this request 'unprecedented' and would not sanction the document leaving the office without express permission of the Foreign Secretary. Rather reluctantly, Chamberlain agreed to let MacDonald have the draft, provided he did not let it out of his possession and returned it immediately.[79] In the light of later confusion about the whereabouts of key documents, the request is worth remembering. Meanwhile, suspicion of the role played by the CPGB and by the Soviet Union in fomenting industrial unrest was stirred up both by the press and by groups of industrialists who sponsored the publication of 'Red Conspiracy Leaflets' with titles like 'How the Reds Work' and 'How the Reds gain control of the Unions'.[80] Labour unrest increased as unemployment rose, particularly after the return to the gold standard made British exports more expensive. A crisis in the coal industry was settled on 'Red Friday', 31 July 1925, when Baldwin agreed to subsidize the mine-owners in order to avert the threat of a general strike, but the solution was temporary and the crisis merely postponed.

The Secret Service Committee, 1925

Although Stanley Baldwin supported firm action against subversion, he remained troubled by the implications of the Zinoviev Letter affair. To his mind, it had suggested a worrying level of confusion and duplication of effort in the intelligence community, as well as a lack of accountability. Concerned to maintain a balance between the defence of national institutions and democracy on the one hand, and the need for good intelligence on industrial relations and Bolshevik subversion on the other, he was wary of giving the secret intelligence establishment too much of a free hand.

In February 1925 the Prime Minister had decided to revive the Secret Service Committee, to review the work of the intelligence agencies—not just SIS and MI5, but all the intelligence bodies, including Scotland Yard, Indian Political Intelligence, and the Government Code and Cypher School—and to recommend changes that 'would conduce to the greater efficiency of the system'.[81] The three most senior civil servants in the land, Sir Warren Fisher, Sir Maurice Hankey, and Sir Eyre Crowe, met first on 26 February 1925. The committee held ten meetings by the end of June, although it did not report until December. The proceedings were dominated by organizational issues—in particular, by proposals that all the agencies should be amalgamated and co-located under a single head (a role in which SIS Chief Sinclair saw himself). But at three meetings of the Secret Service Committee the Zinoviev Letter was discussed specifically: the proceedings reveal the usual tendency of rival authorities to defend their own position and put the blame on others, while failing to bring any new information to light.[82]

On 5 March 1925, at the committee's third meeting, Metropolitan Police Commissioner Brigadier General Sir William Horwood rejected any idea of a lack of cooperation, or capacity, on the part of Scotland Yard. In response to Crowe's questioning as to why it had proved impossible to verify the receipt of the Zinoviev Letter by the CPGB, Horwood suggested Childs's inability to do so 'might have been due to lack of funds'. He insisted that there was 'close and satisfactory liaison between Scotland Yard and the various branches of secret service', and disputed the idea that 'Communists knew what was going on in Scotland Yard and the General Post Office'.

Childs himself, giving evidence at the sixth meeting on 17 March, said his liaison arrangements were so efficient that it was 'impossible' for there to have been any leakage of SIS documents from Special Branch. He added, however, that 'the value of SIS documents to him was usually minute', since owing to 'the diplomatic immunity enjoyed by the Soviet couriers he was never able to prove the receipt of Bolshevist communications in transit to this country'. Childs also complained that he should have been told that SIS had an agent inside the CPGB, and denied that he had ever seen 'C' (the SIS Chief) in connection with the Zinoviev Letter. When questioned closely on the point by Crowe, Childs insisted that he 'studiously avoided any course of action which might be regarded as spying upon the Labour party', and was 'resolutely opposed to using his own organisation for political purposes'.

At the seventh meeting, held on 19 March with both Sinclair and Childs in attendance, the committee discussed a paper sent by the SIS Chief on 18 March 1925 to the Secretary, Nevile Bland, in support of proposals for the amalgamation of the intelligence agencies under Sinclair's own leadership. This document, entitled 'Some recent examples of lack of cooperation, coordination and overlapping between C's organisation, MI5, Scotland Yard, IPI and the Passport Control Department', included a section on the Zinoviev Letter, which Sinclair described as 'a classic illustration of the overlapping inevitable under the present system':

> It was discovered abroad; was addressed to the communist party in England, and enjoined revolutionary action both in civil and military spheres. Thus, under the present arrangement of divided responsibility in the British secret service, it concerned all the three different branches. Surely a system under which such a situation could arise was fundamentally wrong.

He noted that the Letter had been sent to Scotland Yard on 9 October with a request for assistance in confirming its receipt by the CPGB. Owing to 'the interception of letters having been suspended by the Home Secretary and the lack of Agents', Scotland Yard had been unable to provide this help.[83] Childs defended his corner, telling the committee that if he had known about SIS's informant in the CPGB he could have told Sinclair that the information was 'unworthy of confidence':

> He suggested that C should have kept him closely informed of each step in his enquiry and, if his informant had proved valuable, have offered to place his services at the disposal of Scotland Yard. He repeated his opinion that the letter was deprived of importance by the fact that the purport of it was common knowledge and that it was consequently redundant.

Crowe was not about to let this pass: he stressed the importance of the FO's judgement in the affair, and said that 'ruling out all questions of the genuineness of the letter and of what happened to it in this country, he considered the facts which had been elicited concerning the attempt to obtain information about it in London, showed plainly an inherent weakness in the liaison system of our secret service'.[84]

A month after this meeting, Crowe was dead. He was succeeded as Permanent Under-Secretary by Sir William Tyrrell, who had been Private Secretary to Sir Edward Grey and was the most senior of the FO's Assistant Under-Secretaries. Tyrrell was entirely different from his predecessor, in both style and in his approach to his duties in the FO, though the two men had got on well and worked effectively together. As Ephraim Maisel puts it: 'Crowe and Tyrrell were one of the most successful combinations that ever arose in the Foreign Office, not because they worked as a team but because the one was the opposite of his companion... Crowe was the embodiment of the perfect civil servant, while Tyrrell was the symbol of the non-conventional diplomat.'[85] Tyrrell was known for going everywhere and knowing everyone—but some contemporary observers found his deliberately laid-back style worrying. Richard Casey, Special Representative at the Australian High Commission in London, told his Prime Minister, Stanley Bruce, in February 1925 that Tyrrell was 'very clever, very agile-minded, well-known for his ability at discovering "formulae" but without the high principle and sound judgement and knowledge of Crowe'. Casey also noted that Tyrrell was a Catholic, like Gregory (who was promoted to the rank of Under-Secretary in the FO shortly after Tyrrell became Permanent Under-Secretary): 'There are people who affect to be a good deal concerned about the control that will now be in the hands of these two Catholic officials... As a matter of gossip one hears it said that Gregory is "the friend of every Cardinal in Europe".'[86]

Tyrrell, like Crowe, distrusted the Russians, and had chaired an inter-departmental committee on Bolshevik subversion against the British Empire.[87] He took Crowe's place on the Secret Service Committee, which continued to meet throughout 1925, producing a report in November that Tyrrell judged 'very lucid & useful'. However, the report neither mentioned the Zinoviev Letter, nor recommended any radical change to the organization of the intelligence community—despite admitting that 'if there were today no British secret service of any kind... we should not adopt the existing system as our model'.

The heads of the relevant agencies were urged to see each other more often and promote 'harmonious' relations (a dig at the tension between Sinclair, 'a zealous, intelligent and exceptionally competent officer', and the 'highly-strung, sensitive and over-burdened' Childs). The committee's recommendations did little to satisfy Sinclair's ambitions (though they did produce some internal changes in SIS), or to reassure Baldwin about the efficient workings of the intelligence machinery.[88] Meanwhile, the Zinoviev sore was left to fester, so that when it erupted again, it was with a peculiar and shocking force.

4

The Plot Thickens, 1928–1929

'They thought they had buried Zinoviev, but lo and behold, his ghost has arisen.'[1]

In January 1928 the professional life of J. D. Gregory, respected Under-Secretary in the Foreign Office and expert on Russian affairs, tumbled round his ears, triggering a series of revelations that rocked the British political and intelligence establishment and ensured that the Zinoviev Letter was once more in the forefront of the news in the first half of the year. The allegations made in 1924–5 about Gregory's foreign-currency dealings, and their possible connection with the Zinoviev Letter,[2] resurfaced when Prime Minister Stanley Baldwin ordered a Special Board of Enquiry into the conduct of civil servants revealed during a lawsuit against Gregory's friend Mrs Bradley Dyne.

The Board of Enquiry's proceedings were considered so sensitive that the files on them were released only in 1992. Its report, however, with one section devoted to the Zinoviev Letter, was published in the press on 28 February 1928.[3] It prompted some of those who had kept their mouths firmly shut in 1924 to come forward and tell their stories, including Thomas Marlowe of the *Daily Mail* and Donald im Thurn. All this alarmed the Conservatives and reopened old wounds in a Labour Party now preparing for the next general election. Just as the scandal appeared to have subsided, it re-emerged in the early months of 1929 with the arrests in Berlin of Vladimir Orlov and his fellow forgers, and in London of two Special Branch officers who were unmasked as Soviet agents, developments that were alarming to the intelligence agencies.

In the general election on 30 May 1929 Labour gained twenty-six more seats than the Conservatives, and Ramsay MacDonald again took office as Prime Minister. Diplomatic relations with the Soviet Union, broken off in May 1927, were restored in October. But on the same day that the protocol was signed settling the outstanding questions between the two governments, a Soviet diplomat in Paris defected by jumping over the garden wall of his embassy and began to publish further 'revelations' about the Zinoviev Letter, including details of Zinoviev's cross-examination by Dzerzhinsky in 1924.

All this took place against an international backdrop of increasing financial instability, concern at Germany's attempts to break free from the provisions of the Versailles Settlement, and consequent international attempts—which the USA sought to dominate—to settle difficult legacies of the First World War and preserve the peace. Meanwhile, in the Soviet Union, acute economic difficulties and the threat of internal dissent made the Bolshevik regime even more desperate to obtain credits from the West, despite authorizing a continuing high level of propaganda and subversion. It also made Stalin even more determined to eliminate any rivals to his power and led him to launch the drastic programme of economic transformation that would bring with it the Great Terror and the death of millions of Soviet citizens.

To understand the dramatic events of 1928–9, we need first to revisit briefly the events of the preceding two years, when the Zinoviev Letter mystery bubbled under the surface before finally coming to the boil.

'We are at a new kind of war with Russia': Anglo-Soviet relations, 1926–1927

Until 1928, Stanley Baldwin and his ministerial colleagues, not to mention Foreign Office officials like Tyrrell and Gregory, might have been forgiven for thinking that, for the present at least, Russia

Figure 10. Austen Chamberlain, Foreign Secretary 1924–9

could drop down the list of what would today be called policy priorities.[4] During 1926, Foreign Secretary Sir Austen Chamberlain had pursued a policy of 'patience and expectancy', taking the view that the Russians should be left alone 'in the expectation that sooner or later they would discover that they have more need of us than we have of them'.[5] He, and his officials, saw little to be gained by denouncing the 1921 Trade Agreement, expelling Soviet representatives, or breaking off relations, no matter how badly the Bolsheviks behaved. As Gregory put it, 'There is no use in slamming a door which has only got to be opened again...we should only find ourselves six months hence in an embarrassed position, conducting our routine business with the Soviets in a neutral capital and wondering how on earth to resume direct relations.'[6]

This essentially pragmatic strategy had foundered on the strength of the anti-Bolshevik lobby in Parliament, industry, and the press, enraged by the Soviet regime's financial support for the Miners' Federation and the TUC during the General Strike in the summer of 1926,[7] as well as by perceived Russian interference in the Chinese civil war to the detriment of British interests[8] and concern about closer German–Soviet ties, symbolized by the signing of the Treaty of Berlin in April 1926.[9] By the end of the year, demands—including from Cabinet members like Joynson-Hicks, Birkenhead, and Churchill— for some form of decisive action against the Bolsheviks had become, as Gregory remarked, 'well-nigh irresistible', even though he, like Chamberlain, still considered a breach in relations undesirable.[10]

After an incident in which Russia was suspected of tampering with foreign diplomatic bags,[11] Chamberlain felt impelled to send a note of protest on 23 February 1927 to the Soviet Chargé, complaining about his government's behaviour and warning 'in the gravest terms that there are limits beyond which it is dangerous to drive public opinion in the country'; if the Bolsheviks did not mend their ways, he said, the Trade Agreement would be abrogated and diplomatic relations severed.[12] As Chamberlain wrote to his sister Hilda, he sent the note as a compromise, to buy a little time: he dreaded a breach with Russia 'for its reactions on Europe & especially on Germany & the Baltic States', but 'the toes of my colleagues are itching to kick them even tho' it be but a useless gesture'.[13]

As usual, after a predictably indignant riposte the Russians ignored the note, and details of subversive activities continued to build up. British military authorities were particularly concerned about the threat to imperial security posed by Soviet activities in Afghanistan. At the beginning of April 1927, a raid on the Soviet Embassy compound in Peking produced incriminating evidence of Bolshevik propaganda and espionage, while the Warsaw Embassy reported on war material being sent from Germany to the Soviet Union.[14] Anti-Red hysteria mounted in the British press, encouraged by Tory backbenchers. The final breach came as a result of a raid on 12 May by Scotland Yard and intelligence officers on the premises of ARCOS, the Soviet trading organization, after a disaffected employee had passed information to SIS that a British Army Signals Training pamphlet had been photo-copied there.

Though the ARCOS raid was 'hurriedly planned, chaotically executed and failing in its primary objective' (the pamphlet was not found), it was portrayed to Parliament and the general public as an intelligence coup and used to justify the termination of the Trade Agreement of 1921 and the severance of diplomatic relations with the Soviet Union.[15] In fact, the raid and its aftermath were an intelligence disaster, since to justify its actions the government published intercepted communications between the Soviet Embassy in the UK and Moscow, causing the Russians to adopt a One-Time Pad system that meant henceforth no high-grade Soviet diplomatic messages could be read by the British until the Second World War.[16] As SIS Chief Sinclair complained, 'The publication of the telegrams automatically stops their source of supply for some years at least. It was authorised only as a measure of desperation to bolster up a cause vital to Government, which had the facts been fully known at the time, needed no such costly support.'[17] Just as in 1923, the grand gesture of protest had little effect on Soviet policy but scored an intelligence own goal.[18]

The reaction of the Soviet regime was a violent one: the Moscow Embassy reported summary executions throughout Russia of people accused of being British spies, while a number of British officials were threatened with arrest and had to leave the country; SIS were concerned for the safety of their agents in the Baltics. From Moscow, the British Chargé, William Peters, reported that the ARCOS raid had 'pushed all other political events into the background', and was being interpreted as yet further proof of the existence of a Western anti-Soviet bloc. The Soviet government was 'able to present itself as the injured party, and to point to events in London as proving that it was no obsession on its part to think that Great Britain was the centre of anti-Soviet effort'.[19] All this played into the hands of Stalin: increasingly autocratic (he had now removed both Zinoviev and Trotsky from the Politburo), he was convinced—or at least professed to believe—that 'the chief contemporary question is that of the threat of a new imperialist war'.

Thomas Preston, the British agent in Petrograd who had been forced to move to Finland when threatened with arrest, agreed that the effect produced by the rupture of relations was 'tremendous... shaking the Bolshevik Government to its very foundations'. There had been 4,000 arrests in Leningrad alone, and a number of violent incidents, while the Bolshevik propaganda machine continued to promote the threat of war and blame Britain for Russian economic difficulties. It was reported that the OGPU—which had suffered a series of disasters in its overseas operations in the spring of 1927[20]—had been given extraordinary powers to protect the country from 'foreign spies, pillagers and murderers, together with their Monarchist and white guard allies'. Preston added that while some regretted the breach, others failed to understand 'how it was that two great countries—meaning Great Britain and Russia—could quarrel over a document such as the Zinoviev Letter'.[21] The Letter, and its political implications, had clearly not been forgotten by the Bolsheviks.

It remained a subject of interest to some in Britain as well, with occasional press reports and Parliamentary Questions.[22] In April 1927, a slim volume appeared entitled *Anti-Soviet Forgeries: A Record of some of the Forged Documents Used at Various Times against the Soviet Government*, with a foreword by George Lansbury. It contained a detailed history of 'lies and slanders' against the Bolsheviks, and described the work of many forgery 'arsenals', including in Berlin, Vienna, and Britain (the last a reference to 'Mr Singleton').[23] Chapter III, on 'The "Zinoviev" or "Red" Letter,' went through the events of 1924 in detail, giving the text of the Letter and documents related to it, summarizing the Trade Union Delegation's report and quoting extensively from the parliamentary debates at the end of 1924.

Anti-Soviet Forgeries referred to the Letter as an early example of the work of fabricators who were mostly 'Russian "White Guards"—counter-revolutionary *émigrés*'. It gave details of those working in what it called 'Druzhelovsky's arsenal in Berlin', including 'Alexander Gumansky', 'Gerald Ivanovich Sievert', and Vladimir Orlov. Orlov, it said, was 'in the service of the Latvian Intelligence Department', and closely connected with one 'Pokrovsky', supposedly another name for A. A. Belgardt, son of a former tsarist senator, and possibly the same person as the 'Bellegarde' who was to be named in the 1967 book by the *Sunday Times* 'Insight' team.[24] Many of those named (though all had multiple aliases and were spelled in many different ways) were included in a note prepared by SIS in July 1927 on Soviet activities aimed at discrediting evidence obtained by British intelligence. The note also referred to reports that the OGPU was using its penetration of White Russian organizations to distribute false information and documents. Commander Wilfred 'Biffy' Dunderdale, SIS's Head of Station in Paris, had supplied some of the details on which this note was based, noting that as soon as any anti-Bolshevik organization was formed, Orlov took steps to penetrate it by supplying it with spurious documents, and that he was himself connected with the OGPU as well as White Russian intelligence. Dunderdale reported information that Orlov's organization was 'completely controlled by the GPU and with the consent and cooperation of the German S[ecret] S[ervice]'.[25]

As always when Orlov was concerned, the truth was elusive. Druzhelovsky is a case in point. Semen, or Sergiy, Mihailovitch Druzhelovsky, a Russian Jew, had apparently come to Berlin in 1922 from Poland, where he had been in prison for espionage, and had been put in touch with the Orlov bureau by the German authorities. Arrested in 1926 by the Berlin police as an OGPU agent, he was released but put on trial in Moscow in the summer of 1927. During the proceedings he apparently stated that the Zinoviev Letter had been written in his lodgings in Berlin by a Russian émigré with the help of Belgardt and Gumansky, who were working for British intelligence; the forgers received £80 for their trouble.[26] But although this was enough for the French newspaper *L'Humanité* to declare Druzhelovsky '*auteur de la fausse lettre Zinovieff*',[27] no one in an official position was disposed to take the story very seriously. The trouble was, as even the press admitted, that Druzhelovsky, whom *Pravda* called a 'murderer, pimp and profiteer', was a habitual liar who would say any-thing to save his skin. According to SIS, the OGPU regarded him as a valuable agent who would be brought out when required to spread convenient rumours.

Nevertheless, these reports and rumours did not do the reputation of the British intelligence establishment any good, and they made Stanley Baldwin uncomfortable. The familiar image of Baldwin with a pipe, lazily scratching a pig's ears, created a good brand image but belied his political acumen. While holding no brief for Moscow, and appreciating the importance of the work done by the intelligence agencies to counter Soviet subversion, he remained worried that the British public might think that episodes like the Zinoviev Letter showed the government using state apparatus for party advantage. This mattered, in the run-up to a general election due by November 1929, and when by-election results indicated not just a Labour, but also a Liberal, resurgence under Lloyd George, at the expense of the Conservatives, despite the reforming efforts of ministers like Winston Churchill (Chancellor of the Exchequer) and the ambitious Neville Chamberlain (Minister of Health).

At the beginning of 1927, after a leak to the press had resulted in a foreign agent escaping arrest, Baldwin had reconvened the Secret Service Committee in the hope that they might suggest reforms to prevent the politicization of intelligence. He was afraid, as Tyrrell wrote, that 'the political work done at Scotland Yard might at any moment give rise to a scandal, owing to the Labour party obtaining some plausible pretext to complain that a government department was being employed for party politics'. Baldwin was clearly thinking about the Letter. But as in 1925, the committee failed to grasp the nettle, and even the mismanaged ARCOS raid did not rouse them to suggest any radical alteration of existing intelligence arrangements.[28]

By the end of 1927, despite a few 'revelations', the Zinoviev Letter debate had not moved on materially. The breach in Anglo-Soviet relations made little difference to the intelligence agencies, since Bolshevik propaganda and subversion proceeded unabated; in particular, Soviet encouragement of Communist unrest caused severe problems for British interests in China. MI5 continued to keep a close eye on Soviet agents in the UK, and SIS on those overseas: though ARCOS had been forced to move its operations to Antwerp and Hamburg, it continued to function, as did the global network of Bolshevik covert operatives. The next crisis in the Zinoviev Letter saga came, however, neither from diplomatic relations nor intelligence operations, but from a lawsuit.

The Francs Scandal, 1928

J. D. Gregory, now an Assistant Under-Secretary in the FO and a close confidant of the PUS, Sir William Tyrrell, must have thought that the allegations made in 1924–5 about his conduct during the Zinoviev Letter crisis been laid to rest when he had assured Ramsay MacDonald and J. H. Thomas that there was no truth in them.[29] He does not appear to have moderated his behaviour, but continued to speculate in foreign currency together with Aminta Bradley Dyne, even if she generally took the lead in their financial transactions.[30] In 1926 she made a profit of over £23,000 (about £1.3 m today), but in 1927 a loss of over £26,000. By late 1927 she owed her stockbrokers nearly £40,000 (about £2.3 m): not surprisingly, they sued her.

Ironmonger v Dyne was heard in the King's Bench Division of the High Court: proceedings opened on 26 January 1928 in front of Mr Justice Horridge and a special jury. It was inevitable that Gregory's name would come out, for the only way that the stockbroker who had handled the Dyne account could justify offering virtually unlimited credit to a woman of uncertain means and creditworthiness was to say that he had relied on the introduction given by 'a prominent official at the Foreign Office'. During the hearings it emerged that Gregory's finances were inextricably entwined with Aminta's, and that other members of the FO's Northern Department, including Owen O'Malley and Commander H. F. B. Maxse, had been involved in speculative dealings as well. On 1 February the jury took only twenty minutes to find in favour of Ironmonger, with £38,938 (over £2.2 m today) payable by Mrs Dyne.[31] That same morning, at 11.30 a.m., the Prime Minister told the Cabinet that he, the Foreign Secretary, and the Chancellor of the Exchequer had decided immediately to issue a press communiqué announcing a Special Board of Enquiry into statements made during the Dyne case about the conduct of civil servants. It was to be led by Sir Warren Fisher, head of the civil service and Permanent Secretary to the Treasury, with Sir Malcolm Ramsay

(Comptroller and Auditor-General) and M.L.Gwyer, HM Procurator-General and Solicitor to the Treasury, as the other members of the board.They would begin work straight away.[32] Ministers were clearly concerned about press coverage of a juicy scandal—people always enjoy reading about the misdeeds of public servants.

During *Ironmonger v Dyne*, Mr Justice Horridge and the jury appeared incredulous at the evidence offered, not just by Mrs Dyne but by stockbroker Alfred de Waal, who insisted that although she had been 'almost my biggest customer, if not the biggest', he had kept no record of their transactions.[33] Aminta's own evidence was both vague and contradictory: she claimed to have acted only on instructions, yet had clearly been the dominant figure in the financial dealings. Questioning revealed her to be fairly knowledgeable on business matters (she said she had been her husband's business manager since the war), while Gregory, she said, was a man who knew less about business than anyone she knew. This might explain why in early 1924 an account had been opened with his money, but from which she profited. Asked if her husband (who had been required at least once to bail her out) was interested in her dealings, she replied that he was 'only very furious, if you call that an interest'. He was, she said, a 'very complacent person'.[34]

Out of all this, the statement about Gregory's being naive in business matters is perhaps the most believable. A friend of his, Dr J. G. Vance, a former accountant now ordained priest who volunteered to appear before the enquiry as an independent witness, described Gregory as 'a very clever man whose knowledge of Europe is wonderful but whose knowledge of finance is nil'. Gregory himself wrote to Sir Malcolm Ramsay apologizing for being unable to give any precise details about payments traced to him: 'it is very galling to have to confess to such utterly unbusinesslike methods'.[35] It is hard to disagree with the verdict of Charles Blennerhassett, intelligence officer turned stockbroker, that Gregory was 'a man of extraordinary faults' as well as extraordinary qualities; Blennerhassett told the board that he had stopped seeing so much of Gregory as he was 'more and more in the woman's hands'.[36] Certainly, Gregory appears to have been in thrall to Aminta Dyne. This seems the only explanation of why an outwardly sober and respectable civil servant, highly thought of in his profession, married with two children, entered into a long-running, expensive, and indeed unsuccessful financial partnership to speculate in foreign currency—involving some of his Northern Department colleagues, much to his and their later detriment, and possibly other members of the FO and other departments, though this was never proved.[37]

Although the records of the Treasury Board of Enquiry are fascinating, only a part of the proceedings is relevant to the present story. When Ramsay MacDonald learned of the verdict in the Dyne lawsuit and the setting up of the Board of Enquiry, he immediately made the connection with his questioning of Gregory in early 1925 about the deposition sworn by Mrs Dyne's maid, Violet Digby, connecting Gregory's and Aminta's activities with the Zinoviev Letter.[38] On 8 February 1928 MacDonald wrote to Fisher, saying that he had evidence to submit to the enquiry.[39] Invited to appear on 15 February, MacDonald gave the board a copy of Digby's deposition, and told them how Gregory had denied everything when challenged. 'I suppose you all remember the Zinoviev Letter,' he said. 'I never made up my mind whether that letter was a forgery or whether it was authentic, but I always regarded the way in which the matter had been handled by my political opponents as monstrous, a nefarious piece of deceit and fraud.'

MacDonald said that the revelations in the Dyne case had made him wonder whether there was a connection with Gregory's signature of what he called 'the despatch', the note of protest to the Soviet Chargé that MacDonald claimed he had not authorized but was signed off by Gregory on 24 October 1924 and published the following day with the Zinoviev Letter. Perhaps, suggested MacDonald, Gregory did this 'in order to improve the currency market so that his speculations or his friends' speculations might be improved':

> What would be the effect of these speculations if this Despatch had depreciated Russian currency or had any of the other reactions that

might reasonably be expected on the Stock Exchange, in the City? And the connection which is here, and which is quite meaningless until this case came on, the connection which is indicated here between a man in a very tight fix, who has lost a lot of money, and the political situation now becomes possibly very close. As a matter of fact, it may be found to be cause and effect. It may be found to be nothing at all. I do not know.[40]

MacDonald's evidence opened up an unwelcome line of enquiry for the board, and they questioned him closely about it: was he suggesting that an official might have been influenced in the course of his public duty by financial self-interest? If so, it would be a question 'materially affecting the fair name and confidence of the Public Service, and politicians and Ministers and all in the Service'. MacDonald: 'Yes.' He then went on to relate in detail the events of the critical week in October 1924, and Crowe's part in it, stressing that he would 'cease to believe in anything' if Crowe had deceived him. MacDonald was clearly more open to the possibility that Gregory had done so. He did not care, he said, if Gregory disliked the Labour government or himself as Foreign Secretary: 'Why should he not say so? But if I found that was influencing Mr Gregory's work, Mr Gregory would go.'

Pressed again as to whether he was suggesting—as a 'possibility', not an 'allegation'—that an official might have been motivated by personal financial considerations, MacDonald again assented. He hastened to add that he was, nevertheless, very concerned to protect the reputation of the civil service, telling the board of distinguished civil servants that 'if anything happens to besmirch you it is one of the most disastrous things that has happened in our time'. He added, however: 'I must confess I am interested in my own reputation which has never quite been cleared up yet.'

After MacDonald's evidence the board had no option but to include in their investigations the alleged connection between the Francs Case and the Zinoviev Letter. As Warren Fisher told MacDonald:

We are trustees not merely for ourselves, but for the public. We are trustees to you, to Parliament, and to the public of our own country as well as to the Service. We therefore do want to probe the thing to the uttermost and to convince ourselves and then be able to carry conviction having convinced ourselves as to the dimensions and the nature and the degree of this problem... We are not on a question here of a conceivable breach, a gross breach of the delicacy demanded of a public servant, but on the conceivable possibility of a very different order of action.[41]

Fisher and his fellow board members were naturally disturbed about the idea of civil service corruption. Yet they were frustrated in their pursuit of any convincing evidence to support the allegation. For despite MacDonald's conjectures, Violet Digby's deposition, and the suspicions of other witnesses, it proved impossible to show how Gregory *could* have manipulated events to benefit financially from the Zinoviev Letter, let alone that he actually *did*. The board consulted a range of witnesses on whether Gregory and his colleagues could have used their privileged position as FO officials to gain inside information to their financial advantage. Experts from the City were unanimous in agreeing that it was highly unlikely that they could have done this (while making clear their view, shared by the board, that those officials should not have been speculating in foreign currency at all).

This line of questioning was then extended to the Zinoviev Letter: could Gregory have profited financially from the timing of its publication, and the reply to it? Could he have made money out of the destabilization of the financial markets that might follow a political scandal? The financial experts consulted by the enquiry were unanimously sceptical. Even if such a destabilization occurred—by no means certain—it would have been impossible to predict whether rates would rise or fall, and there would have been no way of making sure of cashing in at the right moment. The idea that Dyne and Gregory had organized their speculative dealings to coincide with the publication of the Zinoviev Letter seemed inherently improbable and was not supported by the evidence. Aminta's dealings did not suggest a well-informed or strategic approach, but rather 'gambles (wild gambles at that) upon turn of the market at a time of fluctuations'.[42]

In the end, the board members were forced to conclude that they were barking up the wrong tree in trying to link the Francs Scandal to the Letter. Having reached this conclusion, they were most concerned in their report to stress that Gregory's crime was inappropriate currency dealing, not corruption:

> We are satisfied that there is not the slightest foundation for any of the suspicions which have, in our opinion, most unjustly attached to Mr Gregory in connexion with the events of the 24th and 25th October, 1924, and we beg to report accordingly.[43]

Predictably, this conclusion was greeted with incredulity by Labour supporters. In a pamphlet published in May 1928 by the Anglo-Russian Parliamentary Committee, its secretary W. P. Coates wrote that the board's conclusions were absurd:

> The implications of the Statutory Declaration [by Violet Digby] are in our judgement crystal clear and we have no doubt that our readers will draw the same conclusions as we have made in our own mind. Was it because these deductions were so evident and so damning that the Special Board put up their inflated man of straw and then demolished him?[44]

It is, however, hard to see that the board could have reached any other conclusion on the basis of the evidence presented to them. Gregory had not, examination of his bank records showed, made any gains at the critical time; in fact he had been out of pocket. He could not have known, as the board pointed out in their report, when MacDonald would return to the FO the amended draft of the note to the Soviet government, nor could he have affected the timing of its publication significantly, since Crowe had been the one to insist on its being sent off. For Gregory to sign the note to the Soviet Chargé was, in the circumstances, normal procedure and entirely appropriate. He could certainly have sold a copy of the Letter between 10 and 24 October, but there is no evidence that he did so, and those who did secure copies insisted that they did not pay for them—which seems plausible given the circulation of the Letter in the final week before publication.

Gregory, whose testimony throughout the Board of Enquiry had been both muddled and unconvincing, did not emerge unscathed. For his dealings in foreign currency he was dismissed from the Foreign Service, while O'Malley (whose excuse for his conduct was that they had 'all hoped to get something for nothing') was 'permitted to resign', and Maxse was severely reprimanded and forfeited three years' seniority.[45] There is no doubt that Gregory's conduct was suspicious, and leaves many unanswered questions. Was he naive in both business and politics, as the testimony suggested? The Board of Enquiry proceedings do not answer this, and nor does Gregory's generally uninformative autobiography, published with what many thought indecent haste in 1929.[46] Investigating the Francs affair in 1998, I found the whole matter both highly suspect and puzzling, but, like the board, was unable to find any proof that Gregory—whose judgement was clearly impaired by his association with Aminta Dyne—had actually played any significant role in the manipulation of the Letter. In the absence of further evidence, I can only repeat my judgement in the 1999 report:

> The range of Gregory's close contacts—'C' himself, Polish diplomats, prominent White Russians, City men who were former Intelligence officers—together with his involvement with the Letter in his capacity as a senior FO official, means that any attempt to follow the thread of the Zinoviev mystery leads to Gregory; if not at the centre of the labyrinth, at least in one of its main antechambers... But if political motivation is sought... it can surely be found much more readily in figures like Desmond Morton and Joseph Ball, both senior members of Intelligence agencies, both closely involved with the fortunes of the Conservative party, than it can in J. D. Gregory, whose involvement is clearly indicated but who may, in the end, have been no more than a rash and misguided man led astray for the love of an exotic and extravagant woman.[47]

Gregory had lost his career, and slipped into obscurity; he and Aminta Dyne seem to have lived and travelled together during the 1930s, but I have found no evidence of how they spent the Second World War. Gregory died in 1951; but Aminta, who had turned his life upside down, reinvented herself yet again, moving to Hollywood and—by now in her fifties—making a number of films including *Kiss the Blood off my Hands* (1948) and *Dangerous When Wet* (1953). She died in 1964.

Red Letter Day: revelations in Parliament

If February 1928 had been the month when the ghost of Zinoviev arose, March was the month in which it clanked its chains most loudly. The publication of the report of the Board of Enquiry on the Francs Case began a landslide of 'revelations' about the Zinoviev Letter episode. On 29 February 1928 Baldwin told the Cabinet that he had been asked by MacDonald to provide a half-day of parliamentary time for a debate on the board's findings. Though Baldwin felt it necessary to agree to this request (the debate was later arranged for 19 March), it seemed likely that the Labour Party would take the opportunity to ask for a fresh enquiry into the whole business of the Zinoviev Letter. Some ministers thought this might be a good thing, in order to 'clear up the mystery and set at rest the rumours and suggestions circulated in regard to this matter', but others were doubtful. Any such enquiry would, in effect, be revisiting a matter on which a Cabinet Committee had already pronounced judgement; and the safety of informants overseas had to be considered. Baldwin asked his colleagues to 'consider the political and other aspects of the desirability or otherwise of granting an Inquiry' before any debate took place.[48]

Baldwin and Chamberlain were clearly disturbed by the prospect of reopening the Letter controversy, and hostile Parliamentary Questions in the early part of March indicated trouble ahead.[49] Godfrey Locker Lampson, the Conservative MP (and former diplomat) who had served as Parliamentary Under-Secretary for Foreign Affairs since December 1925, recorded on 3 March 1928 a conversation with MacDonald indicating that the Zinoviev Letter was to be made the subject of a 'further and more definite campaign' by the Labour Party. Locker Lampson's impression was that Labour would focus on four points: how the *Daily Mail* got hold of the Letter; its authenticity; at what point Crowe 'knew he was taking an exceptional course in publishing without the consent of his chief but did so on account of his information about the *Daily Mail*'; and to 'try to elicit why it was that there was no more categorical enquiry in the Foreign Office in regard to the truth or otherwise of certain allegations in the Statutory Declaration'. MacDonald also told him that a number of Conservatives had approached him to express their view that much damage had been done to the prestige of the Foreign Office by recent revelations, and he himself felt 'very badly served by the staff'.[50]

The idea of reopening the issue also alarmed the SIS Chief, Sinclair, who wrote to Tyrrell on 2 March expressing the hope that it would be 'most sternly resisted'. The Zinoviev Letter, he said, was 'obtained by the Secret Service by Secret Service methods. If, therefore, questions are to be answered in regard to this letter, it means that the Secret Service organisation and its methods will no longer be secret.' This would, he said, mean 'the wrecking of the Secret Service organisation which has taken so many years to build up and on which such large sums have been expended', and probably 'the sacrifice of hundreds of lives', since the organization and its methods would no longer be secret.[51] This may seem overdramatic, but SIS and other intelligence organizations relied—as they do today—on obtaining information in secret and with the guarantee of anonymity for their sources. Any enquiry or publicity that threatened to expose sources and methods was unwelcome. Since the end of 1924, SIS had continued to insist, as far as the Foreign Office were concerned, that the Letter was authentic; but at the same time they were keeping a close eye on organizations and individuals suspected of its forgery, with whom for operational reasons it was necessary to maintain contact. Sinclair and his colleagues preferred to keep the whole business—and the question of their own involvement with it—out of the public eye as much as possible.

However, neither the Cabinet nor SIS had any chance of keeping the Zinoviev Letter out of the news at the beginning of March 1928.

On the day Sinclair wrote to Tyrrell, the *New Leader*'s editorial screamed: 'Make the *Mail* talk: the Francs Inquiry and the Zinovieff Letter'. The Francs Scandal, it said, had reopened an 'unsavoury episode' that could not now be closed again without a proper enquiry.[52] Other newspapers agreed: for the media, the board's report had at once revealed a great deal and left a lot of unanswered questions. Some considered it a smokescreen. Sinclair sent Bland a report of a statement made by Chicherin at a Sovnarkom meeting on 3 March: 'A shady lot of Russian and British White Guards and counter-espionage agents joined up around the Zinoviev Letter hand in hand and in close friendship with leaders of the Conservatives and with the enterprising Gregory.' The Labour Party, should, said Chicherin, demand 'a special commission to investigate into it'. He added that such an investigation would not reveal anything compromising to the Soviet regime, as the government had repeatedly denied any respon-sibility for the Comintern's actions.[53]

Then on 4 March 1928 *The Sunday Observer* printed a long state-ment by Thomas Marlowe, the former editor of the *Daily Mail*, now retired and living in France. In it he described how he had come into possession of two copies of the Zinoviev Letter, enabling him to pub-lish it on 25 October 1924. On 22 October, he said, he had received a message from an 'old and trusted friend', informing him of the exist-ence of a document showing the relations between the Bolsheviks and Labour leaders; the Prime Minister knew about it, but was 'trying to avoid publication'. Marlowe's informant said that 'if he could obtain the approval of a third person', he would post him a copy. Marlowe then consulted another 'friend', who said he knew of the document and was indignant at the government's reluctance to publish, though he could not get hold of a copy. Finally, a third 'friend' arrived with a copy of the Letter in his pocket, and Marlowe undertook to give it the widest publicity; shortly afterwards he received the copy from the first 'friend' in the post.

Marlowe insisted that he had paid no money for the two copies— 'the men I dealt with were gentlemen'. He had then proceeded to get the Letter typeset, and notified all the other leading newspapers.

He praised Crowe for his decision, when learning of the imminent publication of the Letter, to send the FO note of protest for publication as well: 'this was the right decision...loyally made in the best interest of the Prime Minister himself'. Marlowe also cleared of any suspicion Gregory, whom he said he had never met and to whom he had certainly never paid any money; he criticized MacDonald for blaming unjustly his subordinates. Marlowe said it was obvious that his own decision as editor of the *Daily Mail* to publish the Letter had forced the FO's hand: without it, he asserted, MacDonald would have succeeded in delaying publication 'until it could do his party no harm', after the election. As it was, the effect of publication was 'unequalled in all the history of general elections. No single event that I have ever heard of produced such direct and definite reaction in the public mind.' For this, said Marlowe, MacDonald had no one but himself to blame.

Marlowe did not name the 'friends' who had approached him about the Letter, and it is impossible to be certain of their identity. As we have seen, the 'old and trusted' friend may well have been former SIS officer Frederick Browning, who admitted giving the Letter to the *Mail* but may have wanted to consult SIS before doing so.[54] The second friend, who was unable to get hold of a copy, could have been Donald im Thurn, though Marlowe denied having any dealings with him.[55] As for the third friend, the list of possibilities is extensive, including the former DNI, Admiral 'Blinker' Hall, any one of a number of senior military figures to whom the Letter had been circulated on or before 22 October, or someone from Conservative Central Office. Members of the intelligence community, including Joseph Ball or Desmond Morton (who later told Miss Bagot that future SIS Chief Stewart Menzies was the culprit),[56] are also possible candidates.[57]

Giving evidence to the Board of Enquiry, MacDonald had voiced his suspicion that:

> the headquarters of the Conservative Association had the Zinovieff letter for days before it was published, and presumably the *Daily Mail* had it for weeks before it was published. I think it will be found that the *Daily Mail* had it before the Foreign Office had it.[58]

No conclusive evidence has been found in the archives to suggest that the Letter was in circulation before the FO received it from SIS on 10 October, although it is not impossible. It is certainly possible that, following its initial circulation, a copy was passed to Conservative Central Office and/or the press, but again there is no proof. The only certainty is that whoever gave the Letter to the *Daily Mail* in October 1924 did so in the knowledge that it would damage the Labour Party's prospects in the forthcoming general election. Marlowe, telling his story in March 1928 in a way that caused a media storm, may well have had his eyes on the next election, as well. The *Daily Mail* was, after all, a very right-wing newspaper. Whatever his motives, Marlowe's statement of 4 March 1928 was reprinted widely, and the events of October 1924 and their possible link to the Francs Case were examined in every detail. MacDonald, in a speech in Middlesbrough on 6 March, asserted that Marlowe's testimony showed that 'The Labour Government was assassinated by masked conspirators', prompting *The Observer* to criticize him for impugning Marlowe's honour.[59]

The re-emergence of the controversy did, however, have a unifying effect on the Labour Party. Hugh Dalton, a member of the Party Executive, had noted in his diary that in 1928 Labour's courage seemed to be evaporating in anticipation of the next election, the leaders divided and the wider party suffering from 'great caution and anti-Leftism'.[60] The idea of having been cheated in the general election of 1924 was something on which they could all agree. At a Labour Parliamentary Executive meeting on 12 March, however, the news that MacDonald had received a letter from one 'Dombrovski' in Paris, offering information on who wrote the Zinoviev Letter, was received with caution. Marlowe's statement had said little on the matter of the Letter's authenticity, other than that MacDonald 'knew' it to be genuine. The Executive agreed that Tom Shaw (who had served as Minister of Labour in the 1924 government) should go to Paris to investigate—'Quite like a film story!' noted Dalton. Shaw reported back on 15 March that Dombrovski's real name was Riczewski, and that he was a 'tuberculous degenerate' and professional forger. He claimed to have been one of those responsible for the Zinoviev Letter, 'acting for the British Secret Service', and offered more information for money. But J. H. Thomas thought it too risky to pursue this further:

> What if these rascals are double-crossing us, and the Government here know what is happening, and we are challenged, during the debate, to deny that we have just sent an ex-Cabinet minister to Paris to pay £20 to bribe two White Russian spies?

Thomas advised postponing any further action till after the debate on 19 March, advice Dalton approved: 'apart from all else, how convenient for the Tories to be able to sidetrack the whole debate from the leak to the *Daily Mail*, back to the authenticity of the Letter!'[61]

The parliamentary debate requested by MacDonald was scheduled for the afternoon of Monday, 19 March. But Marlowe's very public 'confession' now prompted someone else to come forward and tell his story: Donald im Thurn, who felt that he had never been rewarded appropriately for his role in 'discovering' the Zinoviev Letter.[62] Im Thurn's sentiments were shared by his friend, the Conservative MP for Hitchin, Major Guy Kindersley. Kindersley, who later wrote his own account of events, claimed that Major Joseph Ball—who had moved from MI5 to Conservative Central Office in 1927—had told him that the Conservatives were 'rather worried' about the forthcoming parliamentary debate. Finding that Ball apparently did not know about im Thurn's part in the affair, he offered to introduce him, and apparently showed Ball the account im Thurn had prepared regarding his 'disclosure' of the Letter in October 1924.

On the day of the debate, there was a lunch party at the home of J. C. C. Davidson, Chairman of the Conservative Party;[63] present were the Prime Minister, Stanley Baldwin, Attorney General Sir Douglas Hogg, Ball, im Thurn, and Kindersley, who had announced his intention of reading out im Thurn's account of the Letter during the debate. According to Kindersley's account, Baldwin greeted him with the words:

> 'Kindersley, this is the most extraordinary thing'. I replied, 'Yes, sir, it is very interesting.' He replied, 'I don't mean that, but you have kept

Figure 11. Joseph Ball

your mouth shut all these years.' 'Well, Sir', I replied, 'these sort of
things are far too dangerous to talk about.' I always remember this,
because it showed me in a flash that Stanley Baldwin never realized
the enormity of the Soviet system and the lengths to which its rulers
are prepared to go to to attain their ends, and how dangerous it is to
cross their path.[64]

Kindersley, described as 'one of those reliable, plodding, utterly loyal
Tory members who have always constituted the backbone, rather than
the brains of the party',[65] was doing the Prime Minister an injustice
here: he was well aware of the 'enormity' of the Soviet system. But
Baldwin's immediate problem now was what to do about im Thurn's
statement. He could not ignore it: if im Thurn now stated publicly
that the Conservatives had promised him money and refused to pay,
the party 'would be seen not only to have meanly cheated a brave
man, but to have been much more actively involved in eliciting
publication of the letter than it wanted to appear'.[66]

It was too dangerous to allow Kindersley to read out the statement in Parliament: the Labour Opposition would certainly subject him to cross-examination. At the same time, it was a gift to the Conservative cause. Baldwin decided that he would read the statement out himself.

The debate began at 4 p.m., when MacDonald moved that the disclosures in the Board of Enquiry's report were 'of national importance and concern' and should be subject to an enquiry empowered to take evidence on oath. He then launched into a long account of what had happened in 1924, justifying his own handling of the Zinoviev Letter, and describing the whole episode as 'a deliberately planned and devised concoction of deceit, fitted artfully for the purpose of deceiving the public and to influence the Election'. It was not a particularly good performance. MacDonald struggled to reconcile his allegations of bad faith with his defence of the civil service; he seemed to be accusing the intelligence agencies of leaking to the press, drawing an unclear distinction between FO officials and the agencies.[67]

Baldwin, by contrast, was on confident form, realizing that in Marlowe's statement, and the as yet unrevealed account by im Thurn, he held powerful cards. The opening of his speech gave a good idea of how he intended to play them:

> At breakfast this morning, on taking up my *Daily Herald*, my eye was caught by a headline, 'Red Letter Day'. I said, 'Whose Red letter Day?'[68]

He went on the attack immediately by referring to the Campbell case and the draft Russian treaties, taking the House back to the two things that had damaged the Labour government's standing in the summer of 1924. Baldwin then spoke at length about the Letter, and said he had thought Labour were going to produce an affidavit by 'someone who is going to swear that he had forged the Zinovieff letter'. (This was apparently a reference to the evidence from 'Dombrovski' in Paris that the Labour Executive had declined to pursue, and Dalton noted in his diary that at this point in Baldwin's speech Arthur Henderson nudged him and winked; 'Weren't we wise to stop Tom Shaw before he had committed us too far!' Dalton remarked.[69]) Nevertheless,

Baldwin's comment that any supposed forger would 'join a gallant crowd', naming a series of alleged authors of the Letter including Druzhelovsky and 'Bernstein alias Henry Lawrence', gave the impression that the government was on top of all the evidence and did not think much of it.

Baldwin then produced his trump card, announcing his intention to read a statement by 'a gentleman unconnected with office and politics, or with any of those things that make a conspiracy'; he extracted the 'last drop of dramatic juice from the occasion' by revealing im Thurn's name only at the very end.[70] Although Labour MPs were aware of the Marlowe statement from the press, that of im Thurn was new to them, and Baldwin's use of it wrong-footed the Opposition and confirmed the government's dominance in the debate. Labour arguments in favour of a new enquiry did not convince the House: MacDonald's motion was defeated by 326 votes to 132.[71]

There were, of course, many problems with im Thurn's statement, although Baldwin claimed to have checked it as far as he could. It included the assertion that im Thurn had received the complete text of the Zinoviev Letter on 9 October, an assertion that his own diaries belied. He also said he had given his copy of the Letter to a 'trusted City friend' to pass on to the Daily Mail, and that at no time had he received any information from any official source (another assertion contradicted by his diary). His actions, he said, had been 'dictated solely by patriotic motives' and he had not sought or received any payment or reward. In fact, im Thurn's diaries and letters show that he had received some payment for his efforts in 1924, from White Russian sources, and had received a pledge of further payment from Lord Younger, former Chairman of the Conservative Party.[72] A major reason for his coming forward in 1928 was dissatisfaction at the Conservative Party's failure to pay up the agreed balance.

On 2 April 1928, after the debate, Davidson wrote a cheque for £5,000 for Ball to give to im Thurn, who acknowledged it on behalf of his anonymous informant, 'X'. The identity of 'X' was, as noted earlier, uncertain, im Thurn himself apparently using 'X' to denote more than one person, possibly a woman.[73] Now, in his letter to Ball, im Thurn specified details of how the debt was to be paid: apart from the lump sum of £5,000, 'X' was to receive 'from the other source' £250 a year for ten years, and an extra £2,500 at the end, paid to him in Argentina, to which he was travelling 'as a common deck hand' and would 'establish himself as an Argentine national'. This particular X was definitely male, and not, apparently, the same X referred to in the diaries of October 1924;[74] and his future plans were strikingly similar to those of the White Russian officer Ivan Pokrovsky.[75] Writing to Ball on 2 April 1928, im Thurn clearly still felt that the Conservative Party had short-changed both him and Kindersley: however, their desire for honours to reward their patriotic efforts remained unfulfilled.[76]

Despite the Marlowe and im Thurn statements, there was not really any new information in the speeches made in the House of Commons on 19 March 1928. Yet the debate—dismissed by Dalton as 'rather a fizzle'[77]—was an important milestone in the story of the Zinoviev Letter. It showed that, even after three and a half years, the subject could arouse strong sentiments—in both Labour and Conservative ranks. Both sides clung to their established positions about the authenticity or otherwise of the Letter, yet both clearly had doubts. The debate also demonstrated that there was still a great deal more speculation than fact about the events of October 1924. And if Marlowe and im Thurn had been prompted to come forward and tell their stories, it had to be possible that others might do so, too. There might be no enquiry, but it was clear that the last had not been heard of the Zinoviev Letter.

That was certainly the view of the SIS Chief, Sinclair, although the defeat of the motion for a new enquiry pleased him. During March 1928, while preparations were being made for the debate and the press was full of stories inspired by the Francs Case (*Daily News*, 6 March 1928: 'Zinovieff Comes Back'), SIS supplied a number of reports to the FO concerning rumours about the authenticity and authorship of the Zinoviev Letter, commenting that none of them proved it was not genuine. In Berlin, the name of one Anton Schrek was mentioned as a possible forger,[78] while copies of documents from SIS sources in

Russia included a circular issued by the CPGB Agitprop department on 17 March attacking MacDonald for not admitting that he had always thought the Letter a forgery. The CPGB document also mentioned Schrek, and a supposed member of the Polish Secret Service called Peciokowski; Schrek's involvement was also suggested by the Polish General Staff.[79] Meanwhile, MI5 learned from correspondence between W. N. Ewer of the *Daily Herald* (who on Soviet instructions had moved the direction of his network to Paris after the ARCOS raid), and the *Herald*'s chief Foreign Correspondent, George Slocombe, that Sir Basil Thomson, formerly of the Metropolitan Police, had in 1924 been trying to publicize a French 'Zinoviev Letter'.[80] Yet none of these rumours produced concrete evidence about the Letter supposedly sent by Zinoviev to the CPGB on 15 September 1924.

Soviet comment on the parliamentary debate was cautious: Russian proposals for the limitation of armaments were currently being considered by the Preparatory Commission on Disarmament in Geneva, and the public washing of Comintern dirty linen in the British press was unwelcome. The Soviet government was trying to play the role of a good international partner, with its own economic needs in mind. Although the Western powers were inclined to dismiss the Russian disarmament proposals as 'purely a political move', they could not be rejected out of hand.[81] On 22 March 1928, *The Star* printed Chicherin's reply to Baldwin's speech in the debate, alleging that the British government was afraid to hold an enquiry into the Letter, and stating that im Thurn 'obviously' worked for British intelligence. For good measure, Chicherin also repeated the information given at the Druzhelovsky trial in 1927, naming 'Belgardt, Jemtchujnikov and Gumanski' as the forgers, together with the Pole 'Paciorkovsky'.[82]

In the opinion of SIS, many of these rumours about the Letter were spread by those hoping to cash in on the renewed public and official interest, and did little more than to confirm the existence of a large number of 'forgery factories'. It was the breaking up of one of the most active of these—that run by Orlov in Berlin—that was to provoke the next set of 'revelations', almost exactly a year later.

Arrests in Berlin

In the second half of 1928, the Francs Scandal died down and press rumours about the Zinoviev Letter abated. During the autumn all the parties began to prepare in earnest for the next general election, due at some point in 1929. The British government, and in particular Sir Austen Chamberlain and the FO, were preoccupied with discussions leading to the signature in August 1928 of the multilateral Kellogg–Briand Pact on the renunciation of war as an instrument of policy.[83] Indeed, the volume and complexity of international issues he faced overwhelmed Chamberlain, who suffered a total collapse of his health at the end of July 1928, and was unable to return to work until the end of November.[84] MacDonald, too, felt tired and jaded, though he remained Labour's chief spokesman on foreign affairs.[85]

With diplomatic relations still suspended, the Soviet Union was not high on the British government's agenda. The Bolshevik leadership, meanwhile, remained determined to follow a pragmatic foreign policy in pursuit of vital trade and foreign credits, and pursue an active engagement in international affairs. In February 1929, for example, a Soviet initiative led to the so-called 'Litvinov Protocol', signed by Estonia, Latvia, Poland, and Romania as well as the USSR, being added to the Kellogg Pact, a move intended to please the Americans, but also to deter both external aggression and internal dissent.[86] The Soviet regime also made a series of overtures to the British government, with a view to re-establishing relations, but they were received coolly. FO officials repeated, when asked, that there was no question of discussing the settlement of Russian debts without dealing at the same time with Soviet interference in other countries' domestic affairs.[87] Patience and expectancy remained British policy as far as the Russians were concerned. Far more worrying were reports about German remilitarization and a desire for hegemony in Europe.[88]

This was the situation at the beginning of March 1929, when Admiral Sir Hugh Sinclair, Chief of SIS, had a nasty shock. He learned that Vladimir Orlov, former SIS informant and master forger, had been arrested in Berlin, together with associates including Gumansky, Sievert, and Sumarakov, and his headquarters raided (even though it was the German authorities, including the Police, the German Secret Service, and Military Intelligence, who had been funding and supporting Orlov's activities). There seem to have been several reasons behind the arrest, including a falling-out between Orlov and Sievert that led them to incriminate one another, complaints by the US Senator Borah who had been accused of accepting bribes from Moscow in return for US recognition of the Soviet regime, and information dug up by an American journalist, H. R. Knickerbocker, in the course of investigating the Borah story. To add to the mix, W. N. Ewer was told by an American journalist, Frederick Kuh, that the German government had the 'inside story' of the Zinoviev Letter and that the British Labour Party might be able to make political capital out of it.[89]

Sinclair was alarmed by news of the Berlin arrests, and sent a telegram to Frank Foley, SIS's Berlin Head of Station, on 5 March, asking for a full report and copies of any documents uncovered in the raid. He also asked Desmond Morton to produce a comprehensive note on Orlov and his activities. Morton obliged, setting out the background of Orlov's forgery ring and his past relations with SIS. He expressed the view that Orlov, despite his covert ties with the OGPU, was 'no Bolshevik':

> He has always been an intriguer and politician, working his Intelligence Organisation for his own benefit firstly, for the benefit of the Russian Monarchist cause a bad second, while such European powers who have paid him money have been hardly anywhere . . . The severance of personal relations with the British intelligence in 1923 had a great effect on him. From that moment there is no doubt that he commenced forging documents and selling them to anyone ready to buy them, with the united objects of making money to keep himself going, and at the same time doing harm to the Bolsheviks.[90]

Still anxious, Sinclair telegraphed again to Berlin asking for any information on the Zinoviev Letter to be sent 'to me personally'. Foley replied on 11 March that the Berlin police were endeavouring 'to establish by microscopic examination of type whether ORLOFF forged ZINOVIEV letter'. While Orlov and his associates awaited trial, Morton paid a visit to Czechoslovakia during which he seems to have collected further intelligence on the case.[91]

At the same time that Orlov's headquarters were being turned over by the police, J. D. Gregory's memoirs were published in London. Their tone attracted some criticism, not least from MacDonald, who commented that 'nobody was more disappointed' than he at the fate that overtook Gregory, 'but I do wish he had upheld the dignity of the Foreign Office a little bit better when he was writing this book'.[92] *The Manchester Guardian* agreed, complaining that Gregory treated the Zinoviev Letter 'rather as a comedy than anything else': 'Indiscretion is nothing to Mr Gregory, but here he is so discreet as to omit everything one wants to know and to ignore the fact that the Red Letter had very important effects on the history of the Empire.' Gregory's language was a mixture of facetiousness and condescension towards MacDonald and other Labour ministers, though the occasional remark indicated bitterness at his own fate:

> It is no business of mine to say how I first got mixed up with this Red Object...The only thing that I am quite sure about is that I did get mixed up with it and have never been the same man since. It would have been a far more expeditious end, and far less painful, to have swallowed a Borgia pill all at once than exposed myself to this lingering Cheka infection. I should have passed away, if not peacefully, at least rapidly.[93]

The publication of Gregory's memoirs, together with the Berlin arrests, encouraged the British press to rake up the Zinoviev Letter once more. As the *Daily Herald* put it on 18 March 1929, 'The Red Letter has come suddenly into the limelight again.' The *Herald* recalled that Gumansky was one of the people named by Druzhelovsky in 1927, and then by Chicherin in 1928, as responsible for the Letter, under the direction of 'Captain Paciorkovski of the Polish Military Intelligence, and also by the British secret service'.[94] The communist paper *Sunday Worker* published an article on 24 March by 'Outpost'—a byline for W. N. Ewer—headed 'Forgery as a Business: How "Red Letter" makers trade their goods: New Revelations'. This suggested that the Letter had reached London through more than one channel, including Orlov, the Poles, im Thurn and his White Russian contacts, and even through a 'semi-private espionage organisation' based in London and Paris and used by German monarchists. In other words, almost everybody had a hand in either forging or publicizing the Zinoviev Letter.

The *Daily Herald*, however, printed a rather different and much more specific story on 25 March 1929, headed 'Red Letter Sensation'. The Zinoviev Letter, it stated, was 'forged in Riga by an ex-Russian Imperial Army officer, who was urged by certain British interests to "produce material to compromise the Labour Party".' The Russian officer, it alleged, was Pokrovsky, who had subsequently been forced to leave Latvia and was 'now believed to be residing in Buenos Aires'. Pokrovsky had been contacted by a former Russian general in London known as 'Korniev', and asked to produce a document calculated to compromise Labour; Pokrovsky then concocted a draft which he sent to Orlov and Gumansky, and 'submitted to the British Intelligence Service'. A copy of the letter was posted to the CPGB 'in a registered envelope' and a coded telegram sent to advise the British police of its arrival.[95]

This story is almost identical to that published by Oleg Tsarev and Nigel West in *The Crown Jewels*, based on KGB records, seventy years later.[96] The *Herald* claimed its information came from the Berlin police, investigating Orlov and his associates. While that may be true, it is surely likely that information also came from Moscow, particularly given Ewer's Russian contacts. According to the files of the OGPU's Foreign Department, cited in *The Crown Jewels*, the OGPU was very well informed about Orlov's activities: a note on his file, dated 19 March 1929, stated that 'constant taps' were kept on him, although it was not until 1945 that the full extent of his involvement in the international White Guard network became known. The OGPU's information on Ivan Pokrovsky, as stated in *The Crown Jewels*, was confirmed by Gumansky in material received from a private

German intelligence group, the 'Bureau Liser-Rau', while Pokrovsky's move to South America suggests a connection with the 'X' in im Thurn's story. The details about 'General Korneyev', a Russian officer of English origin granted British citizenship in the First World War, are identical to those in the *Herald* article of 25 March 1929. The details of how the Letter reached the British authorities are, in both sources, inaccurate, since the evidence indicates it never reached the CPGB and that the police learned of it from SIS. But the closeness of the accounts in the *Daily Herald* and *The Crown Jewels* is both striking and significant.

All these stories alleged the involvement of British intelligence in the Zinoviev Letter, and might have been expected to provoke both interest and concern in SIS and MI5. Yet in the spring of 1929, it was not these 'revelations' that preoccupied the intelligence establishment, but the discovery that Special Branch had been penetrated by Soviet agents who had for some years been supplying information through a network run by Ewer.[97] Though both MI5 and SIS had been investigating Ewer and his group for some time, the full extent of Soviet penetration only became clear after the arrest on 11 April 1929 of two Special Branch officers, Inspector Ginhoven and Sergeant Jane, together with a former police officer, Walter E. Dale. Dale, who had acted as a private detective for the group, had kept a diary from 1922 to 1927 which showed that 'unremitting surveillance', as an SIS memo put it, had been maintained on all the agencies since at least 1922, that 'the regular connection between SIS, Code and Cipher School, MI5, the Foreign Office and other Departments of Government' was watched carefully, together with the movements and home addresses of staff.[98]

These revelations were a severe shock to SIS and the other agencies, and a blow to their reputation, just at the time when press speculation about their involvement in the Zinoviev Letter was rife. How much of their organization and operations, intelligence chiefs wondered, had been laid bare to the Bolsheviks over the past seven years or more? In that context, it is not perhaps surprising that Sinclair was anxious about the forthcoming trial of Vladimir Orlov.

Foley had told Sinclair in March 1929 that he 'must be prepared for official statement shortly'. But no statement followed: the German authorities thought better of it, perhaps unwilling for their own involvement with Orlov to be aired in court. The trial finally took place in July 1929, when Orlov and Sumarakov were sentenced to four months' imprisonment but released immediately since they had been in custody since March; charges against Sievert, who had suffered a nervous breakdown, were dropped. Harold Nicolson, Counsellor in HM Embassy in Berlin, told Sir Ronald Lindsay (who had now replaced Tyrrell as PUS) that, according to the Russian Ambassador, the German Foreign Office had no interest in reviving the Zinoviev Letter controversy. As Sinclair commented to Lindsay, the German authorities were already satisfied that Orlov had not written the Letter, but had been under pressure from the German Socialist Party to extract a confession from him.[99] (For those interested to know what became of him, Orlov was asked to leave Germany in 1931 and moved his centre of operations to Brussels, under an old alias, 'Orest Borovoi', apparently dying there in 1940 under torture by the Nazis.[100])

By the time Orlov and his associates came to trial, there was a new government in Britain. The election campaign during May 1929 was dull compared with that of 1924. Baldwin ran on a platform of 'Safety First', while the Labour manifesto stated that the party stood for 'arbitration and disarmament', and that 'peace is one of the greatest issues of the Election'. On polling day, 30 May, Labour won a slightly smaller share of the vote than the Conservatives, but more seats: 288 to the Conservatives' 260; the Liberals, though increasing their vote substantially, won only 59. For the first time, Labour was the largest party.

Baldwin resigned as Prime Minister on 4 June, promising that he would not 'worry' MacDonald while Labour was in office, but would conduct a fair fight to regain power: a way of saying 'no more Zinoviev Letters', perhaps.[101] MacDonald took office as Prime Minister for the second time, and after a sharp tussle chose Arthur Henderson as Foreign Secretary in preference to J. H. Thomas (a choice Austen Chamberlain deplored, considering Thomas to be 'by far the abler man').[102] Hugh Dalton was appointed Parliamentary Under-Secretary at the FO: 'Perfect!' he wrote. Interestingly, in the light of previous rumours, one of Dalton's first instructions to his Private Secretary, Gladwyn Jebb, was to make a chart 'showing who in responsible positions in the Foreign Office *were* Roman Catholics'.[103]

During the election campaign, both the Liberals and Labour had announced their intention of re-establishing relations with the Soviet Union. Both countries were interested in expanding trade relations, as well as normalizing day-to-day business. Once in office, however, MacDonald adopted a cautious approach, despite the fact that, as Dalton put it, Russia was 'in the whole field of foreign affairs, the subject on which we are under most pressure from our own Party'. MacDonald made it clear that unconditional restoration of diplomatic relations was not on offer; previous demands for a cessation of hostile Bolshevik propaganda and subversive activities remained a precondition. In the House of Commons on 15 July, he announced, apparently without consulting the Cabinet or the FO, that there would be no exchange of ambassadors between London and Moscow without parliamentary approval, which meant in effect deferring such a move for some months. Henderson may have been annoyed, but accepted that the government could take no chances with its policy towards the Soviet regime: 'Russia has brought us down once,' he told Dalton, 'We can't afford to let it happen twice.'[104]

After negotiations between Henderson and the Soviet Ambassador in Paris, M. Dogvalevsky, a protocol was signed on 3 October 1929 for the settlement of outstanding issues between the two governments, including an exchange of notes providing for the cessation of Bolshevik propaganda.[105] It was approved by Parliament in early November, and in December 1929, for the first time since 1917, an exchange of plenipotentiary ambassadors took place. The British diplomat posted to Moscow was Sir Esmond Ovey, who recorded his first impressions after meeting Litvinov:

> One has on arrival the strongest feeling that one is undoubtedly living in a city and country which either are or imagine themselves to be in

a state of siege... The picture of M. Litvinov's mentality, both as regards his conversation and official utterances, is not very hopeful, nor, I fear, is there very much hope that, were he to adopt a more reasonable attitude, he would have any power to affect the group which not only governs the country but remains, as far as can be ascertained, in almost monk-like seclusion in order to avoid any possibility of contamination with the Western ideas of the heads of foreign missions. To this group, which is the absolute master of the country, he makes no allusion whatever... it is, indeed, a case of 'Hamlet without the ghost'.[106]

The 'ghost' was, of course, the Communist Party of the Soviet Union, over which Stalin was in firm control.

Besedovsky jumps the wall

At this point Zinoviev, who had fallen from grace in 1926, re-enters the story. On 26 October 1929 the *Morning Post* reported that having renounced his support for Trotsky and declared his loyalty to Stalin, Zinoviev had now been appointed leader of the Western European section of the Comintern, and was organizing demonstrations in cities all over Europe. It was perhaps coincidental that the day before, the French conservative daily newspaper *Le Matin* had printed a story including the headline:' *Trois sécretaires fusillés à cause de la lettre Zinovieff*' ('Three secretaries shot because of the Zinoviev Letter').[107]

On 3 October 1929, Grigori Besedovsky, Soviet Chargé d'Affaires in Paris (while Dogvalevsky was signing the protocol restoring Anglo-Soviet relations), became the earliest Soviet diplomat to defect to the West. Accused of counter-revolutionary plotting and illegal contacts with Western intelligence, he made a 'dramatic escape over the embassy wall, pursued by OGPU guards who had orders to return him to Moscow for interrogation and, almost certainly execution'. In 1930, he was to publish his memoirs denouncing Stalin as 'the embodiment of oriental despotism', and revealing OGPU secrets including details of British and Italian officials who had offered their services to the Paris residency.[108] In October 1929, however, he published a number of articles in the French press claiming that according to Dzerzhinsky, Zinoviev had indeed signed the Red Letter without reading it, and that three Comintern clerks, including a female secretary, had been shot as a result.

According to the story in *Le Matin*, which *The Times* picked up the following day (26 October), Zinoviev had, according to Besedovsky's account, seemed very ill at ease and 'distinctly evasive' when summoned to Moscow to account for himself, after the letter he supposedly sent to the CPGB on 15 September 1924, and the British note of protest of 24 October, had been received. After 'examining the letter closely', Zinoviev said that 'he did not remember having actually dictated it, but that it so closely conformed with the general policy of the Third International towards Great Britain that he would certainly have signed it if it had been placed before him, but for the fact that it would obviously have produced difficulties'.[109]

Le Matin reported that Zinoviev then refused to answer any more questions: '*Je n'ai pas signé, un point c'est tout*' ('I didn't sign it, and that's that'). Because of Zinoviev's prominent position at that time in the Politburo and Comintern, his interrogation ended there, although according to Besedovsky the OGPU shot three secretaries, including *une femme très belle*, who had apparently presented the Letter for signature. Dzerzhinsky, said Besedovsky, knew perfectly well that the Letter was genuine, but did not dare to challenge Zinoviev, who was *le pivot du bureau politique*. There were plenty of inconsistencies in the story, and Besedovsky, keen to establish his credentials after his dramatic defection, was an interesting but unreliable informant. But if nothing else, the episode showed the continuing level of interest in the Zinoviev Letter, and suggested that there was still much to discover about the events of 1924.

Politics, the Wall Street Crash, and world depression, combined with international instability encompassing both a resurgent Germany and a troublesome but apparently stable Soviet regime that offered promising trade opportunities, now appeared to put the Zinoviev Letter episode onto the back burner. But it still rankled with Labour, and it still worried the Conservatives and the intelligence agencies. In his letter to Joseph Ball on 2 April 1928, im Thurn had boasted:

> There is no doubt whatever that the letter smashed the Communists, split the Labour Party, ruined the Liberals, upset any chance of revolution and made the failure of the general strike a foregone conclusion and established the Conservative Party on a basis of solidity which has never existed before and which is likely to exist for many, many years to come.[110]

Grandiose claims, and not shared by those of more sober judgement. But such attitudes made it inevitable that stories about the Red Letter continued to circulate, despite the best efforts of those who wanted the whole affair forgotten.

5

The Philby Effect, 1960–1970

'We used to trust our colleagues absolutely. Now we cannot any more.'[1]

In the 1960s a perfect storm of spy scandals, publications, and the defection of the spy Kim Philby—together with Harold Wilson's decision to open official records to the public when they were thirty years old—brought the Zinoviev Letter back to the centre of media, political, and public attention, leading to the first major official investigation based on access to closed archives as well as to all the available open source material. But that did not mean that the Letter had dropped off the radar completely in the intervening years. Between 1930 and 1960, it floated just below the surface of public life, occasionally bobbing above the waves. Neither British intelligence nor the Labour Party had forgotten or forgiven the events of 1924. At certain times, during election campaigns, or when there was an example of what today would be called 'fake news' involving a forged document or a planted story, the Zinoviev Letter was liable to be invoked by politicians of all persuasions.

There were obvious reasons why the Zinoviev Letter was not high on the political agenda during a period that included the rise of Nazi Germany and six years of world war, when the Soviet adversary who signed a pact with Hitler in 1939 became the Soviet ally after the Nazi invasion of Russia in June 1941, and an adversary again with the onset of the Cold War. The Labour government that took office in July 1945 was more preoccupied with domestic subversion and atomic spies than with licking old wounds. The 1950s saw a series of intelligence disasters, including the defection of Guy Burgess and Donald Maclean, but in public perception these tended to be overshadowed by dramatic international events such as the Suez crisis and the brutal Soviet suppression of the Hungarian uprising.

In the early 1960s, Conservative Prime Minister Harold Macmillan was confronted by a series of serious and embarrassing spy scandals, pointing to Soviet espionage against the UK on a large scale (though ironically the episode that led him to resign—the Profumo affair—was more damaging politically than in intelligence terms). But it was the defection of Kim Philby, the former senior SIS officer, that rocked the British intelligence establishment to its core. Though Philby had been under suspicion since 1951, there had been insufficient evidence to prosecute him in the face of his consistent denials. Cleared publicly by Harold Macmillan as Foreign Secretary in 1955, he had remained in close touch with former colleagues right up until the time he fled to Moscow from Beirut in January 1963. Almost to the last, SIS had remained resistant to the idea that one of their former senior officers—a man who had headed the section that dealt with Russia and been privy to all the secrets of their Soviet operations—could be a traitor. Philby's betrayal led all the agencies to look at themselves closely, wondering who else might have been involved, and what other operations might have been compromised, even as long ago as the 1920s. One of the operations they investigated was the Zinoviev Letter, a subject on which the Labour government that took office in 1964 under Harold Wilson could be expected to be sensitive; he and his ministers took office deeply suspicious of potential plots and political chicanery.

It would take far too long, and is not necessary to this story, to trace in detail the history of Anglo-Soviet relations or their respective intelligence organizations during the period 1930–60, or to note every occasion when the Zinoviev Letter was mentioned in the press or in Parliament. But there were some occasions when the Letter cropped up that are instructive in showing its continuing impact on politics—particularly Labour politics—and in setting the scene for the renewed interest in it during the 1960s.

Three elections and two curious Foreign Secretaries: 1930–1960

The second Labour government headed by Ramsay MacDonald lasted a little over two years, and struggled throughout to grapple with the international financial crisis and collapse of confidence in British public finances. In August 1931, with the Cabinet deadlocked over budget cuts, particularly unemployment benefits, Labour gave up the struggle and MacDonald, encouraged by King George V, formed a cross-party National Government. The majority of the Labour Party rejected the idea of such a coalition, accusing MacDonald of selling out to capitalism: Philip Snowden, as Chancellor of the Exchequer, J. H. Thomas as Colonial Secretary, and Lord Sankey as Lord Chancellor were the only ones to join him in the new Cabinet. In September 1931 the National Executive voted to expel the 'National Labour' members.[2] At the same time, pressure from the Conservatives (who wanted to push through trade protection measures) drove the National Government to seek a so-called 'doctor's mandate' to tackle the economic crisis, and a general election was held on 27 October 1931.

In what some saw as an eerie echo of 1924, an incident shortly before polling day recalled the Zinoviev Letter, as well as emphasizing the gulf that had developed between National Labour and the rest of the party. On Saturday, 24 October 1931, Walter Runciman, a 'Simonite' rather than a 'Lloyd George' Liberal—the Liberal Party was also split[3]—made a speech in South Shields stating that in April and August 1931 the Labour government had been anxious about the position of Post Office Savings Bank deposits, a substantial amount of which had been lent to the Unemployment Insurance Fund. This had, he said, 'brought home to the Cabinet the difficulties with which they would

be faced if serious distrust of British credit set in'. Snowden spelled it
out for the voters the next day:

> Mr Runciman's warning to depositors in the Post Office Savings Bank
> and other thrift societies is well founded. The Labour leaders, when
> they ran away, were well aware that I had warned them of the peril
> which threatened the savings of the poor. That peril is passed, due to
> the measures which the National Government has taken. There is now
> no danger, but, if the Labour Party with its programme of huge bor-
> rowing and increased taxation were returned, it would at once become
> a real danger.[4]

The Labour leaders who 'ran away' were, of course, those who had
rejected the National Government. Coming from the man who
had served as Chancellor of the Exchequer in both Labour governments, this seemed to the party like double treachery. Snowden's
statement was reported widely, and had a considerable impact on
those who made most use of the Post Office Savings Bank—the
working classes. He gave the impression, wrongly, that the government could not honour its obligations towards investors because
the money had been spent. For those with savings in the Bank, 'the
notion that the money they had paid over the Post Office counter
might be lost if they voted Labour made the financial crisis seem
real and frightening'. Snowden's biographer concluded that his aim
must have been to promote a last-minute campaign point, with the
Zinoviev Letter in mind.[5]

As in 1924, it is difficult to know whether this episode had any
effect on the result, which was a disaster for the Labour Party. Of the
554 seats won by the National Government, 473 were Conservative
and 13 for National Labour. The rest of the Labour Party was reduced
to only forty-six seats (plus six Independent Labour Party), despite
winning almost one-third of the popular vote. In such circumstances,
people recalled the Letter. The scare started by Runciman and spread
by Snowden rankled, and was recalled during the election campaign
in 1945 by Clement Attlee and again in February 1950, when Herbert
Morrison warned that the 'electoral tactics of stunts and scares is very

much ingrained in the Tory party machine'. On both occasions, it was bracketed with the Zinoviev Letter.[6]

After the schism of 1931 there was no realistic early prospect of another Labour government, and no occasion for the party to resurrect the controversy over the Letter. Even when Zinoviev himself was arrested and executed in 1936 for supposedly plotting against Stalin, the British press remained largely silent on the subject of the Letter. Many in the Labour Party still looked to the Soviet economic model as an example, and saw communism as preferable to the growing threat of domestic and international fascism.[7] While moderate Labour members were concerned about communist influence, and repelled by Stalin's excesses, it is hardly surprising in the political and economic context of the mid-1930s that many others, particularly young people appalled at the growth of fascism, were attracted to the Communist Party—including the 'Cambridge Five', Kim Philby, Guy Burgess, Donald Maclean, Anthony Blunt, and John Cairncross, all of whom were recruited by the KGB at this period.[8] Even after the rude shock of the Nazi–Soviet Pact and the Soviet invasion of Finland in 1939, when the *Daily Herald* proclaimed that 'The Union of Soviet Socialist Republics is dead. Stalin's new imperialist Russia takes its place',[9] some Labour intellectuals still defended the Soviet line.

The National Government remained in power until 1940, under MacDonald (until 1935), Baldwin (1937), and then Neville Chamberlain. The Zinoviev Letter surfaced on one further occasion in the 1930s: a minor incident, but it was to assume some importance during the 1960s. When Anthony Eden resigned as Foreign Secretary in February 1938 because of disagreements with Chamberlain, he was succeeded by Lord Halifax, who shortly afterwards asked to see the FO papers about the Zinoviev Letter. It is not clear whether this was merely from idle curiosity; he told William Strang, by now of Counsellor rank, that he would like to talk to him about 'this old history'. However, Harold Caccia, who had been Private Secretary to Halifax, recollected when consulted in 1966 that the Foreign Secretary's interest 'had been prompted by his Private Secretaries impressing on him the importance of avoiding any repetition of the Ramsay MacDonald question by his placing his initial at the end of any document rather than in the margin or at the top or elsewhere'. Sir Stephen Gaselee, the FO Librarian—one of those who had been troubled by procedural irregularities in dealing with the note to Rakovsky on 24 October 1924[10]—pointed out when sending the file to Halifax's Private Office on 13 April 1938 that 'you will observe that Mr Ramsay MacDonald did not initial draft either above or below; but all the amendments are in his handwriting'.[11] Whatever Halifax's motives, he apparently returned the papers without further comment: and international affairs during 1938 and 1939 surely offered him no opportunity for further consideration of the matter.

By the time a Labour government next gained office, the Second World War was over. A number of senior Labour figures had served in Winston Churchill's wartime coalition, including those who were to dominate the government from 1945 to 1951: Clement Attlee, Ernest Bevin, Stafford Cripps, Hugh Dalton, and Herbert Morrison. For Attlee and Bevin, as Prime Minister and Foreign Secretary, their experience in government and diplomacy was to be invaluable in handling post-war relations with the Soviet Union, now a member of the 'Big Three' alongside the United States and United Kingdom, determined to extract profitable recognition of its major contribution to victory and ready to flex its international muscles to ensure its interests were respected.

The undoubted mutual regard between Churchill and his Labour colleagues in the War Cabinet was eclipsed swiftly by party rivalry during the campaign leading up to the general election held on 5 July 1945, and the Zinoviev Letter soon raised its head. Attlee, warning Labour candidates that it was essential that electors should 'keep their minds fixed on the central issues and to resist any last-minute attempts to stampede public opinion', stated that:

> I am justified in making this appeal because eve-of-the-poll scares are a familiar device of the Tory party. The older electors will recall the Zinoviev Letter scare of 1924 and the Post Office savings lie of 1931.

The simple fact is that nothing would be more harmful to the post-war economic and social welfare of our country than that the Tory party should again have charge of the nation's affairs.[12]

Churchill, unwilling to believe that the country he had led to victory would reject him at the polls, had already caused outrage by his broadcast on 4 June alleging that a socialist government would have to employ 'some form of Gestapo' to implement its policies.[13] He also attacked Labour through what he called the 'Laski controversy', alleging that the Chairman of the Labour Party's insistence that the National Executive, not the leader, should determine foreign policy would make it impossible for Labour to govern authoritatively.[14] 'Many anxious eyes are turned towards us,' Churchill said in a broadcast speech on 30 June; 'A failure by Great Britain to produce a strong, coherent, resolute Government supported by a substantial and solid majority in Parliament, would alter the entire balance, not only of tortured Europe but of the whole world, now struggling to rise again and bring order out of chaos.' He pursued this idea in a letter to Attlee on 3 July 1945—two days before the election—insisting that the controversy could not be laid to rest until 'the public has a statement signed jointly by yourself and the Chairman of the Executive Committee'.[15]

Attlee, who saw the election campaign as 'something of a personal duel between himself and Churchill',[16] dealt with this challenge in the terse and efficient manner that was to characterize his premiership, replying by return of post—and sending his letter to the press—that the Conservative leader clearly did not understand the difference between the Labour Party and the Parliamentary Labour Party:

> Despite my very clear statement you proceed to exercise your imagination by importing into a right to be consulted a power to challenge actions and conduct...I think you underestimate the intelligence of the public and I do not share your belief.[17]

The Manchester Guardian, under the headline 'The End of a Myth', praised Attlee's reply, commenting that Churchill had 'never before been so worsted' since he had become Prime Minister. The paper described Churchill's letter as:

> a last feeble attempt to rattle the bones...As a stroke of the Zinoviev order it is a failure. The Tories could afford to blow that mine five days before the poll and it certainly had Ramsay MacDonald terribly perplexed for three of them. The present one was sprung three days before the poll. Perhaps this reflected some doubts in the mind of the mine-layer...Attlee proved himself no MacDonald. He did not dither.[18]

Attlee thought he had emerged victorious from the episode, too, writing to his brother Tom that 'Winston keeps slogging away at the silly Laski business, but I don't think that he gets the better of the exchanges with me'. As for Harold Laski, who never supported him as Labour leader, Attlee later wrote that he was 'a brilliant chap, but he talked too much...He wanted to be a public figure and an *éminence grise* at the same time. You can't be both. I gave him a try as an *éminence grise,* but he started making speeches at the week-ends. I had to get rid of him.'[19]

The Labour government that took office in July 1945 had too much on its plate in both domestic and foreign affairs, and in coping with constant criticism from the left wing of the party, to pay further attention to old political controversies. In any case, the Conservatives were for some time too stunned by their electoral defeat to give the government a hard time. Nor was there any real mileage in alleging communist influence upon the Labour government. Though rejecting what they saw as an over-simplistic American attitude to communism (there were some in the US who considered a socialist government in Britain to be in danger of 'going over'),[20] both Attlee and Bevin showed themselves to be staunch anti-communists, whether in domestic matters or in a world increasingly polarized into eastern and western spheres of influence.[21]

By the time of the next general election in February 1950, Labour ministers were exhausted by the strain of a major programme of domestic legislation and nationalization, a severe economic crisis, and a period of increasing international tension in the early years of what is now known as the Cold War. The Conservative Party, led by Churchill, had recovered from its defeat in 1945 and was mounting a concerted attack. Herbert Morrison, Lord President of the Council, clearly anticipated trouble during the campaign. He wrote in *The Manchester Guardian* on 18 February 1950 that 'Transport House regards the three days before the poll next week as particularly vulnerable'; Labour, he said, 'has bitter memories of the famous Zinoviev Letter'. Morrison conceded that it was difficult to imagine that a 'Red Letter' stunt could be pulled off in 1950—'I think the electorate would not have it'. Three days later, *The Guardian* observed that 'there was no missing the implication' of such warnings by Morrison and other ministers: 'Labour is too virtuous for that'; but it reminded readers of the details of both the Zinoviev Letter and the Post Office Savings episodes.[22] On 23 February, Labour was returned to office with a majority of only six.

Intelligence and security issues proved to be far more significant for the Attlee governments of 1945–51 than Labour had anticipated: domestic subversion, atomic security, Zionist terrorism, Soviet espionage, and the handling of defectors were only some of the problems they faced. Participation in the wartime coalition meant that Labour ministers had gained useful 'work experience' in these matters: Attlee, Bevin, and some of their colleagues began their period of office already on familiar terms with the secret world. They were not disposed to regard the security and intelligence agencies with hostility or suspicion. As the intelligence historian Dan Lomas put it, as far as Labour ministers were concerned, 'if a legacy of the Zinoviev Letter affair existed, it had died by the end of the Second World War'.[23] Nevertheless, for many of the Labour MPs elected in 1945, unaware of the contribution to victory made by intelligence successes such as codebreaking and MI5's 'Double Cross' system, the reputation of the intelligence establishment, and indeed of the Foreign Office, was clouded with suspicions dating back to the Zinoviev Letter.[24] Attlee faced a constant barrage of criticism from the party's left wing against his government's foreign and security policies, particularly in respect of what was seen as excessive deference to the Americans and unnecessary hostility to the Soviet Union. He and Bevin, however, realized that US money and military muscle were vital to British and European security, while the Soviet Union, resentful of what it saw as the steady encroachment of Western capitalism, continued to extend its influence over bordering countries and beyond.

At home, Attlee and his colleagues had to deal with the problems of communist-inspired industrial subversion, as well as evidence of pervasive Soviet espionage and propaganda (despite the dissolution of the Comintern in 1943). Ministers were cautious in their dealings with the intelligence agencies, continuing with organizational reforms initiated before the end of hostilities (including cutting back the multiplicity of 'secret shows' that had proliferated during the war) and, initially at least, rejecting the idea of covert operations. But to inform their foreign and atomic policies, and to nurture the increasingly close security and intelligence relationship with the United States, Attlee and Bevin recognized the importance of secret intelligence; Attlee had more meetings with the head of MI5 than any other twentieth-century premier. Although aware of the risk that protective security measures against subversion, targeting communists, would be seen by the party as a witch-hunt, Attlee knew, as he noted on a paper for the Cabinet Committee on Subversive Activities, that 'We cannot afford to take risks here.'[25]

The extent of Soviet post-war espionage began to emerge in September 1945, when the defection of GRU[26] cypher clerk Igor Gouzenko in Ottawa revealed the existence of Soviet spy networks in both the US and UK, including the British atomic scientist Alan Nunn May.[27] In 1947 Attlee was briefed, even before the FBI and long before the CIA, on VENONA, the US programme to intercept encrypted Soviet communications and 'the most important counter-espionage breakthrough of the early Cold War'.[28] This led to the unmasking of atomic scientist Klaus Fuchs (codenamed CHARLES or REST) as a Soviet spy early in 1950; later that year another scientist, Bruno Pontecorvo, defected. VENONA traffic dating from September 1945 also revealed the existence of a high-level network of British spies—the Cambridge Five—though their codenames were not 'broken' for some time. This meant that when Kim Philby (codenamed STANLEY), after heading up the SIS section dealing with Russia—in which capacity he had delayed the transmission of intelligence on Gouzenko's revelations—was posted to Washington in 1949, he was inducted into the VENONA secret and promptly told Moscow about it. When Philby learned in April 1951 that Donald Maclean had been identified as HOMER, he was able to ensure that Maclean was tipped off and could slip out of the UK in May with Guy Burgess (whose codename, HICKS, had not yet been broken).[29] Philby himself, recalled from Washington, was interrogated by MI5 on a number of occasions during 1951, but although a report by Helenus Milmo QC stated that he was 'unable to avoid the conclusion that Philby is and has for many years been a Soviet agent', the Director of Public Prosecutions advised there was no legal evidence on which he could be prosecuted; SIS felt the case against Philby was 'not proved' and allowed him to resign from the Service on advantageous terms.[30]

By the time Burgess and Maclean left Britain, Herbert Morrison had replaced the seriously ill Ernest Bevin as Labour's Foreign Secretary in March 1951, and quickly found himself in the middle of a crisis. The unmasking of Nunn May and Fuchs and the defection of Pontecorvo had already shaken American confidence in their British allies (despite the fact that a number of US spies had been identified as well); the disappearance of Burgess and Maclean, and abrupt recall of Philby, made things worse. The British Embassy in Washington reported on 8 June 1951 that the disappearance of the two diplomats had caused a 'major sensation' in the US, with the CIA 'highly disturbed' and the confidence of the State Department in the integrity of FO officials 'severely shaken'. Attlee, alarmed, asked for a report on Burgess and Maclean, and Sir Alexander Cadogan was asked to investigate.[31]

Soon after taking over from Bevin, yet before the disappearance of the two diplomats, Morrison asked to see the files on the Zinoviev

Figure 12. H. A. R. 'Kim' Philby

Letter. He did so after agreeing to place Maclean under surveillance, and when the British Embassy in Washington had asked for Burgess to be summoned home because of outrageous behaviour; there may be no connection, but possibly his interest was prompted by the suggestion of FO officials behaving badly. Roderick Barclay, Morrison's Private Secretary, recalled in 1966 that he had expressed 'mild surprise' when the Foreign Secretary asked for the Zinoviev file, receiving the response that 'surely he was entitled to call for any Foreign Office file he might wish to see without giving any reason'.[32]

Barclay wrote to the FO Librarian on 24 April 1951, saying that Morrison 'wondered whether the Foreign Office archives threw any light on the question of Mr Ramsay MacDonald's connexion with the Letter'. This time, however, unlike in 1938 when Halifax had requested the file, it proved more difficult to assemble the papers. While some were produced by the Library in the usual way, others were retrieved from a cupboard in Northern Department, while more sensitive papers, particularly those containing references to SIS material, had apparently been transferred into the keeping of the Permanent Under-Secretary's Department (PUSD), the name given in 1949 to the department that served as a point of liaison between the FO and British secret intelligence agencies.[33] An appeal was made to the PUS, now Sir William Strang, who had his own memories of the Zinoviev affair; he put together a selection for the Foreign Secretary. In the light of later confusion about the whereabouts of key papers, it is worth quoting Strang's minute to Morrison of 27 April 1951:

> You asked to see the papers about the Zinoviev Letter. The annexed three papers will give you the main lines of the story. There is a short history of the incident in print in N 8467 at Flag A.[34] The Letter as it came into the Office, and the original minutes thereon are in N 7838 at Flag B.[35] The draft to Mr Rakovski, substantially amended in manuscript by Mr Ramsay MacDonald, is in N 8105 at Flag C.[36] If you require further information, I will let you have it if available.

This seems to have been the last occasion when MacDonald's amended draft was noted as being present in the file. Morrison wrote on 6 May: 'What seems to emerge is that Mr MacDonald was not clear in his instructions & it is doubtful if FO shd have acted without explicit & initialled instructions of clear authority. It is very interesting & when we have time we might have a talk.'[37] There is, however, no further evidence of Morrison's interest in the Zinoviev file during the remainder of the Labour government, which was defeated in the general election of October 1951 and replaced by the Conservatives under Winston Churchill.

Intelligence scandals and doubts about security bedevilled the Conservative governments in office from 1951, led by Churchill until 1955, Anthony Eden, and, after the Suez crisis, by Harold Macmillan, and made for uneasy relations between ministers and the security and intelligence authorities. Efforts to identify other British spies named in VENONA messages continued; Burgess was now matched, correctly, to HICKS, but JOHNSON was thought to be Philby, though

the codename actually referred to Anthony Blunt. Suspicions grew
that Philby was the 'Third Man' who had tipped off Burgess and
Maclean. MI5 continued to press for further investigations, while SIS
continued to insist there was no proof; renewed interrogation of
Philby in 1955 produced no conclusive result and Macmillan was
forced by press speculation to name, and clear, him in the House of
Commons.[38] The impression of government disarray and cover-up
was increased in 1956, when Burgess and Maclean appeared publicly
in Moscow, while the reputation of the intelligence agencies was
damaged further by the incident in April 1956 when Commander
'Buster' Crabb disappeared in Portsmouth Harbour while undertaking an unauthorized intelligence operation against Russian warships.[39]
Tense relations between the government and agencies over the Suez
crisis, plus the continued failure to identify the remaining British
spies, made for a difficult decade.

One final appearance of the Zinoviev Letter in the 1950s deserves
mention. In February 1956, Major Guy Kindersley wrote to former
Conservative Party Chairman J. C. C. Davidson announcing his
intention of publishing his own account of the circumstances under
which Donald im Thurn (who had died in 1930) had supposedly
brought the Letter to light in 1924, including an account of the
lunch party at Davidson's house on 19 March 1928.[40] Davidson sent
Kindersley's letter to Joseph—now Sir Joseph—Ball, a businessman in
the City, on 14 March, commenting that 'of course he hasn't a clue
as to what really happened'.[41] Ball replied that he did not think it
right for Kindersley to publish details of a private lunch party, and
that they should tell him so. The three men met in Ball's office on
30 October 1956, and Kindersley was persuaded against publication;
he died the following month. Kindersley had apparently been dis-
tressed that im Thurn had died without receiving the knighthood he
felt had been promised to him, and had written to Davidson to say so.
Robert Rhodes James, who edited Davidson's papers in *Memoirs of a
Conservative*, published in 1966, commented that no such letter was
found, but that:

it appears from what papers do exist on this subject in his papers, that the part Davidson played had been essentially a minor one compared with that of Ball. Until the revelation of 1967, Davidson was convinced that the Letter was genuine.[42]

As Robert Blake notes in the *Oxford Dictionary of National Biography*, Ball was surely 'a quintessential *éminence grise*'. Laski, as Attlee might have said, was not in the same class.

'Quite a pocketful of trouble': spies and suspicion, 1960–1964

Harold Macmillan took over as Prime Minister in January 1957 from Anthony Eden, broken by the Suez crisis.[43] The early years of his premiership were active and successful, leading to triumphant re-election in 1959 (when Anthony Howard, in *The Guardian*, thought that 'to some extent the Labour party even now shows the scars of the incident with the *Daily Mail* and the Zinoviev Letter in 1924').[44] He established a good relationship with the new US President, John F. Kennedy, who took office in January 1961, and persuaded his party to apply to the European Economic Community in order to learn whether the terms of entry would enable Britain to become a member.[45]

Macmillan's last few years as Prime Minister, until his resignation in October 1963, were, however, beset by espionage scandals. Although not related directly to the Zinoviev Letter, their cluster effect had a bearing on the investigations into the Letter in the second half of the decade, so deserve a little attention.[46] In January 1961 Harry Houghton and Ethel Gee, both of whom worked at the Admiralty Underwater Weapons Establishment at Portland, were arrested following a tip-off from a Polish defector, together with their Soviet handler, 'Gordon Lonsdale' (Konon Molody), and, through Lonsdale, the spies 'Peter and Helen Kroger' (Morris and Lona Cohen), all of whom received long prison sentences in March. Macmillan announced the appointment of the Romer Committee to enquire into breaches of security.[47] Even before the Portland trial was over, SIS officer George Blake confessed to having spied for the Soviet Union since 1951, and was sentenced on 3 May 1961 to forty-two years in prison. This meant yet another enquiry, the Radcliffe Committee on Security Procedures in the Public Service (its announcement causing Macmillan difficulty, as he could not say publicly that Blake worked for an organization that did not, theoretically, exist).[48] Then, in September 1962, Admiralty clerk John Vassall was arrested, leading to the announcement in November of the Radcliffe Tribunal of Enquiry.[49]

Macmillan, who hated spy scandals and disliked direct contact with the Security Service, found all this most annoying as well as troubling. He also had a great deal more to worry about than spies, not least the existential threat of the Cuban Missile Crisis in October 1962. But at a time when national security really was threatened by international events, and close relations with the Americans of critical importance, regular reminders of lapses in security were particularly unwelcome. (This might account for the description of his reaction to the news of Vassall's arrest, broken by MI5's Director General Roger Hollis: 'No, I'm not at all pleased. When my gamekeeper shoots a fox, he doesn't go and hang it up outside the Master of Foxhounds' drawing room; he buries it out of sight... Why the devil did you "catch" him?'[50])

In January 1963, after making a disingenuous 'confession' to SIS officer Nicholas Elliott, Kim Philby left Beirut, where he had been working as a journalist (and supplying information to SIS),[51] and fled to Moscow; it was some time before the news became public in Britain, but then it caused a media sensation. Philby's defection, after so many years full of suspicion yet short on proof, was a great embarrassment, particularly in the context of the Anglo-American security and intelligence relationship, a severe blow to the Security Service and SIS, and to Macmillan, who had cleared him publicly in 1955. As Ben Macintyre notes, there arose a 'Great Philby Myth' of a 'super-spy who had bamboozled Britain, divulged her secrets and those of her allies for thirty years, and then escaped to Moscow in a final triumphant *coup de théâtre*'; the truth, as always, was rather more complex.[52]

If Macmillan hoped that after Philby's defection the spy stories would go away, he was to be disappointed. The Profumo affair, in the summer of 1963, was the last straw as far as he was concerned. Although there is some debate as to the extent that national security was compromised by the involvement of the Secretary of State for War, John Profumo, with GRU officer Evgeni Ivanov through their mutual lover, Christine Keeler, the episode was undoubtedly sordid and damaging to the public reputation of ministers, and caused the Prime Minister great embarrassment.[53] This time, it was Lord Denning who was to carry out an enquiry. In the circumstances, Macmillan felt he ought to brief Harold Wilson, who had become leader of the Labour Party in January 1963 on the death of Hugh Gaitskell:

> I had an hour with Harold Wilson and tried to explain to him how the so-called 'Security' services really worked. It seemed to me right to do so and he took it quite well. (He had never heard of 'C'.)[54]

Wilson may have taken it well, but he was not slow to exploit the government's plight when the Denning Report was debated in Parliament on 16 December 1963, alleging that the security services were being run with 'nonchalant amateurism in a world of ruthless professionalism'.[55]

The series of espionage scandals had, indeed, been so relentless that Macmillan wondered whether he was being targeted personally by Soviet intelligence, and consulted Sir Dick White, the former Director General of MI5 who had become Chief of SIS after the Crabb scandal in 1956 (the only man to have held both jobs). White apparently 'told him plainly that the Russians had no assets to organise a plot involving Profumo'.[56] An MI5–SIS working party found no evidence of such a plot, but by the time it reported Macmillan had resigned due to ill health, to be succeeded by Alec Douglas-Home.[57]

The concentration of spy cases in the early 1960s was not coincidental. Soviet intelligence services, which had been reduced and weakened by Stalin's purges in the 1930s and had been in a state of virtual collapse in 1950–1, had been rebuilt in the aftermath of Stalin's death in 1953. A Praesidium resolution in June 1954 'On measures for the strengthening of intelligence work by the organs of state security of the USSR abroad' led to the construction of KGB and GRU networks of 'illegals' in Britain and the US, regarded as the main enemies of the Soviet Union.[58] These developments led to a period of unprecedented growth in Soviet espionage activities in the UK that would only be checked in 1971, with Operation FOOT.[59] For Macmillan, it was less a question of being targeted (though White's confident assertion that the Russians were not capable of it seems somewhat complacent) but rather of being the man in charge at the time.

Of course, it was not all bad news: after all, these successive 'spy scandals' arose when Soviet espionage was uncovered, whether through defector information or through the efforts of British intelligence. Spies were being detected, prosecuted, and imprisoned. Philby's flight to Moscow did, apparently, increase the pressure on both Anthony Blunt and John Cairncross, both of whom confessed to spying in 1964 (although Blunt was not publicly identified as a traitor until 1979, and Cairncross declined to return from the US to be prosecuted).[60] But the 'revelations', trials, and publicity were undoubtedly damaging to the reputation of the intelligence agencies. Philby's defection was the catalyst for what intelligence historian Christopher Andrew describes as 'the most traumatic episodes in the Cold War history of the Security Service', in which both the Director General and his Deputy were to be accused, falsely, of being Soviet 'moles'.[61]

But the Philby episode also had a devastating effect on SIS, many of whose senior officers (though not White)[62] found it hard to accept the full depth of his treachery. All the agencies, encouraged by suggestions from the defector Anatoli Golitsyn and the CIA's head of Counter-Intelligence, James Angleton, now wondered whether they might have been penetrated by other Soviet agents, as yet unidentified. In November 1964 a joint MI5–MI6 working party, codenamed FLUENCY and chaired by Peter Wright, was set up to examine all evidence of hostile penetration of the services, including looking back over old cases; it reported in May 1965 'not merely that both Services had been penetrated by Soviet intelligence but that the penetration continued'.[63] (Both Wright, later of *Spycatcher* fame, and Angleton proved to be deluded conspiracy theorists, but that was not apparent at this stage.) By that time there was a Labour government in power for the first time in thirteen years, Labour having won the general election on 15 October 1964 with an overall majority of five.

Ever since the Profumo affair, an election had been on the cards, and Harold Wilson, who had worked hard to win over those who felt him an unworthy successor to Gaitskell, had been both thorough and imaginative in ensuring the widest possible support for Labour when it was called. He had also, in Ben Pimlott's words, 'watched the polls as an Indian charmer watches a snake', the 'first British politician to take an expert, almost detached interest in their performance and to apply their message to his behaviour'. Up to the end, the polls were close and the outcome uncertain: and although the majority was tiny, Labour's victory was notable as 'the first occasion in peacetime since 1906 that an incumbent Conservative administration had been displaced by a non-Conservative party with an absolute majority'.[64]

It might have been expected that the Zinoviev Letter would come up during the 1964 election campaign. Wilson was outspoken in his criticism of the Tory-owned press and of what he perceived as an anti-Labour bias in the BBC: he had pressed for the political element of the programme *Today's Papers* to be suspended during the election period. Former Cabinet Secretary Norman Brook, now Lord Normanbrook and Chairman of the BBC, declined to do this but said he would ensure impartiality (though Wilson did succeed in getting *Steptoe and Son* postponed on election day so that it was not screened until the polls closed).[65] But no one seems to have mentioned the Zinoviev Letter during the campaign: the only untoward event immediately before polling day was an unofficial strike on the London Underground, which could surely be attributed only indirectly to the Conservatives.

Perhaps the absence of any mention of the Letter is because Wilson's avowed platform for Labour was to look forward, not back: he was, however, to prove very sensitive to the idea of political dirty tricks. After such a long period out of office, it was inevitable that incoming Labour ministers would be suspicious of both the civil service, regarded as innately conservative,[66] and of the intelligence services. There was, as the official history of MI5 describes, 'a widespread delusion' that ministers' correspondence and phone calls were intercepted, and the Prime Minister himself developed a 'fascination with bugging' that was later to verge on paranoia. Wilson gave the Paymaster General, the rather unpredictable George Wigg, a roving brief on security matters: as Cabinet Secretary Burke Trend told the heads of MI5 and MI6, what Wilson had in mind 'was that Wigg should safeguard the Prime Minister against scandals taking him unaware and he did not want to be caught in the position of Macmillan at the time of the Profumo case'.[67] Nevertheless, Wilson and his colleagues developed a good relationship with the civil service, and indeed with the intelligence agencies. The Security Service provided the government with valuable intelligence at a time of industrial unrest, including regular reports on the seamen's strike in the summer of 1966,[68] as well as information on Soviet espionage activities; SIS and GCHQ gave them information on Soviet and Eastern-bloc espionage and subversion overseas.

The hole in the archive: 1965–1967

I little thought, when beginning this book, that I should need to write about the corner of government in which I spent nearly all my career, and about some of the people with whom I worked. But the next episode in the Zinoviev story involves the Foreign Office Historical Section, established in March 1918 in order to provide historical expertise and advice to British representatives negotiating the peace settlements that followed the First World War. The Labour government decided in 1924 to publish a series of *British Documents on the Origins of the War, 1898–1914,* to counter the influence of the famous German series *Die Grosse Politik der Europäischen Grossmächte, 1871–1914;* a central objective of the Foreign Office in publishing documents edited by professional historians has always been that the British government's case should not go by default. In 1944, Anthony Eden signed off on a new series to cover the interwar period (*Documents on British Foreign Policy 1919–1939, DBFP*), and Sir Alec Douglas-Home, as Foreign Secretary, announced in 1973 there would be a series beginning in 1945, *Documents on British Policy Overseas* (*DBPO*), still going strong in 2018.

It takes a very long time to edit one of these volumes, from identifying the material in FO and other archives, making a selection, and adding editorial content, through to publication. For this reason, *DBFP* began with two concurrent series, starting in 1919 (First Series) and 1930 (Second), so that there might be some hope of reaching 1939 before its events had been forgotten; then, in recognition of a public desire to understand exactly how the government had taken the road to war in 1939, the Third Series was initiated in 1947 to cover the period from the German annexation of Austria in March 1938 until the outbreak of war. By 1963 the editors realized they were still falling behind, so a fourth series was initiated, Series Ia, to cover the years 1925–9. The editor of the new series was to be Margaret Esterel Lambert, a formidably clever and eagle-eyed graduate of Somerville College, Oxford, who had joined the Historical Section as a research assistant in 1953 but rose quickly to a senior position, relied upon heavily (and bullied) by the Historical Adviser, Rohan Butler.[69] The other editors in the mid-1960s were Professor W. N. Medlicott (Senior Editor, responsible for the Second Series) and Professor Douglas Dakin (First Series), while Butler, who completed the Third Series, turned his attention to the post-war period.

From the beginning, all editors insisted on editorial independence, making 'unreserved access to the Foreign Office archives and complete freedom in the selection and arrangement of their material' their condition for undertaking the work. So when Margaret Lambert, editing her first volume, *The Aftermath of Locarno 1925–26*, came in 1965 to write a footnote on the Zinoviev Letter and found a number of papers absent from the file, she and her colleagues were dismayed. (The volume that actually covers the events of 1924, First Series, Volume XXV, was not published until 1984, so the problem had not arisen before.) According to her paper, 'Investigation into the Zinoviev file of 1924', the file (N 108/38 of 1924) contained only: the copy of the Zinoviev Letter received from SIS on 10 October 1924, with its covering note; a copy of the letter sent to Rakovsky on 24 October—not the one signed by Gregory 'in the absence of the Secretary of State', but an amended copy bearing MacDonald's name; and the Confidential Print version of the same note.[70] Missing were the draft note to M. Rakovsky, which MacDonald had sent back to the FO, heavily amended but not initialled; a carbon copy of the note dispatched under Gregory's signature; and a number of other documents dating from October to December 1924, all containing references to SIS material though not necessarily related to the Letter.

As Butler noted in a minute of 1 November 1965, the absence of key papers from the file was potentially liable to undermine the authority of *DBFP*:

> Because some historians might not be slow to suggest that these gaps indicate that the Editors have only been allowed to work on files that have been stripped of the most sensitive material and have thus, in effect, been subjected to a form of pre-censorship. In my experience this is of course quite untrue, apart from the different issue of earlier wrong weeding out of ignorance, against which I have made strong representations. The present state of the Zinoviev file, however, makes me fear that it might not prove easy to convince outside historians of the true facts; in which case both the Office and the Editors are liable to suffer severely and unfairly in public estimation.

Medlicott agreed: 'There is no doubt that historians find it hard to believe in such cases that documents do get lost: the suspicion consequently aroused is in direct proportion to the department's reputation for archival efficiency.'[71]

The problem was put before the relevant Deputy Under-Secretary, Sir John Nicholls, and Clifton Child, FO Director of Research and Head of the Library, and an intensive investigation was put in hand. This involved a search of long-neglected cupboards, questioning of archivists and officials past and present, including those in the Permanent Under-Secretary's Department in contact with the intelligence agencies, and in SIS itself, and consulting former diplomats, such as Strang, Caccia, Hoyer Millar (now Lord Inchyra), Barclay, and Alan Campbell, who remembered that in 1951 papers had been produced from a cupboard by a Miss Paget who seems to have been personal assistant to the head of Northern Department from the early 1920s until 1952. Predictably, memories diverged, whether on events in 1924, or the state of the file when inspected by Halifax in 1938 and Morrison in 1951. Views differed as to whether MacDonald's draft had or had not been initialled. Oliver Harvey (now Baron Harvey) wrote to Nicholls that he remembered the draft as corrected by MacDonald and initialled by him 'in the margin only', but marked to be sent off by Crowe: 'It has always struck me that it was so odd of Crowe who was such a stickler for Office procedure that it was sent off without the PM's initials at the bottom.'[72] Butler also spoke to Sybil Crowe, Eyre Crowe's daughter, to see if any of her father's papers might help (the answer was negative).

The details of the investigation are entertaining but inconclusive: the missing Zinoviev papers were not found. A small clutch of correspondence between the head of the FO Security Department and SIS in the early 1950s suggests that at least some of the missing papers, bearing a 'CX' reference, were destroyed as a matter of principle, and that a number of others were 'weeded' in 1953, possibly including the MacDonald draft, since drafts were routinely destroyed.[73] As it became clear that the papers were not going to turn up, Margaret Lambert began drafting a passage to appear in the Preface to the first volume of Series Ia, deploring the 'insufficient recognition of the exceptional historical importance of the Foreign Office political files', and referring specifically to the 'seriously unsatisfactory condition' of the Zinoviev file; scrupulously, she noted that this might not be due to over-zealous weeding, but some other cause.

All this was not just a storm in a Historical Section teacup (when I first joined, we all foregathered formally every day at 4 p.m. for tea, with china cups and excruciating polite chit-chat). While FO cupboards and memories were being searched, the hole in the Zinoviev archive had become entangled with a thorny political issue: Harold Wilson's determination to relax the fifty-year rule governing the release of government documents. The Public Records Act of 1958 had granted for the first time a statutory right of access; government departments were required to transfer records worthy of permanent preservation to the Public Record Office (PRO) when they were thirty years old, to be opened to general public inspection at fifty years, with certain special conditions and exceptions. The Lord Chancellor had overall responsibility for the system, and the power to prescribe closure for longer periods in the case of specific classes of record, including those concerning national security. (When the Conservative Lord Chancellor, Lord Gardiner, introduced the Bill's Second Reading in December 1957, announcing that there were over 46 miles of shelves in the Public Record Office in Chancery Lane, the former Labour minister Lord Alexander wondered whether they contained the 'true inner record of the great story of the Zinoviev letter of 1924'.[74])

The length of the period of closure was criticized from the start by the proponents of what would now be called open government, including academic historians and a number of politicians, especially in the Labour Party. The controversy was fuelled by the privileged access given to Anthony Eden (now Lord Avon) in writing his memoirs, and the Cabinet Secretary, Sir Burke Trend, had already been considering what might be done to address the growing interest in 'contemporary' history and the way in which the accessibility of public records affected research and teaching.[75] Neither Macmillan nor

Douglas-Home had been inclined to engage with the issue, but Trend found Harold Wilson 'predisposed towards fresh thinking upon the whole subject as well as prepared to gloss over official reservations about the early amendment of the 1958 legislation'.[76]

On 5 August 1965, Wilson told the Cabinet that although the Advisory Council on Public Records had recently recommended more liberal access to closed records for 'established historians', this would be too difficult to implement. It would, he said, be possible to reduce the period of closure without damaging the basic objective, which was 'not only to prevent the premature disclosure of confidential information that might be prejudicial to the State but also, and chiefly, to preserve the constitutional principle of the collective responsibility of the Cabinet and the individual responsibility of Ministers to Parliament'. Wilson proposed that the period should be reduced to thirty years, on condition that existing safeguards against premature disclosure were maintained. This would be 'consonant with the Government's policy of liberalising the convention by which public life was regulated', and bring Britain into line with other countries, 'who would otherwise remain free to publish biased and partisan accounts of events in which we had taken part while we should continue to be inhibited from making any adequate reply'.[77]

The change required the assent of Opposition leaders and HM the Queen: while Liberal leader Jo Grimond raised no objection, Conservative leader Edward Heath expressed his concern that a reduction to thirty years could involve embarrassment to politicians and civil servants still alive and active in public life, thereby inhibiting the confidential nature of ministerial discussions and frankness of official advice. Wilson persisted, however, arguing that the reduction 'would let some light and air into our public records without in any way weakening the conventions which regulate the conduct of public affairs in this country'. He also argued that the official history programme should be extended to include peacetime periods and episodes as well as war, and that the FO's practice of publishing selected documents might be extended to other government departments.[78]

Wilson's proposals did not meet with enthusiasm everywhere in Whitehall; the Foreign Secretary, Michael Stewart, considered the thirty-year rule would be an 'almost intolerable handicap to serving members of the Diplomatic Service', and the PUS, Sir Paul Gore-Booth, agreed, arguing that it would undermine the relationship of trust between ambassadors and the governments to which they were accredited. FO officials even discussed with the Cabinet Office the possibility (surely remote) of their two departments being exempted from its provisions. Rohan Butler drew up a detailed paper on the administrative, legal, political, and historical consequences, warning that for the FO they were likely to be 'heavily adverse', and that since there would have to be special arrangements for the exemption of particularly sensitive files, historians would come to 'twig the existence of such special archives', with 'predictable complications'; he also argued that the publication of *DBFP* would be 'downgraded'.[79]

None of this cut any ice with the Prime Minister, his confidence boosted by winning a greatly increased majority in the general election on 31 March 1966. On 10 August he announced in the House of Commons that as both the Leader of the Opposition and the Queen had now given their assent, legislation to implement a thirty-year rule would be introduced. He confirmed that there would be no change in the present arrangements for publishing FO documents, and rebuffed an attempt by Michael Foot to argue for an even shorter period of closure. Acknowledging that some people felt it 'a little unfair to those who started Cabinet work early in life, as I did myself, that they should have all their youthful indiscretions published', Wilson commented that 'Personally, I would prefer to be alive to answer the criticisms.'[80] The following day, George Brown became Foreign Secretary, swapping jobs with Michael Stewart, who now became Minister of Economic Affairs.

As soon as it became apparent, at the beginning of 1966, that Wilson was not to be deflected by opposition or disapproval, discussions began in the FO about the Zinoviev Letter file. It was assumed from the start that when the first thirty-year-old papers were released, this

Figure 13. George Brown, Foreign Secretary 1966–8, with Prime Minister Harold Wilson

file would, as Butler wrote in a memorandum on 'The Zinoviev Letter and the Fifty-Year Rule', be one 'for which historians, and perhaps also journalists and politicians, Russian as well as British, would be specially likely to make a bee-line'. The absence of key papers would inevitably arouse criticism: particularly suspicious would be the missing draft to Rakovsky as amended by MacDonald, and the fact that no trace of correspondence between MacDonald and Crowe, immediately after the publication of the note signed by Gregory and the Letter itself, was to be found in FO archives. After consultation with Child, Butler proposed a pre-emptive strategy, so that if challenged the FO could say it had the matter in hand. This involved the search for Zinoviev documents (already set in train), asking the Royal Archives and other potential sources for copies of any relevant documents they might hold, and issuing strict instructions to departments about the perils of keeping apparently sensitive material 'off the file', citing the Zinoviev case as 'a striking example of how self-defeating such evasive action could be'.[81]

With the agreement of Nicholls and the FO Legal Advisers, a 'Plan of Campaign on Zinoviev Letter' was drawn up, involving instructions to the 'weeders', enquiries of retired officials, possible sources of supplementary material, a circular to departments on sensitive material, a final check on the 1924 files, and the insertion of a special statement in the Preface of the forthcoming volume of *DBFP*; Nicholls undertook to write to the Controller of HM Stationery Office to ask that production of the volume be speeded up so it could be published before the end of 1966.[82] As we have already seen, searches and enquiries failed to produce any documents, but the Royal Archives at Windsor provided thirteen photocopied sheets, including a letter and minute from Crowe to MacDonald, which were inserted in the FO file with a note by the Deputy Librarian, Albert Harrington.[83] The Treasury, asked whether the papers of the 1928 Board of Enquiry might offer any clues, provided copies of the evidence given by four FO officials (Willert, head of News Department in 1924, Bland, Strang, and Gaselee) but declined to hand over that given by MacDonald.[84]

Series Ia, Volume I of *DBFP* was scheduled for publication on Monday, 12 December 1966. On 23 November, Butler sent a minute to the PUS alerting him to the forthcoming volume with its Preface paragraphs about the shortcomings of FO archives, and in particular the Zinoviev Letter file. He annexed Margaret Lambert's paper on the Investigation into the Zinoviev File, and a general brief for News Department on the destruction of documents in FO archives 'in case the press displays interest'. Gore-Booth ruled on 4 December that these papers should be seen by a minister as soon as possible:

> This must clearly go to Mrs White [Eirene White, Minister of State for Foreign Affairs] as early as possible on Monday Dec. 5 ... I am sure we should not 'pretend' in any way, but as this episode is a most sensitive piece of Labour Party foreign policy history, we must be sure to have the best possible answers. I must confess I did *not* realize that this wd. come upon us so soon & suddenly.[85]

On Friday, 9 December, the papers reached Murray MacLehose, George Brown's Principal Private Secretary, who passed them to the

Foreign Secretary on 11 December with a note that he would wish to see them 'at once'. By this time, however, the press had already received advance copies of the volume, and there were a number of stories in the Sunday papers, including 'FO loses Red Letter protest' (*Sunday Observer*) and 'Zinoviev Case: Papers Lost' (*Sunday Telegraph*). Further disobliging reports were published on 12 December, raising questions about other documents the FO had supposedly 'lost', including the Hoare–Laval Pact (which had in fact been saved narrowly from incineration by the historian David Dilks)[86] and the Munich Agreement.[87] *The Times* commented that, forty years later, the Zinoviev Letter affair 'still fulfils the rules of any really first-class mystery':

> It is still good for instant argument, for very many people even now refuse to believe that forgers had been busy. It remains a popular catchword: it has only to be breathed from an election platform and everyone is immediately put on guard, or should be, against an eve-of-poll scare. *Zinoviev Letter!* is almost as spine-chilling, even today, as *Bankers' Ramp!*[88]

The Foreign Secretary, George Brown, was unsurprisingly furious at all this negative publicity, writing to the PUS:

> This is quite intolerable.
>
> 1) If we knew—as we must have—that it was about to become public, why was I not advised? I should not have to learn these things from the newspapers.
>
> 2) It lends considerable point to my present complaint about the lax way files are passed out: the inadequate check on how long they are out: and the apparent disinterest in when or how they come back.
>
> 3) Even today we wouldn't know whether papers had been extracted. There's no evidence on which to blame 'weeders'.
>
> I would like to talk about this case and our general practice. I shall have a lot of trouble over it.[89]

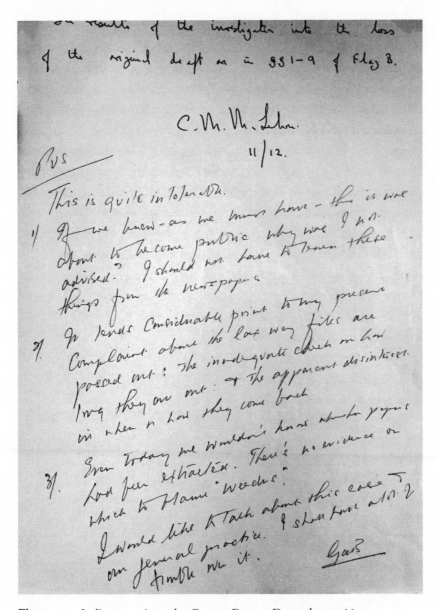

Figure 14. Indignant minute by George Brown, December 1966

A meeting was held on the afternoon of 12 December between Brown, Gore-Booth, George Thomson (Chancellor of the Duchy of Lancaster), and officials, when it was agreed that by the beginning of 1967 'it must be understood, both in the Department and in posts abroad, that an effective system' for checking files in and out must be in operation. Brown was not appeased, however: and when John Rennie, who had succeeded Nicholls as the superintending Deputy Under-Secretary, tried to explain the timeline, the Foreign Secretary scrawled on his minute, 'I received it on the 12th! It had been months in the pipeline.' Nor, he said, had he received any answer to the points in his minute. When Rennie conceded that it was 'unfortunate' they had had so little warning, Brown called it 'the understatement of the year'.[90] (Having had a good deal of experience in trying to bring forthcoming historical publications or document releases to the notice of senior officials and ministers, I have learned that the solution is to spell out possible consequences and 'media handling consider-ations' in the starkest and briefest terms possible, though the trick is to make sure they hear about it *sufficiently* but *not too far* in advance; not always an easy judgement.)

Brown was right that he would have 'a lot of trouble' over the hole in the Zinoviev archive; Parliamentary Questions had already been tabled, and the affair of the Letter, always a sensitive issue for the Labour Party, was being aired in the press all over again, prompting a number of people to come forward with their reminiscences. On 16 December *The Guardian* published a letter from former diplomat Sir Clifford Norton, insisting that Crowe, 'that most upright civil servant', had genuinely believed that MacDonald had authorized the dispatch of the note to Rakovsky on 24 October, prompting a response from the former *Daily Herald* journalist (and, as we now know, Soviet agent) W. N. Ewer that Norton had 'finally settled "Who-dun-it?"' (that is, who passed the Zinoviev Letter to the press), as the answer must be Gregory.[91] Meanwhile, briefing was prepared, in SIS as well as the FO, for the Foreign Secretary to answer questions in the House of Commons on 19 December 1966. But before then, a new set of revelations hit the headlines.

Insights from *The Sunday Times*

On 16 December 1966, with the agreement of the Foreign Secretary, Margaret Lambert, together with Rennie, Child, and Butler, had a meeting with Harold Evans, Managing Editor of *The Sunday Times*, and Hugo Young, his chief leader writer. Evans and Young asked to see the FO copy of the Zinoviev Letter, but were told this was impossible without special permission; they also asked about authenticity, but Lambert explained that as an independent but official historian of British foreign policy the question was not one on which she felt it right to pronounce. Rennie offered to check against the FO text any copy of the Letter that might be produced by *The Sunday Times* (Evans and Young said that the *Daily Mail* had been unable to find theirs).[92]

The reason for the interest shown by Evans and Young was soon apparent, when on Sunday, 18 December, *The Sunday Times* ran a major story by Hugo Young, Lewis Chester, and Stephen Fay (the 'Insight' team): the front page was dominated by a photograph of Madame Irina Bellegarde, 'widow of one of the principals in the Zinoviev plot', under the headline 'Widow solves a 42-year old mystery: Exile group forged the Zinoviev Letter'. It stated that Mme Bellegarde, who had lived in England since 1945, had not previously disclosed what she knew about the Letter 'for fear of bringing some kind of reprisal on close relatives or people directly concerned', but that she felt it safe to speak on learning that the 'annotated copy' was missing from FO files. The cover story also announced that the Conservative Party's role in exploiting the Letter would be revealed.

A 'major report' in the Weekly Review section of the paper gave full details of the story that would be published in book form in October 1967 as *The Zinoviev Letter: A Political Intrigue*. Its main components were, first, Mme Bellegarde's story that the Letter had been forged—on a single sheet of 'genuine Third International notepaper', though it was three pages long—by a group of Russian *émigrés*: her husband, Alexis Bellegarde, her brother Zhemchuznikov, Gumansky, a 'close friend of the family' (and forgery partner of Vladimir Orlov), and an anti-Bolshevik Latvian called Edward Friede. This was essentially an elaboration of the story apparently 'revealed' by Druzhelovsky during his trial in 1927, and repeated by Chicherin in 1928. The second strand in the report was the part played in the affair by Donald im Thurn, based on his diaries as found in Guy Kindersley's papers and made available to the journalists by his son.

Coming less than a week after the reports of the FO's 'lost' files, the *Sunday Times* story was bound to cause a sensation. On Monday, 19 December, *The Times* reported comments by the Conservative MP Sir Gerald Nabarro, whose wife was the niece of Donald im Thurn, described by Nabarro as 'a British Army officer of the greatest integrity and honour, as well as a highly experienced intelligence officer' who had died 'in mysterious circumstances'. He said that im Thurn undoubtedly believed the Letter to be genuine; his service to the Conservative Party had been marked by a silver cigarette case inscribed in 1924 'with the grateful thanks' of the party Chairman. Nabarro cast doubts on Mme Bellegarde's account, and suggested that the missing documents might have been stolen from the FO.[93] Former Labour minister Emanuel Shinwell dismissed this intervention, commenting that it was well known the Letter was 'just a Tory trick like the Post Office savings scare', and it was ridiculous for Nabarro to come along and say it was genuine: 'How old was he at the time, five?' The historian A. J. P. Taylor, always willing to provoke, said he had always assumed it was a forgery, and that in 1924 it had been the Liberals, not Labour, who had been panicked by the Letter: 'Working-class people were as usual sensible: it was the imbecilic middle-class readers of the *Guardian* who were frightened.'[94]

Meanwhile, on the morning of 19 December the Historical Adviser submitted 'first thoughts' on the *Sunday Times* revelations to Rennie, the PUS, and the Foreign Secretary. Butler suggested it was important to keep distinct the questions of the presence in FO files of the Letter, on which 'the Secretary of State can and should say something' when answering questions in the House of Commons that afternoon, and that of authenticity, which he should, for the present at least, refuse to discuss. Butler also pointed out some errors in the *Sunday Times* story, and Professor Medlicott contributed a minute expressing 'slight preliminary doubts':

> Where did the spirited young men get the substance of the letter? From primers and Marxist texts and Z[inoviev]'s speeches, according to Mme B, [but] the letter is much closer to the form and content of other Com[intern] communications to the B[ritish] C[ommunist] P[arty] than this. If it was a concoction of other messages to the BCP then the authors were in much more intimate relationship with the inner workings of the Com[intern] than Mme B suggests...Really there is nothing new except Mme B's unsupported assertion which doesn't ring *quite* true (her picture of gay young things having a good joke at Moscow's expense can't quite be reconciled with the professional knowledge and obvious slick handling of the affair). The Kindersley stuff is a red herring.[95]

In the House that afternoon, Brown dealt with four separate PQs on FO records in one answer, announcing that he had 'instituted certain changes in procedure' to improve security, explaining exactly which papers were missing from the Zinoviev file and making it clear that the copy of the Letter received by the FO in October 1924 had never been missing. Michael Foot, stressing that 'we are even more concerned about interference by the Central Office of the Conservative Party with the files', asked the Foreign Secretary to make a full investigation into what happened with the Letter 'and the fact that Foreign Office officials may have been operating against the interests of the Government at that time'. Another Labour MP, James Dickens, added that the investigation should also look into allegations that the Letter was a forgery, while Emrys Hughes asked that Brown should make sure that 'this record of absolute unscrupulous villainy on the part of the Central Office of the Conservative Party, when £5,000 was paid for a forgery' was not allowed to rest. For good measure, Sir Alec Douglas-Home demanded that Brown should 'acquit the Foreign Office of any collusion with any political party'.[96] Brown dodged all these points, saying merely that if anyone cared to put down a further question, he would be happy to answer.

Brown's performance in the House impressed neither the press nor Labour MPs, who felt he had neither addressed the questions raised in the *Sunday Times* story, nor those about the FO's role in the Zinoviev Letter affair. According to a story in *The Times* of 1 January 1967, under the headline 'Did the FO run a Red scare?', Labour backbenchers were far more concerned about the suspicion that the FO had been in collusion with Conservative Central Office than with whether the Letter was a forgery. On 23 January the Labour MP Ben Whitaker asked the Attorney General in the House of Commons whether he would instruct the Director of Public Prosecutions to 'take proceedings against those responsible for conspiring to utter the so-called Zinoviev Letter in the light of the recent evidence sent to him showing that it was forged'; when the Attorney General denied having received such evidence, Whitaker asked whether, alternatively, he would 'consider the prosecution for false pretences of these officials of the Conservative Central Office, who bought this forgery for £10,000 and have not yet honoured their obligation by paying that money?' The Attorney General replied this was 'a matter of alleged history', about which he had no evidence, provoking some scornful comment from Labour members and in the press.[97]

For a few weeks, indeed, the press could not have enough of the Zinoviev Letter, and examined it from every angle, raking up all the old stories. Robin Bruce Lockhart (son of the Robert Bruce Lockhart who had been in Russia in 1917 and gave his name to the so-called 'Lockhart Plot')[98] took issue with the allegations about J. D. Gregory, who had been his godfather, writing that he had been a dedicated public servant with strong religious beliefs, whose innocence in world matters had brought about his downfall, and the loss of his money as 'the unwitting tool of a woman'. He suggested the involvement of the spy Sidney Reilly, for whom the 'espionage jungle' was his natural habitat and who was expert at covering his tracks.[99]

Yet neither Bruce Lockhart nor anyone else offered any really new evidence to corroborate or disprove the *Sunday Times* reports, or to throw further light on either the authenticity of the Letter or the involvement of Conservative Central Office. In the FO, SIS, and the Security Service the evidence was re-examined, summarized, and cross-checked; but everyone seems to have been working on the same files and reports that had been the subject of investigation from 1924 onwards. By the end of January 1967, these efforts were running out of steam: official and press interest diminished. In July, Ben Whitaker tabled a question in Parliament, asking that the new Committee on Official Histories commission a study of the Zinoviev Letter. Wilson replied that when the new Public Records Bill came into operation in 1968 all historians would be able to see the Zinoviev papers; the purpose of the new official histories was to study episodes that fell within the thirty-year closed period.[100] The Zinoviev Letter disappeared from the news until the autumn.

There was, however, one curious episode early in 1967 when an opportunity to learn more about the Letter was turned down. In January 1967 the FO received a letter from the brother of Rose Hoenig, née Rosenberg, who had been MacDonald's personal assistant for many years, including in 1924, and who had died in April 1966. He said that his sister had indicated that she may have left important papers hidden in her apartment; these had been sealed pending probate, but he was now willing for a search to be made. A brief acknowledgement was sent; but after some months of consideration, the Prime Minister, Foreign Secretary, and Cabinet Secretary all concluded that it would be unwise to try to get hold of these papers: better to 'let the sleeping dogs of the Zinoviev Letter lie'. In the light of extensive minuting about searching for possible sources of information on the Letter, it seems a curious decision; but although no one mentioned Pandora's box, it was clearly on all their minds.[101]

The Bagot Enquiry and Report, 1967–1970

The Labour government had a difficult year in 1967. The euphoria of the increased parliamentary majority in 1966 had soon dissipated in a severe balance-of-payments crisis that summer, while trade-union militancy led to widespread industrial unrest. By 1967 it was clear that another financial crisis was looming, and that substantial cuts in both domestic and overseas budgets would be needed. Meanwhile (as in the late 1940s) the wider Labour Party was critical of what it saw as excessive deference to the Americans (particularly over the Vietnam War), while the government knew they relied on US financial assistance. The Six Day War in June 1967 had thrown the Middle East into turmoil and the Cabinet was divided on a number of issues, including the supply of arms to South Africa.

On 18 November 1967, after months of refusing to allow the possibility even to be mentioned, the government was forced to devalue sterling, leading to the resignation of the Chancellor of the Exchequer, James Callaghan. In the ensuing House of Commons debate on 22 November, mocked for his ill-judged remarks on television about there being no change in the value of the 'pound in your pocket', Wilson flung back a jibe about 'the tendency of the party opposite, who have not repudiated either the Post Office scare or the Zinoviev scare of some years ago'.[102] Ten days later, General de Gaulle vetoed, for the second time, a British application to join the European Economic Community.

During 1967, Harold Wilson also became increasingly convinced that he was 'the victim of a deliberate campaign to bring down his government, planned and executed by the Tory press magnates who were resolved that the election of 1966 must not be followed by another Labour victory'.[103] He suspected Cabinet colleagues of leaks, civil servants of undermining his policies, and the intelligence agencies of fabricating stories of communist influence. That summer Wilson managed to alienate the press, the senior civil service, and the agencies all at once by his clumsy handling of the 'D Notice' affair, involving an enquiry into the leakage of information by Colonel 'Sammy' Lohan, Secretary of the D-Notice Committee, to the journalist Chapman Pincher, exposing the fact that commercial cable companies routinely delivered copies of telegrams for 'security vetting' by the intelligence authorities. This episode, which Wilson himself described as 'in personal terms one of my costliest mistakes'—Ben Pimlott called it 'the prime ministerial equivalent of kicking the cat'—damaged his reputation and led to increased Labour Party as well as public suspicion of the activities of the government, while ruffling feathers all round.[104]

It was against this background that a series of press stories in October 1967 brought the unwelcome (for the government) subjects of British spies, security failures, and political conspiracy to public attention once more. During that month, both *The Observer* and *The Sunday Times* ran major series of articles about Kim Philby. The *Observer* articles were written by the paper's Middle Eastern correspondent, Patrick Seale, who had known Philby in Beirut and had taken over his reporting assignments for *The Observer* and *The Economist* when Philby defected, and journalist Maureen McConville, who with Seale had helped Philby's wife, Eleanor, write her book *Kim Philby: The Spy I Loved*.[105] The first instalment, published on 1 October 1967, announced that the articles were based on a 'special investigation in several world capitals', and gave a detailed account of Philby's career as a spy, as well as Eleanor's story.[106] Although the paper reported that the FO had offered 'no comment', the 8 October edition stated that the security services were now intensifying their probe into what *The Observer* called the 'Suspect Generation—the Communist-penetrated generation of the 1930s which produced Philby, Burgess, Maclean and the atomic spy Nunn May'.

At exactly the same time, *The Sunday Times* published what it called 'the result of a long INSIGHT investigation into the Burgess-Maclean-Philby network', based on hundreds of interviews in the UK and US.[107] The first article, also appearing on 1 October 1967, was headed 'Philby: I spied for Russia from 1933'. Like *The Observer*, *The Sunday Times* claimed its revelations were causing a 'furore' in Whitehall. Certainly, the detailed picture of treachery, and the exposure of what were presented as intelligence failures that had allowed Philby to remain undetected (or at least unprosecuted) for so long, did not make pleasant reading for ministers, the civil service, or the intelligence agencies, even if little of what appeared was unknown to them. Philby himself, in the Foreword to *My Silent War*, claimed that he had decided against publication of the memoir he had been writing since arriving in Moscow, but changed his mind as a result of the *Observer* and *Sunday Times* articles, which, as he put it, 'let some large and fairly authentic cats out of the bag'.[108]

To make matters worse, October 1967 also saw the publication of *The Zinoviev Letter: A Political Intrigue*, based on the *Sunday Times* articles of December 1966. Its chapter titles included 'The Foreign Office: Culpable or Inefficient?' and 'The Spy Who Never Made a Mistake', in which the authors alleged that it was Sidney Reilly who had convinced SIS, and thereby the FO, that the Letter was genuine, concluding that 'the principal culprit for the 1924 landslide against the MacDonald Government was its own master spy'.[109] In the FO, there was particular annoyance about the book's back cover, which reproduced what looked like a piece of FO minute paper, with an official stamp at the top. Headed 'Subject: the Zinoviev Letter', the fake document drew the urgent attention of all departments to a book in which

> the authors purport to establish a number of facts which, if true, will seriously, perhaps irreparably, diminish the reputation of the Foreign Office for sound judgement in the detection of forgery... The official view—consistent, not to say inflexible—is the same as it was 43 years ago; that the letter was genuine, and that the Office acted throughout according to the highest canons of public service.

Clifton Child, the FO Librarian, thought the mock-up 'in the worst possible taste', even as a 'piece of gentle ribbing'. Sir Denis Greenhill, Deputy Under-Secretary, felt even more strongly, minuting:

> I have read this 'smart alec' book with its strong anti-FO bias. This will be continued in the Philby book in which one of the authors is again involved. There is nothing, in my view, which we can do or indeed need to do.[110]

Reviewing the book in *The Sunday Times*, under the headline 'How dead a letter?', the historian Robert Blake found its detail convincing, stating there could now be 'no room for doubt' that the Letter had been forged by 'a youthful group of anti-Bolshevik *émigrés*'. He questioned, however, whether the Letter really made any difference to the 1924 election, and concluded that there was only one lasting consequence: 'the Labour Party's firm conviction that both the Press and the Establishment are in a state of perpetual conspiracy against it'. In 1924, Blake said, this was true, but it was 'a sign of the tenacity of collective political memory' that it should still persist in some sections of the Labour Party nearly half a century later.[111]

One more publication in October 1967 must be mentioned. An article appeared in the journal *Soviet Studies* on 'The "Zinoviev Letter" Case', written by Natalie Grant.[112] Grant was well qualified to write on the subject: born in Estonia in 1901, she had fled the USSR in the 1920s and moved to the US, later working as a translator and analyst in the US legation at Riga between 1928 and 1939. She then worked as a Sovietologist for the State Department in the 1950s, before moving in the mid-1960s to the Hoover Institution at Stanford University in California, from where she wrote her article at the time of the *Sunday Times* revelations in December 1966. Grant, pointing out that the story told by Mme Bellegarde was not new, disagreed with the portrayal of enthusiastic White Russian counter-revolutionaries circulating forgeries to hurt 'the communists'. She observed that those named, whether by Bellegarde or earlier, were, with few exceptions, later exposed as having been, or worked for, Soviet agents.

Pointing out that the Letter could only be seen in its proper perspective if examined against the political context of the period, Grant argued that, to the Bolshevik regime, the accession of the Labour government in 1924 had represented a 'serious reinforcement of the enemy camp' that must be destroyed; the MacDonald government had, she said, been brought down by the Communist Party through the Campbell case:

> The purpose of the 'Zinoviev Letter' lies precisely in the use to which the document was put. With the conspirators who launched the

document, intention to use it to defeat the Labour government in the election played a minor role ... Instead, the 'letter' served to mask the role which British communists had played in causing the defeat of Labour. In this respect, the 'letter' proved of no small benefit to the Communist Party and, on the rebound, to Moscow. It confused evaluation of Soviet political objectives. The Campbell affair receded into the background. Today, the Campbell case barely receives a few lines in accounts of the British elections while the 'Zinoviev Letter' has become a dominating issue.[113]

Grant's thesis is well argued, though in my view attributing too great powers of coordination to a Communist Party that Moscow regarded as underperforming; also, not unnaturally, her analysis of the Soviet political context is surer than that of the British. But she is, in my view, right to dismiss the idea of 'youthful White Guards' forging the Letter on their own initiative.

The articles and books appearing in the autumn of 1967, combined with ongoing investigations connected with the FLUENCY investigation into the hostile penetration of the intelligence services, indicated to the heads of the British agencies that unless an official version of the events concerning the Zinoviev Letter were prepared, the opportunity to establish the truth of the matter would be lost. Those who had been involved in or alive at the time of the episode were fast disappearing, while there was clearly a problem with the paper record. The Cabinet Secretary, Sir Burke Trend, and the FO agreed with the suggestion put forward by the Security Service Director-General, Sir Martin Furnival Jones, that Miss Milicent Bagot, the formidable expert in Soviet communism recently retired from MI5, should be given full access to the archives to prepare a report for internal purposes. She seemed the ideal candidate: knowledgeable, relentless, and with a deep understanding of the context (she is supposed to have been one of the models for Le Carré's research 'queen', Connie), Bagot had joined MI5 from Special Branch in 1931 as a secretary, gaining officer rank in 1949, and was devoted to her work; a martinet in the office, at home she was ruled by her Nanny.[114]

Bagot began work in 1968—the year that the FO's file on the Zinoviev Letter was opened at the Public Record Office. She found more material than she had expected in SIS, Security Service, and FO records, as well as in other departments and in the Public Record Office, in addition to published sources and press cuttings. She drew a blank in a few directions: none of the Service Intelligence Departments came up with any relevant records (despite the fact, she noted sternly, that they were on the distribution list of SIS documents), and the Treasury remained unwilling to disclose the proceedings of the 1928 Board of Enquiry. Having read all these Treasury records in 1998, it is hard to know what they found so sensitive, but they remained obdurate until 1992, even when the FO argued in April 1968 that, as Margaret Lambert pointed out, the fact that MacDonald had given evidence in his capacity as Foreign Secretary surely gave the Foreign Office a reason to see it.[115]

Bagot also interviewed a number of former officials from the intelligence agencies, including from the old Scotland Yard Section SS1 that had moved into MI5 in 1931. She found that some had vivid and apparently accurate recollections of the Zinoviev Letter episode, while others had either forgotten or—like Desmond Morton, she thought[116]—claimed to have done so. Inevitably, those involved at the time sought to present their own role in a positive light, and to gloss over things that might have gone wrong; and even if they did remember the names of those who had provided intelligence as agents in the 1920s, they remained unwilling to give them. Bagot was, of course, an intelligence officer herself and understood how things worked; but the end result was that the personal interviews tended to raise more questions than they answered. The bulk of her research, particularly on the contemporary context of Bolshevik and anti-Bolshevik activities, was done in the archives.

The main points contained in Milicent Bagot's report and its conclusions were set out in the FCO memorandum published in 1999 and have been referred to again in this book, so require only a brief summary here. There were, as she soon discovered, two main problems to be tackled: whether the Letter was genuine, and, if it were a forgery, whether the officials who circulated and acted on it knew it to be a forgery and used it deliberately for a political or personal motive. On the first point, she concluded that despite exhaustive trawling through the files, it was impossible to make a firm assessment of the Letter's authenticity, though it was very unlikely to have been sent by Zinoviev for the instruction of the CPGB. The story that an official working in the Comintern, with access to Zinoviev's secret files, made a copy and arranged for it to reach the SIS station in Riga through an agent (FR3/K, whose identity was never confirmed) seemed, she thought, the least probable answer to the mystery. However, nearly all alternative accounts originated with White Russians claiming to be in contact with networks of informants in the USSR; and the most significant of these networks, Bagot pointed out, was the Monarchist Organization of Central Russia known as 'The Trust', which had been heavily penetrated by the OGPU.[117]

While concluding that the Letter was almost certainly a fake, Bagot conceded that it was by no means clear who had inspired the forgery, though the evidence pointed to the involvement of White Russians, Poles, and Germans. In her view, the assertion by the communist MP Shapurji Saklatvala, during the parliamentary debate of 19 March 1928, that the signature of the draft Anglo-Soviet treaties in the summer of 1924 was followed by a flurry of communications between the Baltic States and Berlin, with the aim of devising 'ways and means...either to frighten [MacDonald] out of his position, or to strengthen his hands and enable him to shake off his extremists', may well have been correct.[118]

As far as the official handling of the Letter was concerned, Bagot was unable to find any definite proof that those who had circulated and acted on it knew or believed it to have been forged at the time. Some officials may have known more about the Letter than they admitted; but there was no proof that any of them commissioned it or had anything to do with its forgery, nor that there was any sort of institutional conspiracy. SIS's insistence on the Letter's authenticity may, Bagot thought, have

> sprung partly from obstinacy and partly from a sense of insecurity as they felt under fire from such prominent Socialists as Parmoor, Trevelyan and Wedgewood, who were bent on the Service's destruction...Nevertheless, the fact that the agent's reports [from FR3/K in Riga] continued to be circulated until at least the spring of 1931 give the impression that SIS genuinely believed in his existence and reliability. On the other hand, Morton's reaction to criticism on several occasions was merely irritation, not the objective investigation of fresh leads.[119]

Bagot found, as I do, the idea of an institutionalized campaign to discredit both the Bolsheviks and the Labour government in 1924 not only unsubstantiated by the documentation, but inherently unlikely.[120]

Before the report was submitted, there had been another public 'flurry' regarding the Letter. In the January 1970 edition of the *Harvard Library Bulletin*, Dr William E. Butler wrote about the discovery of six photonegative glass plates in the Harvard Law School Library, four of which contained a Russian text of the Zinoviev Letter. The negatives were believed to have been acquired in about 1928–9 by a scholar who bought Russian materials in Europe on behalf of the Harvard Law School, and were forgotten until Dr Butler discovered them in about 1968. On each plate, he said, was 'reproduced a single page of 42-line white paper containing Russian script in a very fine hand'.[121]

Butler translated the Russian, and much of his article is concerned with a comparison of the Harvard and FO texts. He concluded that the Russian text in Harvard Law School Library served as the basis for the English text published by the *Daily Mail* on 25 October 1924; that the Harvard plates were 'probably the source of the photographic copies of the Zinov'ev Letter released by unknown persons to Western intelligence services'; and that the Harvard text 'may very well be the original since there is no evidence whatever that the Zinov'ev Letter was actually despatched'. Butler added, in support of his thesis, that the Harvard text was identical to the Russian text sent to Washington by the US Consul in Paris in November 1924 (a copy of which had reached SIS by a circuitous route),[122] except that the Paris text was reproduced from a photograph. Natalie Grant had told Butler about the existence of the Russian text of the Letter in the US National Archives, though she did not mention it in her 1967 article.[123]

Butler did not, of course, know how the FO had got hold of their text of the Letter, nor about the Russian text supplied to SIS from Riga in December 1924. But it was not Dr Butler's scholarly textual analysis that hit the headlines. In February 1970 *The Sunday Times* reproduced a portion of the Harvard text of the Letter, and invited readers to 'help in a historical mystery', if they recognized the hand-writing. The historian Michael Kettle wrote in, sending a specimen of Sidney Reilly's handwriting from a book published in 1931 by Reilly's wife, Pepita, in which she edited her late husband's reminiscences.[124] An expert found them to be by the same hand, though conceding that comparison was difficult when the texts were in languages with different alphabets. Reilly's biographer Andrew Cook is by no means convinced,[125] and even if Reilly copied the Paris text that does not mean he forged it, or had a hand in its exploitation (Bagot discounted Reilly's involvement, although she did not mention the Harvard dis-covery in her report). But the whole thing made for a very good press story, and Kettle wrote to Harold Wilson on 19 February 1970, send-ing a copy of his letter to *The Sunday Times*, and saying the mystery could now be solved; he received a polite acknowledgement, stating that all the relevant documents were available in official archives.[126]

Milicent Bagot submitted her report in August 1970 (by which time the Labour government had been defeated unexpectedly in the general election of 18 June, and Edward Heath was Prime Minister). Although she was undoubtedly frustrated by her inability to answer all the questions about the Letter, despite unprecedented access to the evidence, she was probably not surprised. Her long career in intelligence would have taught her that 'truth' in such matters is always elusive. A decade of revelations, contradictory evidence, speculation, and close study by an insider had not been wasted, however. They had proved that the Zinoviev Letter controversy was not dead, but could be awakened easily. Nor, it appeared, was it true that there was nothing further to learn about the affair, even more than forty years later. The stage had been set for the next act in a mystery that would run for even longer than *The Mousetrap.*

6

New Labour, New Investigation, 1998–1999

'Being open with the British public is a British national interest.'[1]

Throughout my career in the FCO, certain historical mysteries and controversies have recurred at intervals when contemporary events led to renewed calls for an investigation. Some of these were, in the end, laid (more or less) to rest: for example, the Casement diaries, the Katyn massacre, and the fate of the Romanovs.[2] Others, like the Zinoviev Letter, remained unresolved. So when Labour Foreign Secretary Robin Cook commissioned a new investigation into the Letter early in 1998, it was not an unfamiliar subject. But it was to be the first time that we had unrestricted access to all the sources. The Foreign Secretary made it clear he wanted the report to be based on all available evidence, wherever it might be found and whatever it might reveal, and that when completed it would be presented to Parliament and published in full.

Robin Cook was interested in history, and understood that past controversies could distort current policy and the public perception of it. As Chief Historian, I was called into the FCO with other officials over the weekend immediately after the general election on 1 May 1997, to be told by the Foreign Secretary that we must organize an international conference in London later that year on 'Nazi Gold', the

Figure 15. Robin Cook, Foreign Secretary 1997–2001

name for a range of controversial issues to do with the wartime handling of property expropriated from governments and individuals.[3] His instinct was to investigate, get the story out, and deal with the fallout sensibly. When the Zinoviev Letter issue came up in 1998, he took the same approach (even though at first he clearly thought it was ancient history).

The Foreign Secretary's brief was clear: but the fact that the investigation and the publication of the Zinoviev report proceeded smoothly, with the full cooperation of all departments and indeed other governments, owed much to developments in government policy, in the status of the intelligence agencies, and in international relations during the previous twenty years. While the Letter was not prominent in political discourse during this period (though Labour politicians tended to bring it up at times of stress), it had a symbolic importance: in a growing debate in Britain about the need for greater 'openness', whether in government records policy, or in relation to the intelligence agencies whose peacetime existence it became increasingly awkward for ministers to deny; or in the context of the seismic shift in the international scene caused by the fall of the Berlin Wall and the collapse of the Soviet Union. It was also a period of groundbreaking intelligence scholarship, in which two of my distinguished colleagues and old friends, Professor Christopher Andrew, the foremost British intelligence historian, and Peter Hennessy, now Lord Hennessy of

Nympsfield and incomparable authority on the 'hidden wiring of the constitution and the power of the machinery of government in Britain', played an important role.

In Search of the Missing Dimension, 1975–1987

The revelations of the 1960s opened Pandora's box as far as the Zinoviev Letter was concerned.[4] During the 1970s there was a rash of publications on the subject: in scholarly journals, including an article by Sir Eyre Crowe's daughter;[5] in books such as Gabriel Gorodetsky's *The Precarious Truce*, published in 1977; and in correspondence in the press. Amongst the letters printed was one from R. Page Arnot and Andrew Rothstein, who had been members of the Central Committee of the CPGB in 1924 and insisted that at no time had the Letter been seen or discussed by the Committee; and from Robert Woollcombe, whose father Major Malcolm Woollcombe had told him how, when summoned in 1924 to brief the Prime Minister on the authenticity of the Letter, he had 'remained out of sight in an adjoining room with a communicating door' while the Prime Minister's questions and Woollcombe's answers were relayed by Sir Eyre Crowe, standing in the doorway. His father, said Woollcombe, had always believed the Letter to be genuine.[6]

The most comprehensive and provocative contributions to the debate, however, were from Cambridge historian Christopher Andrew, who had made a detailed study of records from a range of sources, uncovering material relating to the activities of the British intelligence community, including the Government Code and Cypher School and Indian Political Intelligence. This research enabled him to demonstrate that it was possible to glean a great deal of information from existing archives, even if the intelligence agencies (whose existence was still supposedly secret) kept their records closed and government departments remained determinedly tight-lipped. In addition to a long article in *The Historical Journal*,[7] Andrew suggested in *The Times Higher Education Supplement* on 14 October 1977, under the headline 'Can the truth about the Zinoviev letter ever be written?', that government restrictions on accessibility to documents about the intelligence services constrained historians to writing 'sanitised' histories of foreign policy.

In relation to the Zinoviev Letter, Andrew argued that the balance of evidence made authenticity more probable than forgery, since forgery presumed 'an improbable degree of gullibility on the part of the Foreign Office in allowing itself to be deceived' and an 'improbable degree of wickedness by the Secret Service':

> If the Zinoviev letter was not genuine, it is difficult to escape the conclusion that the intelligence services engaged in a prolonged and remarkable criminal conspiracy: a conspiracy first to disseminate a forged document and then to authenticate that forgery by a diverse series of further forgeries. Furthermore, that criminal conspiracy (if conspiracy there was) deceived both the incoming Conservative cabinet and all the senior officials of the Foreign and Cabinet Offices. That is not a probable hypothesis.[8]

Later, Andrew would revise his views on authenticity as more evidence emerged. At the time, however, his arguments on the Letter provoked a good deal of comment, including from the veteran historian of the Soviet Union, E. H. Carr, who took the view that while the story of the forgery published in 1967 by the *Sunday Times* 'Insight' team was 'by no means water-tight', it had 'less holes than any of the official accounts'.[9]

But Andrew, who spearheaded the movement to include the 'missing dimension' of intelligence in the writing of history and criticized what he regarded as the excessive secrecy insisted on by Whitehall in regard to intelligence-related matters, was using the Zinoviev Letter to illustrate a far broader point. Writing at a time when the Cold War was at its height and the intelligence services were 'more vital now than they have ever been before in peacetime', he argued that a refusal to admit the existence of the agencies, and the removal of all references to them and their activities from departmental records, led to a distortion of history. All attempts to get to the bottom of the Zinoviev Letter affair, for example, had been 'seriously impeded by the incomplete and bowdlerized nature of the Public Record Office files'.[10]

Christopher Andrew's efforts were applauded and encouraged by Peter Hennessy, then a journalist, who charted in regular articles in *The Times* during this period the gradual development of a ground-swell of opinion, ministerial and official as well as academic, in favour of greater openness in government records policy generally and on intelligence matters in particular. As Hennessy pointed out in November 1977, the unearthing of documents such as a Cabinet memorandum on Secret Service operations after the First World War (found by Andrew in the Lloyd George papers in the House of Lords Records Office) made it increasingly embarrassing for ministers to 'continue the official fiction that no clandestine espionage agencies exist in peacetime'.[11] At the same time, he reported that Conservative MP Michael Latham intended to press Prime Minister James Callaghan about the practice of withholding documents about the agencies, prompted by the publication of David Irving's *Hitler's War*, which Latham considered contained unjustified allegations about a German peace initiative in 1939 that could not be rebutted as the files were closed.[12]

In February 1978, Hennessy published two articles under the general heading 'Growth of the Secret Service'. In the first, 'Grand illusion about MI6 that confused the enemy', he wrote of the 'useful myth' that had persuaded the Germans during the Second World War that it was MI6's 'ubiquitous and omniscient agents' rather than cryptographers that threatened their secret codes, thereby ensuring that the Germans never appreciated the extent of British codebreaking success. In the second, 'Veil of privacy is drawn over modern spies' successes and failures', he wrote that the present 'C' or Chief of the Secret Intelligence Service (Sir Maurice Oldfield, though Hennessy could not name him) was himself a historian, and had little to fear from MPs or fellow historians as there was no Parliamentary Select Committee on intelligence, and that it was very unlikely that the 'weeders' reviewing post-war departmental records would let any intelligence secrets slip through. Hennessy concluded:

> Short of a political calamity in the form of the mythical British Watergate which preoccupies the more perfervid imaginations in Fleet Street, the present day successors of 'Blinker' Hall and Mansfield Cumming are free to experience their successes and failures in almost complete privacy from public gaze, scrutinized only by their ministerial overseers and the Whitehall accounting officers who fillet their budgets.[13]

In the 1970s, those of us working in the FO's Historical Section were warned to be wary of journalists like Peter Hennessy, and forbidden to talk to them without permission. It is easy to see why he ruffled official feathers at the time: indeed, in 1979 the Cabinet Secretary, Sir John Hunt, suggested that 'consideration would have to be given to instructing Departments to cease to have any dealings with Mr Hennessy'. Looking back more than thirty years later, Hennessy confessed to mixed feelings at 'all the distraction that one's pieces caused people who had quite enough to worry about without such pinpricks', particularly 'Jim Callaghan and his irritation at my open government crusade in the late 1970s'.[14] But even though he exasperated ministers and officials alike, Hennessy's articles were very much in tune with the times. It was during this decade that the first books were published disclosing Britain's wartime secrets: 1974 saw the appearance of *The Ultra Secret* by F. W. Winterbotham, former chief of SIS's Air Section, revealing for the first time codebreaking operations at Bletchley Park and the cracking of the German Enigma code; in 1977, Professor R. V. Jones, former scientific adviser to SIS and Assistant Director of Intelligence at the Air Ministry, published his account of wartime scientific intelligence operations in *Most Secret War*; and in 1979 the first volume was published of the groundbreaking official history, *British Intelligence in the Second World War*.[15] The decision to allow these books to be published was taken deliberately after much discussion by ministers, officials, and the intelligence agencies, and they played their part in lifting the veil of official secrecy. At the same time, however, the

Labour government's relations with the intelligence community were by no means untroubled.

Although the Zinoviev Letter does not seem to have come up during the general election campaign leading to a Labour victory on 28 February 1974, the party did face attacks from right-wing interests attempting to damage Labour's prospects by alleging communist influence. Sir Richard Powell, Director General of the Institute of Directors, claimed that Britain owed its industrial troubles to 'Communists, Wilson and Women' (Harold Wilson encouraged communists, and women voted socialists into power, apparently). Chapman Pincher (who had enraged Wilson during the 1964–70 government by publishing 'leaks') wrote in the *Daily Express* that a 'formidable vigilante group' had been organized by 'former Service chiefs, senior ex-members of the Secret Service and MI5 and leading business men' in order to 'protect the nation against a Communist takeover'.[16] Such stories encouraged Wilson in his 'growing conviction that he was the victim of a malign plot to destroy his reputation and bring down his government',[17] particularly since Labour's victory in both the February and October elections in 1974 was very narrow.

Wilson's suspicions about the intelligence community were increased when in May 1974 Chapman Pincher alleged in the *Daily Express* that the security and intelligence authorities had 'serious doubts' about certain junior Labour ministers, and were planning to restrict their access to secret information. Though Wilson rebutted the story angrily in the House of Commons, Pincher insisted that the agency chiefs could 'easily restrict the flow of Intelligence without the Prime Minister's agreement' and had already been doing so. *Time Out*, however, took the view that since it was well known that Wilson had run checks on ministers in the 1964–70 government, it was 'rash' to suppose that the Security Service would operate against Labour MPs without his knowledge. Although the Cabinet Secretary assured the Prime Minister these allegations were untrue, such stories inflamed Wilson's already heightened sensitivities. He believed they originated with the Security Service, though the source may well have been former Deputy SIS Chief George Young, who had decidedly right-wing views and had apparently had lunch with Pincher on the day before the first article appeared.[18]

Though the Wilson government continued to work well on a day-to-day basis with the intelligence authorities, these incidents, allied to his perception that he was under attack from foreign intelligence organizations (he suspected particularly the CIA and the South African Secret Service, BOSS), blighted the Prime Minister's relationship both with the agencies and with the press until his resignation in 1976.[19] Matters were not improved by the fact that Wilson was not told until 1975 of the FLUENCY investigations that had taken place during the 1960s—during his own premiership—into the former Security Service Director General, Sir Roger Hollis, and other MI5 officers.[20] Hollis had been cleared in 1971, and most other leads discounted, although some conspiracy theorists, like MI5's Peter Wright and a few in SIS, remained unconvinced. In 1975, an independent assessor was appointed to oversee all investigations of alleged Soviet penetration of the agencies.[21]

But the fact that the Prime Minister had not been told about MI5's internal molehunt at the time was bound to have a negative effect. During his second premiership Wilson became increasingly distrustful of all except his closest advisers, and worried that a campaign was under way to undermine him. To some, like CIA Director George H. W. Bush, he seemed 'mad', but biographer Philip Ziegler judged he was not mad but living 'on the fringes of a Kafkaesque world where madness was endemic'. Though acknowledging the assurances given by officials that Wilson's suspicions were groundless, Ziegler judged nevertheless 'that something nasty was going on seems probable if not certain'.[22] In hindsight, Wilson's increasing paranoia may have been due to the beginnings of the dementia that would later beset him.

Wilson's successor as Labour Prime Minister, James Callaghan, was far more concerned with the infiltration of the Labour Party by communists and by what Francis Beckett calls 'Labour's increasingly sharp-toothed left wing', including Trotskyist groups such as the

Workers' Revolutionary Party and the faction known as Militant Tendency, than with the possibility that the security and intelligence authorities might hold a file on one of his ministers. Callaghan expressed public confidence in the agencies, and relied on them heavily, as did his Home Secretary, Merlyn Rees, working closely with the Security Service on industrial subversion, while attacking any Conservative attempts to smear Labour by drawing attention to left-wing infiltration of the trade unions or alleging communist influence over policy. In June 1978, following a leak in *The Economist* of draft proposals by a conservative policy group that included the formation of a mobile police squad to counter aggressive picketing, Rees responded by comparing 'innuendoes about Marxism which are designed to cast doubts on the patriotism of Labour Party members' with the Zinoviev Letter and Churchill's 'Gestapo' speech in 1945.[23]

During the Callaghan government, relations between the Labour Party and the trade unions came 'dramatically and disastrously unstuck',[24] and by early 1979, after the 'Winter of Discontent', industrial strife and deep divisions in the party made defeat in the election of 3 May 1979 inevitable. Nevertheless, the Zinoviev Letter popped up yet again in the few days just before the election, as it had on so many similar occasions. On 1 May Michael Heseltine, Conservative spokesman on the environment, said on the BBC's *Nationwide* programme that Labour's Deputy Leader, Michael Foot, should recognize that the party was being infiltrated by left-wing extremists. Foot replied that this was exactly the sort of accusation that was always made against Labour in elections, going back to the Zinoviev Letter affair in 1924.[25] But when William Whitelaw, the Conservative Deputy Leader, warned voters that 'the modern Labour Party is a completely different party from that of Attlee and Gaitskell', he was undoubtedly expressing the view of a number of Labour as well as Conservative politicians.[26] Labour was to remain out of office for another eighteen years, and for much of the period was too preoccupied with internal struggles, and the impact of the policies pursued by successive Thatcher governments, to pay much attention to past scandals. Nevertheless, when Tony Benn, the former Labour minister on the left wing of the party, was challenged on television early in 1980 about the suppression by Labour's National Executive Committee of a report by Reg Underhill on Militant Tendency, he dismissed the report as a forgery like the Zinoviev Letter: 'As far as I can make out it came in plain envelopes from the Intelligence Service.'[27]

During the Thatcher years, Labour was in such a state of internal division that the Conservatives had no need to resort to political stratagems in the elections of 1983 or 1987. The Zinoviev Letter did, however, come up just before the election in February 1992—an indication, perhaps, that the Conservatives, now led by John Major, were less confident of victory than before. *The Observer* reported in February 1992 that a spate of mysterious thefts from Labour MPs' offices (dubbed 'Commonsgate' by Labour MP Peter Hain) had led Labour leaders to believe that Rupert Murdoch's News International was waging a smear campaign to ensure a Conservative victory. For example, *The Sunday Times* published an article on 'Kinnock and the Kremlin', allegedly reporting private conversations between Labour leader Neil Kinnock and Russian diplomats; Labour MP Jack Cunningham (who had computer disks stolen from his office) described this story as having 'as much credibility as the Zinoviev Letter and that other great *Sunday Times* exclusive, the Hitler Diaries'.[28]

According to the official history of MI5, Margaret Thatcher, who served as Conservative Prime Minister from 1979 to 1990, took a greater interest in the intelligence community than any prime minister since Winston Churchill. She relied on the Security Service for intelligence on industrial subversion, and was appreciative of the information she received from both SIS and GCHQ. Overseas intelligence was particularly important at a period when the Cold War was, finally, beginning to enter a thaw. In addition, valuable information was received in the early 1980s from Oleg Gordievsky, the Soviet double agent posted by the KGB to London in 1982, and exfiltrated from the Soviet Union by SIS in 1985 when he came under suspicion.[29] (Gordievsky reported that it was 'generally believed within the KGB that the "Zinoviev Letter" of 1924 was a forgery of the British special services intended as an Active Measure to damage the prospects of the Labour government at the polls'. He himself thought the Letter 'consistent with Soviet policy of the day', and did not think it likely 'that it was a forgery by anti-Soviet Russians in exile'.[30])

After the expulsion by the Heath government of 105 Soviet intelligence officers in 1971 (Operation FOOT), the KGB had struggled to re-establish its human intelligence networks in Western Europe and Britain, while at the same time falling behind the West technologically.[31] Thatcher was very interested in what Gordievsky had to say about these developments, about the KGB's wish to discredit her politically, and about the Soviet government's genuine fear that the West might launch a pre-emptive nuclear strike, an anxiety that peaked in late 1983 during the NATO exercise codenamed Able Archer.[32] Gordievsky also identified Mikhail Gorbachev as a key figure even before he became Soviet General Secretary in 1985, and his intelligence informed the development of Thatcher's policies in the crucial period of *glasnost* (openness) and *perestroika* (restructuring) leading up to the collapse of the Soviet Union.[33]

Thatcher took secrecy seriously, repeating in the House of Commons on numerous occasions that she intended to adhere to the rule of not commenting on security matters. Despite this, her government found itself forced again and again to discuss intelligence matters in public, in a way that made it increasingly difficult to deny the peacetime role of the agencies: from the exposure of Anthony Blunt as the 'Fourth Man' in November 1979, through the Franks enquiry into the Falklands War, and the unmasking of Soviet spies like former GCHQ employee Geoffrey Prime in 1982 and MI5's Michael Bettaney in 1983, to the strident accusations of Soviet penetration and political perfidy peddled by Chapman Pincher and by former MI5 officer Peter Wright.[34] Wright's unreliable memoirs, *Spycatcher*, produced a particularly uncomfortable episode when the Cabinet Secretary, Sir Robert Armstrong, was sent to Australia as a witness in a case brought by the British government in an attempt to suppress publication. Wright was defended by Malcolm Turnbull (who, as I write, is Australian Prime Minister), who tied Armstrong in verbal knots over his refusal to admit the existence of SIS despite acknowledging that Sir Dick White had been head of it, leading the Cabinet Secretary to use the phrase 'economical with the truth'.[35] At the same time, a series of books appeared, by Pincher, Anthony Cavendish, and Nigel West (Rupert Allason) among others, making a series of claims regarding the activities of the intelligence agencies that could not be rebutted publicly without breaching the normal rules of government secrecy.

In addition to his allegations of Soviet 'moles' in MI5, Peter Wright insisted that the Security Service had been investigating Harold Wilson as a security risk: 'up to 30 senior MI5 officers', The Guardian reported, had hatched a plan to leak details of intelligence on senior Labour figures, in what Wright called a carbon copy of the Zinoviev Letter affair.[36] However wild some of these allegations might be, it was impossible for the government to disprove them or prevent them from poisoning any public discussion of the role of intelligence. As the Labour MP Dale Campbell-Savours complained in December 1986 in the House of Commons, when asking the government to set up a judicial enquiry into the alleged attempts by officers of the security services to subvert Wilson's government,

> What has happened to the old values, or was I brought up to believe in a myth?...It is the biggest political scandal of this century. It is a story of collusion between the British Right and the security services. It surpasses in importance the Zinoviev Letter which effectively sealed the fate of the Labour Government in the 1920s.[37]

These developments confirmed the trend towards the desirability, and indeed inevitability, of a more open approach towards the work of Britain's intelligence community, and towards government records policy: the Wilson Committee on Public Records, which reported in March 1981, and the ensuing Modern Public Records White Paper in 1982 paved the way for a more rigorous and accountable system for holding information back, as well as releasing it.[38] Meanwhile, in addition to the more sensational literature, serious intelligence historians were publishing books that showed how much information was already available to those willing to carry out detailed research and look in unlikely places when the official files remained closed: David Stafford, in 1980, published an authoritative account of the work of the Special Operations Executive (SOE); Wesley Wark published in 1985 a ground-breaking study on British intelligence and Nazi Germany in the 1930s, including for the first time details of the Industrial Intelligence Centre, set up originally within SIS to collect intelligence on hostile powers' economic preparations for war; while in the same year, Christopher Andrew's comprehensive history of the British intelligence community, *Secret Service*, drawing on years of research, was an immediate bestseller.[39] All referred to the work of intelligence agencies whose existence the government did not, as yet, acknowledge openly.

Storks and gooseberry bushes, 1985–1996

In 1991, Christopher Andrew quoted the distinguished historian Professor Michael Howard, author of one of the volumes in the official history of British Intelligence in the Second World War, on the traditional view of British intelligence:

> In Britain the activities of the intelligence and security services have always been regarded in much the same light as intra-marital sex. Everyone knows that it goes on and is quite content that it should, but to speak, write or ask questions about it is regarded as exceedingly bad form. So far as official government policy is concerned, the British security and intelligence services, MI5 and MI6, do not exist. Enemy agents are found under gooseberry bushes and intelligence is brought by the storks. Government records bearing on intelligence activities are either industri-ously 'weeded' or kept indefinitely closed.[40]

Yet even as he wrote this, official arguments in favour of greater trans-parency in relation to security and intelligence matters were already winning the day. The Interception of Communications Act, providing for a commissioner to monitor warrants for telephone tapping and a tribunal to investigate complaints, was passed in 1985 after the European Court of Human Rights upheld a complaint by a British businessman about phone tapping.[41] This piece of legislation set the model, and the next decade would see all the intelligence agencies placed on a statutory basis and subject to the oversight of a cross-party Intelligence and Security Committee (ISC). These developments, together with the election of a Labour government in May 1997, were to create the climate in which a new investigation into the Zinoviev Letter would be not only possible, but welcome.

The Security Service Bill came first: MI5's Director General, Sir Anthony Duff, had become convinced that legislation was needed to counter the damage done by Peter Wright and others, and the perception, particularly in the Labour Party, that the Service had become 'a political tool of the right'.[42] By 1988 Thatcher and her Home Secretary, Douglas Hurd, had come round to the argument, though when the Bill was introduced Labour were deeply suspicious of its provisions, arguing that it did not offer sufficient assurances about the political neutrality of the Security Service, and that it gave too much power to what the Labour MP Eric Heffer called 'one of the most authoritarian Governments that I remember'. Not surprisingly, both the Zinoviev Letter and the *Spycatcher* affair were brought into the argument.

Douglas Hurd introduced the Second Reading of the Security Service Bill on 15 December 1988, announcing that a month ago 'no one suspected that we are about to launch a substantial reform of this kind'. He gave a brief history of the Service, slipping in a sly dig at his Labour opponents who, he said, fed on works of fiction paraded as if they were statements of fact: 'I have nothing against the thriller as an art form, but those who unwittingly get their ideas of the Security Service from Sapper, Le Carré or Deighton will not bring much understanding to the Bill.' National security, said Hurd, could only refer to 'matters relating to the survival or well-being of the nation as a whole, and not to party-political, sectional or lesser interests'.

He also confirmed that under the new legislation it would be the duty of the Director General to ensure that the Security Service did not take any action to further the interests of any political party.[43]

Labour MPs were not convinced. Harry Cohen, Labour MP for Leyton and Wanstead, announced that the only aspect of the Bill that he welcomed was the fact that it put the Security Service on a statutory footing. His contribution to the debate illustrates both the continuing potency of the Zinoviev Letter and the reasons for its enduring resonance in the Labour Party. Cohen complained that when the Home Secretary had given his potted history of the Security Service,

> he missed out a key element in the early stages of MI5—that of the Zinoviev letter, which involved MI5 interfering in the politics of the country. It was successful in bringing down a Labour Government. From that, we move on directly to the 'Spycatcher' affair, which is the reason for the Bill. Central to the 'Spycatcher' affair was the plot to subvert the Labour government of Harold Wilson...We know that, if the Service decided to run down a party, it would be biased against the Labour Party and the trade union movement, because of the class nature of the Security Service personnel. On the one hand, there are those on the extreme Right, such as Peter Wright, who are in the service because they are cold warriors and are anti-Socialists, or there are the Oxford-Cambridge set, who we know are the ideal models to act as spies for foreign countries. Neither of those groups had its roots in the working class or in ordinary people, so there is a bias straight away against the trade union and labour movement.[44]

Douglas Hurd dismissed such arguments as old-fashioned, but they were guaranteed to strike a chord with Labour Members and with the wider party—and not for the last time. The Bill passed into law in April 1989, 'elegantly side-stepping the contentious issue of the previous legal basis for the Service's operations by the use of the brilliantly equivocal formula "There shall continue to be a Security Service"'.[45]

The Security Service Act 1989 formed the model for the Intelligence Services Act of 1994 (ISA), which placed both SIS and GCHQ on a statutory footing, and provided the legal basis for issuing warrants and authorizations for all three agencies to carry out their functions. Like the Security Service Act, the ISA required the agencies to be politically neutral, and it established an Intelligence and Security Committee to provide parliamentary oversight for all three, examining their expenditure, administration, and policy.[46] Again, it proved impossible for Labour politicians to debate a piece of intelligence legislation without referring to the Zinoviev Letter. This time it was former Home Secretary Merlyn Rees—now Baron Merlyn-Rees—who brought it up when the Intelligence Services Bill came before the Lords in December 1993.

In contrast to the Commons, there was a general welcome in the Upper House for the Bill when it was introduced on 9 December 1993 by the Lord Chancellor, Lord Mackay. The debate was enlivened by a typically mellifluous contribution from Roy Jenkins, now Lord Jenkins of Hillhead, who reflected that the country was currently in 'calmer waters' as regards the reputation of the agencies, after the scandals of the 1980s. Perhaps, he mused, the fact that Stella Rimington was now Director General of the Security Service had something to do with it:

> There is, somehow, something distinctly if not wholly rationally reassuring about the thought of a woman being in charge of a security service. One feels that she may not go along with some of the wilder pieces of phantasmagoria, which has sometimes engaged her male colleagues. In the same way, the noble Baroness, Lady Park, whether in this House or on television, gives a patina of calm responsibility to all her previously brave and occasionally bizarre exploits on behalf of MI6.[47]

(Baroness Park, formerly a senior SIS officer, had appeared on BBC's *Panorama* programme in 1993 to talk—with permission—about her work.[48])

Lord Merlyn-Rees, however, was less complimentary about the work of the Security Service, despite welcoming the Bill. As Northern Ireland Secretary from 1974 to 1976 he had worked closely with the Service on its responsibilities in the province, and contrasted its performance and attitudes there favourably with what he called the 'canteen MI5 culture' he had observed on the mainland when Home Secretary. He also argued that the government should consider bringing the defence intelligence authorities within the scope of the Bill:

> In 1945 Sir Findlater Stewart recommended to Mr Attlee that the Minister of Defence should be responsible for the security services. I read some-where that that appealed to Mr Attlee because of his attitude regarding the nature of the security of the realm; that it should be from defence. In any event, he had lived through the Zinoviev issue in the 1920s. The nature of that always made him extremely angry. It did not happen. But at least Sir Findlater Stewart put that forward.[49]

The Intelligence Services Act finally became law in November 1994. Its provisions gave both SIS and GCHQ a role in fighting serious crime, and in 1996 the Security Service Act was amended to add a similar function for MI5, in addition to its existing responsibilities for national security and threats to the UK's economic well-being. The Second Reading of the Security Service Bill, on 10 January 1996, led to renewed Labour accusations of the political bias of the agencies, particularly from Ken Livingstone, who said he opposed the Bill because 'treason against Labour Governments has been endemic in MI5 throughout its history'. Livingstone took the opportunity to deliver a long historical survey of MI5's supposed interference in politics (leading the Deputy Speaker to intervene more than once asking him to relate his remarks more closely to the Bill). He began, naturally, with the Zinoviev Letter, and though his account was somewhat garbled it is worth quoting, since it undoubtedly reflected a more general confusion about what actually happened in 1924:

> We all know about the Zinoviev Letter, which led to the downfall of the first Labour Government in 1924. It is now believed to have been pro-duced by two Russian émigrés who were working in Berlin. They passed the forgery to an MI5 officer, Donald im Thurn. Once in the hands of MI5, senior officials realised that its details of an alleged communist plot would be a devastating blow to the Labour Government in the closing days of the election campaign. MI5 leaked the letter to a Tory Member of

Parliament and former intelligence officer, Sir Reginald Hall. It also leaked it to Tory Central Office and the *Daily Mail*, which obligingly ran it on its front page.[50]

(It is interesting to note that once it became possible to talk about the intelligence agencies publicly, Labour politicians referring to the Letter were almost unanimous in attributing responsibility to MI5. Until the FCO report was published in 1999, the part played in the episode by SIS was not known.)

The passage into law of the Security Service Act in July 1996 completed the series of intelligence legislation. Politicians, commentators, academics, and officials could now refer freely to the existence and work of the agencies—in general, though not in specifics—and name their heads openly. In the Foreign Office, we historians were delighted, as it meant that we could include intelligence-related material in our publications more easily, and that records containing mentions of the agencies would no longer be routinely redacted or retained. In a new volume of *Documents on British Policy Overseas* published in 1997 on *Britain and the Soviet Union 1968–72*, for example, documents were printed for the first time from the Permanent Under-Secretary's Department, the liaison department between the FO and the intelligence agencies, whose records are retained under the Lord Chancellor's exemption known as the 'blanket'.[51] These documents revealed for the first time the details of policy formulation leading to Operation FOOT, the expulsion of Soviet intelligence officers in 1971, as well as arrangements made in 1969 to secure the freedom of Gerald Brooke, held in a Soviet prison, in return for the premature release of the Soviet spies Peter and Helen Kroger.[52]

It was, in many ways, the beginning of a new regime: just as it was hoped that the end of the Cold War had made a new beginning in international affairs. For the legislation avowing the intelligence agencies introduced between 1985 and 1996 had as its backdrop a period of momentous change in international affairs. The Berlin Wall had come down, Germany was reunified, the Soviet Union dissolved, and the countries of Eastern Europe were emerging as independent nations after nearly forty years. These developments inevitably had a profound effect on the intelligence organizations operating in what had for so long been thought of as 'the West' and 'the East'.

In Britain, as in other Western countries, there was initially a presumption that there would be a 'peace dividend' (the same misapprehension that had been entertained after the two World Wars). Surely, in a newly harmonious and less polarized polarized international environment, there would be a decreased need for secret intelligence and therefore for large, well-resourced agencies? That sentiment, inspired partly by a desire to cut costs, proved aspirational rather than realistic. It soon became clear that the requirement for secret intelligence had not diminished but evolved, and the laws passed between 1989 and 1996 reflected a change in emphasis rather than a lessening of activity.

Similar adjustments were taking place in the former Soviet Union. As Soviet intelligence expert Jonathan Haslam describes it, after years of 'shadowboxing a massive, imaginary opponent', the Russian intelligence machinery now had to adapt to a situation in which the ideological element of its work had been removed, and find a new role in a changed world. Boris Yeltsin, who had become the first President of the Russian Federation in 1991, divided the KGB into three: the FSB, responsible for domestic intelligence, SVR (foreign intelligence), and FAPSI (communications intelligence). The GRU retained its role as policeman of the 'near abroad', a role that would assume even greater importance at the beginning of the twenty-first century. Although initially economic necessity forced some reduction in sources and manpower, and changes of emphasis, Russia, too, found it needed its agencies, and 'by the mid-1990s cutbacks were being reversed'.[53]

The KGB and its successors also adopted a new strategy in the 1990s of sponsoring and facilitating publications about their work, partly in response to a series of books appearing in Britain. In particular, there had been annoyance in Moscow at the appearance of a history of the KGB published by Christopher Andrew and Oleg Gordievsky in 1990, followed in 1991 and 1992 by two volumes of 'top secret files' on KGB foreign operations.[54] While responding with active measures against both the book and its authors, the KGB Chairman issued an order in September 1990 authorizing the exploitation of KGB archives to project a positive image of the organization. This led to a series of joint projects with Western writers, including four books supposedly based on material received from Philby and held in Moscow.[55] David Murphy, formerly chief of the CIA's Berlin Operations base, and George Bailey, an American writer on Russo-German affairs, were invited to Moscow by the SVR in 1993 to discuss a joint project leading to the publication in 1997 of *Battleground Berlin*, an account of the espionage wars in Berlin between 1945 and 1961, including the story of the construction of the Allied intelligence-gathering tunnel underneath Berlin and its discovery by the Soviets.[56] And from 1995, the SVR also began to publish a multi-volume official history of KGB foreign operations. Meanwhile, however, Christopher Andrew had begun to collaborate with the former KGB archivist Vasili Mitrokhin, who had been brought to the UK by SIS in 1992 with notes he had taken over the twelve years before his retirement in 1984, containing the details of thousands of Soviet agents and intelligence officers and their activities all over the world during the Cold War.[57]

There was, in fact, a positive proliferation of information published during the 1990s on Soviet intelligence and the part it played in international relations, while UK legislation had opened the door for intelligence historians to write more authoritatively on British history as well. The scene was set for the Zinoviev Letter to make its next appearance.

A most extraordinary and mysterious business: looking for the Zinoviev Letter, 1998–1999

When I began my detailed search in the archives for the Zinoviev Letter, the Labour government under Tony Blair, elected with a substantial majority in May 1997, had been in office for nine months, after eighteen years of Conservative rule.[58] The long gap meant that the incoming administration was of an entirely new generation to the two previous Labour governments (1964–70 and 1974–9), in which a number of ministers had served in the Second World War and some, like Harold Wilson, had ministerial experience dating back to the Attlee government. In 1997, although a few members of the Labour front bench had served as junior ministers, and some, like Robin Cook, had considerable Shadow Cabinet experience, the new Cabinet was very inexperienced, as Cabinet Secretary Robin Butler discovered:

> Under those circumstances, it was unsurprising that the incoming ministers looked over their shoulders with a certain personal insecurity. Added to that insecurity was the traditional left-wing conviction that the Civil Service was a reactionary body and that its members, after eighteen years of Tory ministers as bedfellows, had become incorrigibly so.[59]

Nevertheless, the Blair government set out to establish a productive working relationship with the civil service, and for relevant ministers, with the intelligence agencies, then led by Sir Stephen Lander (MI5), Sir David Spedding (SIS), and Sir Kevin Tebbit and then Sir Francis Richards (GCHQ). Everyone had to get to know each other.

The Prime Minister made it clear from the outset that he wanted a coherent narrative for his government across Whitehall, something his forceful Director of Communications, Alastair Campbell, was determined to implement, noting in his diary that Robin Butler agreed: 'all the machine wanted was clear direction'.[60] In the FCO, we in the Historians found this direction extended to us as well: No. 10 wanted to know when we were going to publish or announce something newsworthy. In the previous couple of years, our work on Nazi gold and Holocaust issues, as well as the publication of intelligence material in *DBPO*, had brought us far more into the public gaze than ever before.

In the past, the Foreign Office historians had tended to fulfil a backroom function, our advice channelled to ministers through senior officials. That was, and remains, the norm, but from the mid-1990s

a series of current policy issues with a background of historical controversy meant that we also found ourselves publishing high-profile
reports, representing the government at international meetings, and
speaking at press conferences—once, I even gave evidence before a
Congressional Committee in Washington. As a result the work of the
FCO Historians acquired a raised profile, including in the media. So
we had to make sure we kept on all fours not just with our own FCO
ministers, but with No. 10 as well. Although this could be tricky, their
interest had a definite upside, in that we were encouraged actively to
make our work better known, not just in Whitehall but publicly as
well. All this translated into solid cross-departmental support for the
Zinoviev investigation, including from the Cabinet Office, Home
Office, and Treasury, as well as the intelligence agencies.

The Russian Ambassador in London, HE Yuri Fokine, offered
solid support for the Zinoviev investigation as well. Soon after it
was announced, he provided me with a copy of an article by the
Russian academic Vladimir Petrovich Kozlov on forged Comintern
and Politburo documents, published in a Russian journal in 1996 and
translated for me by Tony Bishop. The article drew extensively on
a book published in Moscow in 1926 called *Anti-Soviet Fakes* (the
counterpart of *Anti-Soviet Forgeries* published in Britain in 1927).
Kozlov discussed the Zinoviev Letter, reviewing the evidence for
its authenticity. While admitting that the content was an accurate
reflection of the Comintern's plans and objectives, he cited internal
mistakes of style, terminology, and nomenclature as clear proof of
forgery, and concluded firmly that 'in the form in which the "Letter"
was published and attached to the British Foreign Office's official
Note, it simply never existed'. As for British evidence, since not all of
it was accessible, 'one can only conjecture as to who prepared the
forgery and legalised it'. But, he added:

> The involvement of [Britain's] special services in this affair is evident, as
> also are the motives behind its manufacture and the timing of its intro
> duction into circulation. The forgery played its own particular political
> role on the eve of the General Elections to the British Parliament.[61]

None of this was new, of course; but it gave a useful indication of the trend of Russian scholarship on the Letter.

First, however, I went through all the British records relating to the Letter that I could identify. I learned that in 1992 the Treasury had, finally, released the records of the 1928 Board of Enquiry into the Francs scandal.[62] This set of files, in class T 281 at The National Archives, proved both voluminous and fascinating, even if ultimately they left many questions unanswered. The relevant volumes of *DBFP* had printed a wide range of documentation, not just on the Letter and the surrounding international context, but also reports from all parts of the Soviet Union in the 1920s on economic, commercial, and military as well as political matters. These provided essential background: the Editors had gathered together a key selection of such papers, avoiding the necessity to read through hundreds of files. But of course I did go back to the original FO files on the Letter, and also on Anglo-Soviet relations as a whole since 1917: research that demonstrated clearly the corrosive effect that Bolshevik subversion and propaganda had across the British Empire. It confirmed my belief that whoever wrote the Letter knew that its sentiments and style, if not its specific content, would not seem unusual in the wider context of Comintern outpourings. It also showed the methods by which the agencies circulated reports to the FO and other departments, and how they were dealt with by their recipients.

Now I moved on to the closed archives of the intelligence agencies. Milicent Bagot's 1970 report was, as I wrote in 1999, the 'touchstone for my researches', as she, too, had drawn on as wide a range of sources as she could. Like her, I found that a surprising amount of material had survived, although none of it told the whole story; and that it was in the archives of SIS that most evidence was to be found, since it was SIS who first received the Letter in October 1924, authenticated and circulated it, later conducting further investigations into it and into forgery rings overseas. The Security Service also held a lot of useful information, including a voluminous personal file on Zinoviev himself (now at The National Archives), and details of the work of the New Scotland Yard liaison sections that had been absorbed into the Service in 1931. I had a lot of help and advice from members of all the agencies, including the GCHQ Historian, the late Peter Freeman, who had a particular interest in the Zinoviev Letter. Peter, a deeply knowledgeable but delightfully quirky man (tiddlywinks champion, demon cricketer, choral singer...), was fascinated by the cryptological side of the story, and had studied all the various texts, in English and Russian, in minute detail. His enthusiasm and encouragement were a great help in tracing a path through the documentation.

I had no problems in getting hold of the material. There is a tendency to think that official historians are shown only what the authorities want us to see, that the wool is pulled over our eyes, or that we have to tailor what we write to an agreed line. In my (long) experience that has never been how it works. Privileged access means being able to see anything relevant to our research, though what we write is, naturally, subject to sensitivity review. That does not mean telling us what to say or how to tell the story, it just means observing the rules, particularly in regard to national security: for example, protecting the identity of sources or methods when dealing with intelligence issues. My search for the Zinoviev Letter in 1998 was restricted not by access, but by what had survived in the archives.

The intelligence agency archives were patchy: unsurprisingly, since the business of the agencies is to collect secret intelligence in the service of the government, not to compile comprehensive archives. By 1998, much early material had long since been destroyed as it was of no operational use, and there were no surviving witnesses to the events of the 1920s. So it was necessary to look further afield. One possible source was the US archives, since during the 1920s the British and American representatives operating in and around the Soviet Union had shared intelligence, and some papers had survived in Washington that had been lost or destroyed in London. I found there interesting information about other Zinoviev Letters, sent to various countries including the US itself, in the early Bolshevik period. In August 1923 a letter supposedly signed by Zinoviev had been addressed to the

Workers Party of America, urging American communists to form cells in factories, farms, and other workplaces. The US Legation in Riga had got hold of a copy of this letter, and sent it to the FBI, who passed it to the State Department. In December 1923, the State Department wanted to publish the letter, as the Senate Committee on Foreign Relations was considering whether to recognize the Soviet Union, and asked the FBI for details of its provenance. The Director, William J. Burns, wrote:

> The original instructions were written in the Russian language and while the Bureau has not been able to obtain a photostatic copy of the same, they were viewed by a party in whom the Bureau has complete confidence. This individual made a copy of the original, which original was signed by Zinovieff, his name being written in English letters.[63]

Zinoviev, however, denied that he had written any such letter. The episode had interesting parallels with that of the letter allegedly sent to the CPGB on 15 September 1924. But I found nothing in the US archives that shed new light on the origins of the British Letter.

And so in July 1998 I went to Moscow, with Tony Bishop, as described in Chapter 1. Although clearly I did not have free access to all archives, I was received warmly by the Russian authorities who gave the impression that they, too, would welcome greater clarity on what really happened during the Zinoviev Letter episode. The two most fruitful sources of documentation for my purposes were the archives of the Russian Ministry of Foreign Affairs and the Russian Centre for the Preservation and Study of Documents of Contemporary History, whose respective directors, Peter Stegny and Kiril Anderson, were more than helpful. In the Foreign Ministry, we found the originals of the notes sent from the British to the Soviet governments via the Embassy in London, including the notorious note protesting about the Zinoviev Letter, sent to Rakovsky on 24 October 1924 and signed by Gregory 'in the absence of the Secretary of State'; also, rather poignantly, MacDonald's letter of 7 November informing the Soviet Chargé that 'the King has been graciously pleased to accept my resignation'. In the Russian Centre, Tony and I examined in detail the records of meetings of the Politburo and of the Praesidium of the Comintern's Executive Committee in 1924. Everywhere, we took copious notes. We found much interesting material, but nothing to suggest that the Letter dated 15 September 1924 was genuine, nor that any part of the Soviet regime had been involved in manufacturing or promoting it. We did, however, find ample evidence that the OGPU had infiltrated White Russian groups in Europe and, indeed, world-wide, and that very little went on in émigré circles on which they were not provided with information. Their views on the Letter were, therefore, likely to be worth taking seriously.

I had a number of useful personal interviews in Moscow. By the time of my visit, Vladimir Kozlov had become head of the State Archive Service of the Russian Federation, and agreed to see me. We had a good discussion, although he confirmed that he had not come across any material on the Letter additional to that mentioned in his 1996 article. He did, however, draw an interesting distinction between different types of forged documents produced at that time: those which showed every sign of being genuine in both form and content, and those which were planted in newspapers as a form of disinformation, with little care given to whether they appeared authentic or not. Russian Foreign Ministry officials, and officials from the SVR who gave me copies of their published history, were friendly and forthcoming in our talks. Overall, the visit was both fascinating and valuable, but it provided corroborative detail rather than any conclusive answers to my questions.

I returned from Moscow, rather dazed by the experience, to piece together everything I had found and to try to reach a conclusion about the Letter. From British sources, I knew now how the Letter had arrived in the UK, how it reached the Foreign Office, and what happened to it thereafter. I also knew that there were a hundred ways in which the Letter could have reached the press, Conservative Central Office, or other interested parties. Military officers, current and former intelligence chiefs and officers, civil servants, politicians, and newspaper proprietors of a Conservative persuasion—that is, nearly all of them—had motive and opportunity to get hold of the Letter and make sure it was publicized. I knew a great deal, from SIS reports, about anti-Bolshevik activities worldwide, and about the forgery rings operating in an interconnected network spread across Europe, often run by people who had worked for British intelligence during or after the First World War. The story was littered with colourful, flamboyant, or enigmatic characters—men like Sidney Reilly and Vladimir Orlov, and the extraordinary Aminta Bradley Dyne; but I also realized that though their stories intersected with the Letter, that did not necessarily mean they played any part in the story.

From Russian sources, I had learned a good deal more about the political infighting in the Soviet regime during the 1920s, about the competing objectives of different parts of the government, and about the tussles, encouraged by Stalin on the principle of divide and rule, between 'old' and 'new' Bolsheviks. I also understood more clearly how, despite the bitter divisions between Russians during the revolutionary period and ensuing civil war, it was perfectly possible for former tsarist officials to serve first White, then Red, interests, and sometimes both at once. If the situation in London in October 1924 were confused, that in Moscow was even more so.

Yet although my researches had uncovered new material, they still confirmed what Miss Bagot had found before me in the 1960s: it was impossible to be certain who had written the Letter, where, or for what reasons, though there were plenty of pointers to what *might* have happened. I could not say categorically that the Letter was a forgery, and though fairly sure that Grigori Zinoviev did not write it, I could not say for certain who did. As for the manipulation of the Letter for political purposes, I took perhaps a more censorious line than Bagot on the activities of some British officials, but agreed that individual political opportunism was more likely than institutional conspiracy.

When the report based on my researches was published by the FCO early in 1999, it received a great deal of publicity. Robin Cook marked its publication with an article in *The Guardian*, entitled 'The Hidden Hand':

> The Zinoviev Letter has been shrouded in mystery for three-quarters of a century. Now the archives have been opened to public scrutiny. Today we are celebrating a remarkable exercise in openness … Publishing this report allows us to bring the maximum amount of material into the public domain without betraying the trust of those who help Britain by cooperating with our intelligence agencies. It is a demonstration of our commitment to be as open as possible, and our recognition that being open with the British public is a British national interest.

The Foreign Secretary paid tribute to the Russian government for the help it had offered in a 'unique exercise in international cooperation'. He noted the main conclusions: first, that 'generations of Labour Party supporters and historians' were right to believe the Letter was a forgery; 'We have no conclusive proof who sent it, but we are confident it was not Zinoviev.' Secondly, the FO had believed the Letter was genuine, principally because 'they got it through MI6 channels— a fact that has not been made public until today'. But, he added, there was no evidence that MI6 had forged it. And finally, there was no evidence of an organized conspiracy against Labour by the intelligence agencies, although there was evidence that some of their officers were among those involved in leaking it to the press and Conservative Central Office. Cook conceded that important questions remained, 'and may always go unanswered'. But the publication of the report celebrated the fact that the Labour government was moving 'from the presumption that the least said the better, to the firm belief that the public has a right to know as much as possible. It is an important democratic principle.'[64]

The report was laid in the House of Commons Library, and, as noted earlier, was generally well received, though some remained sceptical and others bemoaned the fact that the mystery had not been completely 'solved'. Yet even if the report could not state categorically who had written the Zinoviev Letter, nor reach a confident conclusion on the involvement of officials, it had carried the story much further than ever before and in a way that would not have been feasible earlier when well-informed public discussion of the work of the intelligence agencies was impossible. It was hardly surprising that there remained those in the Labour Party who were reluctant to abandon their view that the Letter had been a deliberate piece of political trickery engineered by 'the Establishment' to sabotage the first Labour government in 1924. At a reception to mark the launch of the report, I said to one Labour peer that the Letter was not the reason that Labour lost the general election in October 1924. 'Oh yes, it was,' he replied. 'I'm a Labour romantic. That's what we have always believed, and that's what we believe still.'

7

So Who Wrote the Zinoviev Letter, and Does it Matter?

A hidden limitation of intelligence is its inability to transform a mystery into a secret.[1]

In this book, I have mentioned a number of theories and allegations about the Zinoviev Letter, without giving a firm opinion on how likely or improbable I consider them to be in the light of the evidence. It is now time to lay my cards on the table, both about the Letter's authorship and about the way it was used for political purposes in 1924. I do not want to make this sound too definite: the nature of the evidence relating to this particular political conspiracy rules out a 'Colonel Mustard in the Library with a Lead Pipe' solution.[2] For those readers familiar with the report published in 1999, this may be disappointing; I am not going to renounce its conclusions, and have no startling revelations to uncover. But a rather better-informed synthesis can, I hope, be attempted.

Before that, there are two points that should be borne in mind. First, it is important to remember that no one has ever produced an 'original' of this curious document, and it is possible that one never existed. This is not a new idea, though it has been obscured by arguments about competing texts. In 1930 Sir Wyndham Childs wrote a newspaper article describing the Zinoviev Letter as a 'redundant reiteration' that 'chanced to appear at a psychological moment':

> Very few people are really aware that there *never was* a Zinoviev Letter at all. The document in the possession of His Majesty's Government purported to be nothing more than the English translation of an alleged copy in Russian of an alleged original.[3]

I think Childs was right, in that the English text of the Letter, as transmitted in the telegram dispatched to SIS headquarters in London from Riga on 2 October 1924, may well be the only 'original'. Every other version, in English or Russian, was in all probability derived from the Riga text, either before or after it reached London, including the Cyrillic text supplied by Riga two months after SIS requested it.[4] In my view, this makes all the quibbles about the authenticity of its wording—whether Zinoviev signed himself as President of the Praesidium or of the Executive Committee, for example, or whether the Comintern was ever referred to as the Third Communist International—irrelevant. The Bolsheviks raised textual objections to back up their argument that the Letter was a forgery, as did the CPGB: both knew perfectly well Comintern phraseology was inconsistent and any form of wording was possible, especially in translation, as no two translators would produce an identical English text. Subsequent analysis of Russian texts has little value if there was no Russian original. But the text of the Letter received and circulated by SIS in October 1924 *looked* as if it might have been written by Zinoviev, on Comintern notepaper. That is what matters, and it explains why it was accepted so readily as genuine when it reached London.

The second important point to remember is that during the interwar period Russians, both Bolshevik and anti-Bolshevik, were known globally for their expertise in forgery. After the 1917 Revolution, when normal diplomatic relations did not exist for some time between the USSR and its neighbours and it was not easy to find out what was going on inside Russia, a brisk market developed in forged documents that could provide other governments and their intelligence services with proof of what the Bolsheviks were up to: it was a question of supply and demand. The fact that a high proportion of the Russian intelligentsia who had escaped the Revolution were scattered in exile across Europe and conspiring against the Bolshevik regime facilitated the production of forgeries so good that scarcely anyone could detect them. These included minutes of bodies such as the Sovnarkom, Politburo, and Comintern Executive Committee, and forged letters or communications sent by their officials.

To convince buyers, forgeries had to be highly skilled, printed on the correct paper, signed by the appropriate authorities, and conforming to the authentic style; they must also contain enough truth to inspire the belief that they were genuine. Indeed, some should actually be genuine, in order to instil confidence, with corroborative evidence offered in seemingly unrelated documents. All this made it vital to have contacts with inside knowledge. Once a forger had established a reputation for material accepted as genuine, his output could be very influential, as the likelihood was that all further reports were accepted without close scrutiny; this may have been the case with SIS's unnamed agent, FR3/K, whose output came under question.[5]

Forgeries were perpetrated by the Bolshevik authorities, including the OGPU, military intelligence (the Fourth Department), and the Comintern itself; and by those opposed to the regime, often referred to, collectively, as 'White Russians'. Bolshevik forgeries might be put out as deception material, to spread information that the regime wished to be believed (fake news), to entrap defectors, or to plant stories in the Russian or foreign press that supported the idea of Western plots against the regime. For those opposed to the Bolsheviks, the aim, particularly in the early post-Revolution years, was to pass information to any government or organization that might help overthrow the regime. It made sense to form forgery syndicates, to pool expertise, and to ensure the widest possible market for their products. Unless they had an agent in place, or contacts with access to inside information, these forgers risked their material becoming outdated and consequently less valuable; if it were too obviously culled from the press, customers soon fell away. (SIS severed its formal connection with Orlov in 1923 because of a 'growing suspicion that the information he provided was drawn from his own knowledge and from casual contacts, rather than from secret sources'.[6]) Forgery syndicates therefore worked hard to make contact with defectors or government and intelligence sources.

These two points go some way to explaining why it is so difficult to discover the truth about the Zinoviev Letter mystery. I still cannot say for certain who wrote the Letter, just as I could not do so in 1999, and Milicent Bagot could not do so in 1970. The evidence does not permit certainty. But I do feel I am now in a better position to judge who might have written it, and in what context. Though there are far too many theories to examine every one, I shall review some of the more plausible and say which seems the most likely. To impose some kind of order on unwieldy material, I am going to borrow from Vladimir Orlov (rather appropriately in view of his ubiquity in the story of the Zinoviev Letter) the phrase 'Reds, Whites and Blues':[7] but in this case, I mean 'communists, anti-Bolsheviks, and Conservatives' (the last with both large and small 'c'), all containing potential suspects.

Reds

The most obvious possibility, never entirely disproved, is that Grigori Zinoviev did, in fact, write the Letter addressed to the CPGB on 15 September 1924 and transmitted to London from Riga. As the Soviet Deputy Foreign Minister, Maxim Litvinov, wrote to Soviet Chargé d'Affaires Rakovsky in London on 27 October 1924, the phraseology of the Letter 'really does remind one of the Comintern's'.[8] In Moscow, as well as London, its style and content were accepted as entirely in keeping with Comintern practice. Zinoviev himself said that while he did not write this particular letter, he would in principle have signed a draft in those terms if presented to him, 'but for the fact that it would obviously have produced difficulties'.[9] There are many examples of similar letters, sent to Britain and other Western countries, available for comparison. And although the Comintern was, despite the Soviet government's protestations, subject to party direction, the propaganda arm of the regime had embarrassed the Politburo or Foreign Ministry on more than one occasion by dispatching inflammatory letters to communist parties overseas that conflicted with or undermined the policy the government was trying to pursue.

In London, the initial reaction on the part of the British authorities was to accept the Letter as genuine, and indeed the intelligence agencies, and members of the incoming Conservative government after Labour's fall from power in October 1924, continued to maintain its authenticity. Some, like SIS, had their own reasons for maintaining that stance, even after they, too, became suspicious, but that does not mean all intelligence reports in favour of authenticity were fabricated or disingenuous. A number of reports were sent to the FO from New Scotland Yard suggesting the Letter was genuine, including one based on information from someone with 'forty years' experience of international revolutionary politics' who claimed to recognize Zinoviev's style, and to have personally seen Arthur MacManus, one of the supposed signatories, talking to a *Daily Mail* journalist.[10] Neither statement was conclusive proof, of course, but such reports explain why so many people believed that the Letter had, indeed, been written by Zinoviev.

Zinoviev himself denied writing the Letter, but then he would, wouldn't he? Some of his denials seem equivocal, and in view of the fuss it caused both in Moscow and London, it is unlikely he would have admitted to writing it, even if he had done so. Dzerzhinsky's interrogation of Zinoviev and of Comintern Executive Committee workers shows that he was under suspicion, while demonstrating that Zinoviev's opponents in the party welcomed the opportunity to blame him for poor security. The defector Besedovsky was convinced that Dzerzhinsky knew the Letter to be genuine, but did not dare to challenge Zinoviev, whose position was still too strong.[11]

Nevertheless, there are several reasons why I do not consider it likely that Zinoviev wrote the Letter. The first, based on the records that Tony Bishop and I examined in Russia in 1998, is that so many elements of the Bolshevik regime, from the Chargé in London, Christian Rakovsky, to the Ministry for Foreign Affairs, to the Politburo and even Comintern headquarters itself, seemed genuinely puzzled when they received the British note of 24 October 1924 protesting at the Letter. It was absolutely clear that they had no idea, initially, what the fuss was about; that when they saw the text of the offending Letter, they did not recognize it; and that they were astonished that the Letter should have been published immediately before the British general election. To the Bolshevik authorities, it was clearly a forgery perpetrated as a piece of political trickery.

It is true that the same argument applies to my own researches in Moscow as that brought against the findings of the Trade Union Delegation in 1924: that we were shown only the documentation the Russian authorities wanted us to see. I cannot, of course, be sure that what I saw was the full, original, or unamended record. But the archives are kept meticulously: for Politburo meetings, for example, both agenda and notes of attendance are filed in order. None was obviously missing or tampered with: it would have required a very elaborate operation to falsify them. One could argue that the Letter was so potentially explosive that it was not placed on the agenda, or discussion of it noted, and it is impossible to refute that. But the absence of any record of the Letter, when references to drafts and approval of similar communications are there, and while other documents stress the need to avoid trouble while the Anglo-Russian treaties were still in play, seems to me a strong argument against its authenticity.

When the British note of protest was received on 24 October 1924, some in the Soviet Foreign Ministry, including Chicherin, Litvinov, and Rakovsky, wondered at first whether the Comintern might have sent a letter that they were unaware of—certainly a possibility. But they accepted Zinoviev's denial, partly because he had not been in Moscow at the time the letter was supposedly dispatched. As Chicherin asked Zinoviev in a letter of 12 November 1924:

> Why does the fact not emerge from our evidence of the letter's forgery that the date on the letter related to the time when you were in the Caucasus and could not have signed it? Why did this argument not appear in our messages to London, when it seems to me to be conclusive?[12]

Chicherin was, I think, wrong in judging this argument 'conclusive', even if Zinoviev's unwillingness to use it looks suspicious. Politburo and Comintern records, and some SIS reports, do confirm his absence from meetings in Moscow in the middle of September, though being out of town would hardly have prevented him from writing or signing the Letter.[13] But Zinoviev's denial of authorship was also accepted because the timing was so clearly wrong.

The Labour government's early recognition of the Soviet Union set an important international precedent that, in the regime's difficult economic situation, the Bolsheviks did not want to compromise. The evidence shows that there had been a moratorium on inflammatory missives to the CPGB from the Comintern since the spring of 1924. And despite all the rhetoric about the unacceptably bourgeois nature of the MacDonald government, Soviet documentation, including records of speeches or letters by Zinoviev, indicates a desire for a Labour victory, in order that the Anglo-Russian treaties, with the promise of a much-needed loan, should have at least a chance of getting British parliamentary approval. Although from a British perspective the prospect of such approval always looked unlikely, the Russians seem to have been more optimistic. Rakovsky, who made a short visit to Moscow at the beginning of August 1924, told a special plenary meeting of the Moscow Soviet that he was convinced the treaty would be ratified. Chicherin agreed, adding that even if it were not, 'the mere signing of the Treaty is an event of extraordinary importance—the first step in a new stage in our international relations'.[14]

Russian historian Leonid Mlechin wrote, in a 2007 article on the Zinoviev Letter, that for the Bolshevik regime 'The trade agreement with Britain and the expected loan were a hundred times more important than world revolution.'[15] Why ruin the chance of success at the last hurdle?

Zinoviev said, according to the defector Besedovsky, 'I didn't sign it, and that's that.'[16] On the basis of all the evidence, I tend to believe him. Nevertheless, whoever did write the Letter had access to Comintern notepaper and knew what a letter from the Executive Committee signed by Zinoviev would look like. Gabriel Gorodetsky, in his book *The Precarious Truce*, drew attention to the striking similarity between the 15 September letter and two others sent by Zinoviev earlier in 1924, concluding that they were all forged by the same hand: 'The conceptual consistency of the letters and their deep familiarity with Soviet politics suggests that their authors were in fact Russians who managed to unite plausibility with a tissue of absurdities.'[17] Gorodetsky was pointing an accusing finger at White, not Red, Russians. But it must be at least a possibility that someone else within the Bolshevik regime either forged the Letter to discredit Zinoviev; or, alternatively, engineered the dispatch of a Comintern draft that would otherwise have remained unsent. Rumours of this kind had circulated in 1924, like the story reported by the British Embassy in Stockholm that the Letter had been concocted by a group headed by Trotsky.[18]

Evidence to support this theory is admittedly circumstantial, but it is worth considering. The year 1924 was, as we have seen, a period of bitter internal struggle within the CPSU, a crucial stage in Stalin's campaign to establish dominance, edging out the 'old' Bolsheviks in favour of the 'new', and he was already trying to marginalize Zinoviev and Kamenev, as well as Trotsky. But members of the Central Committee agreed that in the interests of the party an appearance of unity was the most important thing, essential to the retention of power and authority over the Soviet Union. They were willing to sublimate their disputes to the overall imperative of Bolshevik suprem-acy. This was undoubtedly to Stalin's advantage:

> That men like Trotsky, Zinoviev and Bukharin, fighting for their political lives and with much greater gifts of communication, in both speaking and writing, should have voluntarily accepted such a prohibition, shows how strong was the hold exercised by the Bolshevik dogma.[19]

Stalin was not quite ready, in late 1924, to move openly against his rivals; according to Politburo secretary Bazhanov, his confidence had been shaken by the abortive uprising in Georgia against the regime in September.[20] But his tactics in the pursuit of power remained relentless, undermining rivals, promoting his own candidates, and demoting opponents in key committees:

> The adversary was accused of deviation (to the left, the right, or in favour of the kulaks), or of underestimation of something, or overestimation, of forgetting something, of derogation of the precepts of Ilich [Lenin], etc, whereas in reality all the charges were invented and inflated...Stalin had understood that the machine would carry him up, and he did what was necessary to take advantage of it.[21]

This included discrediting, where possible, those whom Stalin considered might impede the consolidation of power in his hands. Zinoviev, energetic and charismatic but erratic and careless of the administrative efficiency that underpinned Stalin's success, was an obvious target, and everything we know of Stalin indicates a willingness to use deception to achieve his ends.

But motive and opportunity do not stack up to solid evidence, and it seems highly unlikely that Stalin would have ordered the deliberate manufacture of a document like the Zinoviev Letter, especially as he, too, was interested in the success of the Anglo-Russian treaties. The possibility suggested in William Butler's 1970 article on the 'Harvard text' of the Letter, that 'Soviet agents deliberately placed a forged Letter in circulation in order to destroy the British Labour Party's ambitious program for the reconstruction of Europe and for British-American collaboration', seems somehow too abstract a strategy for such a tactical operation.[22] Admittedly the Bolshevik regime was paranoid about Western plots, yet the evidence suggests that it wanted to counter the development of anti-Soviet groupings from the stronger base that a treaty with Britain would undoubtedly afford. In international dealings, the Soviets sought to undermine Western solidarity by distraction or by proposing alternative policies; to do that, they had to be a member of the club.

But if Stalin were told, by one of his many informants, or another of Zinoviev's rivals discovered, that a draft of the Zinoviev Letter existed in Comintern headquarters, might they have been tempted to ensure that it was sent, despite (or because of) the trouble it would cause? Perhaps; and the idea recalls the story told to Desmond Morton in October 1924 by the former tsarist naval officer who claimed to have had an agent working in the Comintern Executive Committee offices, an agent who had encouraged Zinoviev to write the Letter and then fled with a copy of it to England.[23] Neither Milicent Bagot nor I were able to authenticate or disprove this story from the archives. It appears, however, that a Russian, 'M', did appear in London in October claiming to have fled from Zinoviev, though there is no hard evidence that he brought any document with him. But since, according to Morton's story, the tsarist officer's Comintern agent had also supplied information to the SIS station in Riga, it is impossible to rule out the possibility that such a letter did exist in Comintern headquarters, even if Zinoviev did not intend to send it, and that through 'M' it found its way to Riga.

All this is speculative, but worth including because of something far more concrete: the unchallenged supremacy established by Russians—both Red and White—in the field of forgery, as described in this chapter. Under its chief Mikhail Abramovich Trillissier the INO, the OGPU's foreign service, specialized in 'faking Politburo minutes, departmental memoranda and false orders of battle', and together with the Fourth Department, was an instrument 'of the country's foreign policy dictated from the Kremlin and by the Party'. Spreading disinformation about Russia's domestic and foreign policy was part of their work. These organizations contained a large number of non-Russian Bolsheviks in their ranks—Latvians, apparently, were particularly well suited to the work—and 'since both civilian and military intelligence services were instruments of a revolution that still defined itself as worldwide, the fact they were heavily populated with non-Russians was seen as not strange but perfectly normal'.[24] They were, of course, well aware what a letter from the Comintern's Executive Committee looked like. While their principal target was White Russian émigrés and Western intelligence services, it is not hard to imagine that either branch might have considered the Zinoviev Letter a useful tool.

The pervasive capabilities of Bolshevik intelligence will be an important factor in considering the role of 'Whites' in the Zinoviev Letter. But before leaving the 'Reds', one more possibility must be explored: that the Letter—genuine or forged—was in fact received and made use of by the Communist Party of Great Britain, as suggested by Natalie Grant in her 1967 article, 'The "Zinoviev Letter" Case'.[25] According to this thesis, the 'Communists', in particular the CPGB, saw in the Letter the opportunity to discredit all their political opponents: Ramsay MacDonald and his colleagues, who had refused to permit the affiliation of communists to the Labour Party; the Conservatives, who could be accused of commissioning and making underhand use of a forged document, thereby undermining their prestige in the eyes of the British public; and Establishment lackeys such as FO officials and the intelligence agencies who were perceived as class enemies.

There is no doubt that the CPGB felt strongly that it had cause for complaint at the Labour Party's antagonistic stance, at a time when membership of the Communist Party was growing, and it was very critical of the government's record; the 1924 CPGB Congress vowed to attack the failures of 'MacDonaldism', regarded as 'a defence of the bourgeoisie against the developing radicalism of the working class'.[26] There was a strong suspicion of 'anything to do with elections, parliament and most of all anything to do with the Labour Party', despite Lenin's earlier ruling that the CPGB should support Labour 'as the rope supports a hanging man'.[27] On this reasoning, the Central Committee of the CPGB (including MacManus, one of the Letter's alleged signatories), disenchanted with Labour and enraged by the government's handling of the Campbell Case (whose importance in the downfall of the 1924 Labour government is, Grant argued, under-estimated),[28] could well have decided to make opportunistic use of a letter from Zinoviev as the 'copingstone of a concerted campaign' against Labour.[29] Crowe expressed the view to MacDonald on 25 October 1924 that the *Daily Mail* must have obtained the Letter from 'some venal informer in the Communist camp', a view commonly held in official circles, and strengthened when SIS told the FO that the Letter had been discussed by the Central Committee, even though that evidence proved unreliable.[30] Though the CPGB consistently denied ever receiving the Letter, no evidence was found that it reached Britain through the postal system, and no copy of it was found when CPGB HQ was raided in 1925, it is nevertheless impossible to refute this thesis conclusively.

Still, it seems unlikely, and partly for reasons to be found in the terms of the Zinoviev Letter itself. The CPGB was, in Comintern eyes, weak and insufficiently active, and though it was urged to throw its weight behind the Anglo-Soviet treaties by supporting the Labour government, there was little confidence this would have much effect. In fact, there was a struggle going on within the CPGB in the early 1920s between the more militant wing, who argued against the grad-ualist approach towards establishing a socialist society exemplified by the policies of the MacDonald government, and those who favoured a more moderate line, encouraged by improved social conditions and a higher standard of living. The same division was mirrored in the trade union movement, with a 'shift from the demand for nothing less than worker's control to militant bargaining'.[31] But the CPGB remained subject to overall direction from Moscow, to what might be seen as a surprising extent:

> The Moscow power struggle affected everything the CP did and every attitude it struck. You might have thought that the power brokers in Moscow had better things to do than watch what their tiny British outpost was up to, but you would be wrong. The CP found itself being lectured like a naughty child for failing to follow the 'correct' line—as most recently laid down.[32]

On the whole, instructions from Moscow were accepted by the CPGB, and the idea that its Central Committee acted on its own initiative to make public a document that, however destabilizing to Labour or Conservatives, could only marginalize the British communists further, seems improbable. None of the reports from SIS or Security Service informants within the CPGB suggested involvement in any such plot. In the end, the CPGB's indignation at being blamed for propagating a document that they claimed never to have seen or discussed seems genuine.

Whites

Most people who have studied the Zinoviev Letter in any detail have concluded that it was probably forged by anti-Bolsheviks, with White Russian émigrés or monarchist exiles the popular culprits (aided and abetted by British, German, Polish, or Russian intelligence, depending on the standpoint of the commentator). Even those who believe that the Letter was concocted by the British intelligence and security services consider that White Russians had a hand in it somewhere. 'White Russians' is, in fact, a rather confusing compendium term, for just as the Bolshevik intelligence organizations contained many non-Russians, the forces arrayed against the Soviet regime encompassed people of many different nationalities, including former members of the tsarist armed forces ('White Guards'), relations both near and distant of the deposed Romanov dynasty, dissident groups within the Soviet Union such as Ukrainian nationalists, those from the Baltic or Scandinavian states, people married to Russians, or mongrel mavericks like Sidney Reilly or Ignacz Trebitsch Lincoln.[33] The result is a confusing calendar of potential forgers.

The 'Whites' were, nevertheless, united in two respects: by their implacable ideological opposition to the Bolshevik regime (even if, in practice, many of them served more than one master and had close connections with Moscow); and by the fact that they had been penetrated or were under close observation by Soviet intelligence or Comintern agents. This meant that the Bolshevik authorities knew a good deal about the 'forgery factories' run throughout Europe by White Russian groups, and also knew that these factories were financed and patronized by foreign governments and their intelligence services, including those of Britain, Germany, and Poland. As soon as a new group of forgers began work, the Soviet authorities were on to it. In November 1924, for example, the Comintern sent a Top Secret note to the Central Committee of the German Communist Party informing them that a telegraph agency, 'Russina', had been set up by White Guards in Berlin, with the help of Berlin Police Headquarters, and had 'already published certain falsified and forged material concerning the activities of the Comintern *Ispolkom* [Executive Committee]'.[34]

Of course, it was not only Soviet intelligence organizations who knew a lot about anti-Bolshevik activities and forgery factories: other countries knew a great deal too, not least because some, like the German government, financed such activities (a not uncommon means of intelligence collection). As far as British intelligence was concerned, in the 1920s the Soviet Union was the prime target, and SIS collected intelligence on anti-Bolshevik as well as Bolshevik activities throughout the world (and, as has been seen, within the UK as well). They were also extremely interested in the European forgery factories, some of which employed people who had worked for SIS in the past, and many of whom were still in touch with SIS stations overseas.

For well-informed agencies like the OGPU or SIS, there was one obvious direction in which to look for the author of the Zinoviev Letter, if it were not genuine: to the pan-European network of forgers, spies, double agents, and political intriguers that had at its heart Vladimir Orlov. To draw a contemporary analogy, Orlov was the spider at the centre of the 1920s equivalent of the Dark Web. As SIS acknowledged, he was a man of real ability and an excellent organizer, and nearly all those whose names were mentioned in connection with the Letter were connected with him and his network in some way. Orlov, like the OGPU, took steps to penetrate any anti-Bolshevik group as soon as it was formed, by supplying it with spurious information, and he provided intelligence to a range of governments in return for financial and practical support. When he set up his bureau in Berlin in 1920, the SIS Chief Cumming gave him £500 and a yearly subsidy on condition that he supplied copies of the intelligence he collected, while the German *Polizeipräsidium* (Police Headquarters) expected the same consideration in return for premises and facilities.[35] He had close contacts with Baltic, French, and Polish intelligence as well.

Although details of Orlov's fantastical career—Greek Orthodox missionary, tsarist secret police officer, SIS agent, confidant of exiled Russian aristocracy, informant of the German Police, master forger, to list just a few of his identities—have been given in earlier chapters,[36] his activities in the 1920s need closer scrutiny in order to answer the question, 'who wrote the Zinoviev Letter?' In the late 1960s, in connection with Miss Bagot's and the FLUENCY team's investigations,[37] Orlov's SIS file was revisited, and a chart compiled of his 'organization', based in part on the information received in 1927 from Biffy Dunderdale in Paris.[38] Here are just some of the strands of his extensive web:

White Russian links:

Grand Duke Kyril Vladimirovich, cousin of the late Tsar Nicholas II who had settled in Germany after fleeing Russia in 1917;

Grand Duke Nicholas, former Commander in Chief of tsarist forces now living in exile near Paris, and heavily involved with monarchist groups;

General Alexander Kutepov, former commander of White Russian forces;

'Brotherhood of Russian Truth' (a network in Berlin set up partly by Orlov, on pseudo-Masonic lines);

White Russian groups in Constantinople, Geneva, and Oslo;

Ariadne Tyrkova Williams (wife of the editor of *The Times*), E.V. Sabline and the Council of Czarist Ambassadors in London.[39]

Bolshevik links:

members of the Soviet Mission in Berlin;

INO Chief Trilissier in Moscow, through former OGPU agent turned forger, Mikhail Sumarakov @ Yakshin, @ Komarov, @ Karpov, @ Pavlonovski;

German links:

Police Headquarters;

Administrative headquarters of the German government;

Interior Ministry;

Defence Ministry;

right-wing private groups linked with German intelligence, like the Nuntia Bureau;[40]

British links:

Frank Foley, SIS Head of Station in Berlin, and his deputy C. H. 'Dick' Ellis, through former journalist and co-forger Count Alexander Nelidov;[41]

SIS representatives Malcolm Maclaren and Frank Marshall in Warsaw, through Polish intelligence contacts;[42]

Harold Gibson, SIS Head of Station in Bucharest;[43]

Rafael Farina, SIS Head of Station in Riga;[44]

Ernest Boyce, SIS Head of Station in Tallinn and Helsinki (who had employed his friend Sidney Reilly to penetrate the Trust, leading to the latter's death).[45]

Orlov's White Russian, Bolshevik, and German links were said to be shared by his close associate Harold Ivanovich Sievert, the former

White Russian intelligence officer now working for the German authorities, who was arrested with Orlov in 1929, although by that time they had fallen out.[46] Through Sievert, other associates linked to Orlov included Druzhelovsky, Gumansky, Gavrilov, and Pokrovsky—all of whom were mentioned in connection with the Zinoviev Letter. The inescapable conclusion is that even if Orlov did not write the Zinoviev Letter, it is highly unlikely that it was forged without his knowledge and, presumably, encouragement.

At this point I should say that the story based on information from Madame Irina Bellegarde, as set out in 1966–7 by the *Sunday Times* 'Insight' team, does not, in my view, hold up against the evidence.[47] Though her husband, Alexis, and his supposed accomplices were almost certainly involved in forgery and anti-Bolshevik conspiracies, at least some of them were also in the pay of the Bolsheviks and were not the naive young men her account suggests. That this group was responsible for the Zinoviev Letter still seems unconvincing in principle and implausible in detail.

A more promising suspect is Ivan Dmitrievich Pokrovsky, formerly an engineering officer in the Russian Navy, whose father had been the head of intelligence for the White Russian General Yudenitch. Pokrovsky was, as noted earlier, the man identified by the OGPU as the forger of the Zinoviev Letter, according to *The Crown Jewels*, the book published in 1998 by former KGB Colonel Oleg Tsarev and Nigel West that led Robin Cook to commission the 1999 FCO report on the Letter.[48] He had also been named in *Anti-Soviet Forgeries*, published in 1927, where he was thought to be identical to 'A. A. Belgardt' (though this is unlikely);[49] and in the *Daily Herald* in 1929, when the details of his supposed flight to Argentina recalled the fate of Donald im Thurn's contact 'X'.[50]

I investigated Pokrovsky's story for the FCO report published in 1999, concluding that although it seemed plausible in many respects, there was no evidence in British archives to suggest that the Zinoviev Letter had been commissioned from this former White Russian intelligence officer, working as a forger in Riga, by 'British Intelligence', and concocted with help from Polish intelligence.[51] Although I thought that the evidence pointed strongly to the Zinoviev Letter's having been written by 'someone in the Baltic States, probably in Riga itself, but who had strong links to the forgery rings operating out of Berlin',[52] I was not inclined to give any greater credence to the Pokrovsky story than to some of the others. I now think that judgement was too cautious. I confess that I was influenced by Tsarev's telling me in Moscow that it was merely 'one version of the truth'; and put off by the fact that the details about how the Letter found its way to London ('posted from Riga to a pre-arranged address for the British Communist Party') did not fit with the archival evidence. Although I still do not feel able to say with certainty that Pokrovsky forged the Letter, he seems a likely suspect.

Gordon Brook-Shepherd, who in his 1998 book *Iron Maze* recounted the Pokrovsky story, admitting it was a 'rum tale', cited an in-house history of Soviet intelligence corresponding to the one I was given in Moscow by the SVR.[53] This includes extracts from reports received by the OGPU in November 1924. A report from Berlin dated 12 November 1924 stated that, according to 'certain information requiring verification', the Letter was allegedly forged in Riga by Lieutenant Pokrovsky, who possessed Comintern headed paper and compiled the Letter from Zinoviev's speeches with 'certain other additions' supplied by Orlov. Pokrovsky was said to have 'connections with British counter-intelligence', who had given him the address to which the Letter could be sent. On 21 November, a report was passed to Trilissier, head of the OGPU's foreign intelligence service, by the Red Army Intelligence Directorate, stating that the Letter had been written in Riga by 'White Guard Intelligence' and sent 'with the aid of the Poles' to London. And finally, a later report on forged documents stated that Pokrovsky had received £500 and a recommendation to Buenos Aires for his work on the Letter.[54] On the basis of such reports, it is hardly surprising that the OGPU identified Pokrovsky as the forger, as set out in *Crown Jewels*.[55]

Of the three principal elements to the story—Pokrovsky as forger, Polish intelligence as facilitator, and British intelligence as instigator—it is for the first that the evidence is most convincing, though still circumstantial. Details of Pokrovsky's career and activities are sparse in British archives, and apparently in those of the OGPU as well. But the evidence suggests that he worked in White Russian intelligence during the Russian Civil War, and retained his monarchist contacts; in that context he almost certainly had dealings with British intelligence representatives operating in the area. After the war, he seems to have moved to Riga, where he joined a forgery syndicate linked with that of Orlov in Berlin, making use of his engineering background to specialize in false information on Soviet naval matters, including the particulars of new Russian submarines, and apparently impressing both the Americans and the French with his reports. According to the note on anti-Bolshevik activities prepared by SIS in 1927,[56] Pokrovsky's fabrications were distinguished by their plausibility, making it difficult, especially for foreigners, to establish that they were not genuine. Both he and his family, according to the note, were 'connected in the closest possible manner' with Orlov, Sievert, and Gumansky.

Based in Riga, and connected with Orlov in Berlin, Pokrovsky would be well placed to produce and disseminate the Zinoviev Letter: to get hold of the materials required (headed notepaper, models of similar correspondence), to check the content with local contacts, and, most importantly, to feed the Letter into the system in a way that ensured its acceptance by the recipient. Riga, an intelligence entrepôt, was the ideal place of origin for the Zinoviev Letter:

> although the expertise required to produce such a forgery lay in Berlin, the members of the Berlin organisation were well aware (because of their own links with British Intelligence) that any attempt by them to feed such a document into British channels would discredit the forgery immediately: as 'C' had assured Crowe, SIS had 'made it their special business' to inform themselves about White Russian forgery rings, especially the one in Berlin...agents operating in and around Riga

were in a better position to know exactly what was going on in
Moscow and to obtain the genuine information which would help
to authenticate the forgery.[57]

Given his background, Pokrovsky is likely to have had contact with
the Riga SIS station chief, Farina, and his colleagues. I have, however,
found nothing to substantiate the claim that 'an Englishman had been
sent to Riga specifically to work with Pokrovsky's forgery organisation';
nor that this person, 'Captain Black', instructed Pokrovsky to write
the Letter and subsequently to leave Europe, travelling with him to
South America. But whoever wrote the Letter was well informed not
just about the situation in Moscow, but also about that in Britain: its
content was, as we have seen, tailored to the political conditions of
the general election campaign. Even if Pokrovsky claimed, according
to Gumansky, that he did not know to what use the Letter would be
put, someone in Riga did.

When Milicent Bagot was investigating the Letter in the late 1960s,
she interviewed a number of people who had served in Riga, or
were in contact with SIS's Riga station, at the relevant time. She was
not impressed by their apparent inability to remember much about
either the Letter or the names of any of their contacts, although she
was unable to substantiate her suspicions. My own view, in the light
of Bagot's and other evidence, is that Farina and members of his
network knew a good deal about what was going on, including about
Pokrovsky's forgery activities, and may have been engaging in some
form of private enterprise, motivated by money, ideology, or both.
Farina was, after all, very anxious to ascertain that his report containing the Letter should have been received safely in SIS headquarters;[58]
the reason for this anxiety was never revealed. Whether that meant
he thought it was genuine, or knew it to be forged, is impossible
to say. But he seems to have been involved to some extent with
Pokrovsky (one story is that Farina provided the £500 for the journey to South America); and the difficulties that Riga seemed to
encounter in asking the quite basic questions put to them about the

Letter by SIS headquarters surely suggest either incompetence or deliberate obfuscation.

It is, of course, possible that Riga's role in the affair was limited to the safe transmission of the Letter. It might have come from a number of sources, including 'FR3/K', who may or may not have worked in the Comintern. It seems likely, however, that the information was obtained from a third party—Pokrovsky, perhaps—before passing it on to the SIS station. In addition to Farina and his colleagues, there were a number of people operating—hustling is probably the right word—in the Baltic States in the 1920s who had worked for British intelligence during or immediately after the First World War. Though no longer employed by the agencies or the military, they retained their personal connections and, of course, their knowledge of how the system worked. (The case of Malcolm Maclaren, who stopped working for SIS in 1921 but remained in Warsaw, and in contact with SIS, was one such example.[59]) Such a 'freelance' former intelligence officer could have mixed freely with British, Polish, or White Russian equivalents; he might also have been at liberty to travel to South America with Pokrovsky when it seemed wise to leave town. Unfortunately, the official record offers no help in proving this theory. As the story told to Desmond Morton by the former tsarist naval officer shows, allegiances were rarely undivided.[60]

The idea that Pokrovsky received help from the Poles with the Zinoviev Letter chimes with various accounts of their role in the affair. The story in the diaries of Maciej Rataj, Speaker of the Polish House of Deputies in the 1920s, that Polish Prime Minister Wladyslaw Sikorski claimed personally to have forged the Letter, seems highly doubtful.[61] On the other hand, the assertion that the instructions contained in the Letter came from the Comintern and were in the possession of the Polish General Staff might contain elements of truth. On a more individual, and perhaps more plausible, level, a Polish intelligence officer called 'Paciorkorwski' (variously spelt) was included in the list of alleged forgers in Druzhelovsky's 'confession' and later by Chicherin. He was said to have been working in Berlin at the time of the Letter and was linked with the forger Schreck.[62]

Checking on this through Polish liaison channels, SIS learned that Captain Edward Paciorkowski was an intelligence officer in Berlin at the relevant time, but that reports of his role in the Letter were much exaggerated. It was, their informant thought, an example of the tendency of the Polish *Deuxième Bureau* to take responsibility for 'every possible and impossible shadowy activity'. The kind of help that he might have offered is unclear; but he may well have been one of the extensive list of people who were well informed on the forgeries produced by Orlov's network, if not the Zinoviev Letter itself. Indeed, it is quite possible that the Polish intelligence authorities, like the Germans, knew a lot about the Letter: but it suited them to keep that knowledge to themselves, not least because of their own close association with Orlov and his connections.

This leaves the allegation, often repeated through the long history of the Zinoviev Letter, that 'British Intelligence' was responsible for commissioning, inspiring, authenticating, and making use of the Letter, in order to discredit the Labour government and the Bolshevik regime, as well as ensuring that the Anglo–Russian treaties were abandoned. Unsurprisingly, this is a line that has been disseminated consistently both by Russian sources and by left-leaning commentators in the West. Brook-Shepherd's justification for taking this view was that the intelligence community contained a 'hard core of what would later be dubbed "Cold War warriors", veterans of the revolutionary era opposed to any idea of political softening towards the Bolshevik regime, whose downfall they still ardently desired'.[63] Certainly the community contained people of this type, but the gap between those sentiments and commissioning a forged Letter to destabilize British politics is a big one. Though the lines between my rather arbitrary division of suspects are somewhat blurred, I propose to deal with this theory in the category 'Blues'.

Blues

I am taking 'Blues' to mean those elements in Britain who are thought to have had the motivation, and in some cases the means and opportunity, to use the Zinoviev Letter against Ramsay MacDonald's Labour government and the Bolshevik regime at the same time. This might include people connected with the Conservative Party itself, its broader circle of supporters including those who controlled the right-wing press, and some members of the military, civil service, and intelligence establishments. This is, of course, a sweeping generalization: by no means all members of the military or civil service, for example, were of a right-wing persuasion. For most Conservatives, dislike of the Labour government did not mean they would have been willing to engage in a political conspiracy to get rid of it; and opponents of the Bolshevik regime were by no means all on the political right. Members of what Labour called the 'Establishment', civil servants, members of the intelligence agencies and the military, as well as the political elite, did not necessarily hold right-wing views, or if they did, did not let them affect the performance of their professional duties. But it is true that a number of those on whom suspicion has fallen, like Joseph Ball, Desmond Morton, and 'Blinker' Hall, were undoubtedly of a strong anti-Bolshevik and conservative persuasion.

In respect of the allegation that the British security and intelligence services were responsible for the Zinoviev Letter, it is not correct to say, as some people have, that according to the FCO's 1999 report 'MI6 forged the Letter'. What I actually said was:

> The most that can be said is that if there were elements there [in Riga] connected with British Intelligence, who felt strongly enough about the Bolsheviks and (in the context of the proposed loan to the Soviet Union) about opposing the Labour government, to commission such a forgery and send it to London to be passed off as genuine, there is no

evidence to suggest that this was done with the knowledge or consent of SIS Head Office.[64]

I hold to this judgement. But that does not mean I think it impossible that elements of British intelligence were involved with the production of the Letter, as I have argued. According to the account given to the OGPU by Gumansky, 'British intelligence in Riga did not establish contact with other British stations in connection with this assignment'.[65] This supports the idea of private enterprise on the part of the SIS station in Riga, without constituting proof. But in terms of any broader conspiracy, neither the documentary evidence nor my own knowledge of the history of the British intelligence establishment suggests that the idea is plausible:

> The idea of an institutionalised campaign, directed by SIS, to discredit both the Bolsheviks and the Labour government is not only unsub-stantiated by the documentation, but seems inherently unlikely. It was just not how the Intelligence Services operated, and implied a degree of cohesion and control, not to mention political will, which simply did not exist...the majority of officials considered it their duty to serve the government of the day faithfully, whatever their private views may be.[66]

There are, however, questions to answer about the conduct of certain officials, including SIS officer Major Desmond Morton, his Chief Admiral Sinclair, and Sinclair's former deputy, Frederick Browning; the former Director of Naval Intelligence, Sir Reginald 'Blinker' Hall; and Major Joseph Ball, MI5 officer and later Conservative Party Director of Research. Other anti-Bolshevik elements, including those in contact with White Russian groups in London, should also be added to the list of suspects.

Ever since the Zinoviev Letter was published, immediately before the 1924 general election, allegations have persisted that it was a dirty political trick cooked up by the Right to discredit the Left. Yet although there are genuine grounds for suspicion about the activities of certain people, there is very little concrete proof. That remains the case. I cannot prove beyond doubt that any member of the Conservative

Party, the Foreign Office, or British intelligence was involved in the manufacture, dissemination, or manipulation of the Letter for political advantage. This is not surprising, since any such conspiracy would have been well masked at the time and its secrets kept. I can, however, review some of the key questions, and offer a possible scenario.

Did the 'Blues' know whether the Letter was genuine or forged? It is clear that different groups had a vested interest in promoting a particular view. For SIS, whose officers had authenticated it on receipt, it was a point of principle and organizational pride to maintain that line, even though, as we have seen, they were soon having doubts about it. Their position was also based on the importance of maintaining absolute secrecy about their own activities. Extensive SIS investigations in the 1920s and later show that they had serious doubts about the Letter; but to admit this would open the door to the kind of discussion they were not prepared to entertain, in order to protect their sources and methods. This is not necessarily evidence of deception or sinister intent. Individuals, including Morton, Sinclair, and Browning, may well have known or suspected the status of the document. If so, they did not commit such knowledge to paper.

Foreign Office officials also had reason to maintain that the Letter was genuine, or perhaps it is more accurate to say that they had no reason to suspect it was not. They received what they called 'corroborative proof' from SIS, and further confirmation when requested. They had handled similar material in the past, and knew the Letter was not out of character for Zinoviev and the Comintern. The idea, spread deliberately (and defensively) by the Soviet authorities, that FO officials, such as J. D. Gregory, were responsible for concocting the Letter seems implausible. The documentation does not support it, or the theory that officials sought to sabotage the Anglo-Russian treaties, or undermine their political masters. In fact, the departmental files, as one would expect, show very little sign of political awareness. My own view is that the way the Letter was dealt with by departmental officials owed more to exasperation with persistent Soviet breaches of the Trade Agreement, and of other pledges to renounce propaganda and subversion, than to any deliberate strategy. On receipt of earlier examples of Comintern provocation, officials had argued in favour of publicity but were overruled by ministers. The Zinoviev Letter was merely the latest in the series, and offered the opportunity to protest openly at Soviet tactics.

Once the Letter had been published and the government had lost office, it became, as has been seen in this book, the focus of Labour disappointment, turning into indignation. The two 'sides' took up rigidly opposed positions that they felt unable to moderate, even though some on the Labour side thought the Letter was genuine, while some Conservatives conceded that it might well be a forgery. In this way the Letter became a point of symbolic political dispute that has lasted for nearly a century. When the Letter was first brought to the Prime Minister's attention, he instructed that its authenticity should be checked, but did not appear to suspect it was a forgery until the confusion surrounding the dispatch of the note of protest to the Soviet Legation and events surrounding the final stages of the election campaign aroused his suspicions. It was the humiliation of electoral defeat, the anger of his ministerial colleagues, and the inconclusive enquiry into the Letter that led MacDonald to become convinced Labour had been the victim of a deliberate deception. The events of 1928 hardened those suspicions,[67] but did not provide the material to substantiate them.

Ministers in the Conservative administration under Stanley Baldwin, taking office in November 1924, also had solid reasons for maintaining the authenticity of the Letter. It underlined why they had won the election, and gave them good cause to abandon the Anglo-Russian treaties and other bilateral arrangements. Also, the Chamberlain enquiry into the Letter relied on the same evidence as that carried out in the last days of the Labour government, emanating from the intelligence agencies and therefore thought to be beyond question. Reopening the question could only lead to trouble. For both political and practical reasons, it was not in the interest of the Baldwin government to entertain any doubts on the issue; just as it made sense for the Soviet government to insist that the Letter was forged, and indeed to encourage the suspicion that the Conservatives were responsible.

Was the Zinoviev Letter commissioned deliberately as a forgery to destabilize the Labour government, or was it employed opportunistically when it arrived in Britain? There is no doubt that the Letter was a gift to the Conservative Party during the election campaign in October 1924, even if it did not affect the result decisively. But that does not necessarily mean that the Letter was forged to order. Despite stories like that of 'Captain Black' in Riga, or the claim that the Letter was commissioned by General Korneyez, a former Russian officer granted British citizenship, who 'requested material that could be used against the British Labour Party in the forthcoming General Election',[68] I have not seen any concrete proof to support this. It is certainly possible that White Russian circles in London, with whom a number of 'Blues' were connected, commissioned it through their connections in the Baltic States. But if such an order were placed, those involved covered their tracks, and kept quiet about it. In short, the Letter may have been commissioned, but reliable evidence is lacking.

Even if it were forged deliberately, to order or just to plant it in the correct channels, that does not mean that the intelligence authorities in London knew it. It seems to me more likely that the Letter's potential usefulness was recognized when it reached London, either within SIS, or when it was circulated more widely. Its content and timing offered obvious potential to damage the Labour government and make sure that the Anglo-Russian treaties were never ratified. For someone with an eye to the political possibilities, it was of no consequence whether the Letter was genuine or not. Despite his insistence that he saw nothing unusual in the Zinoviev Letter, I would put Desmond Morton in that category, as well as his MI5 colleague, Joseph Ball; it is worth recalling their exchange in July 1924 about the handling of Comintern letters.[69] It has also been suggested that the heads of MI5 and SIS, Vernon Kell and Hugh Sinclair, saw a chance to ensure the defeat of a government that it suspected wished to close down the intelligence agencies altogether. Collusion between Kell and Sinclair is certainly a possibility, although the MacDonald government had shown little sign of carrying out earlier promises to cut back on the intelligence establishment. But this is speculation, and I have found no concrete evidence, although as I know only too well from writing a biography of Morton, such intelligence professionals knew how to keep secrets.

Did one or more of the Blues leak the Letter, or otherwise make sure it reached the press? Almost certainly: but the suspect pool is very large. After its arrival from Riga, the Letter passed through GC&CS before reaching SIS, and was then circulated to the Foreign Office and elsewhere in Whitehall. Admiral 'Blinker' Hall, as former Director of Naval Intelligence, had been responsible for codebreaking during the First World War, and was still in close contact with former colleagues, as well as with various clandestine unofficial right-wing intelligence networks; Morton, who authenticated the Letter in SIS, had professional links with such groups, like that headed by Sir George Makgill.[70] Ball was already in contact with Conservative Central Office; Major Alexander of MI5 met Donald im Thurn regularly for lunch; Freddie Browning kept in close touch with the 'C'. This Blue 'Establishment' was a relatively narrow, interconnected group of men with common experience, including service in the First World War. Any one, or small group, of them might have ensured that the Letter reached the *Daily Mail*. In his study of the Letter, Uri Bar-Joseph wrote:

> Given that SIS in London consisted of, perhaps, forty people who functioned in a clublike atmosphere in which the 'need to know' principle was virtually unknown, and that about sixty more officials, mostly from the various intelligence branches, knew of the letter, we can assume that any of them could have leaked it to the press.[71]

While I do not agree that the concept of 'need to know' did not operate in SIS or other agencies, Bar-Joseph is right to say that any member of this community could have leaked the Letter. And, as he points out, when Donald im Thurn was going round London talking about the Letter and the need to secure its publication, none of the senior intelligence figures that he contacted saw fit to inform the Foreign Office or a minister of what was going on.[72]

There is no doubt that a number of people in the 'Blues' category knew more about the Zinoviev Letter than they were ever willing to admit. Donald im Thurn's diaries, though muddled, give the strong impression that some of his contacts in both political and intelligence circles were discussing the arrival of an inflammatory document at the same time as, or even before, it arrived in SIS headquarters, and before it was circulated within Whitehall or more widely. Correspondence between Morton and Ball; press stories about an expected 'bombshell' in advance of the Letter's publication; the unexplained conduct of FO officials like Crowe and Gregory; SIS Chief Sinclair's anxiety about what might become public during Orlov's trial in Berlin in 1929: all these are suggestive of collusion and conspiracy, but they do not constitute proof. The later efforts of Joseph Ball, on behalf of Conservative Central Office, to control the narrative of the Zinoviev Letter and prevent others from telling their own versions of the story suggest that he knew a lot about what actually happened. But there is very little hard fact to go on; rather, there is a good deal of presumption and assumption.

These, then, are my conclusions: that the Zinoviev Letter is unlikely to have been genuine, but may well have been forged by Ivan Pokrovsky with the knowledge if not active assistance of British intelligence officials in Riga; that this story was probably known to at least some members of the British, French, German, Polish—and Russian—intelligence authorities, all of whom were well informed on the activities of the Orlov network; but that in any case, there were enough people in Britain within the security, intelligence, or military communities who neither knew nor cared that it was a forgery, but were willing to make the Letter available to right-wing interests opposed to the Labour government and its Russian policies. I recognize these conclusions are unsatisfactory. But it is the best that can be done based on the evidence. And it does not alter the fact that the Zinoviev Letter was, and remains, a potent political symbol; indeed, it makes it even more extraordinary.

Does it matter who wrote the Zinoviev Letter? Any researcher wants to find 'the answer', and reach a satisfactory conclusion after following the evidence trail. To that extent, it matters. On 11 December 1924 *The Times* printed a letter signed by 'A Traveller', recounting a conversation with a 'very high official of the Soviet government', with whom he had shared a railway compartment. This official described the debate about the authenticity of the Zinoviev Letter as 'quite irrelevant'. It was, he said, effective because it was true, in the sense of being entirely consistent with communist tactics and Soviet statecraft: '*se non è vero, è ben trovato*'. An 'active Russian Communist', he argued, based his moral code on the interests of the party and the proletariat, just as an Englishman believed in fair play and good faith.[73] The Letter achieved its aims, and so for practical purposes was authentic. Ramsay MacDonald, writing in *The Times* in March 1928, tended to agree: 'the important point was not the authenticity of the document but the use to which the document was put'.[74]

It is true that the Letter's impact, and the way it has continued to resonate in British politics for more than ninety years, owe far more to the way it was used than to its authorship. But for the historian, that is not enough. I really wish I did know, beyond doubt, who wrote the Zinoviev Letter, and the details of the political conspiracy surrounding it. For the story of the Zinoviev Letter is, above all, the story of a political conspiracy—and, as I know only too well from my career as an official historian, good conspiracies never die.

Conclusion

Good Conspiracy Theories Never Die

In 2000, the Labour Party celebrated its 100th birthday, and journalist Andrew Rawnsley, in *The Observer*, compiled an A–Z of the movement and its mythology 'to remind them where they came from'. A glance through the alphabet recalls episodes in the Zinoviev Letter story: A for Attlee; H for Harold Wilson, M for Militant Tendency, S for Socialism; poor Ramsay MacDonald gets short shrift under R for Red Flag, as 'the greatest traitor in Labour folklore' for splitting the party in 1931. Z is, of course, for Zinoviev Letter, repeating the usual assertion that it played a key part in bringing down the first Labour government (Rawnsley adding that the equivalent in 2000 was Blair Letters, 'signed columns purportedly written by the Prime Minister believed to be forgeries concocted by Alastair Campbell').[1]

Rawnsley's article was intentionally flippant, aimed at New Labour and what he called 'the Blair glitterati'. But the people, events, and movements included in his list—not just Z for Zinoviev—are a reminder of the part that enduring ideological battles and myths have played in the Labour Party's history, both in and out of government. In that history, the Letter has been one of the most deep-rooted of all the myths, and symbolic of long-running divisions within the party that still persist. It has been invoked in political discourse on a number of occasions since the publication of the 1999 report, not only in connection with Labour politics but also in regard to Britain's relations with Russia, and in connection with any suggestion of electoral 'dirty tricks'. In April 2001, for example, the Australian writer Peter Myers wrote of the Letter:

> The USSR Government claimed that it was forged; a standard 'Left' line is that it was produced by British intelligence (as, they claim, the Protocols [of the Elders of Zion] was [sic] created by the Tsar's intelligence service). Yet, given the deception about the true nature of Bolshevism, authenticity must be considered quite possible.[2]

Myers reproduced extracts both from the Letter, and from Dmitri Volkogonov's life of Lenin, to illustrate his point that the Letter was entirely in keeping with the objectives of Zinoviev and the Comintern. Despite the fact that he is inclined towards conspiracy theory, writing about plots by Jews, Bolsheviks, and global capitalism, Myers's conclusions about the Letter are not ill-founded. In crude terms, the political Right always tended to accept, or at least to allege, the authenticity of the Letter, while the Left saw it, from the beginning, as a political intrigue perpetrated by their political opponents; the Comintern's objective was, avowedly, to spread global revolution.

One could say that all these groups had, and in some cases their successors still have, an interest in promoting the idea of a conspiracy, even if their views on the perpetrators differ radically. Stephen Ambrose, in a 1992 article reviewing a book about the assassination of US President J. F. Kennedy in November 1963, wrote that 'dramatic or unhappy events' often produce conspiracy theories, as people want someone to blame, and are unwilling to believe that 'chance or accident can change world history'. Even when common sense indicates that a theory is implausible, people may still embrace it just because the alternative seems impossible.[3] Ambrose was talking about the idea of a complex conspiracy to assassinate Kennedy by a 'consensus of powerful men'. A later parallel might be the elaborate theories constructed by some to explain the death of Diana, Princess of Wales, in a car accident in 1997. Many people are perfectly capable of understanding that a conspiracy theory is inherently unlikely, while simultaneously holding the belief that 'there must be something in it';

after all, they argue, why would the authorities take the trouble to deny a theory that has no foundation?[4] That phenomenon was just as powerful in 1924, when the Zinoviev Letter episode certainly constituted a 'dramatic and unhappy event' for the Labour Party, as it was in 1963 or 1997.

At the general election held on 7 June 2001, the Labour government led by Tony Blair was re-elected with a large majority, the Conservatives' poor showing leading to the resignation of Conservative leader William Hague. During Labour's second term, British participation in the US-led coalition that invaded Iraq in March 2003 proved an increasingly divisive issue, particularly in respect of the basis on which the government had taken its decisions. It was not, therefore, surprising when the Zinoviev Letter came up during parliamentary discussions on the Iraq War. In the course of the long debate on 22 October 2003 as to whether there should be a judicial enquiry into the British government's decision to take military action in Iraq, Sir Peter Tapsell, who served as a Conservative MP continuously from 1966 to 2015 and was Father of the House from 2010, argued the case for an enquiry with his usual circumlocutory eloquence. In his view, the country had been misled into going to war, and he went even further back than the Zinoviev Letter in seeking a precedent, alleging that the 'so-called dodgy dossier was a rather clumsy update of Bismarck's doctoring of the Ems telegram'.[5]

Later in the debate, government and Opposition MPs clashed over the advice (not at that stage made public) given by the Attorney General, Lord Goldsmith, on the legal basis for the war in Iraq.[6] Tapsell said that:

> By far the most helpful precedent for the Opposition is the fact that when the opinion of Sir Patrick Hastings, the Attorney-General, on the Zinoviev letter was made public, it brought down the first Labour Government.

Bill Cash, the Shadow Attorney General, agreed: 'Absolutely...the Ramsay MacDonald Government fell because the Cabinet effectively pressurised the Attorney-General into giving advice that altered the basis of his previous advice.' Leaving aside the fact that in 1924 the Attorney General's change of advice related to the Campbell case, not the Zinoviev Letter, it is true that the case was the immediate cause of the MacDonald government's resignation, and it was interesting that the Conservative Opposition thought to raise the issue in this context in 2003. Summing up, FO Parliamentary Under-Secretary of State Bill Rammell expressed the view that although the debate had been 'instructive and worthwhile', he was not sure that 'anyone in the House or outside has changed their view in the course of it'.[7] The Iraq Enquiry, led by Sir John Chilcot, was to be announced in June 2009 by Gordon Brown, who had taken over from Tony Blair as Prime Minister in June 2007; Ramsay MacDonald was never able to persuade the House that an enquiry was needed into the Zinoviev Letter.[8]

On 5 May 2005 Labour was re-elected for a third term, the first time in its history that the party had ever achieved such a feat. However, it lost both seats and votes, and the government's majority was reduced, while the Conservatives and Liberal Democrats both made gains. The next five years were turbulent ones for Labour, with growing tensions within the party, exacerbated by the succession of Gordon Brown to the premiership in 2007, and by a series of severe challenges for the government including the global financial crisis that began in 2007–8. In 2010, thirteen years of Labour government came to an end, succeeded first by a coalition of Conservatives and Liberal Democrats until 2015, and then by a Conservative administration in which David Cameron, Prime Minister from 2010, took the decision, under pressure from the Eurosceptics in his party, to call a referendum to decide whether Britain should remain in the European Union. During the previous decade the Letter had continued to crop up at intervals, in the context of tensions in relations between Russia and the West; in books on Anglo-Russian relations and intelligence; and as a subject of historical interest in the media. In 2007, Simon Smith produced an interesting documentary on the Letter for the BBC, 'The Hidden Hand'. But it was in the campaign leading up to the EU referendum, held on 23 June 2016, and in the political fallout from the result in favour of 'Brexit', that the Zinoviev Letter again came into its own, resurfacing, as so often in the past, at a time of heightened political tension.

Commentators in the left-leaning media saw in the referendum campaign another skirmish in the long-running power struggle between the press and politicians, evoking irresistibly episodes like that of the Zinoviev Letter. In an article on 17 June 2016, Martin Kettle, conceding that the parallels between Ramsay MacDonald, the first Labour Prime Minister, and Conservative Prime Minister David Cameron were not immediately obvious, argued that if Cameron were forced to resign after losing the EU referendum, he would become 'the first British Prime Minister since MacDonald' to be 'brought down by the British press, and, more specifically, to be ousted by the *Daily Mail*':

> To say that today's *Daily Mail* relies on forgeries in its long attempt to drive Britain out of the EU, in which Cameron's fall would be more than just collateral damage if it happens, would be false. Nor would the *Mail's* campaign be the sole reason for a Brexit vote. But to say that the *Daily Mail*, then and now, has at its heart a rightwing political project, rather than a purely journalistic project, would not be false at all.

The *Daily Mail's* campaign against David Cameron was, said Kettle, revenge for setting up the Leveson Enquiry into the conduct of the British press.[9] The Prime Minister did, indeed, resign in the aftermath of the referendum result, to be succeeded by Theresa May.

During the referendum campaign the question of Britain's membership of the EU also produced strong differences of opinion within the Labour Party, already divided following the party's failure to gain office in 2015, leading to the unexpected success of the radical left-wing MP Jeremy Corbyn in the subsequent leadership contest. After the vote for Britain to leave the EU, criticism within the party of the approach Corbyn had taken during the campaign produced a leadership challenge, in which he was re-elected with an even larger share of the vote, supported by Momentum, a large grassroots campaigning network formed during his 2015 leadership campaign. These debates within the Left led a number of commentators to look back to 1924. John Medhurst, a Trade Union Industrial Officer and writer on Russian affairs, wrote an article on 16 October 2016 entitled 'Who's Afraid of the Big Bad Communists? Red Scares Then and Now', drawing parallels between the present day and the 1920s, including a short history of the Letter and its impact on the Labour party over the years. The Zinoviev Letter, Medhurst said, had been 'entirely fictional', just as claims that Momentum was a cover for hard-left infiltration of Labour were fictional; he observed with interest that, unlike the 'newly-radicalised Labour party under Corbyn', Labour in 1924 had posed little threat to established power and privilege. In future, he warned, further media attempts to 'subvert and sabotage' the Labour leader could be expected.[10]

When that article was written, there was no indication that on 18 April 2017 Theresa May would call a snap general election on 8 June, in order to increase the Conservative majority, a venture that did not pay off, since the government's majority was reduced and Labour did far better than the pollsters or political commentators predicted. In the run-up to the election (always a classic time for the Zinoviev Letter to raise its head), May accused European politicians of misrepresenting Britain's negotiating position over 'Brexit' in the Continental press, in an attempt deliberately to affect the result. This led several commentators to recall the events of 1924. Gary Gibbon, for Channel 4 News, reflected that not since 1924 had there been an accusation of 'foreign interference' in a British election; and in the *i*, David Levesley referred to the Zinoviev Letter episode as 'an example of what we'd now call "alternative facts"'.[11] The former Labour MP Chris Mullin, in a blog for *The Spectator* on 3 June 2017 headed 'Jeremy Corbyn for PM?', pointed out that in his novel *A Very British Coup*, published in 1982 and subsequently televised, his hero, steelworker Harry Perkins, had been elected Prime Minister on a platform more radical than that of Jeremy Corbyn, including 'withdrawal from the Common Market (been there, doing that)'.[12] The novel had done well, said Mullin, partly because some of the events in it turned out to be true, and the plot was not wholly improbable:'Even moderate Labour governments have traditionally faced attempts to destabilise them by elements in the political and security establishment'; among the examples he cited were the Zinoviev Letter and the alleged undermining of Harold Wilson by the security services.[13]

Faced with this catalogue of contemporary references, who would argue that the Zinoviev Letter is dead and buried? I am sure that commentators on all sides of the political spectrum will continue to refer to it at times of stress or electoral instability, neither of which shows much sign of subsiding as I write. As for the 'truth' about the Letter itself, though the passage of time may make it seem increasingly unlikely that new evidence will appear, I have certainly not given up hope that more might yet be discovered. Even if the British archives hold no further clues, some may well lie in Russian or Baltic archives, or the archives of other countries and their communist parties. In the 1920s, opponents of Bolshevik Russia were spread far and wide, and more and more countries are rediscovering their history. New books on the intelligence landscape of the early years of the twentieth century are also appearing, by scholars familiar with Russian as well as Western sources, and each adds a little more to the picture. The Zinoviev Letter may be dormant; but like all good conspiracy theories, it is not dead yet.

Appendix

The Zinoviev Letter: facsimile of
message L/3900 from Riga, as received
by the Secret Intelligence Service
on 9 October 1924

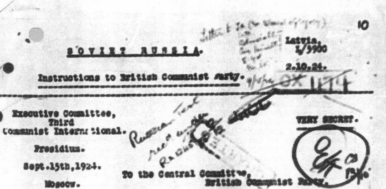

SOVIET RUSSIA.

Latvia,
1/9900
2.10.24.

Instructions to British Communist Party.

Executive Committee,
Third
Communist International.

VERY SECRET.

Presidium.

Sept.15th,1924.

To the Central Committee,
British Communist Party.

Moscow.

Dear Comrades,

The time is approaching for the Parliament of
England to consider the Treaty concluded between the
Governments of Great Britain and the SSSR for the
purpose of ratification. The fierce campaign raised
by the British bourgeoisie around the question shows
that the majority of the same, together with reaction-
-ary circles, are against the Treaty for the purpose
of breaking off an agreement consolidating the ties
between the proletariats of the two countries lead-
-ing to the restoration of normal relations between
England and the SSSR.

The proletariat of Great Britain, which pronounced
its weighty word when danger threatened of a break-off
of the past negotiations and compelled the Government
of MACDONALD to conclude the Treaty, must show the
greatest possible energy in the further struggle for
ratification and against the endeavours of British
capitalists to compel Parliament to annul it.

It is indispensable to stir up the masses of the
British proletariat, to bring into movement the army
of unemployed proletarians, whose position can be im-
-proved only after a loan has been granted to the SSSR
for the restoration of her economics and when business
collaboration between the British and Russian prolet-
-ariats has been put in order. It is imperative that
the group in the Labour Party sympathising with the
Treaty should bring increased pressure to bear upon
the Government and parliamentary circles in favour of
the ratification of the Treaty.

Keep close observation over the leaders of the Labour
Party, because these may easily be found in the leadingstrings of the bourgeoisie. The foreign policy of
the Labour Party as it is already represents an inferior
copy of the policy of the Curzon Government. Organise
a campaign of disclosures of the foreign policy of
MACDONALD.

The IKKI will willingly place at your disposal the
wide material in its possession regarding the activities
of British imperialism in the Middle and Far East. In
the meanwhile, however, strain every nerve in the
struggle for the /

11

-2-

the ratification of the treaty, in favour of a continuation of
negotiations regarding the regulation of relations between the
SSSR and England. A settlement of relations between the two
countries will assist in the revolutionising of the international
and British proletariat not less than a successful rising in any
of the working districts of England, as the establishment of close
contact between the British and Russian proletariat, the exchange
of delegations and workers, etc., will make it possible for us to
extend and develop the propaganda of ideas of Leninism in England
and the Colonies. Armed war-fare must be preceded by a struggle
against the inclinations to compromise which are embedded among
the majority of British workmen, against the ideas of evolution
and peaceful extermination of capitalism. Only then will it be
possible to count upon complete success of an armed insurrection.
In Ireland and the Colonies the case is different; there there is
a national question, and this represents too great a factor for
success for us to waste time on a prolonged preparation of the
working class.

But even in England, as in other countries where the workers
are politically developed, events themselves may more rapidly
revolutionize the working masses than propaganda. For instance,
a strike movement, repressions by the Government, etc.

From your last report it is evident that agitationpropaganda
work in the Army is weak, in the Navy a very little better.
Your explanation that the quality of the members attracted just-
-ifies the quantity is right in principle, nevertheless it would
be desirable to have cells in all the units of the troops, par-
-ticularly among those quartered in the large centres of the
country, and also among factories working on munitions and at
military store depots. We request that the most particular
attention be paid to these latter.

In the event of danger of war, with the aid of the latter and
in contact with the transport workers, it is possible to paralyse
all the military preparations of the bourgeoisie and to make a
start in turning an imperialist war into a class war. Now more
than ever we should be on our guard. Attempts at intervention
in China show that world imperialism is still full of vigour and
is once more making endeavours to restore its shaken position and
cause a new war, which as its final objective is to bring about
the break-up of the Russian proletariat and the suppression of
the budding world revolution, and further would lead to the en-
-slavement of the colonial peoples. "Danger of War", "The
Bourgeoisie seeks War; Capital fresh Markets." — these are the
slogans which you must familiarise the masses with, with which
you must go to work into the mass of the proletariat. These
slogans will open to you the doors of comprehension of the
masses, will help you to capture them and march under the banner
of Communism.

The Military Section of the British Communist Party, so far as
we are aware, further suffers from a lack of specialists, the
future directors of the British Red Army.

It is time you thought of forming such a group, which,
together with the leaders, might be, in the event of an outbreak
of active strife, the brain of the military organisation of the
Party.

Go attentively!

-2-   12

Go attentively through the lists of the military "cells", detailing from them the more energetic and capable men, turn attention to the more talented military specialists who have, for one reason or another, left the Service and hold socialist views.   Attract them into the ranks of the Communist Party if they desire honestly to serve the proletariat and desire in the future to direct not the blind mechanical forces in the service of the bourgeoisie but a national army.

Form a directing operative head of the Military Section.

Do not put this off to a future moment, which may be pregnant with events and catch you unprepared.

Desiring you all success, both in organisation and in your struggle,

With Communist Greetings,

President of the Presidium of the IKKI,

ZINOVIEV.

Member of the Presidium,
McMANUS,

Secretary, KUUSINEN.

Copies to
London,
Esthonia,
Finland,
Legation,
File.

TRANSCRIPTION

SOVIET RUSSIA

Latvia

L/3900

2.10.24

Instructions to British Communist Party

Executive Committee,
Third
Communist International.   **VERY SECRET**
Praesidium.
Sept. 15th, 1924   To the Central Committee,
Moscow.   British Communist Party.

Dear Comrades,

The time is approaching for the Parliament of England to consider the
Treaty concluded between the Governments of Great Britain and the SSSR
for the purpose of ratification. The fierce campaign raised by the British
bourgeoisie around the question shows that the majority of the same,
together with reactionary circles, are against the Treaty for the purpose of
breaking off an agreement consolidating the ties between the proletariats
of the two countries leading to the restoration of normal relations between
England and the SSSR.

The proletariat of Great Britain, which pronounced its weighty word
when danger threatened of a break-off of the past negotiations and compelled the Government of MACDONALD to conclude the Treaty, must
show the greatest possible energy in the further struggle for ratification and
against the endeavours of British capitalists to compel Parliament to annul it.

It is indispensable to stir up the masses of the British proletariat, to bring
into movement the army of unemployed proletarians, whose position can be
improved only after a loan has been granted to the SSSR for the restoration
of her economics and when business collaboration between the British and
Russian proletariats has been put in order. It is imperative that the group in
the Labour Party sympathising with the Treaty should bring increased pressure to bear upon the Government and parliamentary circles in favour of the
ratification of the Treaty.

Keep close observation over the leaders of the Labour Party, because
those may easily be found in the leadingstrings of the bourgeoisie. The foreign policy of the Labour Party as it is already represents an inferior copy of

the policy of the Curzon Government. Organise a campaign of disclosures of the foreign policy of MACDONALD.

The IKKI will willingly place at your disposal the wide material in its possession regarding the activities of British imperialism in the Middle and Far East. In the meanwhile, however, strain every nerve in the struggle for the ratification of the treaty, in favour of a continuation of negotiations regarding the regulation of relations between the SSSR and England. A settlement of relations between the two countries will assist in the revolutionising of the international and British proletariat not less than a successful rising in any of the working districts of England, as the establishment of close contact between the British and Russian proletariat, the exchange of delegations and workers, etc, will make it possible for us to extend and develop the propaganda of ideas of Leninism in England and the Colonies. Armed warfare must be preceded by a struggle against the inclinations to compromise which are embedded among the majority of British workmen, against the ideas of evolution and peaceful extermination of capitalism. Only then will it be possible to count upon complete success of an armed insurrection. In Ireland and the Colonies the case is different; there there is a national question, and this represents too great a factor for success for us to waste time on a prolonged preparation of the working class.

But even in England, as in other countries where the workers are politically developed, events themselves may more rapidly revolutionise the working masses than propaganda. For instance, a strike movement, repressions by the Government, etc.

From your last report it is evident that agitation-propaganda work in the Army is weak, in the Navy a very little better. Your explanation that the quality of the members attracted justifies the quantity is right in principle, nevertheless it would be desirable to have cells in all the units of the troops, particularly among those quartered in the large centres of the country, and also among factories working on munitions and at military store depots. We request that the most particular attention be paid to these latter.

In the event of danger of war, with the aid of the latter and in contact with the transport workers, it is possible to paralyse all the military preparations of the bourgeoisie and to make a start in turning an imperialist war into a class war. Now more than ever we should be on our guard. Attempts at intervention in China show that world imperialism is still full of vigour and is once more making endeavours to restore its shaken position and cause a new war, which as its final objective is to bring about the break-up of the Russian proletariat and the suppression of the budding world revolution, and further would lead to the enslavement of the colonial peoples. 'Danger of War', 'The Bourgeoisie seeks War; Capital fresh Markets.'—these are the slogans which you must familiarise the masses with, with which you must go to work into the mass of the proletariat. These slogans will open to you the doors of comprehension of the masses, will help you to capture them and march under the banner of Communism.

The Military Section of the British Communist Party, so far as we are aware, further suffers from a lack of specialists, the future directors of the British Red Army.

It is time you thought of forming such a group, which, together with the leaders, might be, in the event of an outbreak of active strife, the brain of the military organisation of the Party.

Go attentively through the lists of the military 'cells', detailing from them the more energetic and capable men, turn attention to the more talented military specialists who have, for one reason or another, left the Service and hold socialist views. Attract them into the ranks of the Communist Party if they desire honestly to serve the proletariat and desire in the future to direct not the blind mechanical forces in the service of the bourgeoisie, but a national army.

Form a directing operative head of the military Section.

Do not put this off to a future moment, which may be pregnant with events and catch you unprepared.

Desiring you all success, both in organisation and in your struggle.

> With Communist greetings,
> President of the Praesidium of the IKKI,
> ZINOVIEV

Member of the Praesidium,
MCMANUS,
Secretary, KUUSINEN.

Copies to
  London,
  Esthonia,
  Finland,
  Legation,
  File

Notes

INTRODUCTION

1. Usually known in Bolshevik circles as Grigorii Ovseyevich Zinoviev, he was born Ovsi Gershon Aronovich Radomishelski at Novomirgorod in 1883. Zinoviev also went by the names of Apfelbaum, Shatsky, and Aronoff. He was one of the original Bolshevik revolutionaries, having been a close associate of Lenin in Switzerland and elsewhere since 1908, and had travelled back to Russia with him in the sealed train to Russia in 1917.

2. The Secret Service Bureau, formed in 1909, separated a year later into MI5, the UK's domestic intelligence agency, and MI1(c), responsible for overseas intelligence ('MI' referring to Military Intelligence, the names a hangover from the First World War). From about 1920, the name Secret Intelligence Service (SIS) was commonly used for the overseas agency. Today it is often known as MI6, a name it adopted just before the Second World War. In this book SIS is most commonly used, but in practice the two are interchangeable, as are MI5 and the Security Service.

3. Martin Kettle, 'The EU referendum is a battle of the press versus democracy', *The Guardian*, 17 June 2016.

4. Gary Gibbon on Channel 4 News, 3 May 2017, David Levesley in iNews, 4 May 1027; see further the Conclusion to this book.

5. David Aaronovitch, *Voodoo Histories: The Role of the Conspiracy Theory in Shaping Modern History* (London: Jonathan Cape, 2009), p. 8.

6. The Bolshevik regime had fought a civil war from 1918 to 1920 against a range of opponents seeking to overthrow it. 'White Russian', i.e. anti-Bolshevik, forces had been supported by the Western powers, including Britain, although British Prime Minister David Lloyd George took the view that while he was willing to help bordering states if they were attacked, he was not prepared to use British troops against the Bolsheviks: 'I would rather leave Russia Bolshevik until she sees her way out of it than see Britain bankrupt.' See Gill Bennett, *Churchill's Man of Mystery: Desmond Morton and the World of Intelligence* (London: Routledge, 2006), pp. 45–6.

7. The full text of the Zinoviev Letter, as received by SIS on 9 October 1924, is reproduced in the Appendix to this book.

8. Kim Philby, a senior SIS officer who was also a Soviet spy, defected in 1963. See Chapter 5.

9. Lewis Chester, Stephen Fay, and Hugo Young, *The Zinoviev Letter: A Political Intrigue* (London: Heinemann, 1967).

10. Treasury documents on the Francs Case of 1928 (see Chapter 4) were not transferred to the Public Record Office (PRO, now The National Archives, TNA) until 1992, and were not made available to the cross-Whitehall investigation in the 1960s.

11. Chamberlain made this remark at a meeting of the Locarno Powers in Geneva on 14 June 1927, reported to the Foreign Office on 16 June: see *Documents on British Foreign Policy* (*DBFP*), Series Ia, Vol. III, Enclosure in No. 240.

12. Guy Burgess, Donald Maclean, Kim Philby, Anthony Blunt, and John Cairncross. There are many publications on the Cambridge spies, severally and jointly. For an authoritative account see Christopher Andrew, *The Defence of the Realm: The Authorized History of MI5* (London: Penguin, 2009).

13. For 'Operation FOOT' see Gill Bennett, *Six Moments of Crisis: Inside British Foreign Policy* (Oxford: Oxford University Press, 2013), ch. 5.

14. Robin Ramsay, in *Politics and Paranoia* (Hove: Picnic Publishing, 2008), claimed that right-wing campaigns, carried out by the security services in the 1970s, were Britain's 'Watergate-type experience', but the evidence produced came from conspiracy theorists like Peter Wright and has largely been discredited. Ramsay's account is, however, of some interest in its analysis of the reasons why conspiracy theories are so pervasive, particularly in the US.

15. Mitrokhin escaped to the West in 1992, bringing with him the copious notes he had smuggled out of the KGB archives. The results were published in Christopher Andrew and Vasili Mitrokhin, *The Mitrokhin Archive: The KGB in Europe and the West* (London: Penguin, 1999), and *The Mitrokhin Archive II: The KGB and the World* (London: Penguin, 2005); hereafter Mitrokhin I or II.

16. Data Protection Act (DPA) 1988; Freedom of Information Act (FOIA) 2000. The DPA applies to the UK's intelligence agencies, which are not within the scope of FOIA.

17. Nigel West and Oleg Tsarev, *The Crown Jewels: The British Secrets at the Heart of the KGB Archives* (London: HarperCollins, 1998).

18. The Foreign Secretary has ministerial responsibility for SIS, and also for GCHQ, and thus for their records. Responsibility for the UK's domestic

intelligence agency, the Security Service or MI5, rests with the Home Secretary, and with the Prime Minister.

19. Under the Public Records Act 1958 government departments were required to transfer documents worthy of permanent preservation to the Public Record Office when they were fifty years old (amended to thirty years by the Public Records Act 1967). The records of the security and intelligence agencies and certain intelligence-related records held by departments are retained under an exemption (known as the 'blanket') from the Lord Chancellor under Section 3(4) of the 1958 Act. These retentions are approved in ten-year tranches and each blanket approval must be reconsidered after not more than twenty years.

20. *Parl. Debs, H. of C., 5th ser.*, vol. 306, col. 324.

21. Gill Bennett, *The Zinoviev Letter of 1924: 'A most extraordinary and mysterious business'*, FCO History Notes No. 14, February 1999, Foreign and Commonwealth Office (hereafter HN). It is available online at <https://issuu.com/fcohistorians/docs/history_notes_cover_hphn_14>.

22. As explained in the 1999 report, Miss Bagot's memorandum, dated 1970, remains closed and is not releasable because of the sensitive operational and personnel information it contains (HN, pp. 2–3). However, some of the material, as drawn from her memorandum and cleared for publication in the FCO Report, also informs the present account. For the career of Milicent Bagot, the first female Oxford graduate to be employed by the Security Service (MI5), see Andrew, *Defence of the Realm*, pp. 131, 217, 232, 330, and 550.

23. Cass R. Sunstein, *Conspiracy Theories and Other Dangerous Ideas* (New York: Simon & Schuster, 2014), p. 5.

CHAPTER I

1. Oleg Gordievsky, the former senior KGB officer who supplied information to the British authorities for some years before escaping dramatically to the West when he came under suspicion, reviewed *Crown Jewels* in *The Spectator*, 18 April 1998.

2. West and Tsarev, *Crown Jewels*, p. 43.

3. Kenneth Anthony Bishop (1938–2012) originally studied Russian during his National Service in 1956–8, later graduating from Cambridge in Modern Languages before joining the Foreign Office. An expert on Soviet affairs in the Foreign Office's Research Department, in 1968 he was appointed Conference Interpreter, later Principal Conference Interpreter with the rank of Counsellor, in which capacity he acted as Russian interpreter

for Prime Ministers, Foreign Secretaries, and other ministers and senior officials. He was, as his obituary put it, 'the voice of British leaders from Macmillan to Blair—and in the early 1990s even the voice of The Queen—in meetings with Russian leaders'.

4. The Comintern, or Third Communist International, was the organization responsible for spreading the message of global communist revolution. Established in 1919, it was dominated by the Bolsheviks, whose experience of seizing power successfully in 1917 provided the basis for Comintern strategy. For the history of the Comintern since 1864, when the First International was established with the help of Karl Marx, see Alexander Vlatkin and Stephen A. Smith, 'The Comintern', in Stephen A. Smith (ed.), *The Oxford Handbook of the History of Communism* (Oxford: Oxford University Press, 2014), ch. 10.

5. This was of course the previous British Embassy building, not the new one that opened in 2000. The former Embassy remains the residence of the Ambassador.

6. The Union of Soviet Socialist Republics (USSR), originally comprising Russia, Transcaucasia, the Ukraine, and Belorussia, was established formally on 30 December 1922. Within the British government, the terms 'Russian' or 'Soviet Russian', 'Bolshevik', and 'Soviet' were used interchangeably throughout the early years of the USSR, and I have followed their practice.

7. Vladimir Ilyich Ulyanov (1870–1924) spent much of his adult life in exile, where he adopted a number of aliases, including Lenin. For an account of his early life and return to Russia in April 1917 see Helen Rappaport, *Conspirator; Lenin in Exile: The Making of a Revolutionary* (London: Hutchinson, 2009), and Catherine Merridale, *Lenin on the Train* (London: Allen Lane, 2016). Josef Vissarionovich Djugashvili (1878–1953) had taken the name Stalin ('man of steel') in 1912. On his early life see Simon Sebag Montefiore, *Young Stalin* (London: Weidenfeld & Nicolson, 2007); see also Kevin McDermott, 'Stalin and Stalinism', in *The Oxford Handbook of the History of Communism*, ch. 3.

8. On this abortive conspiracy to overthrow the Bolshevik regime in the summer of 1918, involving British envoy Robert Bruce Lockhart and Sidney Reilly, see Gordon Brook-Shepherd, *Iron Maze: The Western Secret Services and the Bolsheviks* (London: Macmillan, 1998). Brook-Shepherd suggests that the plot 'should really be called the "Lenin plot", with Lockhart and Reilly as the chief dupes in the Allied camp' (p. 109). See also Michael Occleshaw, *Dances in Deep Shadows: Britain's Clandestine War in Russia 1917–20* (London: Constable & Robinson, 2006). Whatever the

truth of this confused episode, it remains notorious in Russia even today as an example of Western perfidy.

9. Mitrokhin I, p. 40.

10. Article by Louise Jury, *The Independent*, 4 February 1999, p. 9. *Sex, Lies and Videotape* was a 1989 film starring Andie MacDowell.

11. In the general election held on 6 December 1923 Labour won 191 seats to the Conservatives' 258 and Liberals' 159, but Labour leader J. Ramsay MacDonald was asked to form a government on 22 January 1924 because of deep divisions on policy and leadership in the other two parties. British Communist Harry Pollitt told the Comintern Praesidium on 30 January that the Labour Party had 'never anticipated that the result would put them in the position of being the government' (see HN, p. 5).

12. On the early history of the party see Keith Laybourn, *A Century of Labour: A History of the Labour Party* (Stroud: Sutton Publishing, 2000).

13. See David Marquand, *Ramsay MacDonald* (London: Jonathan Cape, 1977), p. 247.

14. Sir Patrick Hastings, *Autobiography* (London: Heinemann, 1948), p. 226. On the convergence of Liberals with Labour see David Howell, *MacDonald's Party: Labour Identities and Crisis, 1922–31* (Oxford: Oxford University Press, 2002), pp. 310–18.

15. Liberal leader Herbert Asquith, though critical of Labour, was reluctant to force the government out of office. As A. J. P. Taylor commented, 'It was agreeable to feel that he could put Labour out; even more agreeable not to do it' (*English History 1914–1945*: Oxford: Oxford University Press, 1965, p. 218).

16. According to his biographer, Snowden believed that the function of the Chancellor of the Exchequer was 'to resist all demands for expenditure made by his colleagues and, when he can no longer resist, to limit the concession to the barest point of acceptance': Colin Cross, *Philip Snowden* (London: Barrie and Rockliff, 1966), p. 207. For Snowden's policies as Chancellor and his relations with the Treasury and Bank of England see George C. Peden, *The Treasury and Public Policy 1906–1959* (Oxford: Oxford University Press, 2000),ch. 4.

17. On the overall record of the government see John Shepherd and Keith Laybourn, *Britain's First Labour Government* (London: Palgrave Macmillan, 2006).

18. Marquand, *MacDonald*, p. 330.

19. Dudley Sommer, *Haldane of Cloan: His Life and Times 1856–1928* (London: George Allen & Unwin Ltd, 1960), p. 401. On 14 August 1924 the *Daily Herald* commented that it had been an 'immense advantage to the country

to have Ramsay MacDonald at the Foreign Office' but that 'there are disadvantages in having no effective Prime Minister' (quoted in Shepherd and Laybourn, *Britain's First Labour Government*, p. 145).

20. For the crisis provoked by the Franco–Belgian occupation of the Ruhr in January 1923 see *Documents on British Foreign Policy (DBFP)*, First Series, Vol. XXI (London: HMSO, 1978).

21. For negotiations in 1924 on German reparation, including an Inter-Allied conference that produced agreement on the Dawes Plan, see *DBFP*, First Series, Vol. XXV (London: HMSO, 1985). Marquand described MacDonald's part in them as 'the high point of his Government— perhaps his career' (Marquand, *MacDonald*, p. 351). The Geneva Protocol was never adopted, but the initiative was subsumed within what became the Locarno Treaty in 1925.

22. See *DBFP*, First Series, Vol. XII, for the 1921 agreement, and Victor Madeira, *Britannia and the Bear: The Anglo-Russian Intelligence Wars 1917–1929* (London: The Boydell Press, 2014), ch. 3. Churchill's comment is quoted in David Stafford, *Churchill and Secret Service* (London: John Murray, 1997), p. 103.

23. See *DBFP*, First Series, Vol. XXV, No. 53, and Bennett, *Morton*, p. 64. See also Christopher Andrew, *Secret Service: The Making of the British Intelligence Community* (London: Sceptre edn, 1986), pp. 417–20, and Madeira, *Britannia and the Bear*, pp. 112–15.

24. Speech by MacDonald at the Albert Hall, 8 January 1924: see *The Times*, 9 January 1924.

25. See *DBFP*, First Series, Vol. XXV, Nos 207–8 and No. 205, for a memorandum by J. D. Gregory, head of FO Northern Department, setting out the legal implications of recognition. As noted earlier, the Union of Soviet Socialist Republics (USSR), originally comprising Russia, Transcaucasia, the Ukraine, and Belorussia, was established formally on 30 December 1922. Within the British government, the terms 'Russian' or 'Soviet Russian', 'Bolshevik', and 'Soviet' were used interchangeably throughout the early years of the USSR, and I have followed their practice.

26. Cabinet Conclusions 44(24) of 30 July 1924, CAB 23/48, TNA.

27. See HN, pp. 8–9. The proceedings of the Anglo-Soviet negotiations from April to August 1924 are documented in *DBFP*, First Series, Vol. XXV, ch. III.

28. See Gabriel Gorodetsky, *The Precarious Truce: Anglo-Soviet Relations 1924–27* (Cambridge: Cambridge University Press, 1977), p. 35: 'Recognition had marked the high point in MacDonald's acceptance of Russia, but this soon gave way to obstruction of the Anglo-Soviet negotiations.' Michael Jabara Carley, in *Silent Conflict: A Hidden History of Early*

Soviet-Western Relations (Rowman & Littlefield, 2014), pp. 116ff., considers that MacDonald 'quickly absorbed the Foreign Office culture of hostility and suspicion toward Moscow if indeed he did not already possess it when he became prime minister', but the archival evidence does not support the idea of any significant change of view, rather a growing realization of the intractability of the problem of dealing with the Bolsheviks.

29. Sibyl Crowe and Edward Corp, *Our Ablest Public Servant: Sir Eyre Crowe 1964–1924* (London: Merlin Books, 1993), p. 457. Crowe told his wife that the Anglo-Soviet treaty was a 'ridiculous farce' that might 'even bring down the government'. See also Carley, *Silent Conflict*, pp. 129–31.

30. The British delegation included Victor Wellesley, FO Assistant Under-Secretary, with J. D. Gregory and Owen O'Malley of Northern Department, together with representatives from the Treasury and Board of Trade. The Secretariat included Major Oswald Rayner, who had worked for SIS in Russia in the First World War and joined the FO in 1923: see Bennett, *Morton*, p. 74.

31. HN, pp. 8–9.

32. Asquith used this phrase in a letter to *The Times* on 22 September 1924; see Shepherd and Laybourn, *Britain's First Labour Government*, p. 159.

33. See Robert Rhodes James (ed.), *Memoirs of a Conservative: J. C. C. Davidson's Memoirs and Papers 1910–37* (London: Macmillan, 1969), pp. 192–6.

34. Cabinet Conclusions 48(24), 6 August 1924, CAB 23/48, TNA.

35. For an account of the case see Shepherd and Laybourn, *Britain's First Labour Government*, ch. 7. A more personal view is given in Thomas Jones, a member of the Cabinet Secretariat, in *Whitehall Diary*, Vol. I, *1916–1925* (London: Oxford University Press, 1969), pp. 286–98.

36. Legislation was required urgently in connection with cross-party recommendations for a commission to settle the border between Northern Ireland and the Irish Free State.

37. See Sir Patrick Hastings, *Autobiography* (London: Heinemann, 1948), pp. 237–40. Hastings called the day of the debate on the Vote of Censure 'certainly the most exciting and possibly the most important I have ever lived' (p. 244).

38. *Parl. Debs, H. of C., 5th ser.*, vol. 177, col. 638; for the whole debate see cols 581–699.

39. Marquand, *MacDonald*, p. 379.

40. See, for example, the pamphlet 'Labour's Great Record: an outline of the first six months' work of the Labour Government', available in the University of Warwick digital collections, <http://contentdm.warwick.ac.uk/cdm/ref/collection/tav/id/1868>.

41. See Huw Richards, *The Bloody Circus:The Daily Herald and the Left* (London: Pluto Press, 1997), p. 76. Richards comments that the obituary of Lenin by the *Herald's* Foreign Correspondent, W. N. Ewer, was far livelier than the coverage of the new Labour government.

42. Leon Kamenev (1883–1936) had returned from exile to Russia in 1914 to edit *Pravda*, but was arrested and imprisoned until 1917 when freed during the February Revolution. Although, like Zinoviev, initially opposed to the Bolshevik plan for the October Revolution, he became one of the first members of the Politburo.

43. The Soviet Council of People's Commissars (Sovnarkom) was nominally the executive body of government, but in practice the Bolshevik leaders exercised control over the government machine and Soviet territory through the CPSU. Similarly, the People's Commissariat of Foreign Affairs (Narkomindel) was nominally responsible for foreign policy, but in practice authority lay with the Politburo.

44. See Boris Bazhanov, *Bazhanov and the Damnation of Stalin*, trans. David W. Doyle (Columbus, OH: Ohio University Press, 1990), p. 34. Bazhanov, one of the first defectors from the Soviet Union, escaped in January 1928 and settled in Paris, devoting himself to writing about Soviet ideology and methods. Though his account has to be treated with some caution, it is convincing on the atmospherics of Kremlin power struggles in the early 1920s. Bazhanov commented that Stalin 'had understood that the machine would carry him up, and he did what was necessary to take advantage' (p. 108).

45. See Bazhanov, *Bazhanov and the Damnation of Stalin*, pp. 74–84. Lev Davidovich Bronstein, later known as Leon Trotsky (1879–1940) was one of the leading organizers of the Bolshevik revolution in October 1917, serving the Soviet regime first as Commissar for Foreign Affairs, and then Commissar for War, where he was responsible for the creation of the Red Army. Since 1923, however, he had led a faction opposing Stalin and his growing control over the CPSU.

46. Bazhanov, *Bazhanov and the Damnation of Stalin*, p. 74. See also Alan Bullock, *Hitler and Stalin: Parallel Lives* (London: Fontana edn, 1998), pp. 192–4.

47. Stephen A. Smith has explained that the release in the 1990s of Comintern records enabled a better understanding of the relationship between Comintern and Politburo: see Vlatkin and Smith, 'The Comintern', in *The Oxford Handbook of the History of Communism*. Kamenev himself, in a speech at the 11th party conference in January 1924, referred to the Central Committee as 'standing at the head of the

Comintern' (Moscow dispatch to FO No. 48 of 21 January 1924, N 922/172/38, FO 371/10481, TNA).

48. See Keith Hamilton and Richard Langhorne, *The Practice of Diplomacy: Its Evolution, Theory and Administration* (London: Routledge, 1995), 'Bolshevik Diplomacy', pp. 148ff. On the relationship between government and Comintern see also Carley, *Silent Conflict*, ch. 2.

49. Hodgson was not a professional diplomat, but had spent his career in consular and commercial posts, in Russia since 1906. He was given the title of Chargé d'Affaires and Head of the British Commercial Mission on the recognition of the Soviet government in January 1924. On his role and achievements see Michael Hughes, *Inside the Enigma: British Officials in Russia 1900–1939* (London: The Hambledon Press, 1997), ch. 7, *passim*.

50. Moscow dispatch 924 of 3 October 1924, N 7864/172/38, FO 371/10482, TNA, printed in *DBFP*, First Series, Vol. XXV, No. 256.

51. On the German revolution and its impact on the Russian power struggle see Bullock, *Hitler and Stalin*, pp. 139–42, and Christopher Andrew and Oleg Gordievsky, *KGB: The Inside Story* (London: HarperCollins, 1990), pp. 58–9.

52. Caution is needed, however: an early 'Zinoviev Letter' supposedly sent from Riga to the Communist Workers' Party of Germany (KPD) in 1920, concerning joint military action by German and Russian revolutionaries, was apparently a forgery, and Zinoviev also denied authorship of a letter sent by the US Legation in Riga to the Federal Bureau of Investigation in 1923. See HN, p. 15.

53. See the interesting essay on Zinoviev by Anatoly Lunacharsky, written in 1923 as one of his 'Revolutionary Silhouettes', translated by Misha Glenny in 1967 and transcribed in 1996 for <https://www.marxists.org>.

54. At the end of 1923 the CPGB had been in danger of financial collapse, and had to mortgage its headquarters in order to fight the election: see Trevor Barnes, 'Special Branch and the First Labour Government', *The Historical Journal*, Vol. 22, No. 4 (December 1979), p. 943.

55. Carley, *Silent Conflict*, p. 85, quoting a letter from Litvinov to Christian Rakovsky, Soviet Chargé in London, 23 November 1923, from Russian archives. Born Meyer Wallach, Maxim Maximovitch Litvinov (1876–1951) was a prominent Soviet diplomat.

56. A series of contradictory letters of instruction were sent to the CPGB between December 1923 and the spring of 1924, advising British communists to work methodically 'for the disintegration of the so-called Labour Party' while at the same time formulating a series of demands to the government that suggested support for its remaining in power. For

information on Comintern meetings and letters to CPGB, December 1923–March 1924 from SIS and Russian archives, see HN, pp. 17–19.

57. The letter reached the Secret Intelligence Service (SIS) through its Riga Station. Its authenticity was corroborated by a report from the US Legation in Riga to the State Department, describing a meeting on 18 March at which Zinoviev had stressed that 'the Central Committee must be especially careful to avoid at all costs anything aimed at the over-throw of the MacDonald Government, as this could not suit the interests either of the Soviet Government or of the IKKI'. (US Legation in Riga to State Department, 9 June 1924, US National Archives (NARA), RG 59, 841.00B/38.)

58. The memorandum of 26 March 1924 did not come to light until a copy was found at CPGB headquarters when raided by the police on 14 October 1925: see HN, pp. 19–20.

59. See HN, p. 21. SIS archives include no reports containing instructions of this kind. Comintern Executive Committee archives were made available during my visit to Moscow in 1998, but I found no drafts or references to letters between April and September. The only exception was a let-ter apparently sent by McManus on 12 September, found by the TUC Delegation when it visited Moscow, enclosing a speech given by Zinoviev in August concerning anti-war propaganda. See also Madeira, *Britannia and the Bear*, pp. 120–1.

60. SIS archives, quoted in HN, p. 23.

61. Minute by George Mounsey, a Counsellor superintending FO Treaty Department, 6 May 1924, N 3844/104/38, FO 371/10478, TNA. The file contains a copy of the Comintern letter of 7 April, circulated by Special Branch as part of one of its regular reports on revolutionary organiza-tions in the UK. See also Barnes, 'Special Branch and the First Labour Government', on FO efforts, supported by MacDonald, to suppress information on Soviet propaganda in Britain during the negotiations.

62. Rakovsky, like Hodgson in Moscow, was Chargé, not Ambassador; at the time of *de jure* recognition the elevation of representatives to the rank of Ambassador did not take place, partly because HM King George V objected to according such an honour to a representative of a govern-ment that had murdered his cousins.

63. See *DBFP*, First Series, Vol. XXV, Nos 230–1. The Russian delegation included a large number of Soviet trade unionists in addition to Mikhail Tomsky, a member of the Central Committee of the CPSU and of the Politburo, and B. S. Stomonyakov, Soviet trade representative in Berlin. The Secretariat included Andrew Rothstein, a founder member of the

CPGB now working for the STD in London: the FO had raised objection to the inclusion of his father, Feodor A. Rothstein, who had been accused in the Curzon memorandum of inciting subversion in Persia (ibid., Nos 233 and 235).

64. Foreign Policy Archive of the Russian Federation, Rakovsky collection, quoted in Madeira, *Britannia and the Bear*, p. 122.

65. Carley, *Silent Conflict*, p. 25.

66. A copy of the message from Kuusinen to the CPGB, 10 October 1924, was printed in Jane Degras (ed.), *Documents of the Communist International* (London: Royal Institute of International Affairs, 1960), Vol. II. It is note-worthy that this message was *not* reported to SIS by Riga's agent FR3/K.

67. Report on the Central Executive Committee of the Union in Moscow dispatch No. 1004 to FO, 24 October 1924, N 8251/704/38, printed in *DBFP*, First Series, Vol. XXV, No. 259.

68. See Bennett, *Morton*, ch. 4. For Sidney Reilly, see Chapter 3 in the current volume.

69. Ch. 2 of Mitrokhin I gives a detailed account of Soviet intelligence at this period. See also Andrew and Gordievsky, *KGB*.

70. See Jonathan Haslam, *Near and Distant Neighbours: A New History of Soviet Intelligence* (Oxford: Oxford University Press, 2015), pp. 21–4. The KGB were 'near neighbours' of the Commissariat of Foreign Affairs, while military intelligence headquarters were further out of the centre of Moscow, hence 'distant neighbours'. See ibid., p. 10.

71. See Keith Jeffery, *MI6: The History of the Secret Intelligence Service 1909–1949* (London: Bloomsbury, 2010), pp. 185–6.

72. SVR history quoted in HN, p. 32.

73. The symbol @ is used in intelligence files to denote 'alias', or 'also known as'.

74. According to Orlov, the Blues were Russian monarchists, who planned to reconstruct the old Russian white, blue, and red flag by taking their stand between the Reds (Bolsheviks) and White Russians. See Bennett, *Morton*, p. 45.

75. See ibid., pp. 75–6.

76. On Orlov's employment by SIS, see ibid., ch. 3.

77. The Industrial Intelligence Bureau (IIB), financed by the Federation of British Industries and the Coal Owners' and Shipowners' Associations, was set up by Sir George Makgill at the end of the First World War to acquire intelligence on industrial unrest and the activities of 'subversive' bodies like the CPGB and IRA. For Makgill's activities, and his close connections with British intelligence, see ibid., ch. 4.

78. Marquand, *MacDonald*, pp. 314–15. See also Andrew, *Secret Service*, pp. 425–6.

79. Andrew, *Defence of the Realm*, pp. 146–8. On Childs's concern with communist activities and reports on industrial subversion see Barnes, 'Special Branch and the First Labour Government'.

80. See Andrew, *Secret Service*, p. 426.

81. On the origins of these organizations and their development during the First World War and in the early post-war period see Jeffery, *MI6* and Andrew, *MI5*; on the early history of GC&CS (now GCHQ) see also <https://www.gchq.gov.uk/features/story-signals-intelligence-1914-2014>. See also Bennett, *Morton*, chs 3 and 4.

82. Shepherd and Laybourn, *Britain's First Labour Government*, pp. 132 and 138. See also John Shepherd, 'A Gentleman at the Foreign Office: Influences Shaping Ramsay MacDonald's Internationalism in 1924', in Paul Corthorn and Jonathan Davis (eds), *The British Labour Party and the Wider World: Domestic Politics, Internationalism and Foreign Policy* (New York: Tauris Academic Studies, 2008), pp. 40–5.

83. See Ephraim Maisel, *The Foreign Office and Foreign Policy 1919–26* (Eastbourne: Sussex Academic Press, 1994; 2014 edn), pp. 130–1. Sir Alexander Cadogan (1884–1968) served in China 1933–6, as FO Permanent Under-Secretary 1938–45, and as the first UK Permanent Representative to the United Nations from 1946.

84. J. D. Gregory, *On the Edge of Diplomacy: Rambles and Reflections 1902–28* (London: Hutchinson, 1928), p. 135; Robin Bruce Lockhart, *Ace of Spies* (London: Hodder & Stoughton, 1967), pp. 92–3.

85. The Secret Service Committee was convened initially at ministerial level in 1919, but met again in 1921 and 1922 under the Cabinet Secretary, Sir Maurice Hankey, with Sir Warren Fisher and Sir Eyre Crowe as members—the 'three biggest guns in Whitehall' (Alan Judd, *The Quest for C: Mansfield Cumming and the Founding of the Secret Service* (London: HarperCollins, 1999), pp. 469–70). For the Committee's papers and reports see CAB 127/355–7 and KV 4/151, TNA. A detailed account of the proceedings is also given in Bennett, *Morton*, pp. 37–9, 56–8, and 66–8.

86. Bennett, *Morton*, p. 64.

87. For an interesting analysis of the social and professional environment of those involved in both intelligence and foreign policy-making see Uri Bar-Joseph, *Intelligence Intervention in the Politics of Democratic States: The United States, Israel and Britain* (University Park, PA: The Pennsylvania State University Press, 1995), pp. 320ff.

88. For an account of im Thurn's part in the Zinoviev Letter affair, see Chester, Fay, and Young, *Zinoviev Letter*. Although the details in this book by the *Sunday Times'* 'Insight' team about the origins of the Zinoviev Letter do not accord with documentary evidence that later became available, the authors are properly cautious about im Thurn's activities.

89. See Andrew, *Defence of the Realm*, p. 150.

90. See HN, pp. 28–9. The Russian Volunteer Fleet (RVF) Association had been set up in St Petersburg in 1883 and moved its offices to Paris in 1917 before moving them back to Moscow in 1923. The Anglo-Russian Volunteer Fleet was the RVF's London agent, and one of its directors, Vladimir Sagovsky, was General Manager of ARCOS (the All-Russian Cooperative Society Ltd). See further Chapter 4 in the current volume.

91. The phrase was used in a letter from 'A Traveller' printed in *The Times* on 11 December 1924, describing a conversation with a 'very high official of the Soviet Government'.

CHAPTER 2

1. The text of the Letter, as received by SIS, is reproduced in the Appendix.

2. 'CX' was the designation for material received by government departments from SIS; 1174 was the SIS file number for the Zinoviev Letter.

3. Ispolnitel'niy Komitet Kommunisticheskogo Internationsionala, Executive Committee of the Comintern (referred to either as IKKI or ECCI). Arthur MacManus (1889–1927), leader of the Clyde Workers Committee during the First World War, was one of the founders of the CPGB in 1920 and its first Chairman; he was a member of the Comintern's Executive Committee. Otto Kuusinen (1881–1964) was a founder of the Finnish Communist Party and served as Secretary of the Executive Committee from 1921.

4. British diplomatic and commercial officials in Russia, though restricted in their dealings with their Soviet counterparts, had a range of personal contacts, some from the tsarist period, from whom they received useful information. See Hughes, *Inside the Enigma*, pp. 188–91.

5. See Jeffery, *MI6*, ch. 6. On the use of alternative sources of intelligence see, for example, P. Tomaselli, 'C's Moscow Station: The Anglo-Russian Trade Mission as cover for SIS in the early 1920s', *Intelligence and National Security*, Vol. 17, No. 3 (Autumn 2002), pp. 173–80. Many useful intelligence reports from diplomatic and commercial representatives within the Soviet Union can also be found in *Documents on British Foreign Policy* (*DBFP*), First Series.

6. On the FR/3 group, see Jeffery, *MI6*, pp. 190–1.

7. See HN, p. 34. On Farina, see Jeffery, *MI6*, pp. 188–91.

8. See Chapter 1. Although more than one treaty had been negotiated, for the Soviet government the key treaty was the general Anglo-Soviet treaty whose ratification would pave the way for a loan.

9. For the life and career of Major (later Sir) Desmond Morton, see Bennett, *Morton*.

10. On Cumming's death and Sinclair's background and character see Jeffery, *MI6*, pp. 169–71. On the staffing and structure of SIS at this period see ibid., pp. 162–9.

11. Major, later Sir, Joseph Ball (1885–1961), described as 'a quintessential *eminence grise*', joined MI5 at the outbreak of the First World War and remained in the Security Service until 1927, when he was persuaded by the chairman of the Conservatives, J. C. C. Davidson, to join Central Office as director of publicity. From 1930 to 1939 he was head of the Conservative Research Department and worked closely with Neville Chamberlain. See Robert Blake, 'Ball, Sir (George) Joseph', *Oxford Dictionary of National Biography* (Oxford: Oxford University Press, 2004).

12. Bland was Private Secretary to the FO's most senior official, Permanent Under-Secretary Sir Eyre Crowe.

13. The FO copy of the note is filed at N 7838/108/38G, FO 371/10478, TNA. On Woollcombe see Andrew, *Secret Service*, pp. 488–9.

14. See Barnes, 'Special Branch and the First Labour Government', p. 949.

15. Minutes on N 7838/108/38G, FO 371/10478, TNA.

16. See Bennett, *Morton*, pp. 72 and 81–2.

17. See N 7838/108/38, FO 371/10478, TNA. An account of these developments, including the minutes by Crowe, MacDonald, and others, was prepared for the committee of enquiry into the Zinoviev Letter set up by Austen Chamberlain, who succeeded MacDonald as Foreign Secretary. It is printed in *DBFP*, First Series, Vol. XXV, Enclosure I, in No. 264, and provides a useful summary of events.

18. Further details of Morton's informant and the provenance of the supposed 'corroborative proof' supplied by SIS to Crowe can be found in HN, pp. 36–9; see also Bennett, *Morton*, pp. 80–2.

19. Minute by Morton of 11 October and Bagot report, 1970, quoted in HN, pp. 36–7.

20. In March 1925, Morton submitted an expanded version of his report, stating that according to his informant no full meeting of the CPGB Executive Committee had been held to discuss the Letter, 'partly because most of the members were inaccessible owing to activities in face of the obviously imminent Parliamentary election'. Since at the time of the

supposed receipt of the Letter no election had been called, and did not seem in immediate prospect, this would appear to reduce the reliability of Morton's account still further.

21. Summary of testimony by Childs, SIS archives: see HN, p. 39. See also Chapter 3 in this volume.

22. See Chapter 1.

23. Letter of 3 July 1924 from Morton to Ball, SIS archives, quoted in HN, p. 31.

24. Jonathan Pile, in a privately printed book about Ball, *Churchill's Secret Enemy* (2012), feels that Ball played a more prominent role in the Zinoviev Letter episode than has been acknowledged. That is certainly possible, but Pile is not correct in alleging that material in SIS or MI5 archives has been suppressed that illuminates further the role played by either Ball or Morton. Pile's account is also based on a number of misperceptions about the mechanism of SIS operations in the early 1920s.

25. SIS archives, quoted in HN, p. 39.

26. According to Chester, Fay, and Young, *Zinoviev Letter*, a copy of im Thurn's diary was found in the papers of the Conservative MP Guy Kindersley, who died in 1956. Entries between 8 and 27 October 1924 are reproduced ibid., Appendix A. Chester, Fay, and Young deduced that 'X' was an agent of Polish intelligence, but this cannot be verified, and im Thurn himself implied that his informant might have been a woman, the mistress of a Russian monarchist in London connected to ARCOS: see HN, pp. 42–3.

27. Chester, Fay, and Young, *Zinoviev Letter*, p. 80.

28. SIS archives, quoted in HN, pp. 43–4.

29. Chester, Fay, and Young, *Zinoviev Letter*, p. 185.

30. Ibid., Appendix A.

31. On Marlowe's 1928 article see Chapter 4.

32. Letter of 7 November 1924 to Captain Miller, Scotland Yard, KV 2/3331/3/35, TNA. When questioned by Milicent Bagot in 1969, Morton claimed that a copy of the letter had been posted to the *Daily Mail* by Stewart Menzies, who was to succeed Sinclair as chief of SIS in 1939. Bagot made it clear, however, that she regarded this information as suspect.

33. Statement to Treasury Board of Enquiry in 1928, T 281/30, TNA.

34. See HN, p. 45.

35. Chester, Fay, and Young, *Zinoviev Letter*, p. 199; see HN, pp. 44–5.

36. The original Northern Department draft, amended by Crowe, is in N 8105/108/38, FO 371/10478, TNA.

37. 'What happened on "Zinoviev Friday"' was a question put by the *Sunday Worker* on 4 March 1928, when the 'Francs Case' had brought the Zinoviev

Letter to the forefront of public notice once more: see Chapter 4. The article stated that 'Precise and definite evidence there must be of what happened in the Foreign Office on "Zinoviev Friday".' A copy can be found in KV 2/3331/1/78, TNA.

38. SIS archives, quoted in HN, p. 49. The FO memorandum of 11 November (*DBFP*, First Series, Vol. XXV, p. 436) stated that it had been brought to the FO's attention on Friday afternoon that the *Daily Mail* was to publish the Letter the next day, but Crowe knew early that morning.

39. See Marquand, *MacDonald*, pp. 383–4. The draft as amended by MacDonald has not been found in the archives, so his revisions can only be reconstructed by comparing the draft sent to him by Crowe with the final version sent to Rakovsky. For later discussions of whether MacDonald had initialled the draft in the margin, as opposed to at the bottom of the document, see Chapter 5 in this volume.

40. See Chapter 3.

41. Evidence given by Strang to Treasury Board of Enquiry, T 281/30, TNA. See also Lord Strang, *Home and Abroad* (London: André Deutsch, 1956), pp. 57–8.

42. The final text of the note to Rakovsky is missing from FO archives, but the original, signed by Gregory, was consulted in the archives of the Russian Ministry of Foreign Affairs in 1998, and was reproduced in facsimile as Annex C to the FCO's History Note.

43. Rakovsky to Litvinov, 24 and 25 October 1924; Chicherin to NKID and Politburo, 24 October, to Zinoviev and Litvinov, 25 October, translations of documents consulted in Russian Ministry for Foreign Affairs in 1998.

44. Rakovsky's note of 25 October to the FO is printed in *Dokumenty vneshney politiki SSSR* (Foreign Policy Documents of the USSR) (*DVPS*), Vol. VII, No. 242, and in Cmd 2895, *A Selection of Papers dealing with the relations between His Majesty's Government and the Soviet Government 1921–1927* (London: HMSO, 1927). The note was sent immediately to MacDonald, who returned it to the FO with a minute: 'When I return to town information will be to hand to carry the matter another stage.'

45. Rakovsky to Litvinov, 25 October 1924, translation of document consulted in Russian Ministry of Foreign Affairs in 1998.

46. See Hughes, *Inside the Enigma*, pp. 189–90.

47. Litvinov to Rakovsky, 27 October 1924, translation of document consulted in Russian Ministry of Foreign Affairs in 1998.

48. Evidence given by FO librarian Gaselee to the Treasury Board of Enquiry on 21 February 1928, T 281/30, TNA.

49. Details given by MacDonald to the Treasury Board of Enquiry, T 281/13, TNA.

50. A copy of the *Daily Mail* article can be found on the University of Warwick's Modern Records Centre website, <http://contentdm.warwick. ac.uk/cdm/ref/collection/russian/id/2595>.

51. Commentary by A. MacManus to the *History of the Zinoviev Letter,* published by the CPGB in 1925.

52. Crowe to MacDonald, 25 October 1924, N 8105/108/38, TNA. See HN, pp. 51–2. This copy was inserted in the file from the Royal Archives at Windsor, since the FO copy was missing.

53. MacDonald testimony to Treasury of Board of Enquiry, 1928 (see Chapter 4 in this volume), T 281/13, TNA.

54. The record of the Sovnarkom meeting of 25 October, quoted more fully in HN, pp. 68–9, was transmitted to SIS in Riga report L/3981 of 6 November 1924, and circulated by them to Scotland Yard and the Service ministries. MI5's copy is in KV 2/331/3, fos 12–16, TNA. The letter from MacManus referred to seems to be that of 12 September: see Chapter 3 in this volume.

55. Moscow telegram No. 359, 29 October 1924, N 8210/108/38, TNA.

56. Litvinov to Rakovsky, 27 October 1924, document consulted in the Russian Ministry of Foreign Affairs in 1998.

57. See note 54.

58. A number of reports that seemed to authenticate the Letter can be found in KV 2/3331/3, TNA.

59. 'C' to Crowe, 6 November 1924, N 8733/108/38, FO 371/10479, TNA; minute of 6 November to Captain Miller, KV 2/3331/3, fo. 45, TNA.

60. For Crowe's letter to Lord Haldane of 9 November see Sommer, *Haldane of Cloan,* p. 410.

61. MacDonald's diary, cited in Marquand, *MacDonald,* p. 384.

62. See Carley, *Silent Conflict,* pp. 129–30.

63. Crowe and Corp, *Our Ablest Public Servant,* p. 461. MacDonald said in his testimony to the Treasury Board of Enquiry in 1928 that 'As a matter of fact the Zinoviev letter killed Crowe', although he struck this out from the edited version. In his memoirs, Gregory wrote that 'Crowe and the Foreign Office were one and indivisible ... Appropriately and heroically he sacrificed and filled himself on its behalf' (*On the Edge of Diplomacy,* p. 255).

64. See Maisel, *The Foreign Office and Foreign Policy,* pp. 132–3.

65. MacDonald's speech was reported in *The Times,* 28 October 1924, p. 4, under the headline 'Labour optimism at Cardiff'.

66. See Marquand, *MacDonald*, p. 387; US State Department archives, NARA, RG 59, 841.00B/46, quoted in HN, p. 73.

67. See Jeffery, *MI6*, p. 218.

68. Gregory included some of Morel's speeches on the Red Letter in his memoirs, which shed little light on Gregory's own conduct during the affair. See Catherine Ann Cline, 'E. D. Morel and the Crusade against the Foreign Office', *The Journal of Modern History*, Vol. 39, No. 2 (June 1967), pp. 126–37.

69. See Chapter 4.

70. Further details of Aminta Dyne can be found in Chapter 4.

71. Deposition by Violet Digby, T 281/39, TNA.

72. Testimony by Ramsay MacDonald to Treasury Board of Enquiry, T 281/13, TNA.

73. Evidence given by J. H. Thomas, 20 February 1928, T 281/20, TNA.

74. Article in *Pravda*, 28 October 1924: a translation is in KV 2/3331/3/79ff., TNA. Karl Radek (1885–1939) became a Bolshevik in 1917 but was a member of the Left Opposition movement and was expelled in 1927.

75. Letters from Rakovsky to Litvinov, 13 November and 1 December 1924, translation of documents consulted in the Russian Foreign Ministry archives in 1998.

76. Minute by Gregory of 29 October 1924, N 8475/108/38, FO 371/10479, TNA. Rakovsky's note of 27 October is printed in *DBFP*, First Series, Vol. XXV, No. 264, note 9, and in *DVPS*, Vol. VII, No. 245.

77. Rakovsky to Litvinov, 29 October 1924, translation of letter consulted in Russian Foreign Ministry archives in 1998.

78. This report was reproduced in *The Times* on 29 October, 1924, election day. For Radek's article see note 74.

79. A copy of this telegram is in KV 2/3331/3/67–9, TNA.

80. Moscow dispatch 1079 of 21 November 1924, printed in *DBFP*, First Series, Vol. XXV, No. 268; see also No. 260.

81. A copy of the gist of the Riga report is in KV 2/3331/3/6, TNA.

82. A translation of this interview was sent by the US Legation in Riga to the State Department in a report received on 25 November: RG 59 841.00B/45, NARA.

83. This letter was published in *Anti-Soviet Forgeries* (London: Workers' Publications Ltd, 1927), with a foreword by George Lansbury, setting out details of a number of forged documents. See also Chapter 3 in this volume.

84. See N 8195–6/108/78, FO 371/10478, TNA. MacDonald minuted on 29 October: 'Have no correspondence with these gentlemen.'

85. See reports in *The Times*, 28 October 1924, pp. 7 and 12, and 29 October, p. 8. After his speech in Aberavon on the morning of 28 October MacDonald was overcome by exhaustion and retired to bed.

CHAPTER 3

1. George Lansbury, in the Foreword to *Anti-Soviet Forgeries*, p. xii.
2. Intercepted telegram from Rakovsky to Ministry of Foreign Affairs, Moscow, 30 October 1924, KV 2/3331/3/39, TNA.
3. See A. J. P. Taylor, *Beaverbrook* (London: Hamish Hamilton, 1972), p. 223. According to Taylor, Beaverbrook, proprietor of the *Daily Express*, had 'tried to keep the Red Peril out of his newspapers', as he thought the Zinoviev Letter might 'drive panic-stricken Liberals to vote Conservative and would so ruin the Liberal party'. But this approach was ineffective, 'as the Red Peril raged in Rothermere's newspapers and had the result which Beaverbrook expected'.
4. Litvinov to Rakovsky, 31 October 1924, translation of document consulted in Russian Foreign Ministry archives in 1998. Litvinov expressed the view that the incoming Conservative government was 'scarcely likely to be able to completely disregard the Anglo-Soviet conference and the preliminary treaty', though they could be expected to interpret their election victory 'as a mandate for a very tough policy towards us'.
5. After an electoral defeat, the timing of a government's resignation is at the discretion of the Prime Minister, and may be delayed, for example because of negotiations with other parties, or, as in this case, because of an enquiry related to the election.
6. Jones, *Whitehall Diary*, p. 299. Jones took the note of the meeting on 31 October 1924 in the absence of the Cabinet Secretary, Sir Maurice Hankey.
7. Ibid., pp. 300–1. The formal Cabinet minutes record no more than the decision to appoint a Committee of Enquiry: Cabinet Conclusions 57(24), 31 October 1924, CAB 23/48, TNA.
8. See Chapter 2.
9. See *DBFP*, First Series, Vol. XXV, pp. 437–9. A further note from Rakovsky of 1 November, and a response from Gregory on 4 November are printed ibid.
10. N 8272/108/38, FO 371/10478, TNA. The minute is printed in *DBFP*, First Series, Vol. XXV, p. 438.
11. Berzin to Litvinov, 5 November 1924, document consulted in Russian Foreign Ministry archives in 1998. A telegram from Rakovsky to

Moscow, reporting his conversation with MacDonald, is printed in *DVPS*, Vol.VII, No. 256.

12. See Chapter 2.

13. Exchange of correspondence between Miller and Bland, 4 and 9 December 1924, KV 2/3331/2/94–5, TNA. Berzin's account was confirmed in *Anti-Soviet Forgeries*. See also HN, pp. 76–7.

14. SIS files, cited in HN, p. 78.

15. See Chapter 2.

16. SIS response to MacDonald's enquiries of 3 November 1924, quoted in HN, pp. 77–9.

17. Condensed note prepared by Sir Wyndham Childs of his evidence to the Cabinet Committee of Enquiry, and appended to the Bagot report: see HN, pp. 79–80. Childs subsequently published an article in the *Sunday Graphic* on 6 April 1930, in which he said that the Letter had contained no new ideas or new directions, and that if Zinoviev had sent it, he was a 'blithering idiot'.

18. Cabinet Committee Report on the Zinovieff Letter, CAB 27/354, TNA.

19. Cabinet Conclusions (58)24, 4 November 1924, CAB 23/48, TNA.

20. See *DBFP*, First Series, Vol. XXV, pp. 439–40.

21. Jones, *Whitehall Diary*, p. 301.

22. Memorandum by O'Malley, 7 November 1924, N 8473/108/38, FO 371/10479, TNA. Gregory agreed with these recommendations, noting at the foot of the memorandum that he was in favour of 'allowing the result of the elections to remain the real answer to M. Rakowsky'.

23. The two memoranda are printed in *DBFP*, First Series, Vol. XXV, No. 264, as enclosures to a short minute by Chamberlain, N 8467/108/38, circulated to the Cabinet as CP(484)24. The final version of the note sent to Rakovsky by Chamberlain on 21 November 1924 in response to the Russian note of 25 October is printed as No. 266. Rakovsky commented to Litvinov that Chamberlain had been careful to draw his own conclusions: 'The general impression here is that, on the one hand, the Conservative government is seeking to satisfy public opinion within the party, but on the other hand, it is actually beating a retreat because the note is drafted in such a way that, from our side, it could even remain unanswered.' (Rakovsky to Litvinov, 21 November 1924, translation of document consulted in Russian Ministry for Foreign Affairs in 1998.)

24. Cabinet Conclusions 59(24), 12 November 1924, CAB 23/49, TNA.

25. Moscow telegram 359, 29 October 1924, N 8210/108/37, FO 371/10478, TNA.

26. Translation of *Pravda* article and minute of 7 November 1924 by Maxse, N 8382/108/38, FO 371/10479, TNA.

27. An SIS report from its station in Helsingfors in June 1920, an extract of which was passed on to MI5, had described a split in the Bolsheviks, with Lenin holding together different factions including a 'Jewish party', comprising Zinoviev, Trotsky, Dzerzhinsky, and Bukharin. The report said that the 'differences of opinion are so great that sometimes it looks as though an armed fight cannot be avoided' (KV 2/501/2/19, TNA).

28. Stockholm dispatch No. 437, 1 November 1924, N 8319/108/38, FO 371/10478, TNA.

29. Note to Captain Miller, 11 November 1924, KV 2/3331/3/20, TNA.

30. Riga forwarded this report to SIS headquarters in L/3982 on 6 November 1924. The gist of it was circulated to the FO, Scotland Yard, and MI5 on 19 November: see KV 2/3331/3/6, TNA.

31. Chicherin to Litvinov, November 1924, translation of document consulted in Russian Foreign Ministry for Foreign Affairs in 1998. Ignacz Trebitsch Lincoln (1879–1943) @ Patrick Keelan @ Trautwein was a Hungarian-born spy, right-wing conspirator, and fantasist who had been variously a missionary in Canada, British Liberal MP, German agent, and adviser to Chinese warlords. According to his biographer, he was in China in 1924, until he left for France at the end of October: see Bernard Wasserstein, *The Secret Lives of Trebitsch Lincoln* (New Haven and London: Yale University Press, 1988), pp. 216–17.

32. A copy of Zinoviev's telegram can be found on the website of the University of Warwick, <http://contentdm.warwick.ac.uk/cdm/ref/collection/russian/id/2573>. A number of other documents relating to the visit to the Soviet Union by the TUC Delegation in November–December 1924 can be found on the same site in the useful collection 'The Russian Revolution and Britain, 1917–1928'.

33. During their adventures in Moscow, Tintin and his dog Snowy encounter a group of 'English Communists being shown the beauties of Bolshevism'. I am grateful for this reference to the BBC correspondent Frank Gardner, who retraced Tintin's journey to Moscow in 2011, and discussed the project with me. Although the TUC delegation were not all communists, nor the only visitors to Russia around this time, there are details in the book that suggest this connection.

34. Chicherin to Litvinov, 7 December 1924, translation of document consulted in Russian Foreign Ministry in 1998.

35. Minutes of Comintern Praesidium meeting of 18 November 1924, consulted at Russian Centre in 1998. Details of the delegation taken from the Report published in 1925, and from a collection of papers of Sir George Young, Bt, made available for the purposes of the FCO investigation in 1998; see HN, pp. 21–2.

36. Report for the TUC General Council, 1925; extracts were printed in *The Times*, 18 May 1925. See also HN, p. 22.

37. See Andrew and Gordievsky, *KGB*, p. 67.

38. See Giles Udy, *Labour and the Gulag: Russia and the Seduction of the British Left* (London: Biteback Publishing Ltd, 2017), p. 105.

39. See note 17.

40. Cabinet Conclusions 60(24), 19 November 1924, CAB 23/49, TNA. See also note 23.

41. Memo from Chicherin to Politburo, 21 November 1924, translation of document consulted in Russian Ministry for Foreign Affairs in 1998.

42. See Peden, *The Treasury and Public Policy*, ch. 5.

43. British rule in Egypt had been established in 1882, its principal objective to ensure control over the Suez Canal through which passed key supplies of oil. The Anglo-Egyptian Condominium of the Sudan was established in 1899. In the early 1920s British attempts to reduce administrative and military expenditure in the region encouraged demands from Egyptian nationalists for greater autonomy. During the Labour government MacDonald had held talks with the Egyptian Premier, Saad Zaghlul, but they broke down in September 1924.

44. The following analysis is taken from SIS files, cited in HN, pp. 81–3.

45. SIS archives, cited in HN, p. 87.

46. Jeffery, *MI6*, p. 190.

47. Bagot report, cited in HN, p. 86.

48. See Chapter 1.

49. Foley became head of Berlin station in 1923 and remained there until 1939; during the 1930s he helped many thousands of Jews to escape from Germany by giving them visas. See Jeffery, *MI6*, pp. 194 and 301–2; also Michael Smith, *Foley: The Spy who Saved 10,000 Jews* (London: Hodder & Stoughton, 1999).

50. Bennett, *Morton*, p. 82; SIS files quoted in HN, pp. 84–5.

51. See Chapter 1.

52. Translation of a press intercept of 15 November 1924, consulted in the Russian Foreign Ministry archives in 1998.

53. See Chapter 2; details of contact with the tsarist officer from SIS records, cited in HN, pp. 86–7.

54. Marquand, *MacDonald*, p. 390. Marquand notes that MacDonald was 'badly shaken by the events of the last three months', but there was little serious opposition in the party to his continuing as leader.

55. The first woman elected to the House of Commons was Constance Markievicz, in the general election of 1918, but as a member of Sinn

Fein she did not take her seat. Nancy Astor (Viscountess Astor) took her seat as a Conservative MP after a by-election in December 1919.

56. *Parl. Debs, H. of C., 5th ser.*, vol. 179, cols 68–9.

57. He attended a League of Nations meeting in Rome, and talks with his counterparts in both Rome and Paris: see *DBFP*, First Series, Vol. XXVI, Nos 282–7 and 608.

58. David Low, *Autobiography* (London: Michael Joseph, 1956), p. 162.

59. Cabinet Conclusions 65(24), 3 December 1924, CAB 23/49, TNA.

60. Note from Rakovski to Chamberlain, 22 December 1924, and reply of 24 December, N 9365/108/38, FO 371/10480, TNA.

61. *Parl. Debs, H. of C., 5th ser.*, vol. 179, cols 309–17.

62. Ibid., cols 673, 689–90, and 740.

63. Ibid., cols 671–87.

64. The section heading is part of a *Daily Mail* headline on 23 April 1925: 'Clear them out. The Bolshevik Plotters in our Midst.'

65. A selection of the seized documents was published in Cmd 2682, *Communist Papers: Documents Selected from those Obtained on the Arrest of the Communist Leaders on 14 and 21 October 1925*. See also KV 3/18, TNA.

66. See KV 2/3331/2/76, TNA.

67. See Jeffery, *MI6*, p. 185.

68. See Andrew, *Defence of the Realm*, pp. 152–3. Details of Ewer and of the wider investigation can be found in KV 2/1016, TNA. See also Bennett, *Morton*, pp. 122–7, and Madeira, *Britannia and the Bear*.

69. Boris Savinkov, a Russian nihilist condemned to death for the assassination of Archduke Serge in 1905, had escaped and returned to serve in the Provisional Government in 1917. He then joined White Russian forces and represented them in Paris; his anti-Bolshevik activities were much admired by Churchill. Deceived into returning to the Soviet Union in 1924, he died there in prison.

70. Details of these operations, and of the fate of Savinkov and Reilly, can be found in Mitrokhin I, pp. 43–6.

71. See Andrew Cook, *On His Majesty's Secret Service: Sidney Reilly Codename ST1* (London: Tempus Publishing, 2002), pp. 222–3, for a graphic account of Reilly's death.

72. See Michael Kettle, *Sidney Reilly—The True Story of the World's Greatest Spy* (London: St Martin's Press, 1984), p. 130; Brook-Shepherd, *Iron Maze*, p. 307; Richard Spence, *Trust No One: The Secret World of Sidney Reilly* (Los Angeles: Feral House, 2002), pp. 402–3. On Singleton, see the section 'Cabinets, communists, and trade unions' in this chapter; for Captain Black, see Chapter 1.

73. On Reilly's connections with SIS, see Bennett, *Morton*, pp. 48–56.

74. Cook, *Sidney Reilly*, ch. 12 and appendix 5.

75. Minute by Gregory, 2 May 1925, N 2298/29/38, FO 371/11010, TNA.

76. On Locarno see FCO History Note No. 3, *Locarno 1925: Spirit, suite and treaties* (2nd edn, 2000) <https://issuu.com/fcohistorians/docs/history_notes_cover_hphn_3>.

77. Chamberlain to Joynson-Hicks, 5 May 1925, enclosing a memorandum on the admission of Soviet citizens into the United Kingdom, N 2298/29/38, FO 371/11010, TNA.

78. Minute by Chamberlain, 23 July 1925, N 4335/29/38, FO 371/11011, TNA. Following the Curzon memorandum of 2 May 1923 (see Chapter 1), a series of exchanges between the British and Russian governments regarding propaganda resulted in the Soviet government's agreement to 'refrain from hostile action or undertakings against Great Britain, and from conducting outside of its borders any official propaganda direct or indirect against the institutions of the British Empire' (see *DBFP*, First Series, Vol. XXV, No. 80). At the end of July 1925 Northern Department also prepared a review of Bolshevik propaganda activities during the past six months, based on secret sources: N 4398/29/38G, FO 371/11011, TNA.

79. See documentation in N 4079/29/38, FO 371/11010, TNA.

80. Samples of these leaflets can be found on the website of the University of Warwick: see, for example, <http://contentdm.warwick.ac.uk/cdm/compoundobject/collection/russian/id/3501/rec/1>.

81. See Chapter 1, note 84. The proceedings of the 1925 Secret Service Committee and its Report can be found in FO 1093/67–9, TNA. A detailed account can be found in Bennett, *Morton*, pp. 87–90.

82. Records of meetings are in FO 1093/68, TNA.

83. FO 1093/67, TNA.

84. FO 1093/68, TNA.

85. Maisel, *The Foreign Office and Foreign Policy*, pp. 44–5.

86. Casey to Bruce, 5 February and 30 April 1925, from a collection of letters 1924–9, <http://www.info.dfat.gov.au/info/historical/HistDocs>, vol. 18. I am grateful to Jonathan Pile for alerting me to this collection. Gregory had served as Secretary to a Special Mission to the Pope in 1914–15.

87. On Tyrrell's background and career see Maisel, *The Foreign Office and Foreign Policy*, pp. 54–6. See also John Fisher, 'The Interdepartmental Committee on Eastern Unrest and British Responses to Bolshevik and Other Intrigues against the Empire during the 1920s', *Journal of Asian History*, Vol. 34, No. 1 (2000), pp. 1–34.

88. These changes included a move for SIS to new headquarters in Broadway Buildings, together with GC&CS. On SIS and the 1925 Secret Service Committee generally see Jeffery, *MI6*, pp. 222–7, and Bennett, *Morton*, pp. 90–3.

CHAPTER 4

1. Ramsay MacDonald at Briton Ferry, South Wales, 3 March 1928, reported in the *Sunday Observer* on 4 March 1928.
2. See Chapter 2.
3. The Board of Enquiry's records are in T 281/1–40, TNA, with the proceedings of *Ironmonger v Dyne* as pieces 31–4. The Report, issued on 25 February 1928, was published in the *Observer* and *Manchester Guardian* on 28 February, and as Cmd 3037 of 1928. A copy of this, together with related documentation published in Cmd 3038, can be found in T 281/1, TNA. Part III, dealing with the Zinoviev Letter, is printed in HN, Annex F.
4. Section title taken from letter from Sir Ronald Lindsay, HM Ambassador in Berlin, to Gregory, 3 February 1927, N 551/209/38, printed in *DBFP*, Series Ia, Vol. III, No. 3. Lindsay argued that the 'new kind of war' encompassed economic boycott, propaganda and counter-propaganda and pressure on neutrals, assuming that 'we do not wish to concert this latent war into an armed conflict'.
5. Memorandum by Chamberlain, 16 February 1926, N 640/640/38, printed in *DBFP*, Series Ia, Vol. I, No. 278.
6. Memorandum by Gregory, 11 June 1926, N 2868/1687/38, printed in *DBFP*, Series Ia, Vol. II, No. 56.
7. At the end of the agreement negotiated by Baldwin in 1925 (see Chapter 3), the Samuel Commission set up in March 1926 recommended that government subsidies should be withdrawn and miners' pay cut by 13.5 per cent. When the Miners' Federation refused to accept these terms, there was a lock-out on 1 May and a General Strike was called by the TUC in support of the coal miners. It lasted only for nine days but involved over 2 million workers and brought large parts of Britain to a standstill, including in London where there were armoured cars on Oxford Street. See Keith Jeffery and Peter Hennessy, *States of Emergency: British Governments and Strikebreaking since 1919* (London: Routledge and Kegan Paul, 1983), ch. 5; and Kevin Morgan, *Labour Legends and Russian Gold* (London: Lawrence & Wishart, 2006), ch. 6.
8. In 1925 Russia had begun actively to intervene in the ongoing civil war in China, and was thought to have altered the balance of power and

encouraged serious attacks against British interests, including in Shanghai and Canton, some of which had led to the deployment of British forces in defence.

9. The Treaty of Berlin between the Soviet Union and Germany was signed on 24 April 1926, causing alarm in London, Paris, and Warsaw. Although the treaty seemed unobjectionable on the face of it, there were reports that it cloaked military agreements on the sale and exchange of armaments and for military training.

10. Memorandum by Gregory, 10 December 1926, N 5679/387/38, printed in *DBFP*, Series Ia, Vol. II, No. 350. It was circulated as CP(25)27 on 24 January 1927, CAB 24/184, TNA.

11. See Cabinet Conclusions 2(27) of 17 January 1927, CAB 23/54, TNA.

12. The note from Sir A. Chamberlain to the Soviet Chargé d'Affaires of 23 February 1927 had eleven appendices, setting out details of offending Soviet statements and actions. It is printed (without appendices) in *DBFP*, Series Ia, Vol. III, No. 21, and with all its attachments in a Command Paper, Cmd 2822 of 1927.

13. Letter from Sir A. Chamberlain to his sister Hilda, 27 February 1927, in Robert C. Self (ed.), *The Austen Chamberlain Diary Letters* (London: Cambridge University Press for the Royal Historical Society, 1995), pp. 310–11.

14. See Keith Neilson, *Britain, Soviet Russia and the Collapse of the Soviet Order* (Cambridge: Cambridge University Press, 2006), p. 58; letter from Warsaw to FO, 8 April 1927, C 3560/667/18, printed in *DBFP*, Series Ia, Vol. III, No. 134.

15. A detailed account of the ARCOS raid and the intelligence operations leading up to it can be found in Bennett, *Morton*, pp. 94–106. Security Service files on the raid are in KV 3/15–16, TNA. For Baldwin's statement in the House of Commons on 24 May 1927, in which he referred to intercepted Soviet messages, see *Parl. Debs, H. of C.*, 5th ser., vol. 206, cols 1842–54. The government published a selection of papers on Anglo-Soviet relations from 1921–7, including key documents relating to the Zinoviev Letter, in Cmd 2895 of 1927: it is on the website of the University of Warwick, <http://contentdm.warwick.ac.uk/cdm/ref/collection/russian/id/4611>. Formal notice of the severance of relations was given to the Soviet government on 26 May 1927.

16. See Andrew, *Defence of the Realm*, pp. 154–6. The intercepted documents were published in Cmd 2874 of 1927, *Documents illustrating the Hostile Activities of the Soviet Government and Third International*.

17. Memorandum by Sinclair on the ARCOS case, FO 1093/73, TNA. See Bennett, *Morton*, pp. 95 and 104–5.

18. See Chapter 1.
19. Moscow dispatch No. 342, 19 May 1927, N 2352/209/28, printed in *DBFP*, Series Ia, Vol. III, No. 204.
20. See Mitrokhin I, pp. 48–50.
21. Helsingfors (Helsinki) dispatch No. 7, 16 June 1927, N 3016/209/38, printed in *DBFP*, Series Ia, Vol. III, No. 232; memorandum by Preston on conditions in Leningrad, 27 July 1927, N 3744/309/38, ibid., No. 284.
22. See, for example, Chamberlain's response to questions on 2 March 1927, *Parl. Debs, H. of C.*, 5th ser., vol. 203, cols 356–7.
23. See Chapter 3.
24. Chester, Fay, and Young, *Zinoviev Letter; Anti-Soviet Forgeries*, pp. 6–9. See also Chapter 5 in this volume.
25. SIS note of 14 July 1927, cited in Bennett, *Morton*, p. 93. On Dunderdale, see Jeffery, *MI6*, pp. 199–200.
26. Details given in a telegram from the *Sunday Worker* correspondent in Moscow on 16 July 1927, KV 2/3331/1/90, TNA.
27. KV 2/3331/1/88, TNA.
28. The proceedings of the 1927 Secret Service Committee and related documentation are in FO 1093/70–3, TNA. For further details, including the Committee's consideration of the ARCOS raid, see Bennett, *Morton*, pp. 104–6.
29. See Chapter 2.
30. 'The Francs Scandal' was the term used widely in the press at the time to cover the investigation into the currency dealings undertaken by Gregory and other FO officials, usually in French francs.
31. The proceedings of *Ironmonger v Dyne* are in T 281/31–4, TNA. The subsequent Court of Bankruptcy Proceedings in respect of Mrs Dyne can be found in B 9/1077–83, TNA.
32. Cabinet Conclusions 4(28), 1 February 1928, CAB 23/57, TNA.
33. De Waal's evidence, 26 and 27 January 1928, T 281/31–2, TNA.
34. Mrs Dyne's evidence, 30 January 1928, T 281/33, TNA.
35. Evidence from Dr J. G. Vance, 14 February 1928, T 281/24, TNA. Letter from Gregory to Ramsay, 28 February 1928, T 281/36, TNA.
36. Evidence by Captain Charles Blennerhassett, T 281/5, TNA.
37. A number of other FO officials, and civil servants from other departments, were named during the Board of Enquiry's proceedings and some were interviewed, but all denied wrongdoing and no charges were ever brought against them.
38. See Chapter 2.
39. MacDonald to Fisher, 8 February 1928, T 281/38, TNA.

40. Transcript of MacDonald's evidence, 15 February 1928, T 281/13, TNA.

41. Statement by Fisher on 15 February 1928, T 281/13, TNA.

42. Analysis by Mr T. H. Jones of Dyne's financial transactions April–October 1924, T 281/36, TNA.

43. See Part III of the Board of Enquiry's Report, para. 53.

44. W. P. Coates, *The 'Zinoviev Letter': The Case for a Full Investigation*, with a preface by James Maxton MP (The Anglo-Russian Parliamentary Committee, May 1928). See HN, pp. 62–3.

45. Gregory's testimony to the Enquiry is in T 281/7–9, TNA; Maxse's and O'Malley's in T 281/16 and 17 respectively. O'Malley (who was particularly defensive and arrogant under questioning) was later reinstated in the Diplomatic Service after a determined campaign on his behalf by his friends and in particular by his wife, the novelist Ann Bridge, who described the episode in *Permission to Resign: Goings on in the Corridors of Power* (London: Sidgwick & Jackson, 1972).

46. Gregory, *On the Edge of Diplomacy*.

47. HN, pp. 64–5.

48. Cabinet Conclusions 12(28), 29 February 1928, CAB 23/57, TNA.

49. See, for example, *Parl. Debs, H. of C., 5th ser.*, vol. 214, cols 594–8, 1115–17, 1887–9.

50. Minute by Locker Lampson, 3 March 1928, N 1690/623/38, FO 371/13320, TNA.

51. Sinclair to Tyrrell, 2 March 1928, letter cited in Bennett, *Morton*, p. 119.

52. A copy of the *New Leader*'s article of 2 March 1928 is in KV 2/3331/1/68, TNA.

53. Sovnarkom meeting of 3 March 1928, translation of document consulted in Russian Ministry of Foreign Affairs in 1928. SIS sent a copy of the minutes to the FO on 16 March.

54. See Chapter 2.

55. Letter from Marlowe to Geoffrey Dawson, editor of *The Times*, 18 March 1930, quoted in Bar-Joseph, *Intelligence Intervention*, p. 310.

56. See Chapter 2, note 31. Morton's account of events in 1924 was considered unreliable, whether by intention or because so many years had passed.

57. For a useful discussion of the possible sources from which the *Mail* got the Letter, see Bar-Joseph, *Intelligence Intervention*, pp. 311–17.

58. MacDonald's evidence to the Treasury Board of Enquiry, 15 February 1928, T 281/13, TNA.

59. *Daily Herald*, 7 March 1928; *The Sunday Observer*, 11 March 1928, cutting in KV 2/3331/1/80, TNA.

60. Hugh Dalton, *Call Back Yesterday: Memoirs 1887–1931* (London: Frederick Muller, 1953), pp. 171–5. Dalton (later Baron Dalton, 1887–1962), economist and leading Labour politician, later served as a minister in the wartime coalition and as Chancellor of the Exchequer in the Attlee government, 1945–7.

61. Dalton, *Call Back Yesterday*, pp. 177–8.

62. For details of what im Thurn claimed he had been promised see Chester, Fay, and Young, *Zinoviev Letter*, pp. 175–80.

63. Davidson had lost his seat in the December 1923 election, but had played a major part behind the scenes in the reform of the Conservative Party before joining the Baldwin government as Parliamentary and Financial Secretary to the Admiralty. According to Robert Rhodes James, Davidson was responsible for persuading Joseph Ball, whom he described as having 'as much experience as anyone I know in the seamy side of life and the handling of crooks', to join Central Office as Director of Publicity. See Rhodes James, *Memoirs of a Conservative*, pp. 271–5.

64. Kindersley's account of what happened on 19 March 1928 is quoted in both the Appendix to *Memoirs of a Conservative*, and in Chester, Fay, and Young, *Zinoviev Letter*, pp. 163–4.

65. Chester, Fay, and Young, *Zinoviev Letter*, p. 78.

66. Ibid., p. 178.

67. For MacDonald's speech see *Parl. Debs, H. of C., 5th ser.*, vol. 215, cols 47–59.

68. For Baldwin's speech see ibid., cols 59–72.

69. Dalton, *Call Back Yesterday*, p. 178.

70. Chester, Fay, and Young, *Zinoviev Letter*, p. 167.

71. For speeches by Maxton, Saklatvala, and Thomas, also Hogg (Attorney General), see *Parl. Debs, H. of C., 5th ser.*, vol. 215, cols 72–106.

72. Chester, Fay, and Young, *Zinoviev Letter*, p. 80.

73. See Chapter 2, note 26.

74. See Chester, Fay, and Young, *Zinoviev Letter*, pp. 178–9.

75. See Chapter 7.

76. The truth of the part played by im Thurn in the Zinoviev Letter remains unclear, despite the extensive detail printed in Chester, Fay, and Young, *Zinoviev Letter*: see, for example, pp. 173–82 on his dealings with Conservative Central Office, and his desire for both money and honours. Nevertheless, im Thurn's life and death (early in 1930) remain shrouded in some mystery.

77. Dalton, *Call Back Yesterday*, p. 178.

78. The Security Service file on Schrek is at KV 2/3703, TNA.

79. Sinclair to Bland, 17 March 1928, cited in Bennett, *Morton*, p. 119; see also KV 2/3331/1/32, 40, TNA.

80. A good deal of Ewer's correspondence with Slocombe, who was part of his network, was intercepted by MI5. Details of their activities and correspondence can be found in Ewer's Security Service file, KV 2/1016. TNA; see KV 2/1016/1/81–90 for a useful memorandum on Ewer's connections with the Soviet Union.

81. See documentation in *DBFP*, Series Ia, Vol. IV, e.g. Nos 323 and 334.

82. Cutting from *The Star* in KV 2/3331/1/40, TNA.

83. For documentation on the Kellogg Pact, signed on 27 August 1928, see *DBFP*, Series Ia, Vol. V, Chapter III.

84. See *The Austen Chamberlain Diary Letters*, pp. 325–6. The Chancellor of the Duchy of Lancaster, Lord Cushendun, took charge of the FO in Chamberlain's absence.

85. On MacDonald's frame of mind at this period see Marquand, pp. 402–3, but also 474–6. See also Dalton's views in *Call Back Yesterday*, pp. 181–4.

86. See Warsaw dispatch to FO, 5 February 1929, N 894/13/55, printed in *DBFP*, Series Ia, Vol. VI, No. 67.

87. See, for example, the memorandum by C. M. Palairet, head of FO Northern Department, 7 May 1928, printed in *DBFP*, Series Ia, Vol. V, No. 19.

88. See, for example, documentation in *DBFP*, Series Ia, Vol. V, Chapter II.

89. On these events see Bennett, *Morton*, pp. 119–20. Senator Borah was later exonerated, partly on the grounds that the documents accusing him were found to be forgeries. For correspondence between Kuh and Ewer see KV 2/1016/3, TNA.

90. Note by Morton on Orlov, 5 March 1929, cited in Bennett, *Morton*, p. 120.

91. Bennett, *Morton*, p. 121.

92. *The Manchester Guardian*, 8 March 1929.

93. Gregory, *On the Edge of Diplomacy*, pp. 217–18; quoted in *The Manchester Guardian*, 8 March 1929.

94. A copy of the *Daily Herald* article of 18 March 1929 is in KV 2/3331/1/20, TNA.

95. Copy in KV 2/3331/1/18, TNA.

96. See Chapter 1. See West and Tsarev, *Crown Jewels*, ch. II, for the details in the paragraph that follows in the text.

97. For further details see Andrew, *Defence of the Realm*, Section B, ch. 1. A detailed account is given in Madeira, *Britannia and the Bear*.

98. SIS memorandum, 30 April 1929, sent to the FO on 7 May, cited in Bennett, *Morton*, pp. 123–6.

99. Letters from Nicolson and Sinclair to Lindsay, July 1929, cited in Bennett, *Morton*, p. 120.
100. See Bennett, *Morton*, p. 121.
101. See Marquand, *MacDonald*, p. 489.
102. Letter from Chamberlain to his sister Ida, 6 June 1929, *Austen Chamberlain Diary Letters*, pp. 337–8. On the choice of Henderson see David Carlton, *MacDonald versus Henderson: The Foreign Policy of the Second Labour Government* (London: Macmillan, 1970), pp. 15–18.
103. Dalton, *Call Back Yesterday*, pp. 218–20.
104. Ibid., p. 231. See also Carlton, *MacDonald versus Henderson*, pp. 147–50.
105. The negotiations between Dogvalevsky and Henderson are documented in *DBFP*, Second Series, Vol. VII, ch. I; the Protocol is printed as No. 24, and was published as Cmd 3418 of 1929.
106. Moscow dispatch No. 5 to FO, 15 December 1929, N 6119/55/38, printed in *DBFP*, Second Series, Vol. VII, No. 41.
107. 'Three secretaries shot because of the Zinoviev Letter'. Cuttings from the *Morning Post* and *Le Matin* can be found in KV 2/501/39ff, TNA.
108. See Mitrokhin I, pp. 59–60.
109. *The Times*, 26 October 1929.
110. Letter from im Thurn to Joseph Ball, 2 April 1928, reproduced in Appendix C to Chester, Fay, and Young, *Zinoviev Letter*, p. 205.

CHAPTER 5

1. Harold Nicolson, commenting in 1954 on the defection of Guy Burgess and Donald Maclean. James Lees-Milne, *Harold Nicolson: A Biography*, Vol. II (London: Chatto & Windus, 1981), p. 247.
2. On the financial crisis see Peden, *Treasury and Public Policy*, pp. 237–46, and William R. Garside (ed.), *Capitalism in Crisis: An International Perspective on the 1930s* (London: Palgrave Macmillan, 1993). On the Labour split see Andrew Thorpe, *A History of the British Labour Party* (London: Palgrave, 2015 edn), pp. 78–82; for a detailed account of the disintegration of the Labour government and the breach between MacDonald and most of the Party see Marquand, *MacDonald*, chs 25 and 26.
3. The Liberals had also been divided over participation in the National Government: for the differences between those following Sir John Simon, and those Lloyd George, see David Wrench, ' "Very Peculiar Circumstances": Walter Runciman and the National Government, 1931–3', *Twentieth Century British History*, Vol. 11, No. 1 (2000), pp. 61–82.

4. Runciman's speech, an iteration of it on 26 October in North Paddington, and Snowden's intervention, were reported in *The Times*, 26 October 1931, p. 8, and 27 October, p. 12.

5. Cross, *Philip Snowden*, pp. 316–17.

6. Ibid., p. 321; *The Manchester Guardian*, 29 June 1945, p. 6, 18 February 1950, p. 8, and 21 February 1950, p. 6.

7. Jones, *The Russia Complex*, p. 28; see ibid., pp. 23–54, for Labour policy towards the Soviet Union in the 1930s.

8. On the recruitment of the 'Cambridge Five' see Mitrokhin I, ch. 4.

9. *Daily Herald*, 1 December 1939.

10. See Chapter 2.

11. See papers on FO 370/2919, TNA; and the memorandum by Margaret Lambert, dated 23 November 1966, in FO 370/2929.

12. Attlee's letter was reproduced in *The Manchester Guardian*, 29 June 1945, p. 6.

13. See Martin Gilbert, *Never Despair: Winston S. Churchill 1945–1965* (London: Heinemann, 1988), pp. 32–6.

14. See T. D. Burridge, 'A Postscript to Potsdam: The Churchill–Laski Electoral Clash, June 1945', *Journal of Contemporary History*, Vol. 12, No. 4 (Oct. 1977), pp. 725–39.

15. See Gilbert, *Never Despair*, pp. 52–4.

16. See John Bew, *Citizen Clem: A Biography of Attlee* (London: riverrun, 2016), pp. 335–6.

17. Gilbert, *Never Despair*, p. 55.

18. *The Manchester Guardian*, 4 July 1945, p. 5.

19. Letter from Attlee to his brother, 6 July 1945, quoted in Bew, *Citizen Clem*, p. 336; comments on Laski in Frank Field (ed.), *Attlee's Great Contemporaries: The Politics of Character* (London: Bloomsbury, 2009), p. 107.

20. See, for example, *Documents on British Policy Overseas* (*DBPO*), Series I, Vol. XI, Nos 56, 80, and 131.

21. A detailed account of the Attlee government's approach to the Soviet Union and Western security is given in *DBPO*, Series I, Vols X and XI.

22. *The Manchester Guardian*, 18 February 1950, p. 8, and 21 February, p. 6.

23. Daniel W. B. Lomas, *Intelligence, Security and the Attlee Governments 1945–51: An Uneasy Relationship?* (Manchester: Manchester University Press, 2017), p. 45, and see ch. 1, *passim*.

24. See Andrew, *Defence of the Realm*, p. 319; the suspicion was not confined to MI5, but to all intelligence bodies. On Double Cross, see ibid.,

Section C, ch. 1; on wartime codebreaking, see Ronald Lewin, *Ultra Goes to War* (London: Penguin edn, 2001).

25. Minute by Attlee of 21 December 1947, GEN 183/1, CAB 130/20, TNA, quoted in Andrew, *Defence of the Realm*, p. 381; see Section D, *passim*, and Jeffery, *MI6*, chs 18 and 19, for a detailed account of developments in MI5 and SIS during the early post-war period. See also *DBPO*, Series I, Vol. XI, Nos 35 and 61.

26. Soviet military intelligence, previously known as the 'Fourth', was called the GRU after 1942; it was, as Jonathan Haslam points out, the 'second largest intelligence service in the world' (*Near and Distant Neighbours*, pp. xv–xvii, and 10–11).

27. On Gouzenko's defection and the implications for the Attlee government see Gill Bennett, 'The CORBY Case: The Defection of Igor Gouzenko, September 1945', in FCO Historians, *From World War to Cold War: The Records of the FO Permanent Under-Secretary's Department, 1939–51*, <https://issuu.com/fcohistorians/docs/pusdessays>.

28. Andrew, *Defence of the Realm*, p. 365; see Section D, ch. 3, on the impact of VENONA. See also R. L. Benson and M. Warner (eds), *VENONA: Soviet Espionage and the American Response 1939–1957* (Washington, DC: National Security Agency, 1996); a short but detailed account can be found in Robert L. Benson, *The VENONA Story* (US Center for Cryptologic History, 2012).

29. Over 400 files on Burgess and Maclean and related matters, originating in the Security Service, FCO, and Cabinet Office, were released at The National Archives in October 2015 in classes KV2, KV3, and KV6, FCO 158, and CAB 301.

30. See documentation in PREM 11/4557, TNA, and Andrew, *Defence of the Realm*, Section D, ch. 6. For Philby's own account of these events see Kim Philby, *My Silent War* (London: MacGibbon & Kee, 1968), ch. XII.

31. The Report of the Cadogan Enquiry, carried out in June–July 1951, is in CAB 301/120, TNA. See also papers in FCO 158/118, TNA.

32. Letter from Barclay to Nicholls, 15 March 1966, FO 370/2919, TNA.

33. PUSD took over the functions of the wartime Services Liaison Department, as well as the liaison function of the PUS's Private Secretary in respect of the intelligence agencies: see Jeffery, *MI6*, p. 620. PUSD records can be found in FO 1093, TNA, and see also the FCO Historians' publications relating to PUSD records in <https://issuu.com/fcohistorians/docs/therecordsofthepermanentundersecret> and <https://issuu.com/fcohistorians/docs/pusdessays>.

34. i.e. Chamberlain's minute of 11 November 1924 circulating memoranda on the Zinoviev Letter: see Chapter 3, note 23.

35. See Chapter 2, note 14.

36. See Chapter 2, note 37. However, the draft as amended by MacDonald, though present in the file in 1951, had disappeared in the 1960s.

37. Minutes by Strang and Morrison, 27 April and 6 May 1951, FCO 12/64, TNA.

38. See Andrew, *Defence of the Realm*, pp. 429–33. See also FCO 158/28, TNA, including details of the case put by the SIS Chief, Sir John Sinclair, that insufficient evidence existed to prove Philby was the Third Man, and papers in FCO 158/172, 195, TNA.

39. Full details of the Crabb episode (known as 'Frogman'), and papers relating to the Bridges Enquiry of 1956 into the affair, can be found in CAB 301/121–5, TNA.

40. See Chapter 4.

41. See Rhodes James, *Memoirs of a Conservative*, appendix, pp. 203–4, on which this account of the events of 1956 is based. Ball had retired from Conservative Central Office in 1939, and served in the war as an intelligence officer. After the war he went into the City, and died in 1961.

42. Ibid., p. 204. The 'revelation' of 1967 refers to the book by Chester, Fay, and Young, *Zinoviev Letter*.

43. The section-heading quote is a comment by Harold Macmillan in his diary for 1 July 1961, referring to a list of problems he faced, including the Portland Spy Case: Peter Catterall (ed.), *The Macmillan Diaries: Prime Minister and After, 1957–66* (London: Macmillan, 2011), p. 386.

44. Anthony Howard, 'The Press and the Election: Has it Helped the Right?', *The Guardian*, 9 October 1959, p. 8.

45. On this decision see Bennett, *Six Moments of Crisis*, ch. 3.

46. For a more detailed account, see Andrew, *Defence of the Realm*, Section D, ch. 9.

47. Documentation on the Romer Committee of Enquiry into Breaches of Security was transferred into the public domain in 2017: see CAB 301/248–57, TNA.

48. Andrew, *Defence of the Realm*, p. 491. Documentation on the Radcliffe Committee on Security Procedures in the Public Service is in CAB 301/258–61, TNA.

49. Documentation on the Radcliffe Tribunal into the Vassall case is in CAB 301/265–8, TNA.

50. Alistair Horne, *Macmillan*, Vol. II, *1957–86* (London: Macmillan, 1989), quoted in Andrew, *Defence of the Realm*, p. 493; Andrew points out that

it was, in fact, the Cabinet Secretary who had given Macmillan the information, but it remains a good story in Macmillan's style.

51. See Ben Macintyre, *A Spy among Friends: Kim Philby and the Great Betrayal* (London: Bloomsbury, 2014), pp. 204–5.

52. Ibid., pp. 270–2. See also documentation in CAB 301//269, TNA.

53. Andrew, in *Defence of the Realm*, states that the Profumo affair 'never came close to threatening national security' (pp. 494 and 499–500), but Haslam, in *Near and Distant Neighbours*, cites information that the Russians did, indeed, get valuable information from Profumo via Keeler (p. 207). See also documentation in CAB 301/271, TNA, relating to the role of Stephen Ward.

54. Catterall, *Macmillan Diaries*, p. 575, entry for 11 July 1963.

55. *Parl. Debs, H. of C., 5th ser.*, vol. 686, col. 872. The Denning Report was published as a Command Paper, Cmnd 2152 of 1963.

56. Tom Bower, *The Perfect English Spy: Sir Dick White and the Secret War 1935–90* (London: Heinemann, 1995), p. 310.

57. Andrew, *Defence of the Realm*, p. 500.

58. Haslam, *Near and Distant Neighbours*, pp. 174–5, 206; see also Mitrokhin I, chs 11 and 12.

59. See Bennett, *Six Moments of Crisis*, ch. 5.

60. Andrew, *Defence of the Realm*, Section D, chs 9 and 10. On Blunt, see also Miranda Carter, *Anthony Blunt: His Lives* (London: Macmillan, 2001), ch. 17. Papers relating to Cairncross's confession in February 1964, in the US, are in CAB 301/270, TNA.

61. See Andrew, *Defence of the Realm*, Section D, ch. 10.

62. While at MI5, White had been involved in earlier investigations of Philby: see Bower, *The Perfect English Spy*, ch. 5.

63. Andrew, *Defence of the Realm*, pp. 510–11.

64. Ben Pimlott, *Harold Wilson* (London: HarperCollins, 1992), pp. 309 and 319.

65. Philip Ziegler, *Wilson: The Authorised Life* (London: Weidenfeld & Nicolson, 1993), p. 156.

66. Ibid., pp. 213–14. See also a note of July 1964 setting out Wilson's views on the machinery of government, released in the Cabinet Secretary's Secret & Personal papers, CAB 301/194, TNA.

67. Andrew, *Defence of the Realm*, p. 523; see Section D, ch. 11, *passim*, for the Wilson government's approach to security and subversion 1964–70.

68. Ibid., pp. 527–31. Details of Security Service reports on the seamen's strike and the role of the CPGB can be found in CAB 301/233–4, TNA.

69. I worked very closely with Margaret Lambert, later Pelly (1930–97), from the early 1980s until her retirement in 1990. When I first joined the FO in 1972, she rather terrorized me and the other research assistants, all female (the 'gels'), whipping us into shape; but I benefited greatly from her meticulous scholarship and wide-ranging approach to international history, and valued her as an editorial colleague. Rohan d'Olier Butler (1917–96), Fellow of All Souls, Historical Adviser to the Foreign Secretary from 1963 to 1982, was best known for his monumental study of the early life of Choiseul.

70. 'Investigation into the Zinoviev file of 1924', 23 November 1966, FO 370/2929, TNA. The Confidential Print was a selection of important documents, grouped geographically and circulated to FO posts and departments for the information of diplomatic staff and officials.

71. Minutes by Butler and Medlicott, 1 November 1965. 'Weeding' refers to the process of selection review, carried out before files are reviewed for sensitivity, in order to eliminate duplicates, ephemeral material, etc.

72. Letter from Baron Harvey of Tasburgh to Sir J. Nicholls, 12 March 1966, FO 370/2919, TNA.

73. See correspondence on FCO 12/64, also FO 370/2918–22, TNA.

74. *Parl. Debs, H. of L.,* vol. 206, col. 1154; see cols 1147–81 for the whole debate.

75. See Peter Beck, *Using History, Making British Policy: The Treasury and the Foreign Office, 1950–76* (London: Palgrave Macmillan, 2006), ch. 2.

76. Ibid., p. 39.

77. Cabinet Conclusions CC(65)45, 5 August 1965, CAB 128/38, TNA.

78. Written answer by Wilson to a PQ from Michael Foot, 9 March 1966: *Parl. Debs, H. of C.,* 5th ser., vol. 725, cols 561–3. See also Beck, *Using History*, pp. 39–45. In October 1966 the Cabinet Office prepared a memorandum discussing ways of implementing the decision to extend the range of official histories: see CAB 301/228, TNA.

79. Discussions on these matters can be followed in FO 370/2915–16 and 2923–4, TNA. Butler's memorandum, submitted to Nicholls on 20 April 1966, is in FO 370/2924.

80. *Parl. Debs, H. of C.,* 5th ser., vol. 733, cols 1706–8.

81. Memo by Butler, 7 February 1966, FO 370/2915, TNA.

82. 'Plan of Campaign on Zinoviev letter', 25 February 1966, FO 370/2917, TNA.

83. N 7838/108/38, FO 371/10478, TNA.

84. According to Margaret Lambert, Child had asked for copies of the evidence but had had a very guarded telephone reply from the Treasury, where the incident was evidently highly sensitive still.

85. Minutes in FO 370/2929, TNA.
86. When helping Anthony Eden (Lord Avon) with his memoirs, the historian David Dilks had seen in 1960 the original of the Hoare–Laval Pact of 8 December 1935 (an abortive Anglo-French agreement on Abyssinia) in the FO files, but when he went back to check in 1961, it had disappeared. He found it had been 'weeded' and was in the confidential waste about to be incinerated; he rescued it just in time. Details of this incident are in FO 370/2902, TNA.
87. On 19 December Brown confirmed to the House of Commons that the working papers for the Hoare–Laval Pact and the authenticated copy of the Munich Agreement of 29 September 1938 were both in the PRO. The Hoare–Laval agreement is printed in *DBFP*, Second Series, Vol. XV, No. 336; the Munich Agreement in Third Series, Vol. II, No. 1224.
88. *The Times*, 12 December 1966, p. 11, 'P.S. to the Zinoviev Letter'. 'Bankers' ramp' refers to accusations by the Labour Party that they were misled by warnings from the banking sector in 1931, leading to the damaging split in the party when the National Government was formed.
89. Minute of 12 December by George Brown, FO 370/2929, TNA.
90. FO 370/2929, TNA.
91. Letters from Norton and Ewer, *The Guardian*, 16 and 20 December 1966; see also papers in FO 370/2922, TNA.
92. Private information.
93. *The Times*, 19 December 1966, p. 7.
94. Comments in *The Guardian*, 19 December 1966, 'Zinoviev is Authentic, says MP'.
95. Minute by Medlicott, 19 December 1966: see HN, pp. 89–90.
96. *Parl. Debs, H. of C., 5th ser.*, vol. 738, cols 972–6.
97. *Parl. Debs, H. of C., 5th ser.*, vol. 739, cols 970–1. See also report in the *Morning Post*, 25 January 1967.
98. See Chapter 1, note 8.
99. Letter from Robin Bruce Lockhart printed in *The Times*, 15 January 1967, p. 21, 'A diplomat's downfall'.
100. *Parl. Debs, H. of C., 5th ser.*, vol. 750, col. 326W; see also papers in FCO 12/36, TNA.
101. See papers in FCO 12/36, TNA.
102. For the debate see *Parl. Debs, H. of C., 5th ser.*, vol. 754, cols 1314–48; Wilson's remark is in col. 1342. For his broadcast see Pimlott, *Harold Wilson*, pp. 483–4.
103. Ziegler, *Wilson*, p. 266.
104. See Nicholas Wilkinson, *Secrecy and the Media: The Official History of the United Kingdom's D-Notice System* (London: Routledge, 2009), Section 7;

Harold Wilson, *The Labour Government 1964–70: A Personal Record* (London: Penguin, 1964), pp. 478–82 and 530–4; and Pimlott, *Harold Wilson*, p. 446.

105. Eleanor Philby, *Kim Philby: The Spy I Loved* (London: Hamish Hamilton, 1968).

106. Seale and McConville turned their investigations into a book, *Philby: The Long Road to Moscow* (London: Hamish Hamilton, 1973).

107. The 'Insight' team's story was the basis for Bruce Page, David Leitch, and Phillip Knightley, *The Philby: The Spy who Betrayed a Generation* (London: André Deutsch, 1968).

108. Philby, *My Silent War*, p. xiv.

109. Chester, Fay, and Young, *Zinoviev Letter*, p. 195.

110. Minute by Greenhill, 13 November 1967, FCO 12/36, TNA.

111. Blake review, *The Sunday Times*, 29 October 1967, p. 54.

112. Natalie Grant, 'The "Zinoviev Letter" Case', *Soviet Studies*, Vol. 19, No. 2 (Oct. 1967), pp. 264–77.

113. Ibid., p. 276.

114. See Andrew, *Defence of the Realm*, pp. 130, 330.

115. See minuting from April 1968 on FCO 12/36, TNA.

116. On Morton's role, see Bennett, *Morton*, pp. 82–5.

117. See Brook-Shepherd, *Iron Maze*, Part 5, 'The Scam'.

118. See HN, p. 91; *Parl. Debs, H. of C., 5th ser.*, vol. 215, cols 84–5.

119. Bagot Report, quoted in Bennett, *Morton*, pp. 121–2.

120. HN, p. 92. See also Chapter 7 in this volume.

121. William E. Butler, 'The Harvard Text of the Zinov'ev Letter', *Harvard Library Bulletin* (Jan. 1970), pp. 43–62; see p. 48.

122. See Chapter 3.

123. Butler, 'Harvard Text', p. 50.

124. Pepita Reilly, *Britain's Master Spy: The Adventures of Sidney Reilly* (New York: Harper and Brothers, 1932, reissued by Biteback Publishing in 2014).

125. Cook, *Sidney Reilly*, Appendix 5.

126. The correspondence between Michael Kettle and No. 10 in February–March 1970 is in PREM 13/3251, TNA. Kettle published his own account in *Sidney Reilly—The True Story of the World's Greatest Spy* (London: St Martin's Press, 1984).

CHAPTER 6

1. Robin Cook in *The Guardian*, 4 February 1999, p. 18.

2. Sir Roger Casement, Irish nationalist and distinguished Colonial civil servant, was executed for treason in 1916. His diaries, found when he was arrested, depicted graphically homosexual encounters and their

authenticity was disputed for many years. In April 1943 a mass grave of 4,500 Polish officers was found in the Katyn forest near Smolensk; for many years the Soviet Union insisted Nazi Germany was responsible for the killings, but in 1992 the Russian government released documents proving that the Soviet Politburo and the NKVD had been responsible, and revealing that there may have been more than 20,000 victims. Tsar Nicholas II of the Russian Imperial Romanov dynasty was killed with his family by the Bolsheviks in 1918, but until the remains were discovered in the late 1990s there was ongoing speculation about whether any member of the family might not have perished.

3. Representatives of forty-one countries attended the conference: the proceedings were published in *Nazi Gold: The London Conference 2–4 December 1997* (London: The Stationery Office, 1998).

4. The phrase 'missing dimension' was used widely after the publication in 1984 of Christopher Andrew and David Dilks (eds), *The Missing Dimension: Governments and Intelligence Communities in the Twentieth Century* (London: Macmillan, 1984), but Andrew and others used it in the 1970s as well.

5. Sibyl Crowe, 'The Zinoviev Letter: A Reappraisal', *Journal of Contemporary History*, Vol. 10, No. 3 (July 1975), pp. 407–32.

6. Letters in *The Times*, 20 October and 9 November 1977. Woollcombe was the SIS officer who had circulated the Zinoviev Letter to the FO on 9 October 1924: see Chapter 2.

7. Christopher Andrew, 'The British Secret Service and Anglo-Soviet Relations in the 1920s, Part I: From the Trade Negotiations to the Zinoviev Letter', *The Historical Journal*, Vol. 20, No. 3 (1977), pp. 673–706.

8. Christopher Andrew, 'Can the truth about the Zinoviev letter ever be written?', *The Times Higher Education Supplement*, 14 October 1977, p. 15.

9. E. H. Carr, 'Communications: The Zinoviev Letter', *The Historical Journal*, Vol. 22, No. 1 (1979), pp. 209–10; Christopher Andrew's riposte was printed as pp. 211–14.

10. Andrew, 'Can the truth about the Zinoviev letter ever be written?'

11. Peter Hennessy, 'Spy secrets that may embarrass ministers', *The Times*, 25 November 1977.

12. Peter Hennessy, 'Prime Minister to be pressed about 30-year silence on spy agencies', *The Times*, 30 November 1977, p. 4. Latham complained that in *Hitler's War* (London: Hodder & Stoughton Ltd, 1977), David Irving wrote that a peace initiative brought to London by Swedish intermediary Dahlerus in 1939 had been received favourably by Neville Chamberlain and Halifax, but the relevant file on the episode remained closed.

13. Peter Hennessy, 'Growth of the Secret Service' Parts 1 and 2, *The Times*, 4 and 6 February 1978.

14. See Peter Hennessy, *Distilling the Frenzy: Writing the History of One's Own Times* (London: Biteback Publishing, 2012), pp. 195–6.

15. F. W. Winterbotham, *The Ultra Secret* (London: Weidenfeld & Nicolson, 1974); R. V. Jones, *Most Secret War: British Scientific Intelligence 1939–45* (London: Hodder & Stoughton, 1977); F. H. Hinsley et al., *British Intelligence in the Second World War*, Vol. I (London: HMSO, 1979).

16. See Beckett, *The Enemy Within*, p. 180.

17. See Ziegler, *Wilson*, p. 475.

18. The *Daily Express*, 21 May 1974, and *Time Out*, 30 May 1974. See also Andrew, *Defence of the Realm*, pp. 633–4.

19. See Andrew, *Defence of the Realm*, Section E, ch. 4, 'The Wilson Plot', for further details, and Ziegler, *Wilson*, pp. 477ff.

20. See Chapter 5.

21. Andrew, *Defence of the Realm*, pp. 518–21.

22. Ziegler, *Wilson*, p. 478.

23. Michael White, 'Rees arrests the Tory idea for "political police"', *The Guardian*, 2 June 1978, p. 4. See also Chapter 5.

24. Beckett, *The Enemy Within*, p. 183.

25. 'Foot answers charges of "left infiltration"', *The Guardian*, 2 May 1979, p. 4.

26. See Beckett, *The Enemy Within*, pp. 184–6, and Andrew, *Defence of the Realm*, pp. 660–1 and 666–9.

27. See Michael Crick, *The March of Militant* (London: Faber & Faber, 1986), p. 187. I am grateful for this reference to the former Labour minister Jack Straw, who put me on to it when we sat next to each other on a bus in 2015.

28. *The Observer*, 'Dirty tricks fear over break-ins', 2 February 1992, p. 1. In 1983, *The Sunday Times* had bought the rights to serialize what were claimed to be Hitler's diaries, but they proved to be a hoax.

29. Gordievsky, who has lived in Britain since 1985, has written about his experiences in a number of books including *Next Stop Execution* (London: Macmillan, 1995). See also Mitrokhin I, pp. 559–67, and Gordon Corera, *The Art of Betrayal: Life and Death in the British Secret Service* (London: Weidenfeld & Nicolson, 2011), ch. 4.

30. OVATION (Gordievsky's codename) report 4043, March 1986, KV 2/3331/1/5, TNA. 'Active Measures', *Aktivnye meropriyatiya*, were measures aimed at exerting influence on the political life of a target country, 'misleading the adversary, undermining and weakening his positions, the

disruption of his hostile plans and the achievement of other aims': see Vasily Mitrokhin (ed.), *KGB Lexicon: The Soviet Intelligence Officer's Handbook* (London: Frank Cass, 2002).

31. See Mitrokhin I, ch. 25, and Haslam, *Near and Distant Neighbours*, pp. 234–46.

32. For the impact of this NATO exercise in November 1983, and other Soviet security concerns at this period, see Gordon S. Barrass, *The Great Cold War: A Journey through the Hall of Mirrors* (Stanford, CA: Stanford University Press, 2009).

33. See Charles Moore, *Margaret Thatcher, The Authorized Biography*, Vol. II, *Everything She Wants* (London: Penguin Random House, 2015), pp. 115–17. On developments in the Soviet Union see Jonathan Haslam, *Russia's Cold War: From the October Revolution to the Fall of the Wall* (London: Yale University Press, 2011).

34. For details of these events see Andrew, *Defence of the Realm*, Section E, chs 7 and 9.

35. See ibid., pp. 760–75, on the British government's failed attempt to prevent the publication of Peter Wright's *Spycatcher: The Candid Autobiography of a Senior Intelligence Officer* (New York: Viking Penguin, 1987). See also Malcolm Turnbull, *The Spycatcher Trial* (London: William Heinemann, 1988); and Evan Davis, *Post Truth: Why We Have Reached Peak Bullshit and What We Can Do About It* (London: Little Brown, 2017), pp. 13–16.

36. 'Wilson victory triggered plot to destabilise Labour', *The Guardian*, 14 October 1988, p. 2. See Wright, *Spycatcher,* pp. 369–70.

37. *Parl. Debs, H. of C.*, 6th ser., 15 December 1986, vol. 107, cols 782–3.

38. The Report and the White Paper are printed as Cmnd 8204 of 1981, and 8531 of 1982.

39. David Stafford, *Britain and European Resistance, 1940–45: A Survey of the Special Operations Executive, with Documents* (London: Macmillan, 1980); Wesley K. Wark, *The Ultimate Enemy: British Intelligence and Nazi Germany, 1933–39* (London: I. B. Tauris, 1985); Christopher Andrew, *Secret Service: The Making of the British Intelligence Community* (London: William Heinemann Ltd, 1985).

40. See Christopher Andrew, 'The British View of Security and Intelligence', in A. Stuart Farson, David Stafford, and Wesley K. Wark (eds), *Security and Intelligence in a Changing World: New Perspectives for the 1990s* (London: Frank Cass, 1991), pp. 10–24.

41. See Andrew, *Defence of the Realm*, p. 756.

42. Ibid., pp. 757–78.

43. *Parl. Debs, H. of C.,* 6th ser., vol. 143, cols 1104–6.

44. Ibid., col. 1165.
45. Andrew, *Defence of the Realm*, p. 767.
46. Details of the relevant legislation can be found on the websites of the agencies, or at <http://www.legislation.gov.uk/ukpga/1994/13/contents/>.
47. *Parl. Debs, H. of L.*, vol. 550, col. 1034. Stella Rimington became DG in 1992.
48. On the career of Daphne Park (1921–2010) see Corera, *The Art of Betrayal*, ch. 3.
49. *Parl. Debs, H. of L.*, vol. 550, col. 1054. The Findlater Stewart report is in CAB 301/31, TNA; see Jeffery, *MI6*, pp. 619–20.
50. *Parl. Debs, H. of C., 6th ser.*, vol. 269, cols 285–9.
51. On the 'blanket' and other details of this system see Gill Bennett, 'Declassification and Release Policies of the UK's Intelligence Agencies', *Intelligence and National Security*, 17, No. 1 (Spring 2002), pp. 21–32. Although the regime described there has been updated and to some extent superseded by Freedom of Information legislation, the principles governing intelligence-related records remain valid.
52. *DBPO*, Series III, Vol. I, *Britain and the Soviet Union 1968–72* (London: The Stationery Office, 1997).
53. Haslam, *Near and Distant Neighbours*, pp. 276–7.
54. Andrew and Gordievsky, *KGB; Instructions from The Centre: Top Secret Files on KGB Foreign Operations 1975–1985* (London: Hodder & Stoughton, 1991); *More Instructions from the Centre: Top Secret Files on KGB Global Operations 1975–1985* (London: Frank Cass, 1992).
55. See Mitrokhin I, pp. 25–8. The four books were John Costello, *Ten Days to Destiny* (New York: William Morrow & Co., 1991), about the flight of Rudolf Hess; John Costello and Oleg Tsarev, *Deadly Illusions* (New York: Century, 1993), a biography of Alexander Orlov; Genrikh Borovik (ed. Phillip Knightley), *The Philby Files: The Secret Life of the Master Spy* (London: Little Brown, 1994); and West and Tsarev, *The Crown Jewels* (1998).
56. David E. Murphy, Sergei A. Kondrashev, and George Bailey, *Battleground Berlin: CIA vs KGB in the Cold War* (New Haven: Yale University Press, 1997).
57. See Mitrokhin I, ch. 1. Much of the material brought out by Mitrokhin is now in the Churchill Archives Centre at Cambridge.
58. The phrase 'A most extraordinary and mysterious business' in this section's heading, included in the title of the FCO History Note in 1999, was taken from the *New Statesman* of 1 November 1924, where it was used to describe the Zinoviev Letter affair.
59. Michael Jago, *Robin Butler: At the Heart of Power from Heath to Blair* (London: Biteback Publishing, 2017), p. 263.

60. Alastair Campbell and Bill Hagerty (eds), *The Alastair Campbell Diaries*, Vol. II, *Power and the People 1997–1999* (London: Hutchinson, 2011), p. 3.
61. Translation of article by Kozlov, prepared for Gill Bennett by Tony Bishop in June 1998.
62. See Chapter 4.
63. US National Archives, RG 59 861.00, 2227. The letter was published on 20 December 1923. See HN, p. 16.
64. *The Guardian*, 4 February 1999, p. 18.

CHAPTER 7

1. *Review of Intelligence on Weapons of Mass Destruction: Report of a Committee of Privy Counsellors* (The Butler Report: London: The Stationery Office, 2004), ch. 1, para. 51. Intelligence can be expected to uncover secrets: mysteries are essentially unknowable.
2. A reference to the popular board game, Cluedo, where players have to identify a killer, the location of the murder, and the weapon.
3. The *Sunday Graphic*, 6 April 1930.
4. See Chapter 3.
5. See Jeffery, *MI6*, pp. 189–91.
6. See Bennett, *Morton*, p. 54.
7. See Chapter 1.
8. See Chapter 2.
9. See Chapter 4, note 109.
10. NSY report of 28 October 1924, in KV 2/3331/3/73, 77, TNA.
11. See Chapter 3.
12. Chicherin to Zinoviev, 12 November 1924, translation of document consulted in Russian Ministry of Foreign Affairs in 1998.
13. See KV 2/3331/2/4–27, TNA, for attempts by Scotland Yard and MI5 to check on the movements of Zinoviev, MacManus, and Bukharin at the relevant period.
14. Moscow dispatch No. 832 to FO, 5 September 1924, N 7226/6267/85, printed in *DBFP*, First Series, Vol. XXV, No. 251.
15. Mlechin's article, 'The Zinoviev Letter', published on 25 August 2007 on the Russian-sponsored website *Russia Beyond the Headlines*, refers to declassified Russian documentation, which Mlechin says shows 'that Moscow was truly at a loss: no one knew anything about the letter' (<https://www.rbth.com/articles/2007/08/25/letters.html>).
16. See Chapter 4.
17. Gorodetsky, *Precarious Truce*, p. 41.

18. See Chapter 3.

19. Bullock, *Hitler and Stalin*, p. 198.

20. See Bazhanov, *Bazhanov and the Damnation of Stalin*, p. 98. Hodgson reported in Moscow dispatch No. 884 of 22 September 1924 that the rising seemed to have been started by the Georgian Menshevik party, but that it was possible that the Georgian State Political Department had encouraged the outbreak as an excuse to institute a reign of terror and 'get rid of a number of persons who were regarded as dangerous' (N 7708/630/58, printed in *DBFP*, First Series, Vol. XXV, No. 253).

21. Bazhanov, *Bazhanov and the Damnation of Stalin*, pp. 55 and 108.

22. Butler, 'The Harvard text of the Zinov'ev Letter', p. 53.

23. See Chapter 3, and HN, pp. 86–7.

24. Haslam, *Near and Distant Neighbours*, pp. 25, 29–31. See also Mitrokhin I, pp. 40–4 and 50ff.

25. See Chapter 5.

26. Howell, *MacDonald's Party*, p. 390.

27. See Kenneth Newton, *The Sociology of British Communism* (London: Allen Lane The Penguin Press, 1969), p. 16 and ch. 2, *passim*; also Smith (ed.), *The Oxford Handbook of the History of Communism*, chs 10 and 25.

28. See Chapter 1.

29. Howell, *MacDonald's Party*, p. 395.

30. See Chapter 2.

31. Newton, *Sociology of British Communism*, p. 18.

32. Beckett, *The Enemy Within*, p. 35.

33. See Chapter 3.

34. Translation of documents consulted in the Russian Centre in Moscow in 1998.

35. See Bennett, *Morton*, p. 53.

36. For descriptions of Orlov and his activities, see Chapters 1 and 4.

37. See Chapter 5.

38. See Chapter 4.

39. See Chapter 1 and HN, p. 29.

40. See Bennett, *Morton*, pp. 75–6.

41. See Jeffery, *MI6*, pp. 186–7 and 194–5.

42. See ibid., pp. 179–80, and Bennett, *Morton*, pp. 43–4 and 68.

43. Jeffery, *MI6*, pp. 270–1.

44. See Chapter 2.

45. See Chapter 3 and Jeffery, *MI6*, pp. 183–4.

46. See Chapter 4.

47. See Chapter 5.

48. See Chapter 1.

49. Both OGPU and SIS evidence suggests that 'Belgardt' and Pokrovsky were two people, and it would seem they were in a position to know. Belgardt was, however, presumably the same person as the Alexis Bellegarde named as one of the authors of the Letter in Chester, Fay, and Young, *Zinoviev Letter*.

50. See Chapter 4.

51. See HN, p. 90.

52. HN, p. 88.

53. Brook-Shepherd, *Iron Maze*, pp. 308–9.

54. Passages translated by Tony Bishop from a history of Soviet intelligence published by the SVR.

55. See West and Tsarev, *Crown Jewels*, p. 43.

56. See Chapter 4 and Bennett, *Morton*, p. 93.

57. See HN, p. 88.

58. See Chapter 2.

59. See Bennett, *Morton*, p. 53.

60. See Chapter 3 and HN, pp. 88–9.

61. Chester, Fay, and Young, *Zinoviev Letter*, pp. 61–3.

62. See Chapter 4 and Chester, Fay, and Young, *Zinoviev Letter*, pp. 58–9.

63. Brook-Shepherd, *Iron Maze*, p. 309.

64. HN, p. 91.

65. West and Tsarev, *Crown Jewels*, p. 42.

66. HN, p. 92.

67. See Chapter 4.

68. See Chapter 4 and West and Tsarev, *Crown Jewels*, pp. 41–2.

69. See Chapter 2.

70. See Bennett, *Morton*, pp. 71–5.

71. Bar-Joseph, *Intelligence Intervention in the Politics of Democratic States*, p. 317.

72. Ibid., pp. 310–11.

73. 'If it is not true, it is well conceived.' See *The Times*, 11 December 1924, p. 10.

74. 'A Conspiracy', *The Times*, 5 March 1928, p. 8.

CONCLUSION

1. *The Observer*, 27 February 2000, p. 10.

2. <http://www.mailstar.net/zinoviev.html>. It will be remembered that Orlov was considered by SIS to have been responsible for the Protocols of the Elders of Zion (see Chapter 1). Myers quoted from Dmitri Volgokonov, *Lenin: Life and Legacy*, trans. Harold Shukman (London: HarperCollins, 1994).

3. Stephen Ambrose, 'Writers on the grassy knoll: a Reader's guide', *The New York Times*, 2 February 1992.

4. See Sunstein, *Conspiracy Theories and Other Dangerous Ideas*, pp. 25–6.

5. *Parl. Debs, H. of C., 6th ser.*, vol. 411, col. 699. The Ems telegram, sent to Prussian Prime Minister Otto von Bismarck on 13 July 1870, ostensibly described a conversation between Kaiser Wilhelm I, staying at the spa town of Ems, with the French ambassador, Count Benedetti. Bismarck doctored the text before publication to make it appear as if the two men had insulted each other, and the telegram helped to precipitate the Franco-Prussian War.

6. Lord Goldsmith's advice was published in April 2005.

7. *Parl. Debs, H. of C., 6th ser.*, vol. 411, cols 740–2.

8. See Chapter 4. The Report of the Iraq Inquiry was published in July 2016: it can be found at <http://www.iraqinquiry.org.uk/the-report/>.

9. Martin Kettle, 'The EU referendum is a battle of the press versus democracy', *The Guardian*, 17 June 2016. In 2011, David Cameron had appointed Lord Justice Leveson to carry out a judicial public enquiry into the culture, practices, and ethics of the British press, after the phone-hacking activities of some journalists and news outlets had been exposed.

10. <http://www.novaramedia.com/2016/10/16/whos-afraid-of-the-big-bad-communists-red-scares-then-now>.

11. Channel 4 News, 3 May 2017; <http://www.inews.co.uk>, 4 May.

12. Chris Mullin, *A Very British Coup* (London: Hodder & Stoughton, 1982).

13. Chris Mullin, 'Jeremy Corbyn for PM?', <http://www.spectator.co.uk/2017.06/jeremy-corbyn-for-pm>.

Note on Archival Sources
and Bibliography

In writing this book, I have had no privileged access to closed archives. I have, however, referred in the text to documents from those archives, where they have already been cited either in the FCO History Note, *The Zinoviev Letter of 1924: 'A most extraordinary and mysterious business'*, or in my book *Churchill's Man of Mystery: Desmond Morton and the World of Intelligence*, also written with privileged access. Some of the documents not open in 1998–9 have subsequently been released on Security Service (KV) files, and where possible I have given the equivalent TNA reference.

On our research trip to Moscow in 1998, Tony Bishop and I were given access to a lot of Russian documentation that was not available publicly at that time, though I understand that much of it is now open to researchers. Tony translated documents and passages from the Russian for me, on which I made detailed notes. Such material is referred to in the notes as having been consulted in the Russian Foreign Ministry, or the Russian Centre for the Preservation and Study of Documents of Contemporary History. Some of these documents have subsequently been used by other authors, and cited in their publications with file references that were not available to us in 1998. I have added some cross-references, but it would have been impossible to hunt them all out.

DOCUMENTARY COLLECTIONS

Jane Degras (ed.), *Documents of the Communist International* (London: Royal Institute of International Affairs, 1960)

Documents on British Foreign Policy 1919–1939 (DBFP), complete in 64 volumes in four series (London: HMSO, 1946–87)

Documents on British Policy Overseas (DPBO), Series I–III (London: various publishers, 1984–)

I. N. Zemskov et al. (eds), *Dokumenty vneshney politiki SSSR (DVPS)* Vols VI and VII (Moscow, 1962–3)

BOOKS

David Aaronovitch, *Voodoo Histories: The Role of the Conspiracy Theory in Shaping Modern History* (London: Jonathan Cape, 2009)

Christopher Andrew, 'The British View of Security and Intelligence', in Farson, Stafford, and Wark (eds), *Security and Intelligence in a Changing World*

Christopher Andrew, *Secret Service: The Making of the British Intelligence Community* (London: William Heinemann Ltd, 1985; Sceptre edn, 1986)

Christopher Andrew, *The Defence of the Realm: The Authorized History of MI5* (London: Penguin, 2009)

Christopher Andrew and David Dilks (eds), *The Missing Dimension: Governments and Intelligence Communities in the Twentieth Century* (London: Macmillan, 1984)

Christopher Andrew and Oleg Gordievsky, *KGB: The Inside Story of its Foreign Operations from Lenin to Gorbachev* (London: HarperCollins, 1990)

Christopher Andrew and Oleg Gordievsky, *Instructions from The Centre: Top Secret Files on KGB Foreign Operations 1975–1985* (London: Hodder & Stoughton, 1991)

Christopher Andrew and Oleg Gordievsky, *More Instructions from the Centre: Top Secret Files on KGB Global Operations 1975–1985* (London: Frank Cass, 1992)

Christopher Andrew and Vasili Mitrokhin, Vol. I, *The Mitrokhin Archive: The KGB in Europe and the West* (London: Penguin, 1999); Vol. II, *The Mitrokhin Archive II: The KGB and the World* (London: Penguin, 2005)

Christopher Andrew and Jeremy Noakes (eds), *Intelligence and International Relations 1900–1945* (Exeter: Exeter University Publications, 1987)

Anti-Soviet Forgeries (London: Workers' Publications Ltd, 1927)

Uri Bar-Joseph, *Intelligence Intervention in the Politics of Democratic States* (University Park, PA: The Pennsylvania State University Press, 1995)

Gordon S. Barrass, *The Great Cold War: A Journey through the Hall of Mirrors* (Stanford, CA: Stanford University Press, 2009)

Boris Bazhanov, *Bazhanov and the Damnation of Stalin*, trans. David W. Doyle (Columbus, OH: Ohio University Press, 1990)

Peter Beck, *Using History, Making British Policy: The Treasury and the Foreign Office, 1950–76* (London: Palgrave Macmillan, 2006)

Francis Beckett, *Enemy Within: The Rise and Fall of the British Communist Party* (London: John Murray, 1995)

Gill Bennett, *The Zinoviev Letter of 1924: 'A most extraordinary and mysterious business'*, FCO History Notes No. 14, February 1999, London:

Foreign and Commonwealth Office <https://issuu.com/fcohistorians/docs/history_notes_cover_hphn_14>

Gill Bennett, *Churchill's Man of Mystery: Desmond Morton and the World of Intelligence* (London: Routledge, 2006)

Gill Bennett, *Six Moments of Crisis: Inside British Foreign Policy* (Oxford: Oxford University Press, 2013)

Robert L. Benson, *The VENONA Story* (Washington, DC: US Center for Cryptologic History, 2012)

John Bew, *Citizen Clem: A Biography of Attlee* (London: riverrun, 2016)

Tom Bower, *The Perfect English Spy: Sir Dick White and the Secret War 1935–90* (London: Heinemann, 1995)

Ann Bridge, *Permission to Resign: Goings on in the Corridors of Power* (London: Sidgwick & Jackson, 1972)

Gordon Brook-Shepherd, *The Storm Petrels: The First Soviet Defectors, 1928–1938* (London: Collins, 1977)

Gordon Brook-Shepherd, *Iron Maze: The Western Secret Services and the Bolsheviks* (London: Macmillan, 1998)

Alan Bullock, *Hitler and Stalin: Parallel Lives* (London: Fontana edn, 1998)

James Callaghan, *Time and Chance* (London: William Collins, 1987; Politico's edn, 2006)

Alastair Campbell and Bill Hagerty (eds), *The Alastair Campbell Diaries*, Vol. II, *Power and the People 1997–1999* (London: Hutchinson, 2011)

John Campbell, *Lloyd George: The Goat in the Wilderness 1922–1931* (London: Jonathan Cape, 1977)

Michael Jabara Carley, *Silent Conflict: A Hidden History of Early Soviet-Western Relations* (London: Rowman & Littlefield, 2014)

David Carlton, *MacDonald versus Henderson: The Foreign Policy of the Second Labour Government* (London: Macmillan, 1970)

Miranda Carter, *Anthony Blunt: His Lives* (London: Macmillan, 2001)

Peter Catterall (ed.), *The Macmillan Diaries: Prime Minister and After, 1957–66* (London: Macmillan, 2011)

Lewis Chester, Stephen Fay, and Hugo Young, *The Zinoviev Letter: A Political Intrigue* (London: Heinemann, 1967)

Sir W. Childs, *Episodes and Reflections* (London: Cassell, 1930)

W. P. Coates, *The 'Zinoviev Letter': The Case for a Full Investigation*, with a preface by James Maxton MP (The Anglo-Russian Parliamentary Committee, May 1928)

W. P. and Zelda K. Coates, *A History of Anglo-Soviet Relations* (London: Lawrence & Wishart Ltd, 1944)

Communist Party of Great Britain, *History of the Zinoviev Letter* (1925)

Andrew Cook, *On His Majesty's Secret Service: Sidney Reilly Codename ST1* (Stroud: Tempus Publishing Ltd, 2002)

Gordon Corera, *The Art of Betrayal: Life and Death in the British Secret Service* (London: Weidenfeld & Nicolson, 2011)

Paul Corthorn and Jonathan Davis (eds), *The British Labour Party and the Wider World: Domestic Politics, Internationalism and Foreign Policy* (New York: Tauris Academic Studies, 2008)

John Costello and Oleg Tsarev, *Deadly Illusions* (London: Century, 1993)

Maurice Cowling, *The Impact of Labour 1920–1924* (Cambridge: Cambridge University Press, 1971)

Michael Crick, *The March of Militant* (London: Faber & Faber, 1986)

Colin Cross, *Philip Snowden* (London: Barrie and Rockliff, 1966)

Sibyl Crowe and Edward Corp, *Our Ablest Public Servant: Sir Eyre Crowe 1864–1925* (London: Merlin Books, 1993)

Hugh Dalton, *Call Back Yesterday: Memoirs 1887–1931* (London: Frederick Muller, 1953)

Evan Davis, *Post Truth: Why We Have Reached Peak Bullshit and What We Can Do About It* (London: Little Brown, 2017)

A. Stuart Farson, David Stafford, and Wesley K. Wark (eds), *Security and Intelligence in a Changing World: New Perspectives for the 1990s* (London: Frank Cass, 1991)

Frank Field (ed.), *Attlee's Great Contemporaries: The Politics of Character* (London: Bloomsbury, 2009)

William R. Garside (ed.), *Capitalism in Crisis: An International Perspective on the 1930s* (London: Palgrave Macmillan, 1993)

Martin Gilbert, *Never Despair: Winston S. Churchill 1945–1965* (London: Heinemann, 1988)

Oleg Gordievsky, *Next Stop Execution* (London: Macmillan, 1995)

Gabriel Gorodetsky, *The Precarious Truce: Anglo-Soviet Relations 1924–27* (Cambridge: Cambridge University Press, 1977)

Gabriel Gorodetsky (ed.), *The Maisky Diaries: Red Ambassador to the Court of St James's 1932–1943* (London: Yale University Press, 2015)

J. D. Gregory, *On the Edge of Diplomacy: Rambles and Reflections 1902–28* (London: Hutchinson & Co., 1928)

Keith Hamilton and Richard Langhorne, *The Practice of Diplomacy: Its Evolution, Theory and Administration* (London: Routledge, 1995)

Jonathan Haslam, *Russia's Cold War: From the October Revolution to the Fall of the Wall* (London: Yale University Press, 2011)

Jonathan Haslam, *Near and Distant Neighbours* (Oxford: Oxford University Press, 2015)

Sir Patrick Hastings, *Autobiography* (London: Heinemann, 1948)

Peter Hennessy, *Distilling the Frenzy: Writing the History of One's Own Times* (London: Biteback Publishing, 2012)

Samuel Hoare, *The Fourth Seal* (Surrey: The Windmill Press, 1930)

Peter Hopkirk, *Setting the East Ablaze: On Secret Service in Bolshevik Asia* (Oxford: Oxford University Press, 1984, 2001 edn)

David Howell, *MacDonald's Party: Labour Identities and Crisis, 1922–31* (Oxford: Oxford University Press, 2002)

Michael Hughes, *Inside the Enigma: British Officials in Russia 1900–1939* (London: The Hambledon Press, 1997)

Michael Jago, *Robin Butler: At the Heart of Power from Heath to Blair* (London: Biteback Publishing, 2017)

Keith Jeffery, *MI6: The History of the Secret Intelligence Service 1909–1949* (London: Bloomsbury, 2010)

Keith Jeffery and Peter Hennessy, *States of Emergency: British Governments and Strikebreaking since 1919* (London: Routledge and Kegan Paul, 1983)

Bill Jones, *The Russia Complex: The British Labour Party and the Soviet Union* (Manchester: Manchester University Press, 1977)

Thomas Jones, *Whitehall Diary*, Vol. I, *1916–1925* (Oxford: Oxford University Press, 1969)

Alan Judd, *The Quest for C: Mansfield Cumming and the Founding of the Secret Service* (London: HarperCollins, 1999)

Michael Kettle, *Sidney Reilly—The True Story of the World's Greatest Spy* (New York: St Martin's Press, 1984)

Keith Laybourn, *A Century of Labour: A History of the Labour Party* (Stroud: Sutton Publishing, 2000)

James Lees-Milne, *Harold Nicolson: A Biography*, Vol. II (London: Chatto & Windus, 1981)

Robin Bruce Lockhart, *Ace of Spies* (London: Hodder & Stoughton, 1967)

Daniel W. B. Lomas, *Intelligence, Security and the Attlee Governments 1945–51: An Uneasy Relationship?* (Manchester: Manchester University Press, 2017)

David Low, *Autobiography* (London: Michael Joseph, 1956)

Richard W. Lyman, *The First Labour Government, 1924* (London: Russell & Russell, 1975)

Ben Macintyre, *A Spy among Friends: Kim Philby and the Great Betrayal* (London: Bloomsbury, 2014)

Kirstie Macrakis, *Seduced by Secrets: Inside the Stasi's Spy-Tech World* (Cambridge: Cambridge University Press, 2008)

Victor Madeira, *Britannia and the Bear: The Anglo-Russian Intelligence Wars 1917–1929* (London: The Boydell Press, 2014)

Ephraim Maisel, *The Foreign Office and Foreign Policy 1919–26* (Eastbourne: Sussex Academic Press, 1994; new edn, 2014)

Ivan Maisky, *Journey into the Past: Soviet Ambassador to the United Kingdom, 1932–43*, trans. Frederick Holt (London: Hutchinson & Co. Ltd, 1962)

David Marquand, *Ramsay MacDonald* (London: Jonathan Cape, 1977)

Catherine Merridale, *Lenin on the Train* (London: Allen Lane, 2016)

Vasily Mitrokhin (ed.), *KGB Lexicon: The Soviet Intelligence Officer's Handbook* (London: Frank Cass, 2002)

Simon Sebag Montefiore, *Young Stalin* (London: Weidenfeld & Nicolson, 2007)

Charles Moore, *Margaret Thatcher, The Authorized Biography*, Vol. I, *Not For Turning;* Vol. II, *Everything She Wants* (London: Penguin Random House, 2014 and 2015).

Kevin Morgan, *Labour Legends and Russian Gold* (London: Lawrence & Wishart, 2006)

Keith Neilson, *Britain, Soviet Russia and the Collapse of the Soviet Order* (Cambridge: Cambridge University Press, 2006)

Kenneth Newton, *The Sociology of British Communism* (London: Allen Lane The Penguin Press, 1969)

Michael Occleshaw, *Dances in Deep Shadows: Britain's Clandestine War in Russia 1917–20* (London: Constable & Robinson, 2006)

Ocherki istorii rossiiskoi vneshnei razvedki (*Notes from the History of Russia's Foreign Intelligence Service*), Vol. II, *1917–33* (Moscow: SVR, 1997)

Bruce Page, David Leitch, and Phillip Knightley, *Philby: The Spy who Betrayed a Generation* (London: André Deutsch, 1968)

George C. Peden, *The Treasury and Public Policy 1906–1959* (Oxford: Oxford University Press, 2000)

Eleanor Philby, *Kim Philby: The Spy I Loved* (London: Hamish Hamilton, 1968).

Kim Philby, *My Silent War* (London: MacGibbon & Kee, 1968)

Jonathan Pile, *Churchill's Secret Enemy* (privately printed, 2012)

Ben Pimlott, *Harold Wilson* (London: HarperCollins, 1992)

Bernard Porter, *Plots and Paranoia: A History of Political Espionage in Britain 1790–1988* (London: Unwin Hyman, 1989)

Kevin Quinlan, *The Secret War between the Wars: MI5 in the 1920s and 1930s* (Woodbridge: The Boydell Press, 2014)

Robin Ramsay, *Politics and Paranoia* (Hove: Picnic Publishing, 2008)

Helen Rappaport, *Conspirator; Lenin in Exile: The Making of a Revolutionary* (London: Hutchinson, 2009)

Pepita Reilly, *Britain's Master Spy: The Adventures of Sidney Reilly* (New York: Harper and Brothers, 1932, reissued by Biteback Publishing in 2014)

Robert Rhodes James (ed.), *Memoirs of a Conservative: J. C. C. Davidson's Memoirs and Papers 1910–37* (London: Macmillan, 1969)

Huw Richards, *The Bloody Circus: The Daily Herald and the Left* (London: Pluto Press, 1997)

Patrick Seale and Maureen McConville, *Philby: The Long Road to Moscow* (London: Hamish Hamilton, 1973)

Robert C. Self (ed.), *The Austen Chamberlain Diary Letters* (London: Cambridge University Press for the Royal Historical Society, 1995)

John Shepherd and Keith Laybourn, *Britain's First Labour Government* (London: Palgrave Macmillan, 2006)

Jonathan D. Smele, *The 'Russian' Civil Wars 1916–1926: Ten Years that Shook the World* (London: Hurst & Co., 2015)

Michael Smith, *Foley: The Spy who Saved 10,000 Jews* (London: Hodder & Stoughton, 1999)

Stephen A. Smith (ed.), *The Oxford Handbook of the History of Communism* (Oxford: Oxford University Press, 2014)

Dudley Sommer, *Haldane of Cloan: His Life and Times 1856–1928* (London: George Allen & Unwin Ltd, 1960)

Richard B. Spence, *Trust No One: The Secret World of Sidney Reilly* (Los Angeles: Feral House, 2002)

David Stafford, *Churchill and Secret Service* (London: John Murray, 1997)

Lord Strang, *Home and Abroad* (London: André Deutsch, 1956)

Cass R. Sunstein, *Conspiracy Theories and Other Dangerous Ideas* (New York: Simon & Schuster, 2014)

A. J. P. Taylor, *English History 1914–1945* (Oxford: Oxford University Press, 1965)

A. J. P. Taylor, *Beaverbrook* (London: Hamish Hamilton, 1972)

Andrew Thorpe, *A History of the British Labour Party* (London: Palgrave, 4th edn, 2015)

Malcolm Turnbull, *The Spycatcher Trial* (London: William Heinemann, 1988)

Giles Udy, *Labour and the Gulag: Russia and the Seduction of the British Left* (London: Biteback Publishing Ltd, 2017)

R. G. Vansittart, *The Mist Procession: The Autobiography of Lord Vansittart* (London: Hutchinson, 1958)

Rhiannon Vickers, *The Labour Party and the World*, Vol. I, *The Evolution of Labour's Foreign Policy, 1900–1951* (Manchester: Manchester University Press, 2003)

Alexander Vlatkin and Stephen A. Smith, 'The Comintern', in Smith (ed.), *The Oxford Handbook of the History of Communism*

Nigel West and Oleg Tsarev, *The Crown Jewels: The British Secrets at the Heart of the KGB Archives* (London: HarperCollins, 1998)

Nigel West and Oleg Tsarev (eds), *Triplex: Secrets from the Cambridge Spies* (London: Yale University Press, 2009)

Nicholas Wilkinson, *Secrecy and the Media: The Official History of the United Kingdom's D-Notice System* (London: Routledge, 2009)

Harold Wilson, *The Labour Government 1964–70: A Personal Record* (London: Penguin, 1964)

Peter Wright, *Spycatcher: The Candid Autobiography of a Senior Intelligence Officer* (New York: Viking Penguin, 1987)

Philip Ziegler, *Wilson: The Authorised Life* (London: Weidenfeld & Nicolson, 1993)

ARTICLES

Christopher Andrew, 'The British Secret Service and Anglo-Soviet Relations in the 1920s, Part I: From the Trade Negotiations to the Zinoviev Letter', *The Historical Journal*, Vol. 20, No. 3 (1977), pp. 673–706

Christopher Andrew, 'Can the truth about the Zinoviev letter ever be written?', *The Times Higher Education Supplement*, 14 October 1977

Christopher Andrew, 'More on the Zinoviev Letter', *The Historical Journal*, Vol. 22, No. 1 (1979), pp. 211–14

Trevor Barnes, 'Special Branch and the First Labour Government', *The Historical Journal*, Vol. 22, No. 4 (December 1979)

Gill Bennett, 'Declassification and Release Policies of the UK's Intelligence Agencies', *Intelligence and National Security*, Vol. 17, No. 1 (Spring 2002)

Robert Blake, 'Ball, Sir (George) Joseph', *Oxford Dictionary of National Biography* (Oxford: Oxford University Press, 2004)

T. D. Burridge, 'A Postscript to Potsdam: The Churchill-Laski Electoral Clash, June 1945', *Journal of Contemporary History*, Vol. 12, No. 4 (Oct. 1977), pp. 725–39

William E. Butler, 'The Harvard Text of the Zinov'ev Letter', *Harvard Library Bulletin*, Vol. 18 (January 1970), pp. 43–62.

William E. Butler, 'Comment on "The Zinoviev Letter"', *Soviet Studies*, Vol. 21, No. 3 (Jan. 1970), pp. 395–400.

John Callaghan and Kevin Morgan, 'The Open Conspiracy of the Communist Party and the Case of W. N. Ewer, Communist and Anti-Communist', *The Historical Journal*, Vol. 49, No. 2 (June 2006), pp. 549–64

E. H. Carr, 'Communications: The Zinoviev Letter', *The Historical Journal*, Vol. 22, No. 1 (1979), pp. 209–10

Catherine Ann Cline, 'E. D. Morel and the Crusade against the Foreign Office', *The Journal of Modern History*, Vol. 39, No. 2 (June 1967)

Sibyl Crowe, 'The Zinoviev Letter: A Reappraisal', *Journal of Contemporary History*, Vol. 10, No. 3 (July 1975), pp. 407–32

J. R. Ferris and U. Bar-Joseph, '"Getting Marlowe to Hold His Tongue": The Conservative Party, the Intelligence Services and the Zinoviev letter', *Intelligence and National Security*, Vol. 8, No. 4 (1993), pp. 100–37

John Fisher, 'The Interdepartmental Committee on Eastern Unrest and British Responses to Bolshevik and Other Intrigues against the Empire during the 1920s', *Journal of Asian History*, Vol. 34, No. 1 (2000), pp. 1–34

Natalie Grant, 'The "Zinoviev Letter" Case', *Soviet Studies*, Vol. 19, No. 2 (Oct. 1967), pp. 264–77

John P. Sontag, 'The Soviet War Scare of 1926–27', *The Russian Review*, Vol. 34, No. 1 (Jan. 1975), pp. 66–77

P. Tomaselli, 'C's Moscow Station: The Anglo-Russian Trade Mission as Cover for SIS in the Early 1920s', *Intelligence and National Security*, Vol. 17, No. 3 (Autumn 2002)

David Wrench, '"Very Peculiar Circumstances": Walter Runciman and the National Government, 1931–3', *Twentieth Century British History*, Vol. 11, No. 1 (2000), pp. 61–82

Picture Acknowledgements

1   Courtesy of Foreign and Commonwealth Office
2   George Grantham Bain Collection (Library of Congress)
4   © National Portrait Gallery, London
5   © Associated Newspapers Ltd./Solo Syndication
6   Courtesy of the Foreign and Commonwealth Office
7   Courtesy of the Foreign and Commonwealth Office
8   Courtesy of the Foreign and Commonwealth Office
9   Courtesy of the Foreign and Commonwealth Office
10 Courtesy of the Foreign and Commonwealth Office
11 © Picture Post/Hulton Archive/Getty Images
12 © Associated Newspapers/REX/Shutterstock
13 © Kroon, Ron/Anefo; Nationaal Archief (NL), CC–BY–SA; Filenumber 920-1152
14 Courtesy of the Foreign and Commonwealth Office
15 © Jonathan Mitchell/Photoshot/age fotostock

Index